Making Integral: Critical essays on Richard Murphy

Making Integral: Critical essays on Richard Murphy

~

EDITED BY

Benjamin Keatinge

Dear Enda,

It is wonderful to hear tidings of you. We often talk of you, in Oxford and Marston.

With love from

Bernard O Donoghue

CORK **cup** UNIVERSITY PRESS

First published in 2019 by
Cork University Press
Boole Library
University College Cork
Cork T12 ND89
Ireland

British Library Cataloguing in Publication Data
A CIP record for this book is available from the British Library.

ISBN: 978-1-78205-325-5

Printed in Poland by Hussar Books
Print origination & design by Carrigboy Typesetting Services
www.carrigboy.com

www.corkuniversitypress.com

In Memory of Richard Murphy
(1927–2018)

Contents

Richard Murphy

by ANDREW McNEILLIE

Between our roads, a handful of years,
and then the past all round these shores
haunted by the ghost of the *Ave Maria*
telling the epic of the Cleggan Disaster,
holding today up to yesterday's mirror –
the world kept afloat by running repairs.

The landlady of Oliver's Seafood Bar
calls – from a tale or song of long ago?:
'Your heart beats when you hear my name,'
she laughs and tells it him again, 'Joe, Joe,
your heart beats when you hear my name.'
So Cleggan resounds, the day set fair

waiting for the ferry. And my head full
of memories of sailing to an island –
of corncrakes in the month of June
grinding out their tuneless tune:
such unlikely music. My heart unmanned
to hear it once more, to hear it still

on Inishbofin by Cromwell's fort
and the blind tower, as the ferry departs
and leaves me caught in '68 and '69 again,
days on the cusp of violence as they were,
reminded of all those broken hearts
from 'Droit de Seigneur' to Aughrim –

holding yesterday up to today's mirror
and reading in its guilt-edged frame
the old story of a poet's prescience
who saw tomorrow the day before.
Small wonder then that I should say:
my heart beats when I hear his name.

Acknowledgements

In the compilation of this essay volume, I have been fortunate to receive the advice and assistance of many individuals and institutions. I would like to thank colleagues at the School of English, Trinity College, Dublin and South East European University, Republic of North Macedonia for their support and advice. I am grateful to the New Europe College, Bucharest, Romania for the award of an International Research Fellowship in 2015, which enabled some of the editorial work to be completed. I would also like to thank the staff of the National Library of Ireland, the Library of Trinity College, Dublin and the Department of Special Collections, McFarlin Library, University of Tulsa for their friendly assistance. I am also grateful to the many individuals who assisted me in compiling the exhaustive bibliography on Richard Murphy; they are acknowledged individually in the preface to the bibliography.

For permission to quote from the published and unpublished works of Richard Murphy, I am grateful to Emily Riordan and the estate of Richard Murphy ©. For permission to quote from Richard Murphy, *Poems 1952–2012* (2013), I am grateful to the Lilliput Press, Dublin. For permission to quote from Richard Murphy, *The Pleasure Ground: poems 1952–2012* (2013), I am grateful to Bloodaxe Books, UK. For permission to quote excerpts from 'The God Who Eats Corn' in *Collected Poems* (2000) by Richard Murphy, I am grateful to the Gallery Press in Ireland and Wake Forest University Press in the US. For permission to quote from Richard Murphy, *In Search of Poetry* (2017), I am grateful to Andrew McNeillie and the Clutag Press. For permission to quote from Richard Murphy, *The Kick: a memoir of the poet Richard Murphy* (2017), I am grateful to Cork University Press. For permission to quote from the unpublished works, letters, drafts, notebooks and manuscripts of Richard Murphy, I am grateful to Emily Riordan and the estate of Richard Murphy © and to the Department of Special Collections, McFarlin Library, the University of Tulsa. I am grateful to the Guardian News & Media Limited for permission to use the photograph of Richard Murphy by Jane Bown (© Guardian News & Media Limited, 2018). I am also grateful to Mark Wormald, Pembroke College, University of Cambridge for drawing my attention to Jane Bown's photographs of Richard Murphy at Cleggan. The cover image of St Gormgal's *clochán* on High Island was taken by Avi Ratnayake on 29 August 2016 and I am grateful to him for generously permitting its use and also to Sarah O'Toole and Feicín Mulkerrin for making the trip to High Island possible. For permission to print Andrew McNeillie's tribute poem 'Richard Murphy' (© Andrew McNeillie, 2017) from *Making Ends Meet* (Guillemot Press, 2017) as the epigraph to this volume, I am grateful to Andrew McNeillie and to Luke Thompson of Guillemot Press.

For permission to quote from *The Letters of J.R. Ackerley*, edited by Neville Braybrooke (Gerald Duckworth & Co., 1975), I am grateful to the publisher and to David Higham Associates Limited. I am also grateful to Mary O'Malley and Carcanet Press Limited for permission to quote 'Tracing' and 'The Foreigner' from *Where the Rocks Float* by Mary O'Malley (Salmon Poetry, 1993), as well as 'Craft' from *Asylum Road* by Mary O'Malley (Salmon Poetry, 2001) and 'Rebuilding the St John' from *The Boning Hall: new and selected poems* by Mary O'Malley (Carcanet Press, 2002). For permission to quote from the correspondence of Charles Monteith, I am grateful to Faber & Faber Limited. For permission to quote from the correspondence of Douglas Cleverdon, I am grateful to Francis Cleverdon. For permission to quote from the correspondence of Donald Davie, I am grateful to Carcanet Press Limited. I am grateful also to the BBC Written Archives Centre for permission to quote from copyright materials in its archive connected with Richard Murphy's BBC broadcasts. Thanks are also due to the Lilly Library, Indiana University, Bloomington, Indiana for permission to cite from manuscripts in its archives. For permission to quote excerpts from the correspondence of Ted Hughes, I am grateful to the Estate of Ted Hughes © and Faber & Faber Limited. Excerpts taken from *Gaudete* and *Poetry in the Making* by Ted Hughes are reproduced by kind permission of the Estate of Ted Hughes © and Faber &

Faber Limited. For permission to quote from *Contemporary Irish Writers*, edited by J.D. Brophy (Gale, 1983), I am grateful to Cengage Learning, Inc. Excerpts from 'William Carlos Williams' *Collected Prose* by Robert Lowell are reprinted by kind permission of Farrar, Straus & Giroux. For permission to quote from the correspondence of Theodore Roethke and from the correspondence of Beatrice Roethke Lushington, I am grateful to Beatrice Roethke Lushington. For permission to quote from *My Father and Myself* by J.R. Ackerley (*New York Review of Books*, 1999), I am grateful to the publisher and to David Higham Associates Limited. For permission to quote from *The Dream of the Celt* by Mario Vargas Llosa, translated by Edith Grossman (Faber & Faber, 2012), I am grateful to Faber & Faber Limited. For permission to quote from 'Aughrim in Sri Lanka' by Antoinette Quinn, I am grateful to the estate of Antoinette Quinn.

I owe a great debt of gratitude to all of the contributors to this volume for their outstanding scholarly work and for their diligent responses to my editorial suggestions. I am grateful to the readers at Cork University Press whose considered evaluation of the initial book proposal and of the book manuscript has led to a stronger book. I am also particularly grateful to Mike Collins and Maria O'Donovan at Cork University Press for their patient support of this project as it has evolved. The staff and postgraduate students of the School of English, University College Cork (UCC) were kind enough to invite me to present a paper on Richard Murphy's Sri Lankan poems at UCC in March 2017, and I am grateful for their helpful responses to my paper. I would like also to thank Claire Cunningham and Julien Clancy for inviting me to be involved with the radio documentary on Richard Murphy *His Chosen Islands* first broadcast on RTÉ Lyric FM on 4 August 2017. And I am grateful to other individuals and organisations who have indirectly supported this book project and have celebrated Richard Murphy's poetry in other contexts: Poetry Ireland; Peadar King and the INISH Festival; Jeananne Crowley and the Cleggan/Claddaghduff Festival of the Sea; Seán Coyne and the Connemara Mussel Festival; Andrew McNeillie, the Clutag Press and *Archipelago*; Maurice Earls and Books Upstairs; James Harrold; Theresa Kearney and the United Arts Club; Patricia McCarthy and

Agenda magazine; Brendan Flynn, Des Lally and the Clifden Arts Festival.

I would like to thank the following family members, friends and colleagues for their advice and support during the preparation of this book: Daria Brennan, Arthur Broomfield, Sandra Carroll, Eamonn Casey, Harry Clifton, Philip Coleman, Alexandra Cooney, Jean-Martin Deniau, Estela Eaton, Nelda Eaton, Erwan Fouéré, Michelle Gallen, Goran Georgievski, Andrew Goodspeed, Nicholas Grene, Caitlin Henderson, Isla Henderson, Martha Henderson, Nick Henderson, Vivien Henderson, Heather Henshaw, Mark Hutcheson, Veronika Kareva, Annie Keatinge, Athene Keatinge, Douglas Keatinge, Jim Keatinge, Joanna Keatinge, Rebecca Keatinge, Suzanne Keatinge, Emanuel Lisichanets, Mujdin Livoreka, Eamon Maher, Divna Manolova, Joan McBreen, Emma McNamara, Ruben Moi, Maja Muhic, Hava Mustafa, Jehona Mustafa-Murtezani, Mary O'Donnell, Mary Pierse, Jan Piggott, Zoran Poposki, Sathiya Ramakrishnan, Desmond and Nayomi Rodrigo, Alex Runchman, Piotr Sadowski, Elena Spirovska, Richard and Jill Stevens, Arta Toci, Marija Todorova, David Wheatley and Edward Wingfield.

I am indebted to all members of the Murphy family for supporting this book, and I would like to thank especially the poet's daughter Emily Riordan, his brother Christopher Murphy and Mrs Anne-Marie Murphy. Other members of the Murphy family have also been very supportive, and I am greatly indebted to Mrs Mary Cookson (Richard Murphy's sister), Fiona Murphy (Richard Murphy's niece) as well as Theodora Lee and Caspar Lee (Richard Murphy's grandchildren). It was my pleasure and privilege to meet the poet Richard Murphy while working on this volume on two trips to Sri Lanka in 2015 and 2016. I would like to thank him for his unstinting and generous support in making this book possible and for being so enthusiastic about the project during its genesis. It is a great sadness to me and to the contributors that Richard Murphy has not lived to see the final outcome of our scholarship. This book is testimony to Richard Murphy's unique contribution to poetry and it is published as a tribute to his achievements.

Notes on Contributors

BARBARA R. BROWN is emeritus professor of English literature at West Virginia University, Marshall University Campus, Huntington, West Virginia, where she taught and edited genres of life-writing with an emphasis on memoir. Since her retirement, she has resided in Dublin, where she works as an editor.

SIOBHÁN CAMPBELL is the author of five poetry collections, including *Cross-talk* (Seren Press, 2009), *That Water Speaks in Tongues* (Templar, 2008), *The Cold That Burns* (Blackstaff, 2000) and, most recently, *Heat Signature* (Seren Press, 2017). Her poetry and criticism have appeared in the US, Ireland and the UK, including in *The Hopkins Review, Magma, Asymptote, Poetry Ireland Review* and *Southword*, and her work has been collected into the Troubles Archive of Artworks by the Arts Council of Northern Ireland. She is co-editor of *Inside History: Eavan Boland* (Arlen House/Syracuse University Press, 2017) and editor of *Courage and Strength: stories and poems by combat veterans* (Kingston University Press, 2012). Campbell works in creative-writing interventions, co-operating with groups in post-conflict situations, including in Lebanon and Iraq. She holds awards in the National, Troubadour International and Michael Marks poetry competitions and was awarded the Oxford Brookes Poetry Prize in 2016. She works at the Department of English, the Open University, where she co-chairs the MA in Creative Writing.

EVE COBAIN was awarded a PhD from Trinity College, Dublin in 2017, funded by the Irish Research Council. Her doctoral research examines the significance of music in the poetry of John Berryman and her research interests focus on the 'Middle Generation' of American poets. She is co-editing, with Philip Coleman, a collection of essays entitled *Robert Lowell and Irish Poetry*, and has contributed to essay volumes, including an essay on 'Berryman's Beethoven' to *John Berryman at 100: centenary essays* (Peter Lang, 2017).

Lucy Collins is associate professor of English at University College, Dublin. Educated at Trinity College, Dublin and at Harvard University, where she spent a year as a Fulbright Scholar, she teaches and researches in the area of modern poetry and poetics. Recent books include *Poetry by Women in Ireland: a critical anthology, 1870–1970* (2012) and a monograph, *Contemporary Irish Women Poets: memory and estrangement* (2015), both from Liverpool University Press. She has published widely on contemporary poets from Ireland, Britain and America, and is co-founder of the Irish Poetry Reading Archive, a national digital repository.

Elena Cotta Ramusino is a lecturer at the University of Pavia, where she teaches English literature. She works mainly on Irish literature, twentieth-century authors and modernism. Her book publications include *La produzione giovanile di W.B.Yeats: percorsi di un'identità poetica e culturale* (La Nuova Italia, 1997), *Dal buio alla luce: poesia e poetica in Seamus Heaney* (Cooperativa Libraria Universitaria, 1999) and *Elizabeth Bowen's Other Writing: a study of her non-fictional prose* (Ibis, 2018). She has published articles on Virginia Woolf, Seamus Heaney's *The Burial at Thebes*, and on Elizabeth Bowen; her interest in autobiography and memoir is reflected in her work on Elizabeth Bowen's *Seven Winters*, Hugo Hamilton's *The Speckled People*, and W.B. Yeats' *Autobiographies*.

Gerald Dawe was born in Belfast in 1952. He has published twenty books of poetry and essays, including *Lake Geneva* (2003), *Selected Poems* (2012) and *Mickey Finn's Air* (2014), as well as editing various anthologies of poetry and literary criticism, most recently *The Cambridge Companion to Irish Poets* (2017). He was professor of English and Fellow of Trinity College, Dublin until his retirement in 2017.

Philip Keel Geheber completed his MPhil at Trinity College, Dublin (TCD) in 2008 with a thesis on Richard Murphy that explored the poet's identity politics and representations of history. He then completed his PhD in 2013, also at TCD, with a thesis which contextualised the development of James Joyce's narrative style through a genealogy of the French realist novel. He has published or has work forthcoming in *Genetic Joyce Studies*, *Katherine Mansfield Studies* and the *James Joyce Quarterly* in addition to several edited collections. He is co-editor of the forthcoming *Modernism and Food Studies: politics, aesthetics, and the avant-garde* (University Press of Florida), and currently teaches at Fordham University.

MAURICE HARMON is emeritus professor of Anglo-Irish literature and drama at University College, Dublin and was educated there and at Harvard University. Professor Harmon is an internationally known scholar, critic, literary historian, translator, editor and poet. He edited the *Irish University Review: Richard Murphy special issue* (1977) and *Richard Murphy: poet of two traditions* (1978), the first book-length considerations of Richard Murphy's poetry. His many publications include *Seán O'Faoláin: a life* (1994), *The Dolmen Press: a celebration* (2001), *Selected Essays* (2006) and *Thomas Kinsella: designing for the exact needs* (2008). He edited with introduction and notes *No Author Better Served: the correspondence of Samuel Beckett and Alan Schneider* (1998). He is also a poet, and recent collections include *When Love Is Not Enough: new and selected poems* (2010), *Loose Connections* (2012) and *Hoops of Holiness* (2016).

BENJAMIN KEATINGE is a Visiting Research Fellow at the School of English, Trinity College, Dublin. He is co-editor of *France and Ireland in the Public Imagination* with Mary Pierse (Peter Lang, 2014) and *Other Edens: the life and work of Brian Coffey* with Aengus Woods (Irish Academic Press, 2010) and he has published on several aspects of Richard Murphy's poetry including in *The Cambridge Companion to Irish Poets* (2017). He has also discussed Richard Murphy's work at conferences, on radio and in interviews with the poet.

JAMES B. KELLEY first came to know Richard Murphy and his poetry while pursuing a PhD in English at the University of Tulsa. He is professor of English at Mississippi State University, Meridian, where he teaches courses in literature, theory, linguistics and writing. He has published on popular culture, queer theory, twentieth-century American poetry, African-American writing and pedagogical aspects of literary studies. His current book project examines the status of *To Kill a Mockingbird* in classrooms, literary criticism and popular culture.

ANDREW MCNEILLIE was born in North Wales in 1946 and schooled there. Like Richard Murphy, he read English at Magdalen College, Oxford. He is the author of *An Aran Keening* (Lilliput Press, 2001), a work considerably indebted in its origins to Murphy's *Sailing to an Island* (1963). While working in publishing, most recently as the literature editor at Oxford University Press, he founded the Clutag Press, and is the editor and publisher of the literary magazine *Archipelago*.

MICHAEL A. MOIR, JR is associate professor of English at Georgia Southwestern State University in Americus, Georgia, USA, where he teaches courses in modern poetry, modern British literature, Irish literature and postcolonial/world literatures. His research has been published in the *Canadian Journal of Irish Studies*, the *New Hibernia Review*, *Études Irlandaises*, and the *Irish Literary Supplement*. He is currently at work on a study of Louis MacNeice's radio plays.

BERNARD O'DONOGHUE was born in Cullen, County Cork in 1945. He is an Emeritus Fellow of Wadham College, University of Oxford, where he taught medieval English and modern Irish poetry. He has published eight collections of poetry, including *Gunpowder*, winner of the 1995 Whitbread Prize for Poetry, *Farmers Cross* (2011) and *The Seasons of Cullen Church* (2016). His *Selected Poems* was published by Faber in 2008. He has published a verse translation of *Sir Gawain and the Green Knight* (Penguin Classics, 2006), and is currently translating *Piers Plowman* for Faber.

JOSEPH SENDRY is professor emeritus in the Department of English at the Catholic University of America, Washington DC, where he offered courses on Irish literature, James Joyce and the Victorians. He has established a publication record on Richard Murphy's poetry with articles on *The Price of Stone* and *The Mirror Wall* and a review on *Collected Poems 1952–2000* (Gallery Press, 2000) for *Poetry Ireland Review*. His scholarly contributions also include work on Tennyson, Hopkins and Edward FitzGerald.

TARA STUBBS is associate professor in English literature and creative writing at Oxford University's Department for Continuing Education, and a Fellow of Kellogg College, Oxford. Her particular interests lie in twentieth-century Irish and American literature. Her monograph *American Literature and Irish Culture, 1910–1955: the politics of enchantment* was published by Manchester University Press in November 2013 (paperback, 2017). Most recently she has published articles and book chapters on the American modernist poet Marianne Moore and Englishness, on W.B. Yeats and contemporary American culture, and on T.S. Eliot and transatlantic culture. Her second monograph *The Modern Irish Sonnet: revision and rebellion* is forthcoming from Palgrave Macmillan.

TOM WALKER teaches at the School of English, Trinity College, Dublin, where he is Ussher Assistant Professor in Irish Writing. He has published widely on Irish literature, including essays on Denis Johnston, Flann O'Brien, Derek Mahon, Austin Clarke, John McGahern and Patrick McCabe. He is the author of *Louis MacNeice and the Irish Poetry of His Time* (Oxford University Press, 2015) and he is currently working on a project entitled 'Yeats and the Writing of Art' funded by the Irish Research Council.

MARK WORMALD is Fellow and director of studies in English at Pembroke College, University of Cambridge. He has written widely on nineteenth- and twentieth-century poetry and fiction. With Terry Gifford and Neil Roberts he co-edited *Ted Hughes: from Cambridge to collected* (Palgrave Macmillan, 2013) and *Ted Hughes, Nature and Culture* (Palgrave Macmillan, 2018). *The Catch: fishing for Ted Hughes* is forthcoming from Little Toller Books. He is editor of the *Ted Hughes Society Journal*.

Abbreviations

The following abbreviations have been adopted and follow quotations in the text:

P   Richard Murphy, *Poems 1952–2012* (Dublin: The Lilliput Press, 2013) / *The Pleasure Ground: poems 1952–2012* (Tarset: Bloodaxe, 2013)

K   Richard Murphy, *The Kick: a memoir of the poet Richard Murphy* (Cork: Cork University Press, 2017)

In the references:

Tulsa Richard Murphy papers, 1951–1982. 1988.014. Department of Special Collections, McFarlin Library, University of Tulsa

Introduction

BENJAMIN KEATINGE

Richard Murphy was one of Ireland's most distinguished poets whose poetry has left an indelible imprint on Irish letters. Following his death, aged ninety, on 30 January 2018, many tributes were paid. President Michael D. Higgins recalled in *The Irish Times* that Murphy 'had a great reading voice and was the second poet to be chosen, after Dylan Thomas, when the BBC first began to broadcast poetry read by living poets'. In the same article, poet Mary O'Malley remarked that 'He was the only person I knew from the literary world that knew the place I came from as I knew it, the families, the boats, the gossip'. Bernard O'Donoghue, meanwhile, reminded us that 'in the 1960s he was one of the leading figures in English poetry published in Britain and Ireland, in the company of Larkin, Hughes and Heaney'. And Maria Johnston recalled her own first reading of the sonnet 'Natural Son' and how the formal mastery of that poem nevertheless contains a barcly concealed anxiety and restlessness. As Johnston suggested, 'the poem seemed to create a room, but not a safe space, one filled with tensions and profound ambiguity'.[1]

The happier occasion of Richard Murphy's ninetieth birthday on 6 August 2017 was also marked by several tributes. Gerald Dawe wrote in *The Irish Times* that Murphy has always been a 'poet of other people' whose poems 'are not about himself at all', rather, they are 'about "others" and their reality'.[2] The ways in which fellow writers have recognised the gift of Richard Murphy to reach across boundaries of class and social background to understand others' reality is striking and is perhaps one of the keys to his work. In introducing his collected poems *The Pleasure Ground: poems 1952–2012*, Murphy said that he 'remember[ed] with gratitude all the friends, fellow poets, relations, editors, publishers and readers … who have helped and inspired me to write' (*P*, p. 16). The central concern of this volume of essays is to show how Richard Murphy has made 'integral' in his poetry a set of diverse experiences, his own and those of others, along with incidents from the wider panorama of history and geography, in ways which show the poet seeking definition of himself through others. To adapt a phrase from Murphy's poem 'Double Negative', his poetry exists in the realms of possibility where 'the stranger on the mailboat' meets 'the stranger on the quay' (*P*, p. 112).

The particular challenge for Richard Murphy is the fact of his Anglo-Irish background, a background which forms the agon of his poetry. His searching engagements with the limits of Irish life are founded on his early displacements – Irish, British and colonial – described in 'Liner' as taking him 'half way around the world' to find that 'home is like a foreign country' (*P*, p. 193). Murphy's later, self-confessed 'passion for building in granite' that he describes in the poem 'Stone Mania' reflects the poet's efforts to shelter himself against these disruptions (*P*, p. 157). In 'Little Hunger', Murphy presents himself:

> Looking for pink stone
> In roofless houses huddled by the sea
> To buy to build my own.   (*P*, p. 111)

But his poetic persona here is ghosted by the landlords of pre- and post-Famine Ireland and thus his 'work' of 'dismemberment' re-enacts past injustice and a burden of guilt weighs upon the process of acquisition, destruction and reconstruction (*P*, p. 111). The poet is all too aware that the solidity of his own dwelling – 'Threshold, lintel, wall;' – when viewed historically, is founded on the 'exility' and exclusion of others (*P*, p. 111), just as in 'Stone Mania' his 'obsession with building' results, on the social plane, in his neglect 'all this summer' of 'the friends whom I might have seen' but for his building projects (*P*, p. 157).

The poet's misgivings in 'Little Hunger' and 'Stone Mania' are part of his self-consciousness of the privileges of his education and background as a child of the British Empire (Murphy's father was the last British mayor of Colombo) and as the son, on his mother's side, of a Big House – Milford, at Kilmaine, County Mayo – where the walled demesne garden of Murphy's original 'Pleasure Ground' was located. In the elegy he wrote to his grandmother Lucy Mary Ormbsy, titled 'The Woman of the House', Murphy would elegise his grandmother's 'kindness', not just to her family, but to strangers, victims of 'the wounds that poverty caused' which she would attempt to 'cure' by way of makeshift medical care for local 'labourers' (*P*, pp. 30–1). Nevertheless, the poet is aware that such ameliorative care is 'useless' when set against the 'impossible wrong' of Irish history (*P*, p. 30), wrongs which he would go on to explore more widely in *The Battle of Aughrim* (1968) and *The Price of Stone* (1985) in poems which would seek restitution in a relationship of self and other that 'excluded nobody' (*P*, p. 16).

Many critics of Richard Murphy's poetry have considered his work to record his own 'impossible' situation as a belated Anglo-Irishman in mid-twentieth-century Ireland. Indeed, the perception of a compensatory mechanism at work by which, in Terence Brown's words, 'insecure assertions of an Irish identity' are made 'that a man or woman of Catholic nationalist stock feels no need to make' has been widespread.[3] As Patrick Crotty notes in his introduction to a selection of Murphy's poems in *Modern Irish Poetry: an anthology*:

> Murphy is perhaps the last Anglo-Irish poet, fascinated by native modes of existence which appear more instinctive than his own … the speaker in these poems is excluded from the world of unselfconscious intensity …[4]

But if Murphy feels 'excluded' by his own origins from a more spontaneous Irish world around him, it is also an exclusion that helps him to recognise his own paradoxical affinity with those marginal voices that his poetry has celebrated. It is his feelings of alienation from his patrician inheritance, wonderfully recorded in his memoir *The Kick*, that condition his relationship to the marginal figures with whom he identifies: the heroism of Pat Concannon

in 'The Cleggan Disaster', the idioms of 'Pat Cloherty's Version of
The Maisie' (so brilliantly elucidated by Bernard O'Donoghue, who
further explores Murphy's 'plainstyles' in his essay here), the beauty
of the itinerant girls in 'Morning Call'. The question is not necessarily
one of compensation, guilt or social reparation; this would imply an
unbridgeable gulf between the poet and the outsiders of his poetry.
Rather, Murphy feels himself to be analogously 'excluded' from the
received social conventions of his class in a way that is comparable to
those 'others' who populate his poetry. It is Murphy's own occupation
of variegated social space that endows his poetry with its 'respect
for ordinary people, for the particularity of their society' and which
facilitates, in the words of Gerald Dawe, 'the creation of an entire
world' that excludes no one, least of all the poet himself.[5]

The question of assimilation, social and literary, has had a direct
bearing on Murphy's critical reputation. Paradoxically combining,
in his early poems, an Anglo-Irish sensibility against a more Gaelic
environment, to write narrative poetry of the western seaboard (his
prize-winning coda to 'The Cleggan Disaster' titled 'Years Later' was
submitted for Guinness Awards at the 1962 Cheltenham Festival under
the pseudonym of 'Fisherman'), Murphy had established links in the
1950s with Liam Miller's Dolmen Press in Dublin (which published
his 1955 volume *The Archaeology of Love*), and 'The Cleggan Disaster'
was included in the 1962 *Dolmen Miscellany*, edited by John Montague
and Thomas Kinsella. *The Kick* implies, however, that Murphy never
felt fully at home in literary Dublin and his exclusion from the
editorial team behind the *Miscellany* 'confirmed [his] attachment
to the part of Ireland bordered by the Shannon on one side and the
Atlantic on the other' (*K*, pp. 189–90). One should not discount,
however, the significance of Murphy's earliest publications from
Dolmen, which issued individual editions of 'Sailing to an Island',
'The Woman of the House' and 'The Last Galway Hooker' in 1955, 1959
and 1961 respectively.[6] Indeed, as Lucy Collins shows in her essay on
'Richard Murphy's Island Lives', when the manuscript of *Sailing to an
Island* (1963) was accepted by T.S. Eliot at Faber & Faber in April 1962,
Murphy still had to ensure his existing publication commitments with
Dolmen did not conflict with his new status as a Faber poet.

Nor should we overlook Murphy's early reviews in *The Spectator* and the *Times Literary Supplement* in the period 1950 to 1956. Eve Cobain demonstrates in her essay how Murphy's engagement with American poetry began in the review he wrote on Robert Lowell's *Poems: 1938–1949* in *The Spectator* (10 November 1950), which would be followed by other reviews on *The Oxford Book of American Verse* in *The Spectator* (2 February 1951) and *Collected Poems* by Robert Frost (4 May 1951) to name just two other titles from almost fifty reviews from these years, all of which are listed in the Bibliography to this volume.

Here one finds suggestive paths of influence which can help us trace the poet's early development. We learn from *The Kick* that Murphy 'attended few' lectures during his time as an undergraduate studying English at Magdalen College, Oxford (*K*, p. 81); but even if 'Tolkien was inaudible', there are unmistakable marks of at least some of the traditional Oxford curriculum in Murphy's poetry, and its confluence with the contemporary poetry Murphy would review in the early 1950s gives us some clues as to how poems like 'Sailing to an Island', 'The Cleggan Disaster' and 'The Last Galway Hooker' were arrived at. Murphy would later acknowledge that 'Pieces of *Beowulf* and the *Aeneid* are still visible in his work'[7] and it is evident, for example, that the 'Years Later' coda from 'The Cleggan Disaster' is a variation on the *ubi sunt* motif and that the heavily alliterative style of 'Sailing to an Island' is indebted to Anglo-Saxon models. But it is equally helpful to know that the poet published a review of W.S. Graham's volume *The Nightfishing* under the heading 'The Continual Sea' in the *Times Literary Supplement* on 8 July 1955, in which he notes that 'Fishing will always be dangerous and cold', praising Graham's 'grip on experience which the villanelles of the universities never communicate'.[8] Murphy's own sea poems are indebted to his 'experience' of the 'continual sea' *and* to the learning of 'the universities' in ways that need still to be expertly navigated. Collins' essay and that of Philip Keel Geheber offer some important interpretative coordinates to what Geheber characterises as Murphy's 'fluid geographies'.

Another hitherto unturned stone in scholarship has been Richard Murphy's extensive relationship with the British Broadcasting

Corporation (BBC), which enabled broadcasting of much of his early work with parallel publication in *The Listener*.[9] As Tom Walker convincingly demonstrates in his essay 'Richard Murphy: radio poet', the aural possibilities of radio influenced the younger Murphy, leading to the commission of the symphonic *The Battle of Aughrim*, broadcast by the BBC to coincide with its publication by Faber & Faber on 16 September 1968. Walker demonstrates the extent to which Murphy's talent was nurtured by his producers at the BBC – notably Douglas Cleverdon – as well as by his editor at Faber, Oxford contemporary Charles Monteith. Indeed, Murphy's career often benefitted from the help and advice of friends whose literary judgement he valued. Tony White was, for many years, the poet's trusted literary advisor, while Dennis O'Driscoll would subsequently play an important role in Murphy's completion of the fifty-sonnet sequence from *The Price of Stone*, a fraught compositional process which is charted most fully in Murphy's *In Search of Poetry* (2017). In her essay 'What Price Stone? The shaping of inheritance into form in Richard Murphy's *The Price of Stone* sonnet sequence', Tara Stubbs traces the linguistic ironies in some of the key sonnets, and defends that volume against the charge Edna Longley levelled against *The Battle of Aughrim*, a poem she found 'programmatic in its design and designs'.[10] This perception may owe something to the compositional method adopted by Murphy, who always considered poetry as a deliberate process whereby 'the page' is like a 'score' in music and must 'hold in its net the music of poetry, and prevent words from swimming into measureless prolixity' (*K*, p. 139). Murphy's fear of 'prolixity' may have led to a sometimes 'programmatic' approach, but such an approach reflects his twin view of 'poems as buildings and as music',[11] the construction of which entails a deliberate compositional technique, one which formed the basis for his best poetry. In Mark Wormald's essay on 'Richard Murphy and Ted Hughes', we encounter two important poets who retained what Wormald calls an 'imaginative sympathy' for one another's poetic vision even while diverging in technique, style and subject matter. As Wormald shows, both Hughes and Tony White were instrumental in helping Murphy engage with the propitious subject of High Island, leading the poet in the direction of such Hughesian achievements as 'Seals at High Island' or the musicality of 'Nocturne', both published in Murphy's landmark 1974 volume *High Island*.

Murphy received yet another helping hand from J.R. Ackerley, literary editor of *The Listener* from 1935 to 1959, and Ackerley's 'detailed critique of "The Woman of the House"' resulted, according to Murphy, in 'a much improved version' being published in *The Listener* (*K*, p. 117). Indeed, Ackerley disarmed the young poet with his 'deliberately déclassé' appearance when they first met, in February 1951, and further alarmed Murphy by announcing "'I'm homosexual'" in a London tavern (*K*, pp. 115–16). As *The Kick* illustrates, the feelings of guilt and secrecy surrounding such pronouncements in post-war England is hard to exaggerate. In this volume, James B. Kelley re-reads *The Price of Stone* by re-contextualising the 'cruising sonnets' (notably 'Gym', 'Portico' and 'Convenience') in the context of that volume's oscillation between heterosexual and 'queer' identities.

Ackerley's sympathetic guidance of the young poet would be further substantiated in his later response to Murphy's 'The God Who Eats Corn', which he described in a letter as 'a highly dramatic poem about something of the most urgent and deepest importance'.[12] This view is affirmed by Michael A. Moir, Jr in his essay, which reads the poem in terms of 'pastoral space', illustrating how aspects of Murphy's childhood 'pleasure garden' – transplanted by the poet's father, Sir William Lindsay Murphy, into colonial Rhodesia at a time of political unrest and decolonisation   succumb symbolically and actually to the 'voodoo climate' in which:

> ... Tolerant water
> Eases roots, but cannot cool the racist fever.   (*P*, p. 103)

Horticultural metaphors are also explored in Joseph Sendry's detailed examination of the trope of aftermath in Murphy's poetry, in which he notes that etymologically 'aftermath' originally meant second (and inferior) growth after a first harvesting. The implications for Richard Murphy's poetry are clear: the losses at the Boyne and at Aughrim 'sowed a myth' (*P*, p. 61) which continues to reverberate in Ireland. The implications of this 'Bygone cannon, bygone spleen' (*P*, p. 63) is also the focus of Siobhán Campbell's examination of conflict in what is a personal reading of Murphy's *The Battle of Aughrim* by one of Ireland's leading poets.

This volume also foregrounds the achievement of *The Kick*, which is surely a masterpiece of (Anglo-) Irish memoir; both Barbara Brown and Elena Cotta Ramusino provide a strong basis for such an evaluation in their essays. And as Maurice Harmon notes in his significant critical survey of Richard Murphy's *oeuvre*, Murphy's 'post-Yeatsian' outlook is one of 'division and distress' which evinces a postcolonial awareness of the inadequacies of the Anglo-Irish inheritance; hence the search 'for grounds of pleasure that excluded nobody' (*P*, p. 16).

It is the collective contention of these essays that Richard Murphy's voice should be better heard and that he is a poet of today rather than a poet representing a 'bygone' era. In an Ireland still riven by social and sectarian divides, he reminds us of the origin of our current 'borders and bigotries' (*K*, p. 197) and in doing so proves himself, in Siobhán Campbell's words, a poet who 'seems to speak directly to our *now*'. At a time of ecological collapse, he urges us to 'quicken [our] tune' and to 'improvise, before / The combine and the digger come' ('Song for a Corncrake', *P*, p. 121). At a time when technological innovation is fetishised and marketed, Murphy urges the continuance of 'craft' so that certain older models may 'renew ... rebuild ... prolong' themselves in the present day and find a new place 'down tomorrow's sea-road' ('The Last Galway Hooker', *P*, pp. 39–40).

If Murphy's voice 'has been shunted aside' in some of the ongoing cultural debates around identity and belonging in Ireland, as Gerald Dawe has tellingly noted, in other contexts his voice has been listened to.[13] Michael Longley comments in his Ireland Chair of Poetry lecture on 'The West' that it was Richard Murphy who 'first attracted the attention' of Longley and his contemporaries to the glories of the western seaboard through his 'majestic narratives' of the sea in *Sailing to an Island* and his 'consummate nature poems' in *High Island*.[14] Longley is well known for his beautiful poems of birds and flowers, especially at Carrigskeewaun in County Mayo, which has been Longley's spiritual home for several years. Equally noteworthy are the bird poems of Mayo poet and ornithologist Seán Lysaght, whose 'Corncrake' and 'Storm Petrels' reflect Murphy's earlier example.[15]

Connemara poet Mary O'Malley has said that 'The poems of Richard Murphy were very important to me … because I knew the territory', and several of her own poems are written very much in dialogue with Richard Murphy.[16] In 'Tracing' she recalls Murphy's own conversations with her fisherman father:

> a poet and a fisherman
> tracing the genealogy of pucáns. Back
> to the summer of nineteen-twenty-seven,[17]

this date being the year of Richard Murphy's birth. In this male world of boats and boatmen, O'Malley maintains her independence, charting her 'own course' in order to 'keep afloat';[18] but her awareness of 'the voice of an Englishman' in her home environment ('wherever he got the name') is one which ultimately helps O'Malley to establish her own poetic identity.[19] Her upbringing in Connemara and her knowledge of the lore of boats lead her to sympathise instinctively with Murphy's respect for maritime traditions, and she echoes Murphy's sense of these continuities in her poem 'Rebuilding the St John':

> … They are re-building
> the St John closer to Homer's specifications
>
> than Brussels'. This is no postcard, it is a place,
> a boatyard where craftsmen use what is to hand
>
> to follow patterns handed down, inscribed
> on the sand at low tide, measured out in the sea's sound.[20]

Indeed, O'Malley's definition of poetic craft itself is made in the terms Murphy dramatised so effectively in 'The Cleggan Disaster' in describing the choice facing Concannon as he battles the waves:

> It's all about knowing when
> to cut the nets on a fine
> catch and run before disaster
> and when to risk the vessel
> for a haul of silver.[21]

Other contemporary poets have echoed Murphy's blend of solitude, spirituality and the sea, as, for example, the remarkable poem 'Stormbound' by Paddy Bushe published in *Voices at the World's Edge: Irish poets on Skellig Michael*.[22] Here the 'rock, sea and star' (*P*, p. 135) of Murphy's High Island are part of a similar search for meaning, a 'need' to locate 'the stone steps' passage' to fasten the 'pitiful, tenuous hold' of 'This onlooker' surrounded by sea, stone and silence. The anxious communion with 'Cove and cliff / … lake, mill and chapel' (*P*, p. 135) in Murphy's 'High Island' anticipates many of the themes explored by contributors to Bushe's volume.

One senses, therefore, that Richard Murphy's voice has become an integral part of our poetic consciousness. Several contemporary poets are exploring areas – topographical and thematic – which were pioneered by Richard Murphy. In its critical engagement with his work, this book presents new coordinates through which to interpret Murphy's lifetime achievement.

1

Division and Distress in the Poetry of Richard Murphy

MAURICE HARMON

Richard Murphy has had direct experience of a crumbling Big House, an estate run wild from lack of care, ancestral figures, and family heirlooms that spoke of history – a duelling pistol, Rangoon prints, a Crimean medal; a divided family background, colonial Protestant Anglo-Irish on one side and conquered Catholic peasant on the other; divided education, Irish and sensory on the one side and British and rational on the other; divided aspiration that contrasts the rigidity of the rectory and the military with the wildness of the cottage and the sea; a divided sexuality that makes women attractive but men desired. If some poems endorse the Big House, rectory and family aristocracy, others are critical of their cold superiority, greed and indifference to cultural heritage. Negotiating a space between the rigidity of the rectory and the freedom of the countryside, his poetry has focused on topics that had been absent from Irish poetry in the post-Yeatsian period. Although Austin Clarke had initially imitated W.B. Yeats' romantic treatment of the landscape, Clarke's concentration on the distresses of the Irish Catholic conscience clarified a subject that resonated with many people but was foreign to Richard Murphy. While Patrick Kavanagh's uncompromising portrait of the hardships and limitations of farming life, which he had made indicative of spiritual and psychological restriction, spoke eloquently of familiar Irish experience, it had little appeal for the young Anglo-Irish poet whose first collection, *Sailing*

to an Island (1963), set him apart. Together with Thomas Kinsella
and John Montague he belonged to an emerging generation with
a different sensibility. The presence of division together with the
consequential distress is found throughout his work but becomes
central to sonnets in *The Price of Stone* (1985).

Murphy's portrait in 'The Woman of the House' of his grandmother
Lucy Mary Thomson Ormsby (1873–1958), who delivered him in
Milford House, County Mayo in 1927, is affectionate and respectful.
He commemorates her kindness, sense of fun and unfulfilled artistic
ambitions. Above all he emphasises her success in overcoming the
division that existed between Big House and cottage: she cared for
people who lived on smallholdings of five acres or less, who loved
her and called her the healer. She reshaped the family legacy in a
positive manner and belonged to a more gracious time, as Murphy
acknowledges when describing his Ormsby grandparents at Milford
House:

> Time can never relax like this again:
> She on a side-car with her sketch-book,
> He writing a sermon in the library
> Till lunch, then fishing all the afternoon.   (*P*, p. 32)

How one handles one's inheritance is something Murphy has thought
about:

> Through our inheritance all things have come,
> The form, the means, all by our family:
> The good of being alive was given through them,
> We ourselves limit that legacy.   (*P*, p. 32)

His poetry and prose memoirs recover a personal and familial
heritage, examining his own position within a family that has
produced men who fought and died for King and country, worked
in the colonial service, or served the Church. The idea of giving one's
life to poetry was not an option that they valued. When he was sent
to Wellington College, a school with a pronounced military tradition,

he found it difficult to adapt. When he fled Oxford and went to live in Connemara to write poetry, his flight arose from the conflict between the pressures of academic life and the desire to become a poet. Out of that stay at Lecknavarna, close to nature, he later wrote a warmly personal sonnet for *The Price of Stone* in which the cottage speaks to him. The poem is a metaphor for poetry's resonant gravity and accumulated strength:

> Did you need my poor virgin concrete shell
> No family cared to live in, just to write
> Poetry, worshipping my waterfall,
> Abased in loneliness by lust at night?
>
> Still flowing steadfast in a flagstone cleft
> Of stunted alders clinging on, it pours
> With resonant gravity, bringing the gift
> Of widespread raindrops crafted to great force.
>
> Hearing that strong cadence, you learned your trade
> Concerned with song in endless falling, stayed.   (*P*, p. 208)

His Ormsby grandmother persuaded him to return to his studies.

Tensions between obedience and freedom pervaded many areas of Richard Murphy's life. In the first place, the obligation to be true to family values, to behave as expected, to conform to the Protestant ethic and the corresponding desire to escape from these restraints were ongoing struggles. Primarily he wanted to go outside the walls of the rectory, to experience the life of those who lived on the great Galway plains and close to the sea. Fundamentally it was a conflict between head and heart, between an English education with its emphasis on rationality and an Irish indulgence of instinct and feeling. An early expression of this desire came in the poem 'Sailing to an Island' (published on its own by the Dolmen Press in 1955), which describes an attempt made by Murphy with his brother Christopher, friends and other family members to escape from their restricted lives by sailing to Clare Island, once home to the pirate queen Granuaile. The

ill-judged journey ended in failure; they were driven off course by a
storm and found sanctuary in the harbour of Inishbofin, where they
were welcomed by bemused islanders, including Pat Concannon,
who later instructed him in sailing. They found not the romantic
world of a fabled queen but a real world where men caught fish for
the Cleggan market. The poem's powerful rhythm and language
respond to and recreate the exciting risk-taking of the sea journey:

> Orders thunder and canvas cannonades.
> She smothers in spray.   (*P*, p. 20)

The Big House demesne has its Pleasure Ground, but Murphy
dreamed of the vaster and more varied pleasure grounds available
to people whose imaginations were shaped by sea and sky, rock and
cloud. In his mind the sea itself was the ultimate pleasure ground.
He would spend twenty years in Connemara, where he owned and
skippered two Galway hookers, the *Ave Maria* and the *True Light*.
When his first major collection, also called *Sailing to an Island*, was
published in 1963 it was made distinctive by the inclusion of poems of
the sea, 'Sailing to an Island', 'The Last Galway Hooker', 'The Cleggan
Disaster'. His yearnings in that cottage by the Lecknavarna waterfall
blended with the romance of the sea. 'The Last Galway Hooker'
commemorates inheritance as one might record family history,
giving the names of her owners, and setting down how the poet came
to own her. Its Anglo-Saxon quality – a four-stressed line and long
caesura – adds to its dignity. Murphy speaks with authority as he
takes his stand in native, Catholic culture.

It is a proud moment, proudly recorded. He has restored and
renewed the boat and calls, in a Yeatsian echo, upon certain old men
to be his instructors. He respects good workmanship, admires craft,
skill and material, whether wood, stone or word. The poem ends on a
positive hope, in essence a commitment that he may handle the boat
well in the future. That need is satisfied in his account of the Cleggan
disaster and his admiration for the skill and courage of the boatman
Pat Concannon. Throughout, Concannon keeps his head, survives,
and the poem – realistic, literal, restrained, feeling always held in

check – steers clear of emotive language and heroism. The fisherman respects the sea and is sure of his boat:

> With Cong Forest timber, oak, elm and larch;
> Long supple pine oars, thole-pins of holly
> And a grapnel forged by the Cleggan smith.   (*P*, p. 49)

The narrative develops slowly, builds in details of the fishing, mackerel flooding into the nets. Stressing the upheavals of the ocean and the virtues of good seamanship, this poem also has an Anglo-Saxon quality – here, too, a man pits himself against the sea-road. When the storm hits, Concannon responds, will hold out, will not cut and run, but use the weight of the catch in the ebb tide to draw the boat away from the rocks; he endures through thunder, lightning and high waves. The experience is nightmarish, boats are lost, men drowned, an upturned hull threatens them, they see a raised arm. Concannon does what he knows is best:

> He knelt against the stem, his palms bleeding,
> His eyes, dimmed by the scurf of salt,
> Straining to give shape to the shadows they saw
> That looked like men in the milder water.   (*P*, p. 52)

Blinded by the sea, he survives, but when, Murphy wonders, will the widow's son say:

> 'Forget about the disaster,
> We're mounting nets today!'   (*P*, p. 55)

The Battle of Aughrim (1968) was written between 1962 and 1967. As usual Murphy wrote slowly and meticulously and after much preparation and thought. It is his most serious and complex examination of his own family, who had fought on both sides; his English ancestors were rewarded with 70,000 acres of land for their support, reduced to 350 acres in Mayo by the time the poet was born. Murphy records in *The Kick* what started his writing this long historical poem:

I was alone in Mary Coyne's cottage for an hour while the family were away at Mass ... The previous day had ended with me kneeling down in the kitchen with the family while Mary recited the Rosary ... A question uppermost in all Irish minds in our agricultural past – *who owns the land*? – occurred to me so strongly that I took an envelope from the pocket of my donkey jacket and wrote those words ... One written word led to another, with crossings out, more or less in this rough form:

> Who owns the land where musketballs are buried
> Under whitethorns on the esker, in the drained bogs
> Where flocks of sheep browse and redcoats waded?
>
> (*K*, pp. 196–7)

The battle itself was decisive in determining Protestant supremacy in Ireland. The Irish army, supporting the Catholics, fought for the deposed King James II. The English army fought for James' daughter and heir, Queen Mary, who had been raised as a Protestant, and her husband, King William, William of Orange, and supported the Protestants. Murphy's interest was personal as well as impersonal:

> Now I wanted to look inward at the divisions and devastations in myself as well as in the country: the conflicts, legends, rituals, myths and histories arising from possession of the land – why we still had borders and bigotries.   (*K*, p. 197)

His plan is to show both sides of the conflict. In *The Irish Times* of 17 May 1973 he described the poem as an attempt

> ... to get clear a division in my mind between England and Ireland – between an almost entirely English education, an English mind and Irish feeling. I tried to reconcile the two by focussing on the battle (in which my ancestors fought on both sides), finding out all I could – what it was really about and what people thought it was about; putting in different points of view, the errors and atrocities in which myths are made, and drawing up an evaluation of what the religious conflict meant;

what it meant in the past and how the past is still influencing us. It did, for me, reconcile the Irish, Catholic and Protestant. The equation was drawn up and there it is …'[1]

Although responsive to the Protestant story, Murphy is sympathetic to Catholic losses – the decline of Catholic influence, the Flight of the Wild Geese with Sarsfield, the long drain of emigration. The poem is complex, interactive and resonant, the manner stylised, studied and impersonal. He takes possession of the subject, masters its factual elements; the issue of land possession and exclusion touches on his family history and has determined his place in society: class, customs, memory and behaviour. His treatment is objective; he talks to local people, collects folklore, absorbs memories, reads historical accounts as he seeks to learn what he can about the battle. He likes well-built stanzas and rhyme, with the result that much of the poetry has a sturdy, fitted quality. Four poems in Part I are in couplets. There are pictorial descriptions, several vignettes, peasant scenes, battlefield incidents, aristocratic settings, portraits of leaders – the Marquis of St Ruth, Patrick Sarsfield, Colonel Henry Luttrell – and while weighted with historical and factual detail – the positioning and movement of soldiers, tensions between officers, the state of the poor, aristocratic lifestyle – the poem has significant aesthetic force as it focuses on the question of land ownership. It begins with the question that persists, 'Who owns the land where musket-balls are buried …' (*P*, p. 61), and 'To whom will the land belong / This time tomorrow night?' (*P*, p. 82):

> Who cares which foreign king
> Governs, we'll still fork dung,
> No one lets *us* grab soil:　　　(*P*, p. 78)

Murphy's Ormsby ancestors on his mother's side helped to establish the Anglo-Irish Ascendancy world that has defined his personal history, education and attitudes. But he has not ignored the situation of the losers, and deals bluntly with bloodshed and brutality: the unburied dead spread across four miles. This theme runs as an undercurrent through the poem's four sections; the poem is pictorial rather than dramatic, static where it might be advancing, fragmented and select. It has memorable scenes – 'Orange March', 'Casement's Funeral', 'Slate', 'Rapparees', 'The Wolfhound'; 'Rapparees' stands out because of its subtle fusion of the human and the natural world. 'The Wolfhound' is memorable for its portrait of the hound guarding her dead master:

> She lifts her head to cry
> As a woman keens in a famine for her son.   (*P*, p. 92)

In a repeated trope in Murphy's poetry, images join contemporary detail with the past – the dog-rose ditch was once defended by pikes, hikers bathe where cavalry traitors passed.

When he had finished the long poem, Murphy went on to write more personal poems. That distinction may have obscured the fact that *The Battle of Aughrim*, despite its objectivity, was deeply personal, involving family and inheritance, injustice and dispossession. That Irish people had had their land taken so that he and his kind could be rewarded struck him forcibly when he began to consider the plight of itinerants who lived in wattle tents or in caravans on the side of the road. The guilt occasioned by their historical exclusion motivated him to take responsibility for individual families. Poems in the collections *High Island*, *Care* and *The Price of Stone*, and the Sri Lankan poems, are personal in so far as they express his relationship to, observation of, or engagement with a variety of subjects in a variety of places, including, above all, the west of Ireland. Ceylon (now Sri Lanka), where he had lived as a child and where his father was mayor of Colombo, is also an important locale; its alien world contrasts with the familiar surroundings in Cleggan. *High Island* (1974) has three complementary worlds: the exotic world of Ceylon; that of the Irish itinerants, apart from the settled community and close to nature; and that of the islands, High and Omey. Now the sea and the western coast, particularly that part of it centred about the small village of Cleggan, were the focus of his attention. Others relate the poet's attempts to teach an itinerant boy to read, and this corresponds to the poet's memories of being taught to write in Ceylon. Poems about that British colony draw a vivid picture not only of the little boy's experiences in a strange and disturbing place but his unease and feeling of isolation in a foreign culture and climate. Many of the short poems, including 'Stormpetrel', 'Granite Globe', 'Nocturne' and 'High Island', are objective and detached; they take pleasure in finding language appropriate to accurate portrayal, while other poems, particularly 'Seals at High Island' and 'Pat Cloherty's Version of *The Maisie*', continue with the idea of the sea as pleasure ground, though the approach is not so much celebratory as empathetic and engaged.

It is not easy to describe why 'Seals at High Island' is so powerful. It creates a general feeling of movement – voices, noises, action, sea, animals – and the poet observer in surging interaction. They fuse, echo, repeat in constant rhythmic interplay, as in the opening stanza: 'reverberate', 'Clacking', 'bark', jaws open, caverns reverberate, seals bark, the ocean's mouth opens hugely and closes (*P*, p. 143). Throughout the five six-line stanzas the rhythm washes back and forth mimicking tidal wave and animal movement, both sexual and vocal, one line advances steadily, another comes and goes as though interrupted, the imagery is visual and concrete – 'grey bull', 'brindled cow', 'green water', 'black shoals', 'winged feet', 'fierce mouth' and 'scarlet flower' (*P*, p. 143). The poet is the intense observer, this is his language, and these rhythms carry his responses. Movement in every line, increasing and decreasing, opens and closes in glorious sexual union, a 'holy ceremony' (*P*, p. 143). He is almost a participant but reminds himself of the differences between animal feelings and his. Slowly the poem withdraws from the ceremony's climax. Still there is action, the great bull's penis withdrawn like a 'carnelian candle', the cow 'ripples ashore', a rival male swims to attack the 'tired triumphant god', their fight brilliantly captured – heads 'rear', surf boils, 'jaws open', blood jets (*P*, p. 43). There may be a loosening of sexual tension but no diminishment in linguistic and imaginative power. The poem winds down, moves from celebration and joy to sadness, a post-coital *tristesse* – mourning in requiem, a jarring replacement and the reprise of the ocean's tongue, now bitter, which swells in the cove and 'smothers their sweet song' (*P*, p. 144). Murphy is a deeply sexual poet, although the sexuality is often disguised. Here it is in the orchestration, in the symphonic accentuation and performance. The poem is totally achieved, a triumph of language and control, entirely appropriate that it should introduce the poems that Murphy wrote between the meditative *Battle of Aughrim* and the multiple voices of *The Price of Stone*.

By comparison, 'Pat Cloherty's Version of *The Maisie*' is restrained. Where the seal poem swells on the page, this sea narrative is relaxed; where the former is written in the immediacy of the scene, the latter recalls a sad story of loss at sea many years later. The narrative voice is subdued, unassertive and exact in recall. He tells the truth, he says, and we believe him; the meaning discloses itself by degrees, its modest manner both conceals and reveals. The omens are not good – they miss Mass to catch the tide, drowning follows the family, the hooker is burdened with its cargo of flour. On the mainland, people light candles in the church when they see the hooker 'smothered up in darkness' (*P*, p. 14). The helmsman Kerrigan did what he could, held her steady through wind, rain and hail, faced her into the hurricane but the sea claimed him. The crewman Barrett could not save him and he also drowned. The boat foundered with Kerrigan's wife below:

> The woman came up from the forecastle
>   she came up alone on deck
>   and a great heave cast her out on shore
>
> And another heave came while she drowned
>   and put her on her knees
>   like a person'd be in prayer
>
> That's the way the people found her
>   and the sea never came in
>   near that mark no more   (*P*, p. 114)

The poem ends with the recovery and burial of each of the three bodies. The narrative is simple, direct and devoid of literary embellishment although the technique is sophisticated and the poetic intelligence exquisite in its use of vernacular speech, positioning of indented lines, internal echoes and avoidance of punctuation. The powerful and passionate syntax of 'Seals at High Island' has been replaced by a low-keyed lament for ordinary people who go down to the sea in ships and are lost.

If 'Seals at High Island' is an emotional roller coaster, the two poems about storm petrels are more refined. 'Stormpetrel' addresses a bird through a variety of metaphors – 'Gypsy of the sea', 'Guest of the storm', 'Waif of the afterglow', 'Pulse of the rock' (*P*, p. 140) – and each of its four five-line stanzas is delicately handled, images animate the lines which are varied in length. The poet uses alliteration and a preponderance of monosyllables: in stanza one, 'winter', 'wambling', 'whaleroads', 'wake'; in stanza two, 'storm', 'sweeps', 'sooty', 'smelling'; each initial image is animated in active verbs and vivid images – 'sweeps', 'sooty grey coat', 'Barefoot across a sea of broken glass' (*P*, p. 140). The language is lilting, lightly moving, and the poetic touch playful and admiring. 'Nocturne' is even lighter and more human as it finds metaphorical ways to mimic the voices, movements and attitudes of the birds. It begins with sounds – the sound of a blade tapping on an oak table, waves sobbing – then it moves to colour light bleeding on the horizon as the sun sets – then comes movement – birds fly in, they communicate, one coming in, one signalling from a nest, forming a symphony of vibration, all the birds calling. Sounds suggest feelings – 'complaints', 'passion' – and individual voices – the parallel is between bird and human, one voice has to be heard by another amid all the cries:

> Come back!   come back!
> I'm here   here   here
> This burrow   this   wall this hole
>
> Ach!   who kept you?   where've you been?
> There   there   there
> It's all over   over   over   (*P*, p. 142)

Birds fly in and find their mates in loneliness and passion; the relationship between them is conveyed in human terms, in a human context of appeal and comfort, in overcoming obstacles. The poem moves to recovery, as his poems often do – a cottage restored, stone turning to gold, a church resurrected from sand, girls returning from a night of love, seals consummate their relationship, the poet refits a hooker, rescues an itinerant family, meets Tony White, who becomes his soul companion, discovers a monastic site on High Island, which he buys.

The poem 'High Island', *Ardoileán*, is a hymn of resurrection. As the son of a Protestant Anglo-Irish family and one who longed to cross from the rectory to the cottage, in this poem Murphy has come into his own. What he sought in Lecknavarna is now all about him. The poems in *High Island* are acts of imaginative possession – he is alert, responsive, passionately and exactly engaged. He lives among the people, makes a living from the sea, gives employment, connects with craftsmen of the area. It is not all pleasant and rewarding. His attempt to educate an itinerant boy fails, his sponsorship of an itinerant family meets with local opposition, he is conscious of how different he may be seen by other, more rooted members of the settled community and knows that his accent always sets him apart even though he dresses down when he skippers the hookers in order to disguise that difference. But friends who visited include Charles Monteith from Faber & Faber, Ted Hughes, Sylvia Plath, Theodore Roethke, C. Day Lewis and Thomas Kinsella. In London he has titled family and friends. There is always the risk of his homosexuality being discovered. But he has found a personal voice that adapts to many different topics and a technique that adjusts to different rhythms and tones. His relationship with the western seaboard, where he feels at home and can engage with creatively, contrasts with his childhood memories of Ceylon with its strange creatures, native servants, exotic religious ceremonies and the isolation of the compound in which his family lived. There he felt bewildered and threatened with loss of identity. When he listened to the repetitive sound of the coppersmith, he tried to counter its foreign sound:

His *took took took*
And his *tonk tonk tonk*   (*P*, p. 130)

– which the poet never understood – by repeating an English word such as 'beat' (*P*, p. 130). The tension results in a loss of consciousness, his brain 'melting' and the compound spinning around, 'Till I and the bird, the word and the tree, were one' (*P*, p. 130). The risk of losing identity in the foreign place is the underlying theme in the Ceylon poems, whereas in the Cleggan poems identity is repeatedly confirmed. The fourteen-year-old itinerant boy has the opposite reaction. For him written words are alien and of no practical use:

If books resembled roads, he'd quickly read:
But they're small farms to him, fenced by the page,
Ploughed into lines, with letters drilled like oats:
A field of tasks he'll always be outside.
If words were banknotes, he would filch a wad;
If they were pheasants, they'd be in his pot
For breakfast, or if wrens he'd make them king.   (*P*, p. 124)

The principle of natural freedom is one the poet respects. He makes it the lesson in 'Care' where the kid goat has become so spoiled by what the children feed him that he loses his instinct to avoid the poisonous yew. Freedom is at bottom what the poet values in several of the Cleggan poems; it is inherent in the life of fishermen, pulses in the poem about seals and those about birds – corncrake, petrel, swallow, swan or heron – and fundamental to how he sees the entire region and those who live there. Itinerants are free even if they are guilty of sexual abuse in the starkly gothic 'The Glass Dump Road', and it is what he admires in Tony White's philosophy of being free of possessions and what is at the heart of the enthusiastic portrayal of the girls who flood into his home after a night of revelry in the boats. 'Morning Call' delights in their wildness and sensuality. The mood resembles 'Seals at High Island'. They step into his house like fillies and wake him from his bachelor bed; he opens his door to 'a flood' that freshens his 'brackish pools' (*P*, p. 165), they are excited, bursting with young life, fearful of what will be said at home, two beautiful itinerant girls, not in silk kimonos:

> Lovely as seals wet from fishing, hauled out on a rock
> To dry their dark brown fur glinting with scales of salmon
> When the spring tide ebbs. This is their everlasting day
> Of being young. They bring to my room the sea's iodine odour
> On a breeze of voices ruffling my calm as they comb their long
> Hair tangled as weed in a rock pool beginning to settle clear.
> Give me the sea-breath from your mouths to breathe a while!
>   (*P*, p. 165)

That prayer expresses the poet's feeling of loneliness and his longing to participate in sensual life. That exuberance contrasts with the complications of homosexuality. 'Moonshine' clarifies one aspect of Murphy's personality: despite wanting to be accepted by people, he is essentially a loner and this makes relationships difficult. The issue is worded clearly and ironically in this poem, which is a tangle of contradictions from the opening statement:

> To think
> I must be alone:
> To love
> We must be together.

to the conclusion:

> Alone I love
> To think of us together:
> Together I think
> I'd love to be alone.   (*P*, p. 147)

The forces of being alone and being together cause division and pain, and there is no solution. 'Displaced Person' brings the issue of relationship into even sharper and more distressing relief. How does the homosexual fare when making love to a woman? He is divided and troubled, forced into pretence so that love itself is betrayed, and he feels guilty.

> Those years ago, when I made love to you,
>   With fears I was afraid you knew,
>   To grow strong I'd pretend to be
> A boy I'd loved, loving yourself as me.
> I played his part so open-eyed that you
>   Believed my artful ploy was true.
> To show I'd nothing false to hide
> And make you feel the truth of love I lied.   (*P*, p. 172)

Understandably, the issue has not been explicit in much of the earlier poetry, but in *The Price of Stone* (1985) and *The Kick* (2002/2017), Murphy writes more openly about sexual ambivalence.

In the collection *The Price of Stone*, Part II consists of fifty sonnets in which particular places and objects, all associated with the poet, speak in the first person, a process Murphy calls 'ventriloquised autobiography'.[2] Taken as a whole they provide a varied portrait of his life and times. The usual prose form of autobiography is sequential, divided into separate chronological incidents, narrated by a single voice. Here the customary mode of a single voice is exchanged for a wide range of different voices, the chronology interrupted to focus on chosen subjects in specific places. Instead of progression we encounter unexpected halts where the eye of the poet is trained on particulars, the reflective process is slowed for close inspection, comment, reconstruction and shaped responses, as the structures speak, directly or indirectly, about their history and his life. Included are schools he attended – Baymount in Dublin, Cathedral Choir School in Canterbury, Wellington College and Oxford – and places in which he resided, including Milford House in County Mayo, where he lived as a boy; Connemara, where he spent twenty years between Cleggan, Inishbofin, High Island and Omey Island; and Knockbrack ('speckled hill') in Killiney, County Dublin, where he was living when he wrote the sonnets. The objects include the folly on Killiney Hill, the lead mine in Carrickmines, a wattle tent in which itinerants lived on the side of a road, a gym he attended, the ship on which he travelled home from Ceylon as a boy, and many more. While writing a poem in four quatrains about the 'Folly', he hit upon the idea of reducing the final quatrain into a clinching couplet, not a summarising thought as in Shakespeare. Seeing the 'Folly' as a symbol of Anglo-Irish decadence, he thought of identifying with the obelisk and allowing it to speak. It was, he realised, a way of escaping from his own personality and into another persona. By allowing the object to speak in its own voice he enjoyed an unexpected freedom and avoided being openly confessional.[3] From the initial, self-defining 'I rise' the opening stanza is assertive, confident and defiant (*P*, p. 177). The second stanza explains how the obelisk came into being: it was built by an exploitative aristocracy, who made the poor work hard, while they ascended its stair, 'To admire the land they owned and wish for more' (*P*, p. 177). The tower is bisexual: the sun's 'seed' enters through the old grey stucco, moonlight makes its 'witch-pap cone obscene', the couplet describes it as a proud, tumescent, ugly phallus: 'scrawled with muck, I crest the hill' (*P*, p. 177). Sexual dominance, an extension of decadent supremacy, adds to the idea of immoral power. The relevance for the aristocratic, bisexual poet is clear. 'Lead Mine Chimney' continues the theme of the rich getting richer and the poor getting poorer. A chimney that was once part of a thriving mine is now useless, 'Not puffing smoke out any more, disjointed / By age ...' (*P*, p. 178). The appearance it gives of purpose is deceptive.

The 'Portico' at Dún Laoghaire, County Dublin stands on rocks facing the sea and looks towards the Martello tower at Sandycove, associated with James Joyce and *Ulysses*. At its back lie the harbour, boat house and yacht club with a long pier that extends out to the lighthouse at the mouth of the harbour. To its right lies a promenade that runs as far as Sandycove. It is an attractive building; in summertime children play there, people sunbathe on the roof, courting couples find privacy there, at night-time homosexuals meet. In Murphy's heightened account it is a place of degradation. All the details of the poem contribute to his transformative vision. Texture and tone reflect his darker side. The contextual images are of darkness, 'noose', fog, 'mud', and men cruising for sex (*P*, p. 179).

The notion of deadness resides in references to 'rocks', the ashen sea, 'decay', and the insistence that there is nothing admirable here, nothing to attract the stoic mind; this is not a temple to the Hindu goddess of reproduction and decay (*P*, p. 179). It refers to itself as a 'concrete cloister' in which ghosts seek life-restoring blood (*P*, p. 179). Here is a new kind of subsidiary 'deviate church', whose devotees have succumbed to a black hole where they perform homosexual acts (*P*, p. 179). After a reference to seedy Bacchic hymns the couplet condemns the ugly and piercing music of this deviate church and its enactment of 'ithyphallic' art:

> My hymns are hog-snorts, squealing bottle-glass
> Screwed underfoot, a wave's foghorn caress.   (*P*, p. 179)

The voice is ambivalent, both repelled and attracted. The ambivalence in 'caress' is significant: the poet is drawn here, risk is part of the attraction. Ventriloquism has a dual purpose in the sonnets. Buildings speak in their own voices but what they say expresses what the poet wants them to say; their objectivity is masked.

The autobiographical relevance of 'Nelson's Pillar' lies in its being the voice of colonial power. More objective and cerebral than 'Portico', it speaks of force, style and a sense of isolation in an impoverished rebel city whose populace is indifferent to the history of its construction. To them it is alien. It knows it is a stake in the heart of the city, a cold British force that may rule the waves but can never control the beggars who gather at its plinth. To them it is merely a terminus for trams, as Joyce, too, noted in *Ulysses*. Compact, well-managed and self-defining, the sonnet speaks contemptuously of the 'puerile skill' of those who blew it up, and sums up the divided, limited nature of colonial power that is heard in the couplet's reference to its 'chiselled voice' (*P*, p. 180). Key words – 'Doric column', 'square abacus', 'plinth', 'masons' – combine towards particular effects (*P*, p. 180). As in 'Folly', the voice speaks for an aristocracy in decline, power 'Dismasted and dismissed' (*P*, p. 180). The opposition between the speaker's head and the city's heart results in decapitation. Only the voice remains to speak truly of a place where emptiness prevails, not intelligence, the fissure echoing the division in the poet between English rationality and Irish feeling.

The question of voice recurs in the more relaxed 'Wellington Testimonial', witty, objective and playful as it entertains the metaphor of 'Needling' in its dual sense of towering and penetrating, both a smirk and a 'spit', which also has a secondary meaning of ejected saliva (*P*, p. 181). The word 'polished' (*P*, p. 181) is associated with 'spit and polish'. Duality persists in 'dressed' (*P*, p. 181), meaning to put clothes on and to shape stone. Unlike Nelson's Pillar the monument does not have an interior staircase and has lost its capacity for curiosity. All it is good for now, as the couplet once again identifies, its 'sole point', is 'to maintain a clean laconic style' (*P*, p. 181).

In lyric poetry the paraphrasable content is less important than the aesthetic accomplishment. In these sonnets thematic issues can be found without much trouble and, once discovered, remain prominent as evidence of the poet's concerns. Murphy's interests are political, social, sexual, familial and personal. But finding linguistic vitality, finding the poem's inner life, is endlessly engaging. We respond to new verbal combinations, fresh revelations or insights, and since Murphy's intellectual control is clear, his structural strength and syntactic control never in doubt, we have to focus on other areas. Beneath the rigorous architecture and syntax lies the range of feeling we expect in a sonnet. In 'Georgian Tenement', the third in a cluster of poems set in Dublin, Murphy's playful imagination is uppermost. The tenement speaks in the language of ordinary men. What the poet has to say gives way to how he says it, as the poem moves through a metaphorical linking of legal terminology – 'high court', 'session', 'verdict', 'wrong', 'decreed' – together with a linking chain of words like 'dry rot', 'airtight', 'Death and cremation', and 'soft floors' (*P*, p. 182). The links are sometimes on more than one level and the density of verbal relationships is pleasing. In a shift of strategy Murphy writes a narrative that faces the consequences of being 'rebuilt': the construction of an ugly office block (*P*, p. 182). The contrast is with 'whores' whose immoral earnings increase; the word 'turnover' equates remuneration with bodily position (*P*, p. 182). Alert to historical relevance, Murphy commemorates the efforts of the young to save the eighteenth-century buildings – 'Young lovers of old structures' – and the response of the gardaí with 'riot gear and water gun' (*P*, p. 182); their actions prove fatal for the building's preservation. The couplet adds a note of regret to a poem that has been a lament for lost beauty in the face of decay, 'banal' renewal (*P*, p. 182), idealistic resistance and unstoppable destruction:

> Would that your free hands in my spongy wood
> Could cure fungosity, make my flaws good.   (*P*, p. 182)

While youthful idealism is attractive and what whores make goes up in value, a graceful historical building is allowed to decay and die.

If the underside of Dublin life is glimpsed in the canal-bank whores, a more insidious activity is shown in 'Gym'. 'Vice-regal walls' keep the aristocratic association, which is once again debased in a context of imperial domination, secrecy, shame and 'heartless' male performance (*P*, p. 183). Linking words point to role-playing, 'body culture' as a mask for gay sexuality, 'back street' location, 'spurious', 'retreat', 'mime' function as disguises, and this idea is carried forward in 'Discreetly couched', 'ingled', 'masked', 'steam', 'immune', 'tableaux' (*P*, p. 183). The mime continues. All is not as it seems, the scene is 'full of cock and bull' (*P*, p. 183): the language, hitherto disguised, where words are 'spurious', is blunt – the freedom to act and speak is grotesque, symmetrical aristocratic architecture persists, but what it hides is shameful. Here men are lodged, laid, in a shameful 'cell'; 'penetralian' includes the idea of shrine and mystery, secret and hidden; here they 'come to grief', here they have no immunity from decadence and deceit, here mime and masquerade are stripped away and the contemporary fear of AIDS only adds to their shame (*P*, p. 183). Once again it is not the theme that counts as much as the play of words, their capacity to delight. Although dealing with secretive behaviour, a dark presence in the city, the poem, transcending its subject in a triumph of art, gives aesthetic pleasure.

The narrative strength that Murphy introduces to the sequence is seen generally in its biographical content as well as in the many individual voices and tonal changes but also in the ability which he has often demonstrated to give a particular poem an entirely credible and persuasive presence. 'Carlow Village Schoolhouse' compares the poet's search for a secure footing in poetry in 'Much as you need a sonnet house to save / Your muse' to his great-grandfather Richard William Murphy's need in the small village of Nurney for the 'grave / Façade' of the Church of Ireland school, whose training in rationality saved him from the deleterious effects of poverty (*P*, p. 186). The poem, as Murphy reminds us in his notes about it, is about the power of the word to bring people out of destitution.[4] The schoolhouse confirmed the master's desire for order, thought, stability, status, comfort and freed him from being a pauper but cut him off from the poor Catholics: 'Such symmetry he gained from me, you got / By birth, given his names' (*P*, p. 186). The poet never liked being called Murphy; it was too common. In 'Birth Place' he easily accommodates history. That the voice of Milford, his ancestral mansion, should speak of its history, the history of the family and their activities, is a mark of its character. Words evoke different historical narratives – 'absentee' landlord, 'rebel' burnings, and the death of 'old relations' (*P*, p. 191). Throughout, the tone is elegiac as well as historically objective. That the building admits to being 'scared', 'expecting death', and its fear that this birth may be another death, highlights a counterforce (*P*, p. 191). His birthing cries are accompanied by the noise of carts taking 'mouldy' books away to be burnt, a conflagration echoing the earlier 'rebel match' (*P*, p. 191). That image of destruction and death is offset by the nurturing activity of bees industriously making honey. Opposing themes of birth and death, nurturing and destruction exist side by side.

The hexagonal shape of the honeycomb reminds us of the Hexagon building the poet built on Omey Island and its mood of centripetal serenity. A boy leading a pony about a pond in 'Birth Place' is also nurturing, providing water for the young mother. The moment of birth transfigures all that death. The couplet confirms the natural richness of the moment and the event, the comfort of the life-giving sun:

It shone like honey on doorsteps of brown bread.
The August evening kissed her worn out head.   (*P*, p. 191)

The preceding 'Connemara Quay' focuses on death and decay in boats which have been allowed to rot; as a boy home from his Canterbury school Murphy played in the 'hulks' (*P*, p. 190). Here, unlike 'Birth Place' – also dealing with decay and decline but ending on a comforting note – water does not give nourishment, desolation wins. The twin themes of loss and potential, another expression of restriction and freedom, are taken up over and over in the sonnets. The more we read them the more their thematic concerns emerge and, more importantly, the more their drama of recurrent and interconnecting words and strategies become pulses of happy recognition. As in any good poem we discover richer significance by repeated readings. Not only do the sonnets enliven the inner life of the poem through verbal connections, play, levels of meaning and dynamic power, they provide links of various kinds throughout the sequence. The placing of poems neither in an order that is biographically chronological nor in accordance with when they were written creates another layer of achievement; the sonnets connect through the repetition of significant words, particular themes and identifying attitudes. Hence, we become aware early on of the poet's preoccupation with the purpose and power of poetry; the house of the sonnet is architecturally sound, carefully constructed line by line, quatrain by quatrain, clinched in the final couplet and internally bound by strict rhyme and verbal linkages to become a home for the Muse.

Murphy's habit of gutting the *Oxford English Dictionary* for particular words brings an austerity to the text that seems to be off-putting but is effective. Within the first six lines of 'Beehive Cell', 'pyramidal headroom', 'eremitical boredom' and 'cerebellic souterrain' work well in the context (*P*, p. 225). The actuality of his appreciation of wood, stone and good craftsmanship is confirmed by his belief in the disciplined form of the sonnet. Furthermore, if he deals with decadent behaviour, injustice and personal failing, he is faithful to the power of poetry to save us from spiritual destruction. He and his class have little political power and religion has been devalued; he has not joined the army or become a clergyman. But devotion to poetry, however admirable, is not the whole story. He is often distracted by other interests and concerns. In 'Ice Rink' the poet delights in descriptions of the movements, reflections, exaltations, athletic tricks and the 'pure fun' of the skaters on the rink (*P*, p. 185). Like 'Ice Rink', 'Liner' is self-delighting, as the ship speaks to the child. One can only take pleasure in the metaphorical language that describes the progress of the ship in aristocratic terms and mentions dolphins and petrels. But, to the Anglo-Irish Protestant child who has lived in Ceylon, 'home is like a foreign country' (*P*, p. 193). To feel alien in one's own country is his heritage. Poems about birth and death obelise the complex fate of being Anglo-Irish, not fitting into the family's cultural contexts is challenging, an issue that is teased out in a number of sonnets. 'Connemara Quay' concludes with the question and affirmative answer, 'What did you think you might do? Now you know' (*P*, p. 190). The freedom he felt includes the uses of different voices as well as the freedom to stretch rhetorical wings or to grasp the nettle of intricate verbal bindings. As in reading Shakespeare's sonnets, we make a distinction between the poet's self and these fictive selves and between each of the selves. The creation of multiple voices is a major dramatic achievement – they speak in character, embody particular values, turn the focus of their evidence on the poet, who does not shirk what they say but brings them alive in changing styles.

'Rectory' returns to the issue of decay and rising damp; the metaphors of dogs, 'dog-collar', 'chain', 'leap', 'licking', 'loose', 'sniff', 'bitches in heat', 'dog-rampages', 'pups', create a dynamic sequence (*P*, p. 196); the rectory, which has associations with obedience, control and a moral climate, is challenged by animal spirits and natural urges; the two conflicting forces meet: dogs 'feel blessed' not through the chain of command but the perfume of sweet lavender in a lady's dress (*P*, p. 196). Boys may be kept on a leash but bitches 'make mixed marriages' (*P*, p. 196). The poem acknowledges that the freedom enjoyed by animals is not available to the boys, who are 'lockjawed' in the name of Protestant authority (*P*, p. 196). 'Letterfrack Industrial School' joins these issues in a beautiful Connemara landscape and is a passionate response to the fate of boys who have been sent to this remote school where they are confined without hope, checked by the material of the crafts they learn – 'metal, wood, thread, hide' – and by beatings (*P*, p. 197). Verbal blows illuminate their plight. The boys are 'Podded', 'stunted', 'bruise[d]', 'hurt' and packed indiscriminately together – 'Orphans', 'felons', 'bastards' and 'waifs' who are 'branded' for life with the stigma of their incarceration (*P*, p. 197). One, 'Dressed as a girl', found freedom and was 'saved by a thieving gypsy' (*P*, p. 197). Their condition appeals strongly to a poet who has himself known restriction, isolation and loneliness. The beauty of the landscape and its freely flowing waters abide like a heavenly vision, whereas those confined 'abandon hope' (*P*, p. 197). It is a deeply felt satire on injustice and inhumane treatment.

Murphy expressed the same compassion and empathy for itinerants in other sonnets and in *High Island*. Freedom is key, and its twin, wildness. Human beings should not be cabined and confined, subjected to rectory rules, should not be made feel inferior, should not be stupefied, or stunted for reasons of class, religion, race or sexual orientation. Murphy's moral stance is clear. The placing of school poems in a cluster underlines what he felt and what he experienced as he developed these attitudes and beliefs. At 'Baymount' he was confined, deprived of family, bereft of love, lonely, bullied and expected to undergo revolting tests of courage (*P*, p. 198). 'Canterbury Cathedral' opened doors to poetry through voice training; he pays tribute to discipline and liberation:

> Now, you've come back, not to sing the *Te Deum*
> In my nave, but to retrieve from your song's ground
> The love you gave me then. Above the triforium
> It soared to reach martyrs in stained glass crowned.   (*P*, p. 199)

Once again, the underlying themes of poetic vocation, trained use of language and form come to the forefront. The Canterbury poem illuminates what the school represents in its calm, measured movement and linking terms – 'tuned', 'trained', 'filled', 'poured', 'milled' – the feeling present in the rhythms of the first quatrain representing a warm memory of boyhood pleasure, of climbing into the triforium and the circular movement of his return. 'Choir School' is a companion tribute; 'Suntrap' recalls the blissful period spent at

Milford with his mother and the Ormsby grandparents when he
and his siblings were brought home to safeguard them from the
war; in that carefree time 'learning and love made peace' (*P*, p. 201).
The poem is another tribute to craftsmanship, the pleasure ground
of language, the imagination's ability to make the past live in the
present, the 'cottage weaver's warp and woof' the freedom of spirit,
the benevolent continuity of tradition (*P*, p. 201). Wellington College
is where he rejected the idea of a military career and turned to poetry
(*P*, p. 205); Oxford is where he was trained to be critical, not creative
(*P*, p. 206). The positioning of 'Lecknavarna' almost immediately
after highlights the growing attraction of poetry in his young life,
as does 'Killary Hostel' (*P*, pp. 208–9). He was, he writes, 'Hooked
here in boyhood on the Tir na nÓg myth'. 'Convenience', which is
placed between (*P*, p. 207), narrates the incident in Piccadilly when,
young and unemployed, he was trapped by a blackmailer pretending
to be a policeman who accused him of being 'homosexual', a word he
dreaded being applied to himself and even more for the repercussions
in his family should his name appear in a newspaper (*K*, p. 105). The
internal division was indelible: he was a split personality compelled
to live a double life, to seek furtive loves, to be other than he seemed,
to pursue his own vocation and seek salvation in words.

Part roofless oratory, part restored hut, in other words an image of
the poet, 'Miners' Hut' has a split personality. How often, he reflects
in his notes, has he 'sacrificed the oratory of thought for some new
act that involved men building or excavating'.[5] The problem was
deeply ingrained. As he has often demonstrated, he enjoys activity
– sailing in the hooker, designing the Hexagon or miners' hut when
he could have been writing poetry or living a contemplative life.
Some of these activities have led to the writing of poems. He sailed
the *Ave Maria* and wrote 'The Cleggan Disaster'; he designed the
Hexagon and wrote 'Hexagon', he restored the miners' hut and wrote
'Miners' Hut'. Over the course of his life the chronic division between
activity and creativity has meant that his output was smaller than it
might have been. It is the price of stone syndrome, the temptation to
acquire property instead of writing a poem: 'Divided mind ... action
or contemplation ... the conflict in myself ... the struggle that goes

on and on … '.[6] In 'Miners' Hut' the search for gold by former owners of High Island desecrated the oratory, 'a desecration of corbelled cells' that hermits in the ascetic Culdee tradition had built to seek personal salvation (*P*, p. 214). In reading Murphy's reflections behind the sonnets we realise that the complexity of his thinking does not always emerge in the poem. The sonnet form is not conducive to the working out of argument. It compresses, abbreviates, summarises and is not capable of teasing out complex thoughts. It is more suitable for the release of feeling, 'will sound like a fault: wheatear, shearwater' (*P*, p. 214); the song of the birds is the voice of poetry. The key he keeps in his 'desk drawer' will unseize 'tongue-tied stonework' and make the hut 'sound' in its ruins (*P*, p. 214). Instead of being bound, the hut will be relieved, instead of being silent and dead it will sound and live. The paradigm of life and death, restriction and release, persists.

'Hexagon', on the facing page, is another hermit's hut, the poet's sanctuary where he escapes from the world and devotes himself to reflection. There he has all he needs – 'Oak bed, a hundred books, a staunch teak door …' (*P*, p. 215); it is his Lake Isle of Innisfree. He has no need to write: he has his 'isolation', the 'Sun and the moon', serenity and security, with distraction shut away (*P*, p. 215). He lives the dream in a building designed for the contemplative life which he seldom lived.

'New Forge' is another version of the earlier vision. He lived there for thirteen years, wrote *The Battle of Aughrim* and 'The God Who Eats Corn' there, but tragic events intruded: Tony White died, as did Murphy's divorced wife, Patricia Avis. In addition, his responsibility for some Travellers brought him additional anxiety. These wild people lived apart from the settled community and were removed from the contemplative serenity he dreamt about. In 'Horse-drawn Caravan' he speaks of their rowdy, drunken ways (*P*, p. 218). 'Old Dispensary', one of a cluster of poems about Travellers, speaks defiantly of the settled community's attack on a place where 'a lazy breed / Of verminous, ditch-born tinkers might live' (*P*, p. 219). 'Wattle Tent' also opposes wildness and freedom to imprisonment and confinement following on from 'Prison', in which Murphy visits a young Traveller in prison and is saddened by his condition. He sees the sonnet form as another kind of prison as to what can be said in its restricted 'musico-mathematical structure'.[7]

Over and over he admits to personal failing. He fails in a personal relationship because of his preoccupation with building. He failed his wife Patricia Avis when their daughter was born. 'Roof-tree' is a relentlessly personal rebuke for his failure. Instead of celebrating the birth of their child, he employed men to rebuild their house, Lake Park in County Wicklow. The child's cries were answered by the harsh noise of hammering and 'stupefying knocks'. The couplet hands down a clear judgement:

> To renovate my structure, which survives,
> You flawed the tenderest movement of three lives.   (*P*, p. 187)

The poem reverberates with intrusive sounds and active verbs, its verbal links create the music of disruption and insensitive, selfish preoccupation. In 'Red Bank Restaurant' Murphy expresses anger at another type of selfish preoccupation seen in politician and literary critic Conor Cruise O'Brien, who betrayed him. Filled with personal venom, the poem is a satirical but limited portrait of a vain, witty, rapacious, self-protective and malign man, a Faustian figure whose 'cold brilliance' the poem identifies (*P*, p. 188). Sexual betrayal is something the poet understands; in truth his vehemence is compromised. The positioning of the poem beside 'Roof-tree' makes the point of O'Brien's disturbing impact on the home of the young couple, which has been adversely affected by Murphy's obsessive behaviour and now by disruptive, loveless intercourse with the young wife and mother. This is a different kind of mirroring from the icy reflections in the ice rink.

Murphy's general concerns come together in 'Friary', the ruined cloister of Ross Errilly, near Headford in County Galway. He reflects on change, the destruction of a forest, the transition from paganism to Christianity, and the 'desecration' of the friary 'stacked' with 'tombs' and exposed to violation (*P*, p. 224). In these contexts he considers the evidence of transience in the friary itself, the tombs of arrogant 'donors' who invested money in vain to earn salvation: their bones 'unresurrected'. That failure contrasts with the fate of lovers who, in a kind of salvation or rebirth, live each time their names are read on tombs; they are 'buried in rhyme, … / Engraved in words that live each time they're read'. 'Young leaf-growth' and rain which 'harps on ruins' lead to ruined towers, 'leprous sores' and 'lecherous gargoyles'; tender promise gives way to ugliness – 'peeping toms' and 'thieves' (*P*, p. 224). Murphy's belief in the power of words to confer resurrection is limited by the knowledge that innocence, mystery and love are always threatened. Once again he laments the reality of transience, balancing the promise of growth and sexuality with the actuality of destruction and loss. That tragic intermingling leads on to accounts of miraculous birth in the next two sonnets. 'Beehive Cell', the penultimate sonnet, tells the story of the birth of a child by a woman on her own on High Island helped by a mysterious hand.

The concluding sonnet, 'Natural Son', written in the poet's own voice, celebrates the birth of his son William. Murphy and Anya Barnett became lovers after Tony White died, their son was born in January 1982 while Murphy was writing the sonnets at Knockbrack. She wanted to live with him, but he preferred what she called 'our semi-detached relationship', he in one house, she in another. At the same time, as she knew, he needed partners who were gay; his sexuality was also 'split-level' (*K*, p. 306). In *The Kick* Murphy writes, 'although I loved her, I could never become her single-minded lover' (*K*, p. 337). The destructive consequences included desire, conflict, anger and remorse. Written in a fluid movement, the sonnet chooses the metaphor of womb, tomb, house and harkens back to the many other references to room and cell and the release of life throughout *The Price of Stone* sequence:

> No house we build could hope to satisfy
> Every small need, now that you've made this move
> To share our loneliness, much as we try
> Our vocal skill to wall you round with love.　　(*P*, p. 226)

In the published volume, 'Natural Son' is placed at the end of the sonnets, although written before 'Knockbrack' (*P*, p. 184), which returns to the poet's 'dislocated life'.[8] In his notes Murphy writes: 'Perhaps it's time to let the house where the sonnets have been written speak … where I've spent more than two years trying to make poems that will last … never mind if they are forgotten … their making is what matters … so let "Knockbrack" have the final word as the colophon of a beginning with "Folly."'[9]

> Coming to speculate, you stayed for good:
> Your fortune in the gold market of whins.
> Avuncular pines admonished you to brood
> On dark tale ends with woodcut colophons.   (*P*, p. 184)

Modestly regarding himself as no more than a poetic handyman, Murphy's ambition was to adapt a structure that had in the past been 'perfected by consummate sonneteers'.[10] An ambition articulated at Lecknavarna and completed in *The Price of Stone*.

2

~

Richard Murphy's Plainstyles

BERNARD O'DONOGHUE

In my essay "'Pat Cloherty's Version of *The Maisie*", Richard Murphy',[1] I suggested that in that poem Murphy created a new poetic language, achieving an effect of plainness through a form of highly worked intricacy. I want to pursue that suggestion here by claiming that in other poems, particularly in the early part of his career but not only there, Murphy has developed other kinds of plainstyle, all different and often an amalgam of sophisticated poetic devices working in conjunction with representations of Irish dialects or accents. It is the same kind of project that J.M. Synge carried out in his celebrated plays set in the west of Ireland.[2]

The quality in Murphy's poetry that I want to emphasise with the term plainstyle is its accessibility.[3] It is striking, I think, that across a wide range of linguistic registers, themes and metrical forms, his poetic language always has an immediate communicative impact. Even when he uses technical boating language in poems like 'The Last Galway Hooker', terms like 'trammel and spillet' do not detain the reader (*P*, p. 36). This is not just because they can be looked up; they have something of the quality of any technical language when reading at all means a readiness to encounter an unfamiliar set of terms.[4]

First though I want to recap briefly what I said in the essay about 'Pat Cloherty's Version of *The Maisie*'. I argued there that in reporting – even reproducing, as he claims – the language used by Cloherty in describing the tragic events, Murphy at once took advantage of the vividness of the original narrative ('hugging it   hugging it   O my dear', *P*, p. 113), but also created a new language drawing on the established devices of poetic narrative. I ended by quoting T.S. Eliot's observation about Yeats: 'in becoming more Irish, not in subject-matter but in expression, he became at the same time universal' (*P*, p. 279). It is a familiar phenomenon in the history of poetics: for example, in Wordsworth's claim to write in a 'language' of 'a man speaking to men'.[5]

What I want to do here is to return to that subject and to broaden out its reach in a number of ways. Most crucially, something further needs to be said about what I mean by 'plainstyle'. 'Plain style' is a term that in modern criticism is often taken back to the developments in rhetoric associated with the name of Peter Ramus in the sixteenth century.[6] The ambition that Ong attributes to Ramus, which has explained his being taken up by American critics of the New England School, was to achieve 'plaine delivery of the Word without painted eloquence'.[7] This 'retreat from rhetoric'[8] was linked to the emergence of the kind of language associated in England with such Protestant set pieces as Foxe's *Book of Martyrs* (1563), as in its celebrated sentence given to Latimer to address his fellow martyr Ridley: 'Be of good cheer Master Ridley and play the man, for this day we shall light such a candle in England as will never be put out.' The image of light is typical, as Ong makes plain: 'The medium by which light is transmitted seems to act as though it was not there, whereas the medium of sound is felt rather as though it were acting to sustain and to give resonance to sound.'[9] I will return towards the end to consider briefly the place of the visual and the auditory in Murphy's poetry.

I am not concerned to dwell on what Murphy in the 'Battle Hill' sections of *The Battle of Aughrim* calls the 'credal war' (*P*, p. 61) and 'credal slaughter' (*P*, p. 99) of the century after Ramus. But one thing I do want to stress is the concern with history which is central to the effect of many of his most important poems, notably *The Battle of Aughrim*. To see how I think the issue of plainstyle language fits there, I want to take issue with a negative response to the language of that poem which seems to me precisely to miss the point and the distinction of the poem, and indeed of Murphy's poetic project in general. In the course of his review of the American edition of

High Island in the *New York Review of Books*, Donald Davie –
who, as the author of two very distinguished books on diction and
syntax in English poetry, *Purity of Diction in English Verse* (1952)
and *Articulate Energy* (1955), might have been expected to be more
open to the inventiveness of Murphy's historical prosody – calls the
language of *The Battle of Aughrim* 'prosy, strained and wooden', going
on to say, 'To the American critic, it is just this prosiness and flatness,
what Tom Kinsella has called "verse of the lowest possible intensity",
that will seem to be the English sheep dog in this Irish garden. The
Englishman Larkin, they may feel, handles these muted instruments
with more finesse.'[10] This seems odd in a number of ways, but it raises
some interesting issues. 'Verse of the lowest possible intensity' might
recall Patrick Kavanagh's 'true note' played 'on a dead slack string'
(though Murphy, with his prosodic exactness, is not at all like that).[11]
And it seems strange to invoke Thomas Kinsella in this context, since
his translations, both of *The Táin* (1969) and of poems in his *New
Oxford Book of Irish Verse* (1986) in which he uses his own translations
exclusively, can be seen as masterpieces of plainstyle translation. It is
difficult to see him levelling the charge of 'flatness'.

What is less odd perhaps about Davie's characterisation is what
might seem to be the reaction of a Movement enthusiast of the 1950s
– for 'the Englishman Larkin', for example (though again the 'muted
instruments' do not seem to describe him very aptly) – against the
originality of Murphy's employment of a more vigorous, prose-
derived poetic form for his history poems. What does Davie (or
Kinsella) mean by 'verse of the lowest possible intensity'? He must
mean something purely formal: a flatness of voice rather than subject.
Part of what I want to argue is that Murphy steers a very distinctive
course between the free verse of the modernists and the formal
regularity of the Movement poets who reacted against modernism.
His course is distinctive in form: possibly unique in his generation.
But it is most significantly distinctive in turning to historical subjects
and historical sources. The writer he is closest to in this way – though
he is very different from him in other ways – is Seamus Heaney, who
famously said, 'A formal distinction is never strictly formal ... [but]
at once formal but also emotional.'[12] The language a writer uses is not

historically, or even morally, neutral. And what Murphy and Heaney have most in common is a readiness to engage in the details of history – something which both modernism and the Movement poets were reluctant to do.

'Now', Part I of *The Battle of Aughrim*, ends with a short poem called 'History', placing the poet himself in a physical context where 'Touch unearths military history' and he finds 'Bones and bullets fingering my mind', concluding with a claim very uncharacteristic of its time, and unpopular in its time, the blunt observation 'The past is happening today'.[13] The second section, 'Before', starts with 'Legend', a poem which illustrates again Murphy's readiness to respond to a received story:

> The story I have to tell
> Was told me by a teacher
> Who read it in a poem
> Written in a dying language.
> Two hundred and fifty years ago
> The poet recalled
> Meeting a soldier who had heard
> From veterans of the war
> The story I have to tell.   (*P*, p. 70)

This is establishing a literary authority for the re-evocation of the battle, 'Ireland's defence / From the colonists' advance', when Murphy's ancestors:

> Lit matches, foddered horses, thirsted, marched,
> Halted, and marched to battle.   (*P*, p. 70)

This is followed by another received authority, 'St Ruth's Address to the Irish Army' (*P*, pp. 71–2), translated by St Ruth's secretary after the event and quoted by Rev. George Story in his contemporary account of what happened at Aughrim, *An Impartial History of the Wars of Ireland* (1693). In his appendix 'Writing *The Battle of Aughrim*' (*P*, pp. 254–9) Murphy tells us that it was Martin Joyce, the National teacher at Aughrim, who advised him on what books to read about the events at Aughrim, including Story's 'true blue' account. Murphy says Story's book is 'miscalled' or mistitled: that is, it is not an 'impartial' history.

In 'Pat Cloherty's Version of *The Maisie*', Murphy took over Cloherty's verbatim account and adapted it to the formalities of his poem. The language that resulted from the adaptation and incorporation of other, non-oral sources in *The Battle of Aughrim* had naturally been very different. But in both cases a clear and plain register of language is being created which still shows the materials of which it is composed. The appendices to *The Pleasure Ground* (drawing often on his memoir, *The Kick*) give a revealing insight into Murphy's process of composition, sometimes showing how the actual wording of his sources is woven into a new language in the poems, sometimes in a more general way, quoting overheard exchanges as in 'Photographs of Inishbofin – May 1960 – *A dialogue between two boatmen*' (*P*, pp. 249–50). Another unmistakable affinity here is with Yeats' observations about poetic language and its relationship to 'Written Speech'.[14] Yeats praises Lady Gregory for becoming 'the founder of modern Irish dialect literature';[15] Gregory herself said the language she was attempting to create was 'the English spoken by the Irish people, which keeps so much of the idiom of the Irish original'.[16] In a famous passage in the first section of *Autobiographies*, 'Reveries over Childhood and Youth', Yeats discusses the matter of plainness and written speech in terms that are very applicable to – and maybe influential on – Murphy's practice.

> Personal utterance, which had almost ceased in English literature, could be as fine an escape from rhetoric and abstraction as drama itself … I tried from that on to write out of my emotions exactly as they came to me in life, not changing them to make them more beautiful. 'If I can be sincere and make my language natural, and without becoming discursive, like a novelist, and so indiscreet and prosaic,' I said to myself, 'I shall, if good luck or bad luck make my life interesting, be a great poet; for it will no longer be a matter of literature at all.'[17]

It is notable, too, that Yeats says he came to this insight by 'reading verses describing the shore of Ireland as seen by a returning, dying emigrant', and, though he 'knew the verses were badly written', his 'eyes filled with tears'.[18] It is another response to a received, raw language. It is clear that Murphy's poetic language meets both of Yeats' ideals here in creating 'a language to write about Ireland in': both 'the English spoken by the Irish people' as in the *Maisie* poem, and his own 'natural language'.

Murphy's description of his procedures in the appendices to *The Pleasure Ground* shows his consciousness of these lexical factors. The other poem that links most obviously to the discussions there is 'The Cleggan Disaster' (*P*, pp. 48–55) and the note on its provenance (*P*, pp. 251–3).[19] In that note Murphy gives as the source of his poem Pat Concannon's story of the disaster, 'in his own words, arranged for continuity' (*P*, p. 251). The arrangement is not only for continuity, though; this is a plainstyle which is closer to standard language than in the Pat Cloherty poem: less vivid, but highly effective as a narrative style. It is a clear language of observation rather than direct reportage. It is the last of the three narrative poems which make up Part I of *Sailing to an Island* (1963), before the more familiarly structured lyric poems of the book's Parts II and III. It is interesting that in *The Pleasure Ground*, 'The Cleggan Disaster' is promoted to be the final poem from the volume, perhaps as a culmination of the volume's poetic technique. I talked about it briefly in the Cloherty essay, concluding that 'although there are vernacular touches like "The oarsmen were calling Concannon to let go, / Take it easy for a while", or the more self-conscious "Darker it's getting" … the prevailing language is a kind of standard English narrative, very successfully employed' (*P*, p 276). I want to consider this slightly more extensively now, in the light of the report of Concannon's language in *The Kick*.

There are two very obvious differences from the treatment of the received story in the Cloherty poem which came later. First, a lengthy lyrical narrative is developed from Concannon's short account (for which of course we have to take Murphy's eloquent version on trust). The second difference is that, while the *Maisie* poem retains Pat

Cloherty's first-person narration, 'The Cleggan Disaster' is in the third person with occasional first-person quotations, though even those are not that closely derived from Concannon's account. For example, in *The Kick* Concannon is reported as saying, 'When one of the lads heard his own brother crying in the water, he caught him by the hand, but the hand slipped from his grasp and sank under the boat' (*P*, p. 251; *K*, p. 144). In the poem the pathos of the event is given a rather Gothic telling:

> One of the crew said he heard his brother
> Shouting for help, two oars away;
> Yet when he hollered, there was no reply.
> In a flash of lightning, a white hand rose
> And rested on the gunwale, then slowly sank.   (*P*, p. 52)[20]

This is a rather extreme example of a kind of romantic, seafaring excitement that Murphy adds to the narrative, which will be chastened by the closer representation of Cloherty's speech in the later poem. Both are, of course, literary languages; but it tempts us to argue that between *Sailing to an Island* and *High Island* eleven years later Murphy has become more confident in his employment of local language. A comparison with Heaney is apt again: in his poem 'Casualty' Heaney describes himself in his exchange with the fisherman in the pub as 'shy of condescension' (as he is also in his exchanges with his mother in 'Clearances', no. IV where 'I'd *naw* and *aye* / And decently relapse into the wrong / Grammar').[21] In earlier Murphy there is a shyness of condescension that stops him adapting a local voice that is not his own. Later, through acclimatisation perhaps, he has the confidence to represent local language in its full unfamiliarity, or to invent a new argot that represents it with great poetic success.

There is another distancing device in 'The Cleggan Disaster', which also serves to draw it back towards the orthodox literary centre, distancing it from its local curiosity. The events of 1927 which Concannon relates to the poet are being recalled in 1961, so Murphy appends a kind of *ubi sunt* coda, headed 'Years Later': 'Where are the

red-haired women … Where are the barefoot children … Where are
the dances in houses' (*P*, pp. 54–5). We are reminded of the tendency
towards questioning in late Yeats (and the phrase 'Years Later' has a
Yeatsian air to it). But the start of this coda – 'Whose is that hulk on
the shingle / The boatwright's son repairs' (*P*, p. 54) with its question
about ownership – is more forcefully reminiscent of the beginning of
The Battle of Aughrim, the poem which follows it both chronologically
and in the arrangement of the poems in *The Pleasure Ground*. In *The
Kick* (again reproduced as an appendix to *The Pleasure Ground*),
Murphy tells us that he started writing *The Battle of Aughrim* 'in the
"disaster" village of Cleggan on the morning of the second Sunday in
July 1962', that is, immediately after the 'Cleggan' poem. He also says
in the same passage that as he drove through Aughrim, the question
of land possession – 'a question uppermost in all Irish minds in our
agricultural past – *who owns the land* – occurred to me so strongly that
I took an envelope from the pocket of my donkey jacket and wrote
those words, in case I might forget them during a day of chatting to
tourists … One written word led to another, with crossings out, more
or less in this rough form:

> Who owns the land where musket balls are buried
> Under whitethorn on the esker, in the drained bogs
> Where flocks of sheep browse and redcoats waded?'   (*P*, p. 255)

It is as if the full implication of the *ubi sunt* stanzas in the coda to 'The
Cleggan Disaster' has suddenly dawned on him. But the crucial point
about the 'Years Later' coda is that it is a reversion to the poetics of the
English tradition, as distinct from the Irish vernacular. Throughout
his career Murphy has been an immensely gifted prosodist. It is hard
to imagine him, for example, going through the demanding energetic
process to bend the language to his will that Heaney describes in his
essay on Wordsworth and Yeats. Poetic language comes naturally to
him, which is why the achievement of a poem like 'Pat Cloherty's
Version of *The Maisie*' is so remarkable in the way it abjures that
skill to achieve an entirely different effect. The home key throughout
Murphy's writing career – one which is remarkably sustained in the

traditional poetic plainstyle of the sonnets of *The Price of Stone* – is
the established poetic language of the English tradition. He has an
excellent ear, whether it is responding to the evenness of the central
tradition or achieving his effects by departing from it.

But, to conclude with his departures from the poetic norms of
that tradition, we can see that, although there are developments in
the way Murphy uses vernacular and other kinds of plain language
through his writing career, his ideal of clarity, founded on received
language usage, should be viewed as being in a direct line of descent
from Yeats. It can best be understood in the light of the most famous
claim for his own usage made in Yeats in his 'General Introduction for
My Work': 'I tried to make the language of poetry coincide with that
of passionate, normal speech … It was a long time before I had made
a language to my liking.'[22] Indeed the whole of part 'III. Style and
Attitude' in the great Yeats essay could be seen as a guiding star for
Murphy's poetic project. Not that this endeavour begins with Yeats,
even if he expresses it most importantly. Irish writers in English had
returned obsessively to this ambition to bring Irish accent and 'voice'
(the recurrent term) into English poetry, from the writers of *The
Nation* in the 1840s onwards.

In his ambition to achieve the plainness of what he called
'passionate syntax', Yeats said in his very late essay 'An Introduction
for My Plays': 'I have spent my life in clearing out of poetry every
phrase written for the eye, and bringing all back to syntax that is for
the ear alone.'[23] In their shared pursuit of clarity and intelligibility,
Murphy diverges from Yeats in this ideal. His plainstyle draws
largely on images of the visual, rather than what T.S. Eliot called 'the
auditory imagination'. Even in 'Pat Cloherty's Version of *The Maisie*', a
poem whose language and expression is drawn closely from a spoken
source, the imagery and detail is more visual than auditory. Heaney's
poem 'North' ends with a famous image of clarity:

'… Keep your eye clear
as the bleb of the icicle,
trust the feel of what nubbed treasure
your hands have known.'[24]

Ong's description of the transparency of the medium of light, quoted at the start here, is a perfect image for the plainness and clarity that writers like Richard Murphy aim at. Clarity is still a hallmark of his later poetry, even when the subjects are very different, in volumes such as the memoir-like *The Price of Stone* or the 'karmic picture' of *The Mirror Wall*.[25] The aspiration towards clarity and transparency in language is a common one. By drawing richly on varying dialects and narrative forms to represent the different historical and geographical worlds he has moved in and described, Murphy has achieved his objective in a way that is rare and which has been found inspirational in later poetry for which documentary clarity has been an ideal.

3

'As if the sun shone': Love and
loss in Richard Murphy's poems

GERALD DAWE

There are not many poems about divorce, and the experience of separation between those who had once been united. Richard Murphy's account of the legal sitting in London in June 1959 which severed his marriage to Patricia Avis forms an important part of his memoir *The Kick: a life among writers*, and is the subject of his poem 'Grounds', 'a poem that I revised and published forty years later' (*K*, p. 167):

> To needless echoes – 'Yes, m'Lud,'
> 'No, m'Lud' – and I had lost you,
> Lost everything we had gone through.   (*P*, p. 35)[1]

The sense of loss, being lost, and of leaving a life behind, unfinished, incomplete, pervades Richard Murphy's life as a poet. In the concluding stanza of 'Grounds', he admits to 'a dream' in which his ex-wife appears:

>   … sick
> And lost in rain on a high cliff
> Crying and careless where you walk.
> A lighthouse flashes far, far off:
> But I cannot, though I try to, speak
> To stop the harm in all I've done
> Dragging you down and down.   (*P*, p. 35)

49

In a letter to Philip Larkin dated 18 September 1977, Murphy alludes to the death of his wife earlier in the month. Patricia Avis,[2] with whom Larkin had had an affair in the early 1950s[3] when he was working as a librarian in Queen's University, Belfast, had struggled with alcoholism. 'Was it twenty years ago you [Larkin] visited us at Lake Park in the Wicklow Mountains, when we were busy making plans, such as re-seeding worn-out pastures, for an idyllic future? Well, well.'[4] That 'idyllic future' was not to be but the letter continues with a telling reflection on Murphy's part about his own future:

> This recent summer [1977], while I was at home, I built a studio in the garden: it sounds quite simple, but it really was a lot of hard work and done at a frightful cost in time and money. I'll have to get this mania for building under control before it ruins me. At least I hope my friends will enjoy visiting Cleggan, now I have more rooms.[5]

It is a letter full of memories and the offer of hospitality and revisiting places, such as Hull, where Larkin had been based since moving there in 1955 to take up the post as university librarian. But the reference here to 'this mania for building' formed itself into the poem 'Stone Mania', which recapitulates the loss of connection between loved ones and friends as a result of Murphy's 'mad obsession of building more rooms' (*P*, p. 157).[6] It was as if the rebuilding of old houses elides into a metaphorical version of his dedication to making poetry, with the crucial distinction that Murphy actually was physically re-building what had been in the process of destruction and decay, the unavoidable rule of loss:

> But for my mad obsession of building more rooms
>   to entertain them in time to come:
> Because these times are apt to elude us, we die, or our
>   friends drop dead before we can say
> I'd love you to see and enjoy the house whose construction
>   has kept us entirely apart.   (*P*, p. 157)

This life between love (of building) and loss (death but also the loss of love) is at the centre of Murphy's achievement as a poet. With the publication of the neatly constructed *Poems 1952–2012* in 2013, the reader has now the opportunity to chart the journey between both moral and aesthetic dimensions of what could be called Murphy's country. Bookended by 'The Pleasure Ground' (*P*, pp. 13–16)[7] as a prose introduction and by an appendix of over thirty pages of notes and readings, *Poems 1952–2012* has the definitive look of being a complete edition of all the poems which Richard Murphy wishes to keep in print.

It is a shaped and deliberated volume with clearly established timelines divided into six parts with dates identifying how, where and when Murphy's poems first emerged. 'So, on the 25th August 1952', we learn in Murphy's 'Author's note on the provenance of "Sailing to an Island"' and recounted in a little more detail in his memoir *The Kick*:

> … my brother and I set out, with our nine-year-old nephew, John Caulfeild [*sic*], and my employer's daughter, Alison, a talented sculptor, as passengers, from the quay of Rosroe near the mouth of the Big Killary harbour. We were planning to go to Clare Island, a place renowned for legends. We never got there. Contrary winds brought us instead to an island I had never heard of, called Inishbofin.
>
> A week later, alone in the pre-famine Coast Guard cottage on the quay at Rosroe, I wrote the first draft of a poem about our rough passage and change of course that led to a change in my life.   (*P*, p. 245)

This change in direction, at the whim of natural sea conditions, would not only lead to Murphy's lasting identification with the Atlantic coast and the westerly islands but also produce two key enduring emblems of his writing life – the sea journey and the house on land:

> … after some fortuitous redirections, including marriage and divorce, through Crete, Brittany, Wicklow, London, and back to Inishbofin in 1959, the poem I had drafted at Rosroe, revised

and revised, emerged in 1963 as the final version of 'Sailing to an Island'.   (*P*, p. 245)

The poem's 'journey', in other words, from inception in September 1952 to its completion, took over a decade to write and conclude.[8] It was finally published by Faber & Faber as the title poem of the volume *Sailing to an Island* in 1963, which included early work by Murphy such as *The Archaeology of Love* (1955) and *The Last Galway Hooker* (1961), both of which had been published in 'limited edition[s]' (*K*, p. 188) by the enterprising Liam Miller's Dolmen Press. It was from these earliest publications that the poet, then in his late twenties and early thirties, established his reputation alongside, among others, Thomas Kinsella and John Montague as one of the leading poets of the rising generation – post-Yeats, certainly, but also post-Kavanagh (who died in 1967) and, in curious ways, already post-national. Murphy would explore in his long epic-like meditation *The Battle of Aughrim* (1968) the cultural fate and political liabilities of his Anglo-Irish upbringing in a divided society. 'I had written', he remarked:

> … enough externally about boats and the sea [in *Sailing to an Island*]. Now I wanted to look inward at the divisions and devastations in myself as well as in the country: the conflicts, legends, rituals, myths and histories arising from possession of the land – why we still had borders and bigotries.   (*K*, p. 197)

But there is an equalising and powerful sense of the world beyond these concerns – a world that he uncovered in his own roots in the west of Ireland as well as through the colonial taproot which links such a (by now, largely vanished) world with the global British imperial system; this is the context for his fine portrait of his father, 'The God Who Eats Corn', first published in 1964. The dramatisation of that imperial experience in many poems set in his childhood in Ceylon (as it then was) and his returns to Sri Lanka meant in effect that 'Ireland' would not be viewed as a 'Celticised' myth-kitty, but rather as an integrated site in which history plays out its conflictual role with effects upon individuals and families named consistently throughout his writing. Their homes and localities are not merely backdrops to the poet's personal life and conundrums but have an austere life of their own. For these lives and landscapes present an objective reality which Murphy depicts almost like a visual artist, studying the way people live *in* their own surroundings, their folkways and customs, not as an outsider, but more as an observer who once belonged in the various places where he has (albeit temporarily) lived his own life.

The poems fit together in the almost anonymous way of the folk tradition, particularly poems inflected by the west of Ireland. Murphy's subdued voice sounds in keeping with a classically reserved narrative:

> Slate I picked from a nettle-bed
> Had history, my neighbour said.
>
> To quarry it, men had to row
> Five miles, twelve centuries ago.   (*P*, p. 66)

The 'slate' of the poem's here and now links back to another time, the seedbed of Murphy's present out of which contradiction and contrast find their own equilibrium, their tone and controlling diction: in effect, their authority. Yet there is an ironical and haunted aura that moves across these poems in spite of their clarity and well-made, spruce definition.

The doubting illusion of mastering the sea finds another level in the pre-eminent themes of the irreconcilability of loss and the impermanent consolations of love. Murphy's poems are keenly aware of physical decline and decay. The only form of resistance to such conditions in terms of loss, both human and historical, is through building and construction. The fifty sonnets which form the keystone of *The Price of Stone* (1985) literally form themselves into an architecture of love and imagined survival that withstands the inevitable ravages of time, the fall from prestige (and grace) into eccentricity or the quixotic sense of self-regard.

If Philip Larkin's 'girl on the poster' in 'Sunny Prestatyn'[9] is transfigured grotesquely into a mocking cartoon figure because 'She was too good for this life', the follies, chimneys, porticoes, pillars, tenements, schoolhouses, barns, quaysides of *The Price of Stone* convey a sturdy grammarian's resilience in their own making. What survives of and from them all is a kind of loving. And it is of love's complications that so many of Murphy's finest poems speak where the sensual, uncertain, at times violent and/or repressed look of self-protection is released by the poet's attention to physical detail. In 'Jurors', it is the murdered woman's assailant, 'his boots to be analysed / And a few ribs they found of her chestnut hair' (*P*, p. 119); in 'Ball's Cove', a love test turns into another (likely) killing rather than '"A sad accident"':

> … a lobster fisherman said:
> 'She pushed him off,
> I can prove it. I was near the cove
> Hauling pots, and I heard her laugh.'   (*P*, p. 138)

For love, like much else in Murphy's writing, is a double negative:

> Alone I love
> To think of us together:
> Together I think
> I'd love to be alone.   (*P*, p. 147)

Even the occasion of bringing his partner and first child 'home' causes the retrospective questioning to begin in 'Roof-tree': 'How did you celebrate?' and ends with the resounding self-indictment: 'You flawed the tenderest movement of three lives' (*P*, p. 187). Men and women, young and old, settled in their lives or fugitive from a way of life, the dramatis personae of Murphy's poetry includes the names of the great and the good, the historic, the theatrical, the unknown. Family, friends and lovers, the hinted at, the eavesdropped, the provident, the inconsolable and the uncontactable all cross the stage. From Tony White on the Inishbofin quayside in 'Double Negative' (*P*, p. 112), the twin elegies written to him in 'Tony White 1930–1976' and 'Tony White at Inishbofin 1959' (*P*, pp. 160–1), about White's 'greater love of craft in word and deed' in 'Bookcase for *The Oxford*

English Dictionary' (*P*, p. 162) and later revisited in 'Tony White's Cottage' (*P*, p. 212), to Wittgenstein and Roethke trying to heal themselves and the irreplaceable deficits of a childhood recollected in love, these personal losses are all shadowed by a sense of fleeting transient life evoked here in 'Trouvaille':

> Bunches of primroses I used to pick
> Before breakfast, hunting along a limestone lane,
> To put at her bedside before she woke;
> And all my childhood's broken promises.   (*P*, p. 150)

Friendship, too, merges with a sense of the precariousness and vulnerability of loss, its immanent presence abounds, or, more literally, abides in the image such as 'Visiting Hour' dedicated *'for Thomas Kinsella in 1980'* on his hospital sickbed:

> How can I comfort you? What can I say?
> You seem so far away, though near me now,
> Sedated in that iron bed
> Behind a curtain I'm afraid to draw:
> With languished head
> Propped on a pillow, mute and weak.
> Would it be better not to speak?   (*P*, p. 173)

The questions are left like hooks hanging in the air, reproachful, unanswerable. In keeping with all this distinguished array of friends and companions, workmen and men of the sea, women and lovers, the perfect pitch of 'Mary Ure' as:

> She walks by Lough Mask in a blue silk gown
> So thin the cloudy wind is biting to the bone
> But … talks as lightly as if the sun shone.   (*P*, p. 151)

is troubled elsewhere. Poems such as the disturbing 'The Glass Dump Road' (*P*, p. 127), the sexual turbulence of 'Seals at High Island' (*P*, p. 143) – one of Murphy's greatest poems – and the enigmatic beauty of 'Niches' – 'Lovers I've lost are sleeping in the house I've left' (*P*, p. 155) – contextualise the recurring figure of an outsider, such as

Tony White, and those, as in 'Last Word', who bring Murphy's mind
back to his poetic beginning:

> Years pass into dust
> With drills, hammers and saws
> Remodelling an old house
> Whose walls of silence
> Keep a granite hold on my loss.   (*P*, p. 241)

Murphy's overarching achievement can be read as a continuous
musical score with the keynotes of love and loss, as sounded here,
the dominant themes. 'Years' that 'pass', the desire and necessity of
'remodelling' and the 'old house' – such a constant in the imaginative
terrain of the Anglo-Irish – and those 'walls of silence' which are
prefigured in 'The Pleasure Ground' of the self and the 'granite' that
seems both changeless and unspecific, holding intact the egocentricity
of 'my loss'. But the loss that Murphy's poems recount is not self-
restricted or site-specific. They bear the hallmarks of an imperishable
love of language and the poetic craft of enunciating what is seen and
what remains under the surface of an imagined life, evoked here in 'A
River of Notebooks':

> Winkling through dictionaries for bait.
> Poetry feeds on the refuse of time
> Against whose current it swims.   (*P*, p. 236)

The Elizabethan-like symmetry varies from the ornately philosophical
teasing of 'A Nest in a Wall':

> Your country and mine, love, can it still exist?
> The unsignposted hawthorn lane of your body
> Leads to my lichenous walls and gutted house.
> Earth has almost lost your kind of beauty.
> Although we have no home in the time that's come,
> Coming together we live in our own time.
> Make your nest of moss like a wren in my skull.   (*P*, p. 159)

to the near travesties of love and sexual passion in 'Rites of Passage' (*P*, p. 238) and in the troubling distortions of 'Portico' (*P*, p. 179) and 'Gym', where denial and desire struggle with the social structuring of feeling:

> See how my fabric, full of cock and bull,
> Grotesquely free, though ruled by symmetry,
> Lays you in some small penetralian cell
> To come to grief, past all immunity.   (*P*, p. 183)

If history has remaindered the political and ideological eminence of Anglo-Ireland, the artistic prestige associated with several of its diverse offspring has become an essential part of modern Irish writing's critical reputation worldwide: from Goldsmith and Wilde, Yeats and Beckett, to Bowen and MacNeice. It is a curious tale to relate that the notions which Murphy inherited from his father – of rule and order, 'his [father's] pride in the British colonial service' and 'what he perceived as criticism of its injustice by one of his sons [Richard Murphy] who owed his good education to that service' (*K*, p. 214) – should produce their own formal eloquence in Murphy's poems. For the father equals both love and loss on a personal as well as wider cultural and political front:

> Tall in his garden, shaded and brick-walled,
> He upholds the manners of a lost empire.
> Time has confused dead honour with dead guilt
> But lets a sunbird sip at a gold creeper.   (*P*, p. 107)

But the sense of loss also implies a loss of spiritual and political faith in the postcolonial legacy Murphy's father embodied:

> While he reads Homer's *Iliad* in Greek
> Rhodesian forces arm for a civil war.
> Pyres are kindling under *Pax Britannica*
> As black politicians school themselves in jail.   (*P*, p. 107)

Murphy is unflinching, too, in his rendering of the brutality of decolonisation, as the end of that particular history in Ceylon/Sri Lanka is marked by 'Death in Kandy':

> On a bend where drivers park
> To show tourists the Mahaweli
> River that borders the former
> Great University of Ceylon
> I saw a skeleton
> Picked clean by dogs and crows,
> A nameless victim like Anura
> Stretched on a burnt-out tyre
> Under the vertical sun
> Of smiling resplendent Sri Lanka.   (*P*, p. 235)

Violence is never too far under the surface; it resonates throughout Murphy's work, producing its own shocking lure and amazement. Even love, like sexual union, turns into the mythic passion and physical force of 'Seals at High Island':

> … an old rival, eyeing the deed with hate,
> Swims to attack the tired triumphant god.
> They rear their heads above the boiling surf,
> Their terrible jaws open, jetting blood.   (*P*, p. 143)

The relinquishing of love in 'Grounds' (*P*, p. 35), like the unexpected intrusion of 'Two beautiful teenage girls from a tribe of tinkers' in 'Morning Call' (*P*, p. 165), offers a perfect example of just how much true poetry expresses the complications of human feeling alongside the anecdotal ironic glance at how Murphy himself is seen by others in 'Walled Up':

> He danders down the forge lane
> From the coastguard station to the shop
> With a string bag for a message
> They've told him to bring up,

> And when he meets my garden wall
> He asks, politely taking off his cap,
> 'How are the prisoners in Mountjoy Jail?'   (P, p. 126)

Poetry turns into a controlled zone, neatly laid out with natural resources taken from the pleasure ground of both home and abroad and built to outlast the damage of time and the bloody legacy of history.

In *The Price of Stone* – a sequence of sonnets, inlaid, compact, allusive and mesmeric – the desire for structure literally takes over as the poet's voice shifts into ventriloquism. It is a strange, estranging act whereby the poem pretends to be something else: a hut, hexagon, pier bar, ice rink, roof-tree, industrial school, through which the poet speaks his mind; and a slightly antithetical Hitchcockian mind it is, too, for example in 'Georgian Tenement':

> The high court of dry rot, after a long
> Unreportable session behind airtight doors,
> Has mouthed a verdict. Rafters know what's wrong.
> Death and cremation. Up with my soft floors.   (P, p. 182)

If 'England' features little in Murphy's poetry, the English in which the poems are written reminds us of diction as clear as a bell and distinguished by an inherited civic consciousness, classical education and sense that the lucidity of expression does not necessarily deny deeper resonances, undisclosed depths, even trickery and play. Where Yeats may stand formally behind some of his achievement, Murphy can also, undoubtedly, be read in the same terms that he uses to describe Philip Larkin's style: 'translucent' and 'richly complex'.[10] For Murphy is an intriguingly available poet and his poems, like those of Robert Graves, have all the bright music of great love songs such as in the previously mentioned 'Mary Ure':

> Bare feet she dips across my boat's blue rail
> In the ocean as we run under full white summer sail.
> The cold spray kisses them. She's not immortal.

Sitting in her orchard she reads 'Lady Lazarus'
Aloud rehearsing, when her smallest child lays
Red peonies in her lap with tender apologies.

She walks by Lough Mask in a blue silk gown
So thin the cloudy wind is biting to the bone
But she talks as lightly as if the sun shone.   (*P*, p. 151)

In a valuable interview with John Haffenden from 1981, Richard Murphy remarked of that early move to the west coast of Ireland:

> What I really wanted to do was to simplify my life and to find a kind of bedrock on which I could build, and to get to know the heart of the country in which I'd been born, which was totally different to the world in which I'd been brought up, Ceylon and England. It was a kind of exploration, my coming to Connemara ...[11]

One of the most impressive things about Richard Murphy's poetry is just how alive it is to the west of Ireland: its history and people, the landscape and customs of making a living (as Murphy did) from the sea. His poems, gathered around this vision and experience in *Sailing to an Island* (1963) and *High Island* (1974), have justly become classics in and of their own time. But it is not as pastoral that they really live; for the western islands and the terrain are emblematic presences that dramatise an intense prolonged imaginative struggle for personal and cultural identity. Traversing this geography of the mind, Murphy auspiciously reinvented in *The Battle of Aughrim* an historical frieze of war and conflict in the late seventeenth century spliced through with images drawn, almost cinematically, from twentieth-century Ireland. The characteristic imaginative strain of these volumes right up to *The Price of Stone* (1985) and *The Mirror Wall* (1989) is towards an ordered and orderly world.

If the sea is the challenge the individual fights, so, too, is history. There is a personal courage marked throughout these poems, all the more fascinating because it is increasingly rare, rendered almost meaningless as the high romantic belief in the self's discovery of otherness and conflict has been turned by most media into the petulant narcissism of 'lifestyle'. The elegiac tone of some of his finest poems, for example those dedicated to Patricia Avis, or to his 'mentor' Tony White, or the immaculate lyric quoted above, dedicated to his friend, the actor Mary Ure, are defined by an unvarnished clarity. The grand meditations on the lives of his grandmother, 'The Woman of the House', and father, 'The God Who Eats Corn', as with the best-known novels of J.G. Farrell,[12] present an unflinching view of the complex moral universe of the colonial Anglo-Irish.

The counterweight of Ceylon/Sri Lanka in poems such as 'Coppersmith', 'The Fall' and, painfully, in 'Death in Kandy' show Murphy's artistic ability to explore other worlds and understand their separateness, their uniqueness. The lucid, confident voice which tells the stories of these poems, far from being confessional or smugly self-regarding, demonstrates how emotional power is like a physical force which drives beneath the surface brilliance of the poetry. It takes only time to hear this utterly unique and patient music.

NOTE

This essay draws upon two reviews by the present writer of Richard Murphy's poetry: 'A Geography of the Mind', a review of Richard Murphy's *Collected Poems* (*Irish Times*, 11 November 2000) and 'Outlasting Fashion', a review of Richard Murphy's *Poems 1952 2012* (*Dublin Review of Books*, no. 43, 21 October 2013), to whom kind acknowledgement is made.

4

~

Richard Murphy's Island Lives

LUCY COLLINS

The trope of the island has played an important role in the poetry of the British Isles for generations. Even at the time of Ireland's Literary Revival at the close of the nineteenth century, the representation of island life already had important precursors, permitting new writers to explore ideas of cultural purity and spiritual revelation within the context of a literary tradition.[1] In the twentieth century, J.M. Synge's celebrated book *The Aran Islands* (1907) confirmed the already longstanding perception of the islands off the west coast of Ireland as places of origin, unspoilt environments still free from the troubling influence of modernity. Yet the island is often suggestive of binary states: sea and land, escape and containment, alienation and connection. Richard Murphy, who emerged as a poet in Ireland in the 1950s, made life in the west of Ireland more than just the subject of his poetry. He spent long periods there, not only rendering the Atlantic coastline vividly but also re-thinking geographical and poetic landscapes persistently in his work.[2]

Throughout the British Isles, island poems form an important part of any consideration of private and shared modes of identity, and specific descriptions of climate and landscape become a focus for emotional and spiritual quest. For poets such as Máirtín Ó Direáin, raised on Inis Mór, and George Mackay Brown, who spent most of his life in the Orkney community, island experience was essential both to personal identity and creative development. For others the island was figured as a means of escape or renewal, rather than as a permanent dwelling place. To spend a period of time in comparative isolation, often in extreme weather conditions, prompted processes of reflection that have yielded important work from contemporary poets as diverse as Eiléan Ní Chuilleanáin (b. 1942) and Jen Hadfield (b. 1978).[2] At certain times these journeys have acquired a specific cultural resonance. During the Irish Literary Revival the west of Ireland – and specifically its island communities – became an essential inspiration for writers and artists, though the work itself would be read and exhibited in Dublin or further afield. The periphery thus becomes 'a site of roots and identity ... affirming ethnic and cultural solidarity to counter the postcolonial crisis of fragmentation and heterogeneity';[3] the fact of its distance from centres of political and cultural power is thus integral to its meaning. When W.B. Yeats advised Synge to travel to the Aran Islands in search of authentic subject matter, he saw perfection of the art, rather than of the life, as the chief purpose of the journey.[4] Yet the necessity for direct engagement with the source of inspiration shapes both the personal and artistic quest. Arthur Symons was another Revivalist writer who made the journey westward to the Aran Islands, and Heather Clark has noted the complex blend of 'spiritual completion and psychic unease'[5] felt by him during the journey: 'we seemed ... to be venturing among an unknown people', wrote Symons, 'who, even if they spoke our own language, were further away from us, more foreign than people who spoke an unknown language and lived beyond other seas'.[6]

This perception of difference registered by Symons and others alters the spatial representation of the island experience and intensifies its association with binary states. The very remoteness that makes the island an escape from oppressive modernity, or from the pressures of everyday life, can also engender feelings of disorientation that can have profound psychological effects. As Gilles Deleuze has argued:

> Dreaming of islands – whether with joy or in fear, it doesn't matter – is dreaming of pulling away, of being already separate, far from any continent, of being lost and alone – *or* it is dreaming of starting from scratch, recreating, beginning anew.[7]

Disorientation and creativity are not necessarily oppositional states, however, and the characterisation of the island as 'a specific becoming or mutual achievement of land and water'[8] emphasises the state of 'islandness' as one that is always in process, as Philip Keel Geheber also argues in his essay in this volume. Thus, the transformative power of the island lies not only in the new experiences it offers to the traveller – and the capacity of these experiences to inspire creative response – but also in its fundamental questioning of fixed notions of identity, whether individual or collective. These categories are themselves troubled by the island encounter: Deleuze argues that even inhabited islands are, in effect, 'deserted' and those who choose to live there are 'uncommon humans ... absolutely separate, absolute creators'.[9] For Richard Murphy, then, to gravitate towards the island, both as dwelling place and as artistic inspiration, is to articulate a profound sense of separateness that had shaped his life from an early age.

The duality that is seemingly inherent in the meeting of land and water demands further investigation, however. The archipelagic turn in literary studies has drawn attention to texts that reconfigure the dynamics of margin and centre through their representation of seascapes and maritime histories. As Jonathan Pugh has argued, these texts tend to interrogate the binaries of sea and land, or island and mainland, and permit a more dynamic approach to individual and collective histories.[10] This process is a transformative one that 'takes us beyond reductive categories that diminish islands to states of mimicry, to instead foreground how island-island movements and middle passages are cognitive spaces of metamorphosis in their own right'.[11] This perspective problematises the Revivalist characterisation of the western seaboard as, in Yeats' words, a world 'that has never found expression', as John Brannigan has persuasively argued.[12] As well as assuming meaning within a Dublin-based literary and theatre culture, these islands were part of a larger pan-Celtic imaginary, and a place of origin for the diaspora in America and elsewhere.[13]

From this perspective the relationship between peripheral spaces plays an important role in the formation of cultural identity, especially where migration has forged lasting links between communities. The geopolitical landscape of the Irish and British archipelago has been shaped by the same imperial past that may be read in Richard Murphy's biography, and his essay 'The Pleasure Ground' draws attention to the transition from his childhood in Ceylon and in Milford, County Mayo to his adult life in Connemara. Yet Murphy's multifaceted cultural identity, which included periods living in Dublin, London and South Africa, is at odds with his description of himself as 'unalterably Anglo-Irish'.[14] The shifting angles of view offered by this experience are best expressed by the island imaginary which, together with its registration of tidal flows, facilitates Murphy's exploration of the self both in place and out of place. His inventive juxtaposition of tradition and innovation in language, as well as his cosmopolitan outlook, affirms him as a poet of the archipelago.

Murphy began his career in poetry as one of a group of talented young poets to emerge in Ireland in the 1950s, encouraged by the setting up of the Dolmen Press, the first Irish-based poetry publisher of note since the Revival years.[15] Murphy's earliest experience of publishing was gained as a reviewer for *The Spectator* and the *Times Literary Supplement*, however, establishing an early dichotomy between his role as a critic in the London literary scene and as a poet in Ireland. Maurice Harmon's juxtaposition of 'the trained intelligence and critical faculty of his English education and the more emotional, more earthy Irish side' can be traced back to this first phase of his literary career.[16] Early poems 'Creragh' and 'My Three and Twentieth Year' were published in *The Bell* and *Envoy* respectively, in December 1950, but within three years Murphy was publishing poems regularly in *The Irish Times* and his reach had expanded to include *The Listener* and the *New Statesman*. The Dolmen Press published his first collection, *The Archaeology of Love*, in 1955, and the same year brought out *Sailing to an Island* as a presentation booklet.[17] This pattern of publishing limited editions of single poems was repeated in 1959 when Liam Miller printed Murphy's *The Woman of the House*, occasioning some heated exchanges in the columns of the *Times Literary Supplement* concerning the present state of poetry. By 1961, with a growing reputation internationally, and poems in *Listen*, *Encounter* and *Poetry* (Chicago), Murphy was moving out of the orbit of the Dolmen Press. His transition to Faber & Faber, which would publish his second collection *Sailing to an Island*, entailed some disentangling of these earlier commitments, however. Before signing to the British publisher, Murphy had agreed for some poems from the typescript of his new volume to appear in the *Dolmen Miscellany* and was pleased that this – and the publication of *The Last Galway Hooker* in pamphlet form by the Dolmen Press – was acceptable to his new editor Charles Monteith. Monteith's letter to Murphy on 9 May 1962 speaks of the desire 'to get the bibliography right at the very start' and his facilitation of Murphy's transition between publishers is noteworthy.[18] In particular, his request for details of the poems that had already appeared in the Dolmen Press version indicates a supportive attitude to the poet's creative process at this stage in his career.

The Last Galway Hooker, with drawings by Ruth Brandt, had an initial print run of 500 copies. It contains a two-page preface by Murphy, recounting the journey that would form the substance of the poem 'Sailing to an Island'.[19] This experience, as well as finding textual form in a variety of different printings of this poem,[20] is closely linked by Murphy to a period of significant personal and creative change:

> … alone in the pre-famine Coast Guard cottage on the quay at Rosroe, I wrote the first draft of a poem about our rough passage and change of course that led to a change in my life … after some fortuitous redirections including marriage and divorce, through Crete, Brittany, Wicklow, London, and back to Inishbofin in 1959, the poem I had drafted at Rosroe, revised and revised, emerged in 1963 as the final version of 'Sailing to an Island'.
>
> (*P*, p. 245)[21]

Murphy's decision to return to the west of Ireland after the dissolution of his marriage to Patricia Avis coincided with an important transition in his writing career. At the same time as his publishing practice was taking an international turn, the poet himself was – both physically and creatively – moving to a place of origin, deeper into the west. For Murphy this place of origin was both figurative and literal, drawing on memories of the overgrown garden in his grandparents' demesne house in Mayo described in his essay 'The Pleasure Ground' which serves, significantly, as preface and title to *Poems 1952–2012* – an idyllic space of childhood exploration: 'So I went back to that older earlier unfenced romantic pleasure ground in the treeless hills of Connemara on the edge of the sea' (*P*, p. 16). By taking up sailing on his move to Cleggan, Murphy linked this experience to a form of creative discovery, a resituating of the self not only in space but also in time, a process suggested by J. Edward Chamberlin as being analogous to maritime navigation:

> For any navigator, it is never just a matter of noticing signs. Like trackers in the desert or readers in the library, they need to interpret these signs – and the ways of interpretation, like the scripts of different languages, vary widely and need to be learned in different locations and different cultures. Furthermore navigational directions are always relative rather than absolute.[22]

Literature of the sea captures modes of transition, not only through the representation of journeys, but also by means of the temporal relation between narratives of the sea and of land. There has been much debate about whether maritime developments initiate economic and social change, or simply reflect these shifts some time after they have taken place.[23] What is clear is that in different archipelagic zones, at particular historical moments, specific dynamics of land and sea emerge. While the close interaction of the Galway, Mayo and Clare coastlines with their offshore islands suggests an interlocking identity, the tension in Murphy's early work between the settled nature of rural communities and the restlessness of life near and on the sea produces new explorations of personal and shared identity, which facilitate his participation in island life while maintaining networks of association with artistic and intellectual communities elsewhere.

Sailing to an Island marks this reimagining in spatial terms. The book is divided into three parts and all three of the poems in Part I engage directly with the fated character of life at sea.[24] These poems enact a process of risk-taking that will shape Murphy's personal and creative life, and problematise notions of a secure community. His decision to move to Cleggan, and to earn a living there, is matched in daring by his choice of rural subject matter, at a time when his peers were cultivating urban and cosmopolitan perspectives.[25] The book begins in unsteadiness: the opening lines of its title poem reveal the contrary forces at work in the collection as a whole – the tidal pull between earth and sea, past and present. Here the line breaks intensify this effect:

> The boom above my knees lifts, and the boat
> Drops, and the surge departs, departs, my cheek
> Kissed and rejected, kissed, as the gaff sways   (*P*, p. 19)

This instability marks the self-conscious nature of the poet's position in the space between, and his interrogation of, the dynamics of movement. The geometry of the boat's structure alerts the reader to the role of form in determining our understanding of both text and situation, and in suggesting the new poetic modes on which Murphy will elaborate in subsequent collections – the contained and measured lyrics of *High Island*; the symphonic composition of *The Price of Stone*.

In spite of the immediacy of experience here, 'Sailing to an Island' is also freighted with the past. The trip to Clare Island is attended by myths of the pirate queen, but the attempt to 'locate' her eludes the sailors. The space of the island is a form of mirage, hidden by spray, and the boat remains in a threatening zone of jagged rocks – a form of purgatory within which the sailors struggle to make headway. The circularity of the sound patterns affirms this vigorous stasis: the alliterative effects of Clare Island with its <u>c</u>rags and <u>c</u>astles, and the broad-vowel sounds of the brazen Granuaile and her descendants, yields to a five-line stanza of entrapment (*P*, p. 19). Here Clare Island is shown to combine history and legend, real and imagined worlds. Its solidity as a place of earth and stone amidst the wildness of the sea increases the speaker's focus on this goal. The journey, beset with the practical problems of bad weather, is subject to an almost supernatural force in a seascape littered with 'hideous rocks' and 'an extinct / Volcano ... / Guarded by hags' (*P*, p. 19). The shape of the poem reflects the tidal nature of this adventure; stanza lengths fluctuate and sound patterns shift to accommodate the extremity of the danger:

> Now she dips, and the sail hits the water.
> She luffs to a squall; is struck; and shudders.
> Someone is shouting. The boom, weak as scissors,
> Has snapped. The boatman is praying.   (*P*, p. 20)

This contrast with the singing boatmen of the first stanza is also part of the poem's device of repetition and change. It suggests both entrapment and flux – resonant states for marginal maritime communities in mid-twentieth-century Ireland confronting the social and economic limitations of their isolation at the same time as they endured persistent physical danger. The speaker is not of the island community and stands at some distance from these experiences. His fear is increased by the conviction that the boat was one of those involved in the Cleggan disaster of 1927, when a massive storm killed forty-five men:

> We in holiday fashion know
> This is the boat that belched its crew
> Dead on the shingle in the Cleggan disaster.   (*P*, p. 20)

When, eventually, the crew reach Inishbofin, their plans for Clare Island abandoned, the poet notes the difference between himself as a 'holiday' sailor and those for whom the sea is an essential part of life. Here island knowledge is not a kind of folk language but a practical skill and a means of survival. The reticence of the island men suggests the difficulty of reclaiming the past: 'They are slow to tell / The story again ...' (*P*, p. 21), so that the speaker must remain in the present, on the margins of conversation that nevertheless yields pleasure. After a night of drinking the poet relives the lurching motion of the boat:

> The bench below my knees lifts, and the floor
> Drops, and words depart, depart, ...   (*P*, p. 21)

affirming the circularity of experience and, paradoxically, the stasis of the day's aborted journey. Though here it seems to reinforce his novice status, subject to all the extremities of experience, we know that this is the kind of life he will go on to make his own.

The vivid materiality of the boat itself is among the most striking achievements of this poem and it continues to be a practical marker of Murphy's involvement in this peripheral community, both in life and in poetry. Until the twentieth century boat design and building was a central part of the indigenous craft of island communities and it remains an important marker of their tradition. In 1959 Murphy bought the *Ave Maria*, the last of the old sailing hookers built in Galway, and in the winter of that year wrote 'The Last Galway Hooker', the second poem in the Faber volume.[26] Prefaced by an explanatory note clarifying some of its descriptive terms, the text advertises the specificity of experience and the importance of its vocabulary to the authenticity of the work. This synthesis of language and materiality is a significant dimension of Murphy's achievement as a poet. Bernard O'Donoghue notes 'the versatility of the language Murphy develops .... There is a wonderful, controlled heteroglossia in his poetry.'[27] This can be seen as characteristic of the archipelagic mode, in which the relationship between language and place is constantly renegotiated. The 'Metrical Note', which precedes the poem in the 1963 edition of *Sailing to an Island*, implicitly connects the rhythm of the tercets to this linguistic context; it notes the four stresses of each line and the unequal pattern of these, building on the destabilised rhythm of 'Sailing to an Island'. The effect of the rhythm is to draw attention to the absent fourth line that would complete the structure of meaning in key ways. This mixed sense of potential, and of loss, shadows 'Sailing to an Island' from the beginning, despite its impressions of a fresh start. In this way Murphy's transitions between London, Inishbofin, Rhodesia and Dublin during this period are shown to bring the poet both inspiration and anxiety.

This poem, too, is conscious of the material past, and the ways in which this is closely interwoven with topography. The boatwright's hammer and the civil-war gun both sound across the same terrain, suggesting connections between actions separated by time, and implicitly linking human violence with the threatening force of nature. Creation and destruction are brought into close proximity by the endurance of seafaring communities. The craft of making, celebrated here by boatwright and poet, crosses the generations from father to daughter, yet the materiality of the boat is closely linked to its role in nature:

> Songs of disasters wailed on the quay
> When the tilt of the water heaved the whole shore.
> 'She was lucky always, the *Ave Maria*',
>
> With her brown sails, and her sleek skin of tar,
> Her forest of oak ribs and larch-wood planks,
> Cut limestone ballast, costly fishing gear, ...   (P, p. 36)[28]

The given and the made combine to give the boat its strength, and are themselves a record of the changing fortunes of the island community. Though she is the fastest fishing boat, there is nothing to protect the *Ave Maria* from market forces, when the price of fish comes 'down to nothing' (P, p. 37). Her transformation into a yacht changes her function from work to leisure: she is 'like a girl given money and a home' (P, p. 37) and her self-renewal is part of the larger island story of reawakening to new possibility. The burst of hyphenated words – 'pitch-pine', 'Smooth-running', 'ash-blocks' – catches the smooth transition of the vessel and her renovated elegance, but the war and its deprivations intervene and she soon returns to utilitarian mode (P, p. 37).

The fate of human lives entwined with the sea is developed in this poem through the boat's next owner, who was 'Best among the boatsmen of Inishbofin, / She his best buy' (P, p. 38). The gendered binary is made much of: the feminised sea controls the sailor's emotions, prompting his fear of disaster and his pride at overcoming it. In a maritime equivalent to Patrick Kavanagh's Maguire, 'he never married, was this hooker's lover' (P, p. 38).[29] This dependent existence, caught between life of the sea and a retreat into alcohol, suggests the natural rhythms of seafaring, which the poem's tercets relentlessly preserve. The restlessness of this man moves through the text to the speaker himself, communicated in the craft of boat and of poem.

'The Last Galway Hooker' could be seen as the necessary precursor to perhaps the best known of Murphy's early poems, 'The Cleggan Disaster'. Begun in 1959, its imaginative lineage can be traced back to the Clare Island trip of 1952 which was also the starting point of 'Sailing to an Island'. Indeed the links between these poems, and the extent to which Murphy's form evolves to test and deepen his engagement with coastal histories, suggests the formation of a poetic archipelago disrupting simplified readings of Murphy's literary and cultural identity. Rather than moving imaginatively between centre and periphery, the poet commits to his representation of the seafaring community through different poetic modes. The habitual sailor, as Barry Cunliffe outlines, builds up:

> … a familiarity with the environment through which he travel[s], [is] able to assess the movement of his craft in relation to the sea and the winds, to interpret the signs of land still out of sight, and to recognize the shape of land once it became close enough to be visible.[30]

In 'The Cleggan Disaster' Murphy explores the limits of knowledge at the same time as he links the interpretative acts of both seafaring and reading communities. His return to this tragedy is a necessary one and the lengthening of form acknowledges the significance of his subject matter and affords space for the dramatic unfolding of events. In stanzas oscillating between five and eight lines, the poem conveys the changing energies of wind and tide and expresses the risks taken by the sailors:

> … It was cold and late October.
> The hulls hissed and rolled on the sea's black hearth …
>
> (*P*, p. 48)

The formal control of these early stanzas intensifies our awareness of the ungovernable sea, the knowledge of what is to come, and lucidly evokes a literal calm before the storm:

> Five pieces of drift-net with a mesh of diamonds
> Were paid from each stern. The webbed curtains hung
> Straight from the cork-lines, and warps were hitched
> To the strong stems and the pine oars boarded.
> The men in the boats lit their pipes and rested.   (*P*, p. 48)

The stillness here speaks of the meditative power of Murphy's best work, and the responsiveness of his language to the demands of its subject matter. Soon issues of judgement are foregrounded within the narrative of the poem: Concannon ignores the advice to cut his nets, hoping to use them as a way of riding the storm. The interdependence of the community and the sea is part of the poem's texture and is exemplified in the figure of this man; on land he merely marks time, but his commitment to the community – in adhering to the custom of giving away fish to those who need it (a custom also alluded to in Murphy's poem 'Largesse' from *High Island*)[31] – shows his understanding of the collective nature of island life.

The crew are subject to larger forces; they are on board out of necessity, their land too poor to yield a living. The skipper thus emerges as a singular figure, more in tune with seafaring itself than with his men. The raw violence of Concannon's handling of the blue shark is followed by the release of the mackerel shoal so plentiful it could sink the boat. It expresses the energies of life beneath the surface of the ocean and tests man's capabilities to withstand this power. The Gothic character of this scene, with its alternating darkness and colour, the rising wind and the cry of the woman, prefigures the nightmarish experience as the storm takes hold. Here Murphy interweaves the harsh realism of the fisherman's daily life with the imaginative intensity of the night's events in ways that are at once true to, yet transcend, the particularity of the historical moment. The force of the storm renders the sea as a rocky landscape, a transformation of matter that challenges the act of representation itself. Refusing to cut the nets loose, the sailor retains his sense of purpose; the stanza becomes regular in rhythm and complete in rhyme, before being cast again into formlessness:

The moon couldn't shine, the clouds shut her out,
But she came unseen to sway on his side
All the waters gathered from the great spring tide.

As he slid from the cliff-slope of a heaped wave
Down the white and violet skin of turbulence
Into the boiling trough, ...   (*P*, p. 51)

The fear of being drowned out to sea, where they would not be found nor receive a proper burial, becomes a concern for the men. If, as Shin Yamashiro asserts, 'oceanic history is inseparable from fatality',[32] then Murphy's text not only tries to render the immediacy of the fishermen's response but contemplates their participation in a long narrative of human striving against overwhelming forces. The hallucinatory dance intensifies the sense of the sea as a liminal space, where identities merge and change, and perceptions are permanently altered. This powerful transformative force also works on the imagination, transporting Concannon between the sensations of past and present and rendering the sea an atemporal zone. Here the boundary between symbolic language and material reality is removed: metaphorical sea horses become animals with mane and hoof, blood and bone. The disorientation that marks the close of the narrative stems directly from Concannon's blindness – with its overtones of Greek tragedy – but also expresses the impossibility of finding order in the chaos of the sea. His impairment means that he cannot bear witness to the bodies of the drowned fishermen, laid out in the cleared fish store, intended that night for dancing. The perspective of the poem is thus forced to shift towards the omniscient view, to the voice of cultural memory that carries the events across time. The final section of the poem, headed 'Years Later', comprises five stanzas, each with eight short lines. Each asks a question in a variation of the *ubi sunt* motif; each offers an indirect answer. This ebb and flow – the five-line query followed by a three-line response – traces the movement of this story through time, the unbreakable connection between the community and the sea paradoxically strengthened by the losses of that night.

These three powerful poems demonstrate Murphy's shifting perspectives on the life of the sea, and its enduring effects. For Eamon Grennan, however, they demonstrate the poet's outsider status:

> the poignantly unspoken but indelible meaning of all three of these poems resides … in their speaker's failure to become what he calls 'truly Irish,' … revealing in stark outline the very split in his consciousness and personality which they are designed to heal.[33]

That these poems are 'designed to heal', though, is questionable. Rather than providing an Irish poetic identity that Murphy – at least for a time – may have espoused, these works problematise binaries through their shifting perspectives and diverse linguistic strategies. Practically, too, Murphy's engagement with island communities in the west of Ireland would grow and change. In 1969 he purchased High Island, where many of the poems in his 1974 collection of that name were written. In a letter to Philip Larkin, Murphy described it simply as:

> ruins of an early Celtic Church, beehive cells built in the seventh century, uninhabited for the last 900 years, known as High Island, because of its cliffs, it lies a few miles out in the ocean, has no harbour and is thronged by birds, rabbits and seals.[34]

He would contemplate the issue of ownership more deeply in his memoir *The Kick*, however, noting that 'High Island can never be possessed because it will always remain in the possession of the sea' (*K*, p. 250). The poems of *High Island* bear out this observation. From the copulating seals of the opening text to the violent stories interwoven through memory and direct speech, these works move deeper into investigations of human relationships and motivations. Tim Robinson dwells on the delicate balance between different forms of experience in Murphy's work,[35] a dynamic that first comes to prominence in *High Island*, in the interweaving of personal and shared memory. The relationship between human and natural worlds changes here, too, as Murphy experiments with the auditory and visual properties of language:

> Wings beating on stone
> Quick vibration of notes   throats   tongues
> Under silverweed   calling   and calling
>
> ('Nocturne', *P*, p. 142)

Sometimes the dynamics of self and other are obliquely realised; elsewhere, frank expression – such as the erotic meditation of 'Sunup' – releases powerful feeling into the sensual world of Murphy's language. Less concerned with the sea than with island life, these poems move beyond the interstitial sense of arrival that inflected the maritime poems. Here the definition of islandness as 'a metaphysical sensation that derives from the heightened experience that accompanies physical isolation' might be responsible for this deepening engagement.[36] As Eamonn Wall puts it, 'alone on High Island, Murphy serves as a medium between the *pagus* and the *disciplina* ... he negotiates a place in this tradition for modern language, for an Enlightenment-influenced worldview'.[37]

In this way Murphy's engagement with his environment is the key to his creative development. His understanding of place emphasises both continuity and change, through the sea's endless process of transformation and renewal:

> One day the shore will be swept clean, the next covered by weed; the single wave itself rises and falls. Perpetually renewing and destroying, the sea proposes a beginning and an ending, an alternative to our landlocked state.[38]

Profoundly altering our concept of time, this experience permits past and present to assume a new relation. For Murphy the space of the poem – and of the book – is one where both geographical and temporal boundaries can be transgressed to better represent the multifaceted, contingent nature of the self. In the unpublished draft essay 'The Pursuit of Islands' he reflects on the processes of discovery and loss:

Though it was a pity to have lost something small, beautiful and irreplaceable, as the culture of these islands was in certain aspects, it would all be gone so soon that it would be hopeless to observe what still remained, and impossible to go back to what was gone. Was it true, I wondered, this business of going back, a thing we are always told is wrong? I don't think it is wrong, indeed at certain points in most lives it is necessary.[39]

Yet to go back, in these terms, is also to go forward. As the work of *Sailing to an Island* shows, and as Murphy's later poetry bears out, histories are constantly reimagined within new temporal and linguistic frames. In the second half of the twentieth century, familiar structures of political and cultural power have been altered by the emergence of diverse perspectives – and new forms of representation – that offer new ways of reading past and present. Archipelagic poetry addresses this changing spatial imaginary by attending to the relationship between places and identities hitherto deemed marginal. Richard Murphy's enduring engagement with these environments in his poetry is neither nostalgic nor escapist, rather it speaks deeply to the radical displacements of our age.

5

Fluid Geographies: Richard Murphy's poetics of place

PHILIP KEEL GEHEBER

In the autumn 2011 *Poetry Ireland Review*, Richard Murphy published the first of three sets of excerpts from his manuscript in progress 'Transgressing into Poetry'. These chapters of the manuscript consist of materials from notebooks compiled as repositories of ideas for the poems of *The Price of Stone* (1985) as they were in development, and excerpts from these notebooks have since been published in a fuller volume, *In Search of Poetry* (2017). The first set of excerpts, 'Notes for Sonnets', includes reflections for the sonnet 'Pier Bar' from an October 1982 notebook, in which Murphy reminds himself to 'Bring the sea into the bar ... sea rhythms and sounds ... boat rhythms ... not for nostalgia ... there's more to say than to sigh about the sea at this crossing of a boundary in my life ... my literal transgressing.'[1] While 'Transgressing into Poetry' forms the backdrop of *The Price of Stone*, the notes are emblematic of the overarching project of Murphy's 'lifelong transgression', as he calls it in the notes towards 'Carlow Village Schoolhouse', notes which focus on his great-grandfather and namesake Richard William Murphy's role in the decline of the Irish language (he was master of the Church of Ireland parish school in Nurney during the Famine).[2] The 'literal transgressing' and 'lifelong transgression' Murphy signals in these notes is his test of the received limits of class, sexuality, language and sectarian division. He uses geography as a way to test the boundaries of these and calls to mind the geological definition of 'transgress': 'Of the sea: to spread over (the land)'.[3]

Murphy's instinctive amalgamation of seascape and built structure permeates his poetic project as he merges the sea and land into a single topography, 'a sky and water landscape', as he notes in his 1958 travel essay 'Charm of Eire'.[4] While Maurice Harmon has highlighted Murphy's basic belief in 'the truth of place',[5] ultimately Murphy's project aims at the legibility of space, especially at the confluence of land, sky and sea. He notes to himself to 'keep filling the notebook with ideas for sonnet dwellings'[6] that inhabit and interpret this landscape. His poetic project of reconstruction, a reimagination mirrored in his architectural and nautical pursuits, exemplifies the processes Laurence J. Kirmayer describes in his discussion of traumatic memory, 'Landscapes of Memory: trauma, narrative, and dissociation'. According to Kirmayer, 'disruptions give rise to an effort to interpret and so to smooth, stabilise, and recalibrate', hopefully 'to create a specific narrative landscape'.[7] Murphy seeks to refashion a narrative landscape that is inclusive of all Irish sects and divisions, refusing to give priority to any single controlling gaze over Irish geography. His geographic sense is neither explicitly Anglo-Irish nor explicitly Catholic or Gaelic Irish, but one that is always in flux and intimately related to the creative and destructive processes of the sea. He inhabits binary divisions by imagining a western landscape through what Bertrand Westphal terms 'transgressivity' and then populates this space with structures that are best characterised as Foucauldian heterotopias. Murphy's transgressive, heterotopic geography of the west relies on the confluence of materiality, history and imagination to create a new Irish landscape of plurality.

Born into an Anglo-Irish family in 1927, in the wake of the Anglo-Irish Ascendancy's fall from power, Murphy inherits a landscape of decay and disarray from this Anglo-Irish tradition. He characterises his grandmother at Milford House in County Mayo as a 'Mistress of mossy acres and unpaid rent' in the poem 'The Woman of the House' (*P*, p. 29) and as the 'mistress of a beautiful disorder, living on the last trees of a once great forest' in the 1963 version of the essay 'The Pleasure Ground'.[8] John Wilson Foster's 'The Landscape of Three Irelands: Hewitt, Murphy and Montague' describes this inheritance as a 'patrimony of scatter and decay at the hands of modernisation',[9] and this patrimony has severed Murphy's moorings and left him adrift on the shifting tides of twentieth-century Irish socio-politics.

For some critics, like Terence Brown in 'Poets and Patrimony: Richard Murphy and James Simmons', Murphy's intense interest in the west and the seascape as a pleasure ground is based on the insecurity of this inheritance. The sea 'in its terrifying disinterested fashion', Brown comments, 'renders caste distinctions, between Anglo-Irishmen and native Irishmen, of no import. Offshore in a storm men are simply men.'[10] Brown interprets Murphy's interest in the sea as an effort to obviate distinctions of caste, but Murphy seems more interested in confronting and subverting these distinctions, especially as they are inscribed on the landscape. Murphy's remedy for decay is enacted in his efforts to reintegrate shared histories in his poetry and architectural projects. His topography exhibits the dilapidated Big House, the overgrown demesne, imperial remnants and monuments, Famine cottages, abandoned quays, beached boats and crumbling early Christian sites. Mark Kilroy's reading of the 'Connemara Locale' throughout Murphy's early career sheds light on how his poetic focus shifts in its employment of landscape, 'a world bounded by the ever present sea and coast, its people and history'.[11] Thus, *Sailing to an Island* (1963), Kilroy notes, is Murphy's 'poetry of transition rather than of arrival' and illustrates 'the impracticality of clinging to the West in his search for identity'.[12] Then *The Battle of Aughrim* (1968) is centrally concerned with exploring Murphy's dual identity and the way that facticity of ancestry relates to place. Finally, in *High Island* (1974) the poet is 'Characteristically alone' and consciously an outsider, 'but he has established, if not a home, an order. The whole movement can be seen as a freeing from locale.'[13]

Murphy's poetics of place makes the next logical leap in *The Price of Stone*, of which he comments in a 1984 broadcast by the Australian Broadcasting Commission (ABC): 'The freedom I got from letting a building or structure speak in the first person released me into writing all the rest.'[14] As in the notes on 'Pier Bar', Murphy views this newfound freedom as a 'literal transgressing', and the poet's persona is subsumed by the structures that populate his Irish topography and interrogate both personal and communal history as well as the relationships of built structures to place. Murphy is certainly interested in topographical representations, and Kilroy's sense of his poetic development of this theme is an effective surface reading of how he 'orders the world by situating each person and object in landscape and history'.[15] However, Kilroy foregrounds this interest as Murphy's quest to establish a stable identity. 'Here the concern with locale reflects a search for identity', Kilroy writes, 'a search which is in the end only partly successful. No matter how much he immerses himself into the area, Murphy remains the outsider.'[16] Others propose similar readings of Murphy's identity politics as expressed in his topographies. In *Irish Literature: a social history*, Norman Vance closely aligns Murphy with Yeats and 'the benign paternalism of doomed Anglo-Ireland', diagnosing his efforts as a 'post-colonial guilt' which seeks an 'anxious, willed sense of identity with the "meere [*sic*] Irish"', particularly fishermen and islanders'.[17] Similarly, Brown argues that Murphy's poetry exhibits a 'topographical imperative' whereby 'the almost talismanic recitation of place-names is, were irony not present, recognizable as a recurrent reflex response of poets of Protestant background to the vexed question of their possession of an authentic Irish identity'.[18]

While these readings are correct in suggesting that there is some romanticising, nostalgic impulse at work in Murphy's interest in the Irish west, they reductively rely on the same rigidly imagined genealogical essentialism that Murphy's poetry seeks to disrupt. Instead of a mere attempt to establish credentials to pass muster for inclusion into a specific group, Murphy's interrogation is also internal. Neal Bowers characterises this simultaneous, irreconcilable double movement as the central paradox of Murphy's poetry, wherein 'Murphy's outward movement toward the past and toward the Irish landscape, which has often been characterised as detached observation, is actually, at the same time, a push into himself, into his own interior'.[19] Exterior mirrors interior in Bowers' formulation, and Murphy's fluid and plural sense of identity with respect to class, nationality, sexuality and vocation illustrates his embrace of difference and refusal to essentialise or recognise the stability of authenticity. The ever-shifting Irish relationship to land ownership serves as one model for Murphy's sense of the falsity of stable, authentic categories which can provide a sense of undisputed origin.

Sovereign ownership of the land is the central concern of actors in Irish history, and Murphy asks in the opening line of 'On Battle Hill', the first poem in the long sequence *The Battle of Aughrim*, 'Who owns the land ... ?' (*P*, p. 61). The Williamite forces' victory in 1691 at Aughrim guaranteed Anglo-Irish control of the soil until independence, and Murphy recognises this is how Robert Miller, Murphy's ancestor, first came into possession of the estate he would rename Milford (*K*, p. 43). While the land itself is relatively static and seemingly permanent, possession of it can swiftly trade hands, so Murphy's question becomes all the more relevant after the demise of his class. Terence Brown sees this question as Murphy's attempt to prove and justify his native Irish roots, suggesting that it is

> ... not a question a dispossessed native would ask; nor is it one that a planted occupant dare ask as he validates possession by work and improvement. But it is the sort of question a poet perplexed about his contemporary social position can, particularly when he knows that in attempting an answer he will summon up an impressive array of ancestors to help authenticate his own identity.[20]

Earlier in the twentieth century, Yeats, perhaps believing he could forestall the loss of Anglo-Irish sociopolitical power, upheld and memorialised that class' set of ideals. Julian Moynahan points out in *Anglo-Irish: the literary imagination in a hyphenated culture* that Yeats' summary and celebration of the Anglo-Irish 'as a type of aristocracy' as they are being eclipsed is really 'an effort to preserve what is dying out as a precious legacy of cultural memory'; he is effectively, as Moynahan sardonically notes, 'pipe[ing] a former ruling class to its grave'.[21] Yeats may as well have been Cúchulainn fighting back the waves, as the fate of Lady Gregory's demesne suggests. Murphy noted in a letter to his parents after visiting Coole Park in 1950 that

> ... not a stone of the foundations remained, but, to elaborate on Isaiah, waving ash-trees and tall hay were in the place of

> it. The pleasure-ground was improved for being twenty years
> neglected, the glass-house smashed, the shrubs overgrown, trees
> half-fallen across paths.[22]

Decay of the once great estates of this caste was imminent, yet twenty
years' neglect improves the Pleasure Ground. As Murphy's parents
contemplated moving back to Ireland in 1949, he described for them
'the general and inevitable decay of everything, which is only too
evident all over Ireland' and noted, with the metaphor of a sinking
ship, that 'there are now very few places which have not more or less
gone under with their inhabitants'.[23] Murphy inherits this cultural
memory of land ownership from his Anglo-Irish tradition, and he
exorcises the mythologised past in an effort to uncompromisingly
undermine its divisive effects.

Murphy's initiation into the politically fraught Anglo-Irish
relationship to the land came as a child at Milford House, his maternal
family's 'seat' in County Mayo. After 'the Pleasure Ground sank
through decay into oblivion, as the old people died and the young
left the country', Murphy recalls, 'I searched for grounds of pleasure
that excluded nobody, till I found them by living with friends I loved
among people on or near the sea' (*P*, p. 16). In essence, he must climb
over the garden walls, seeking the inspiration and means to construct
a cohesive and continuous narrative outside the parcelled landscapes
of antagonistic traditions into which he was born, without forgetting
the root of that asymmetric power relation: the British Empire and
shipping it controlled for commerce and conquest. Much of his keen
awareness of the sea links between the colonies and Britain, as well
as the sense of colonial displacement those distances engender, were
sown in his early life. We must remember Murphy was born into
complicity with this imperial project: his father was the last British
mayor of Colombo, Ceylon (Murphy spent most of his first eight
years there), and was instrumental in peacefully handing over power
to native Sri Lankans (*K*, pp. 32–4). His father was later governor
of the Bahamas, where Murphy worked as his aide-de-camp (*K*, pp.
95–101).

Thinking about how Murphy leaves the meticulously arranged space of the Pleasure Ground into the wilds of the 'desolate, uncultivated, storm-bound' Connemara coast (*P*, p. 15) and then eventually comes to the sea (physically as a young boy, and then later imaginatively as a poet) in his construction of space, I suggest that Bertrand Westphal's theories in *Geocritcism: real and fictional spaces* (2011) and his foreword to *Geocritical Explorations: space, place and mapping in literary and cultural studies* (2011), in which he propounds a geocritical method for thinking about space as the coherence of heterogeneity, are illuminating concepts to draw upon. In the latter book Westphal defines his three primary concepts of *spatiotemporality* (highlighting the inextricable merger of space and time, especially the way in which 'temporal metaphors tend to spatialize time'), *referentiality* (the links between world and text, referent and representation), and *transgressivity* (which makes space fundamentally fluid).[24] Westphal foregrounds his theory on the dissonance between perception of space and representation of space and draws on concepts like Foucault's *heterotopia*, Deleuze and Guattari's *deterritorialisation* process (both of which I will return to), Henri Lefebvre's production of space, and Edward Soja's 'Thirdspace'. For Westphal 'geocritical analysis locates places in a temporal depth in order to uncover or discover multilayered identities, and it highlights the temporal variability of heterogeneous spaces' in a way that focuses on a polysensuous approach to places ('*places* meaning concrete or realized spaces') and a multifocalisation that 'tends to relativize Otherness' by not privileging a certain point of view.[25] This theory lends itself well to Murphy's poetic project, particularly as one thinks about his changing relation to place outlined by Kilroy. The most important concept for my purposes here is transgressivity, which Westphal defines as a state that 'characterizes the forces continually acting upon heterogeneous spaces, forces that make them a multiple "territory of germination"' and is inherent in dynamic representations of space.[26] The longer definition explains that

> the state of transgressivity is the name we give to the perpetual
> oscillation between center and periphery, to the reconciliations

of peripheral forces operating with respect to the center. It corresponds to the principle of mobility and animates the examined life. It will not weigh in on the scale of values sanctioned by a preconceived hierarchical legitimacy. The limit is integrated into a dynamic field where that which evolves in the periphery is destined to approach the center according to a law of interference. Consequently, transgression is neutralized: it is not necessarily affected by a negative nuance but corresponds to a simple act of border crossing inherent to the system ...[27]

Transgressivity allows the intersection of various qualities and relations without hierarchically privileging any of them. It holds multiple conflicting views in suspension by bringing into focus oscillations and mobility between the centre and periphery in addition to the interference of the centre by the periphery as these power relations inhere in geographic space.

In Murphy's poetic engagement with the Irish west, the sea and land unite to form a contiguous surface upon which he situates his transgressive sites. These two seemingly oppositional entities frequently fuse, as in 'Afternoon at Home', where the poet watches the 'sea dissolve into the line of rock in steam',[28] and in 'Sailing to an Island', where the sea becomes an extension of the landscape and 'There are hills of sea between us and land' (*P*, p. 19). Similarly, in 'The Cleggan Disaster', which recounts the fisherman Pat Concannon's experience of the 1927 storm that drowned twenty-five men in the Cleggan/Rossadilisk area, the sea is protean in its assumption of characteristics of the west-coast landscape. There is a 'cliff-slope of a heaped wave' and 'Three cliffs of waves' which, to Pat Concannon, 'look like rocks' (*P*, pp. 51–2). Additionally, boats act as if they are in a landscape amidst the maelstrom that reverses the land/sea divide. A 'keel like a scythe cut a clear white swath / Through the gale's acres', and an overturned boat becomes wallowing livestock:

> Down the valleys of this lull, like a black cow
> In search of her calf, an upturned hull
> Wallowed towards them.   (*P*, p. 52)

While these images seem to construct the sea as extensions of the land, to be parcelled, swathed and harvested, it also signals the danger of such hubris. The boat, like the wandering cow, is overturned, all of its crewman drowned. Off this coast, as John Goodby notes, 'the sea is represented as a primal landscape whose threat allows the proving of a core self, free from the burden of a divided identity'.[29] Rather than an effort to free oneself of a split identity, it seems, on the contrary, that the fluid topography is a way to embrace different identities with a natural space that resists dominance.

For a citizen of the globalised network of the British Empire the sea has become one more metaphoric landscape for dominance, unifying and linking all of the distant British possessions. Like Elizabeth Bowen, whom Roy Foster argues 'felt most at home in mid-Irish Sea',[30] Murphy seems most comfortable in littoral spaces which allow him to maintain physical separation from metropolitan London with cultural access to the metropolis, an interesting reinforcement of the colonial's relationship to place. This sense of his comfort is best illustrated by the links Murphy established between Cleggan/Inishbofin and London. Renowned poets, including Plath, Hughes and Roethke, as well as representatives of the London elite like Charles Monteith of Faber & Faber, visited him in the Irish west. Monteith characterises his sense of Murphy's and the west's importance by comparing it to Lady Ottoline Morrell's Garsington as the rural gathering place for the Bloomsbury Set in a letter of 30 November 1960. He notes that he had met Toby Robertson, the theatre director, 'and heard that he'd been on the Bofin and how much he enjoyed it all. If things go on like this, Days Hotel will turn into the Garsington of the '60s!'[31] Monteith's romanticising of Murphy's hospitality in the west matches Murphy's view of Connemara, 'that older earlier unfenced romantic pleasure ground in the treeless hills … on the edge of the sea' (*P*, p. 16). Murphy's family tradition has its roots in the routes of the sea, which is one possible explanation for what he means when he sees the Pleasure Ground's origins in it. The sea mimics the form of a garden, in 'The Drowning of a Novice', providing an extension of cultivated Anglo-Irish demesnes:

the sea grew white

Flowers in her garden
    petalled with spray.   (*P*, p. 41)

While it seems that this horticultural metaphor should guarantee the safety of the novice boatman, it is the 'petalled … spray' that gets the boatman lost and eventually overturns his boat and drowns him. In 'Liner', the ship is:

… steaming home, ploughing your peace of mind,
With the bow-wave poise of a duchess coaching through
Her deep blue shire; …   (*P*, p. 193)

Here the sea is a province controlled by the empire and necessary for communications and transport between colonies. Murphy's liner (and other boats) serves as an illustration of Michel Foucault's 'heterotopia par excellence' which is

a floating piece of space, a place without a place, that exists by itself, that is closed in on itself and at the same time is given over to the infinity of the sea … it goes as far as the colonies in search of the most previous treasures they conceal in their gardens.[32]

These ships are the dynamic 'nowhere' that tie the coloniser to the colonised, the network that extends state power.

It is the ship, the '*fleet in being*', that Deleuze and Guattari draw upon in *A Thousand Plateaus*, in their discussion of deterritorialisation and the sea.[33] They define the sea as a smooth space, one which is difficult for a state/war machine like the British Empire to control, and the specific problem is 'the task of occupying an open space with a vortical movement that can rise up at any point'.[34] To grapple with smooth space, which is 'vectorial, projective, or topological',[35] states attempt to striate space, or close it and apply metrics that aim 'to transform into a dependency of the land, with its fixed routes, constant directions, relative movements, a whole counter-hydraulic of channels and conduits'.[36] Striations make smooth space into closed systems: Britain, Ireland, Ceylon and the Bahamas are all relatively positioned within the network of striated British seas. Murphy's liner in its shire, as well as the Homeric 'whaleroads' ('Stormpetrel', *P*, p. 140) and the 'sea-road' (of 'The Last Galway Hooker', *P*, p. 40), all assert control over this space. But 'the multiplication of relative movements, the intensification of relative speeds in striated space, ended up reconstituting a smooth space or absolute movements'.[37] One no longer goes from point to point, but occupies, like Foucault's ship, a space to follow a vector. It is within this swinging pendulum of striated-smoothed space that Murphy populates his topography, with buildings, boats, islands.

Murphy captures a sense of transgressivity and smoothed space in a later poem entitled 'Sri Lanka'. This poem was composed after the sonnets of *The Price of Stone* and, as in that collection's conceit of a place addressing the poet, the island recounts its serially colonised history. The speaking island illustrates Westphal's sense that 'transgression imposes heterogeneity' along with different temporalities and spatialities. 'Sri Lanka' depicts the island as a 'heart-shaped', 'brand name[d]', spiced 'ham / On early spice trade navigators' charts' (*P*, p. 233). Through the names given to the island Murphy highlights the plurality of relationships in a single place. The English name 'Ceylon', which traces its roots to the Tamil *Eelam*, is conspicuously absent from the poem, though the island calls itself 'a white king's gem' (*P*, p. 233). In a single line Murphy gives it the 'brand names' 'Taprobane, Serendip, Tenarisim' (*P*, p. 233), each of which derives from a different linguistic-tradition's act of naming the same place. This poem's focus on naming illustrates Murphy's continuous interest in etymologies that reveal layers of cultural miscegenation in the wake of colonisation and trade. For instance, he remarks in the notes to 'The Last Galway Hooker' that 'the word "hooker" may have been derived from the Dutch "hoeker", a fishing vessel that had plied off the west coast of Ireland for centuries' (*P*, p. 248). Returning to Sri Lanka's nominative layers, 'Taprobane' derives from the fourth-century-BCE Greek geographer Megasthenes or it could be from the Sanskrit *Tambrapani*, 'great pond'; 'Serendip' is a Persian name derived from the Arabic name for the island *Serendib*; 'Tenarisim' is Arabic and means 'isle of delight'; finally, 'Sri Lanka' is the Sinhala and Sanskrit name meaning 'resplendent island', and Murphy notes that 'Sri', 'meaning illustrious or exalted, was an honorific comparable to the "Great" in "Great Britain"' (*K*, p. 307). Each of these names for the island bears the trace of political powers attempting to 'colonise' it by naming and striating the spatial relation to it. However, the island no longer occupies a peripheral position, but its relation oscillates between several centres just as its name oscillates between temporalities and linguistic regions. As Deleuze and Guattari illustrate, the process of striation undermines itself, and this plurality of names re-smooths the space. Sri Lanka's transgressivity is made manifest in its smoothed relation to many dominant cultures over time, and this polychronic, polytopic past – to use terms deployed by Westphal – is what enables the personified Sri Lanka to 'seem as I am' (*P*, p. 233). In other words, the island's ontology is located in transgressivity. Just as Murphy's family and class had become dispossessed and Milford decayed, making his relation to place seem as it was, shifting linguistic markers in 'Sri Lanka' highlight how Murphy recognises and represents the polychronic, transgressive nature of space.

Freed from the burden of ownership, Murphy can assert a transgressive gaze over the landscape/seascape. Westphal notes that this 'transgressive gaze is constantly directed toward an emancipatory horizon in order to see beyond a code and territory that serves as its "domain"'.[38] One early attempt at such an emancipatory act is illustrated in the early poem about Murphy's failed trip to Clare Island, 'Sailing to an Island'. Contrasted against Milford House and the groomed Pleasure Ground is the archetypal western Irish landscape. Clare Island is a space where 'hideous rocks jag', there is 'a purgatory / Guarded by hags and bristled with breakers' with 'its crags purpled by legend' (*P*, p. 19): in short a no place, a mythological waypoint, an antithesis of the Anglo-Irish landscape. The voyage to the island involves seven hours of tacking in a rotten-hulled boat where drowning is a distinct possibility. However, they never arrive. Murphy's attempts to treat the sea like a striated, conquerable space fail. Ultimately, they must succumb to the 'wakeful / Waters that draw us headfast to Inishbofin' (*P*, p. 20), a less fabled destination.

The sea ultimately resists all efforts at striation. Class, fathers, houses and wealth all have no influence on man's ability to survive on the sea. Thus, the sea 'is a pleasure ground', as Terence Brown writes, 'upon which a man may employ his powers of strength and skill in the knowledge that no ordering principle can ever exercise complete dominion over its spirit'.[39] Subjected to a similar controlling force of the sea, Murphy can only look back at Clare Island as his dreams of reaching it are 'Washed over rails' (*P*, p. 20). The transgressive gaze need not necessarily reach and possess the 'emancipatory horizon' it is directed upon; Westphal notes 'transgression equally lies in the swerve, in the new trajectory, the unexpected'.[40] The spontaneous reception party on Inishbofin welcomes the poet back from his ill-advised sailing: 'But tonight we stay, drinking with people / Happy in the monotony of boats,' (*P*, p. 21). For Murphy the sea is a transgressive space, a universal leveller that is at once a source of pleasure and danger, and an embodiment of the ever-revolving process of striation and smoothing.

Extending this spatial reading to the landscape, in the wake of the Anglo-Irish Ascendancy, the redistribution of land ownership re-smooths the space striated by Anglo-Irish control and cultivation. Murphy reminded himself in his notebooks on 1 April 1969, just after he had bought High Island with the encouragement of his friend Tony White: 'I know that High Island can never be possessed because it will always remain in the possession of the sea. Its virtue will grow from its contemplation not its use' (*K*, p. 250). Any efforts by an owner to use High Island (or Sri Lanka) by striating the space surrounding it will be unsuccessful since that process undermines itself and the sea reverts to smoothness. Just as the islands are in the possession of the sea, the land continually experiences a flux in ownership. So Murphy's buildings are characterised like these islands, adrift in a smooth, fluid topography.

Murphy's fluid geography is more apparent in comparison with Yeats' depictions of Coole Park, fixated as they are on demesne ownership and family continuity, with Thoor Ballylee being a phallic reminder of Anglo-Norman rule underlined in Yeats' concern for the textual inscription of ownership. The movement Yeats imagines in 'Coole Park and Ballylee, 1931' traces striated space, where the poet imaginatively follows the water's path from under Thoor Ballylee's window ledge, a mile 'undimmed in Heaven's face', down 'Raftery's "cellar" drop', then underground until it can 'rise in a rocky place / In Coole demesne' and flow into the lake.[41] Here the journey is secluded, unknown, and inaccessible to most people, closed to them through its patrimonial land connection. Though water is 'the generated soul' for Yeats,[42] it traverses a hidden path to his source of inspiration, friendship and patronage. Unlike Yeats' buildings and demesnes, Murphy's landmarks are beyond conventional topological definitions and he employs transgressivity to merge their various contradictory traits in order to contemplate how history and memory construct place.

Turning to one final site from *The Price of Stone* that exemplifies all of these readings of the fluidity of place, 'Hexagon' is emblematic of Murphy's transgressive structures in that collection. The hexagonal studio that he built on Omey Island in 1974, with its 'calm rupestral concentricity' (*P*, p. 215), contradicts the style and scale of typical Anglo-Irish construction. It synthesises a simple stone polygonal shape with the principle that architecture should blend in and highlight its natural surroundings, almost becoming another feature of the landscape. Murphy remarks that he 'wanted it to look as if it had grown out of the rock like a rupestral plant, or as the formal development of a granite outcrop on a hill, not as an alien ivory tower'.[43] It is a site which illustrates Foucault's sense of the heterotopia as one in which 'all the other real sites that can be found within the culture, are simultaneously represented, contested, and inverted',[44] a Westphalian polysystem. Murphy notes in a 12 September 1982 notebook that his sonnet 'Hexagon' aims at a:

> ... reconstruction in verse of that ideal building, the Hexagon, behind and above the graveyard on Omey island ... walls of dressed and undressed granite salvaged from ruins of cabins that once may have housed families of ten children but now are considered unfit for cattle.[45]

The salvaged stone carries the memories of the earlier cabins or cottages just as local granite heightens the 'rupestral' sense of the construction. Its hexagonal shape at once recalls the beehive cells of medieval west-coast monks, as well as the perfectly proportioned geometric constructions and layouts of Anglo-Irish architecture and even the cross-sections of some follies. Five sides have windows which give various views of the surrounding landscape and seascape: 'five views and a wall with books'. There is a bookcase made out of 'Parana pine' (Brazilian pine) for the *Oxford English Dictionary*, representatives of material and linguistic colonisation. Finally, the bed is made from 'oak planks from Cong Forest'.[46] Just as 'The heterotopia is capable of juxtaposing in a single real place several spaces, several sites that are in themselves incompatible',[47] the Hexagon juxtaposes these incompatible elements, unifying them in a transgressive oscillation. It is even a 'heterotopia … of compensation', which carries forward a colonial legacy, 'creat[ing] a space that is other, another real space, as perfect, as meticulous, as well arranged as ours is messy, ill constructed, and jumbled'.[48] Murphy's Hexagon blends all of these contradictory elements into the single construction.

Furthermore, Omey Island is a tidal island, and Murphy's poem illustrates how the space between it and the mainland daily enacts the striation and smoothing of space. When the tide is out, there is a clearly signposted 'road' on the seabed; when the tide is in, the space is re-smoothed and the road vector is effaced. This tidal action is 'a system of opening and closing that both isolates [heterotopia] and makes them penetrable'.[49] During the flood tide, 'closing the strand, comes to embrace / Our isolation' (*P*, p. 215). While the poet is stranded on Omey Island for the duration of the flood tide, 'Blue arms interlace' (*P*, p. 215), leaving the poet 'alone here in a cell, like a hermit, or a hermit crab … a pagan cell for the cult of poetry'.[50] From the Hexagon's perspective, the interlacing of the sea as it surrounds the island and cuts it off from the mainland seems a welcome repose, part of a natural, fluid process of reasserting the dominance of the sea. Elsewhere, however, the sea's power is less a comfort than a destructive power enabling creation. 'Omey Island' presents the sea's overwhelming force as it is:

> Gathering more and more power
> To rampage over the island, or disgorge
> Enough raw granite to face a whole new town.   (*P*, p. 118)

The sheer force of the rampaging waters as they reassert smoothness reveals the 'raw granite' that can be used to construct a town, to re-striate space. In these images of the Hexagon and Omey's relation to the sea, Murphy contemplates the cyclic nature of this fluid geography, puzzling out 'how to balance the destroyer against the creator who needs to destroy in order to create'.[51]

Indeed, Murphy's poetic project continually queries how these processes of creation and destruction alter the landscape for a time but are always subject to an entropic process of decay and degradation. Built structures within this fluid geography are, for Murphy, transgressive heterotopic sites which can embody these cycles, as in *The Price of Stone* where each structure's voice reflects concerns of oscillation. The poems embody these concerns of land ownership, cultural constructions of place, and the continual flux of these multiplicities in the same way that the built structures do. Murphy notes this poetic transgressivity by asking himself in relation to the sonnet 'Family Seat':

> Now when walls are being pulled down and bungalows put up in parks of the old demesnes, why am I still writing sonnets? It could be because the ingrown need for what has been lost goes on … the sonnets are my hexagon, my beehive cell, my folly, and my walled garden … which deprive no one of land they need to live on, keep nobody out, can be overrun, and not go to seed.[52]

Given the collapse of the Anglo-Irish Ascendancy and redistribution of demesne lands, Murphy imagines a topography that does not give priority to any single group's claims. He maintains these conflicting views of geography in suspension within a poetic topography that does not claim land to exclude others from its use. Instead, transgressive sites moored within this fluid geography give voice to the multiplicity of relations in the Irish landscape.

6

~

Richard Murphy: Radio poet

TOM WALKER

On 1 August 1950 Richard Murphy found his way into a radio studio for the first time. Under the supervision of the producer Mary Treadgold – author of the wartime children's classic *We Couldn't Leave Dinah* (1941) and one-time sharer of an office with George Orwell – he recorded a six-minute talk in response to W.B. Yeats' recently published *Collected Poems* (1950). The talk was broadcast a fortnight later on the BBC's General Overseas Service.[1] Murphy at this time was an aspiring young writer trying to make his way in literary London in time-honoured fashion. Not long down from Oxford and yet to put a poem into print, he had recently started publishing reviews in *The Spectator*. By getting on the radio he might be viewed as trying to get a foothold in Grub Street's most recent incarnation. For in the post-war period and particularly with the launch of the Third Programme in 1946, the BBC had emerged as 'an important patron of creative writers'.[2] Murphy benefitted occasionally from such patronage: he had several critical interventions aired in the early 1950s and several of his own poems were broadcast, as this essay will explore. He was never, though, a full-time BBC employee nor a particularly frequent broadcaster or writer for radio to compare with figures such as Louis MacNeice, Dylan Thomas, C. Day Lewis or Ted Hughes. Nevertheless, he should be viewed as more profoundly a radio poet than his early attempts to build a metropolitan literary career or his later intermittent contact with the medium might suggest.

The small radio segment on Yeats posits the need for a close relationship between poetry and ordinary language, yet still seeks a sense of the poetic as a special linguistic or experiential category:

Yeats is a great poet by virtue of managing to speak 'like a man speaking to man at exactly the same time as in mood and language he is being most truly poetic'.[3] In doing so it shares preoccupations with Murphy's other critical pieces of the time. In a *Spectator* review of 1950, Murphy heralds Robert Lowell as a striking talent in part because of his adherence to the poetic through his 'stern and strong' metre and 'direct and resonant use of assonance and alliteration and rhyme'. He is concerned, though, that Lowell's use of poetic effects can at times be excessive.[4] By contrast, a long letter written to *The Spectator* criticises the handling of technique in T.S. Eliot's *The Cocktail Party* (1949) as an 'attempt to make verse indistinguishable from prose'.[5] Another review describes Ezra Pound as having gone too far in rectifying 'the purism of previous poets' by 'adopting too frequently a syntax that derives from the language spoken today by men of inferior habits of speech'.[6] These early critical interventions repeatedly scrutinise the work of Murphy's immediate forebears and contemporaries against some elusive balance between the ordinary and the poetic in relation to form, language, mood and subject matter – a yardstick by which Yeats seems best to succeed. Poetry has somehow to find a mode and register through which both to belong in the modern world and still be able to assert its distinctiveness.

The next talk that Murphy proposed, unsuccessfully, for broadcast was on 'The Language of Modern Poetry'. The surviving outline worries away at the problem of using a contemporary diction undifferentiated from spoken language or prose, on the one hand, and the difficulty of trying to assimilate the archaic into modern poetry, on the other.[7] By now Murphy was in contact with the Talks Department producer P.H. Newby (future controller of the Third Programme and Booker Prize-winning novelist), who commented on an internal memo that he found the script a bit 'too Olympian' for broadcast. He thought, though, that the young Irish critic had 'a good voice and a point of view'.[8] Encouraged, Murphy wrote a letter wondering:

> … if you have already done Robert Lowell? … I am particularly interested in narrative verse. He is working on a narrative poem at present, and he already has developed a strong narrative style.

Alternatively, Valentin Iremonger's first collection of poetry (1941–1946) is just coming out … he is probably the best of the completely post-Yeats Irishmen, and I think he has written good poems quite unaffected by the great man's tone of voice, gesture, etc. Anyway, an intelligent and refreshing change from Irish minor romanticism.[9]

In looking to Iremonger as a poet who has moved beyond the perils of imitation or 'minor romanticism', Murphy's career-long negotiation with Yeats' legacy in Irish poetry is already looming large. However, Murphy's interest in the potential of narrative verse signals another emerging route of development for modern poetry, not least in the dialectical wake of Yeats' symbolic lyricism.

Soon afterwards Newby commissioned a twenty-minute talk from Murphy on 'Narrative Poetry Today' for the Third Programme.[10] Recorded on 27 March 1951, it was broadcast that July and printed in *The Listener* soon after.[11] The talk places the current primacy of prose over poetic narratives in relation to historical and social changes in the nineteenth century. Due to the breaking up of a settled order of society and common religious beliefs, 'poetry which assumed that certain ways of conduct and thought were common to its readers lost half its force and significance'.[12] A resulting shift from communal terms of reference to the poet's individual experience has left narrative poetry uncertain. Also detrimental have been the changes to diction and technique wrought by experiments in symbolism and non-metrical verse:

> Narrative verse needs a settled quality of language and style, which will make it wittingly and continuously acceptable without interruption to the reader. It has, of course, a purity of its own that is just as essential to it as the purity aimed at in symbolism was at one time to lyric. It must assume that the reader knows and will accept its techniques, so that tricks of vocabulary, alliteration, assonance and so on, can be reduced to a barely noticeable part in the construction and movement of a large complete work.[13]

Conversely, reviving narrative verse offers a means of keeping, amid modernity, the poetic in play once again with the communicative and communal. Murphy sees signs of such a revival among his contemporaries: Day Lewis' and W.R. Rodgers' narrative poems are praised for their stress on experience and realistic observation; Lowell can sustain a meditation for verse paragraph after verse paragraph through the energy of his style; in *Four Quartets* Eliot has taken the important reversing step of imposing 'his own idea of order on experience'. The talk's end rallies to the possibility that a new narrative poetic form will emerge to offer 'an alternative, on the larger, unified scale, to the fragmentary, moment by moment record of experience in small occasional poems'.[14]

Murphy proposed, unsuccessfully, a follow-up 'programme of readings from modern narrative poems', including works by Pound, Day Lewis, Rodgers and Robert Frost.[15] More dramatically, the aspiring poet also soon devoted his own creative labours to narrative-verse's revival. Leaving London and moving to Connemara in April 1951, he attempted to write in isolation there a long poem that fused the ancient and modern in setting the pursuit of Diarmuid and Grania in Blitz era London. As he later recalls in *The Kick* (2002/2017), the result was a failure:

> I poured into lines of blank verse the passion I felt while typing, but, when I went back and read them, they sounded wilful and turgid. Each effort to revise produced no better result, yet I continued struggling to revise a narrative form of poetry many critics believed the modern novel had made obsolete. I had no talent for fiction.   (*K*, p. 120)

Murphy sent about a third of the poem to MacNeice, asking him to forward it to the journal *Botteghe Oscure*.[16] MacNeice's reply admits that the 'poem doesn't really "get" me. I daresay I am quite wrong but I find it in detail over-written and on the intellectual and/or moral plane not as gripping as it is intended to be.'[17] A successful writer and producer in the BBC Features Department, MacNeice also later rejected 'the long-winded epic' (*K*, p. 129) for broadcast. Such setbacks should not obscure, however, the realignments of contemporary-poetry's techniques and relationship to its audience that Murphy was seeking to promote at this time, nor his interrelated investment in the potential of narrative verse to bring about such realignments.

The poem from Murphy's austere western-Ireland sojourn that did make it onto the airwaves was a short one: 'Wittgenstein and the Birds' (*K*, p. 129). It was chosen by John Wain for the second of his *First Reading* broadcasts in May 1953.[18] A monthly magazine of new verse and prose, the programme's first outing had provoked controversy: it opened with Wain polemically proclaiming his suspicion of 'anything that suggests sprawling or lack of discipline'.[19] Murphy, unlike Wain, was not named in the October 1954 leading article in *The Spectator* that first identified 'the Movement'; neither was he included in the anthologies most associated with its inception, D.J. Enright's *Poets of the 1950s* (1955) and Robert Conquest's *New Lines* (1956).[20] Yet his critical ideas and creative aspirations at this time were operating somewhat in parallel with those associated with the Movement. Appearing (alongside Wain) on *Literary Opinion* on the Third Programme in September 1954, he had argued that poetry's future lay in turning away from 'journalism' and 'self-expression' towards 'a style which is controlled and cool'.[21] Presenting *New Verse* a year later, he praised Philip Larkin's accuracy and clarity of expression, but was worried by his work's lowered poetic horizons, querying what made it 'better than an equivalent novel, apart from the concentration and the memorable words'.[22] In response to *The Spectator*'s 1954 Movement-identifying leading article, he had also written a letter calling for a more ambitious effort to look on words as nothing less than 'the source and the ruin and the salvation of life'.[23] Murphy's commitment to classical objectivity, conscious simplicity and clarity of expression, when placed alongside his ongoing faith in poetry's transformative powers and live engagement with the work of Yeats, Eliot and Pound, looks not so much like a Larkinesque rejection of modernism altogether as a dialectical commitment to 'Modernism by other means'. That phrase is used by Clive Wilmer to account for Donald Davie's somewhat puzzling mid-1950s association with the Movement.[24] At the time Davie was living in Dublin and wrote to

Murphy to praise his 'use of syntax' and 'pruning away of mannerisms' on receiving a personally inscribed copy of *The Archaeology of Love* (1955).[25] Twenty years later Davie's views on Murphy's work were somewhat more critical. In *The New York Review of Books* he described the language of *The Battle of Aughrim* as 'prosy, strained, and wooden', yet he still recognised the parallels between Murphy and the Movement in commenting that readers may feel that 'Larkin … handles these muted instruments with more finesse'.[26]

Murphy, in broadcasting his critical views and then trying to write narrative verse for broadcast, seems to make an implicit investment in the potential of radio itself to act as a restorative medium for poetry. Several other writers associated with the BBC around this time were approaching the creative possibilities of radio in distinctly positive terms in the context of a changing broadcasting environment. There is a 'particular moment in the UK' in the late 1940s and early 1950s to be recovered, as Paul Long describes, 'in which radio generated a range of ideas about its aesthetic possibilities and essence as well as its potential cultural and social role'.[27] Accounts of the cultural impact of radio before the war often highlight the ambivalent response of writers and intellectuals to the new technology. Many took enthusiastically to the airwaves, but radio also provoked metaphysical and sociopolitical anxieties in its offering of a voice without presence and through its potential for acting as a means of furthering 'social control' and the 'homogenization of mass culture'.[28] As Emilie Morin suggests, Yeats was 'intensely engaged in broadcasting with the BBC' for much of the 1930s, pioneering 'new writing techniques, germane to the demands of radio', while also being reluctant to have a wireless set in his house.[29] Yet in the context of mid-century Britain, the BBC had 'emerged from the war with an enormously enhanced reputation' in having managed to contribute to the war effort and also still provide space for a plurality of voices and a significant cultural programme.[30] The advent of the Third Programme further increased the scope for creative work that would still, in relative terms, be delivered to 'a bigger public than any other form of publication', as Laurence Gilliam (the head of features) emphasised to potential writers in the pages of *The Radio Times*.[31] There were certainly tensions between the experimental and public-service impulses underpinning the new service.³² Nevertheless, in 1947 MacNeice could emphasise that the bureaucratic restrictions of the BBC were surmountable in the pursuit of art:

> Broadcasting is plastic; while it can ape the Press, it can also emulate the arts. Yes people will say, that is theoretically true but in practice you will never get art – or anything like it – out of a large public institution, encumbered with administrators, which by its nature must play for safety and to the gallery. This is not the place to dispute this at length but I would maintain that in this country such an institution cannot be really authoritarian; with ingenuity and a little luck a creative person can persuade (or fool) at least some of the administrators some of the time.³³

In 1971 D.G. Bridson, one of MacNeice's colleagues in the Features Department, looked back with some satisfaction on the powerful cultural influence the Third Programme had yielded: 'Without its encouragement, the work of the *avant garde* in literature and music would have been far slower to find a national audience.'³⁴ It seems that from the late 1940s until the Third Programme's demise in 1970 the BBC provided a means for new and challenging writing to reach a relatively wide audience in a civic space existing at a crucial remove from the demands of the market or the state.

Radio was seen as offering great possibilities specifically for poetry. In a 1945 pamphlet entitled *Poetry and the Microphone*, George Orwell observed that 'the broadcasting of a poem by the person who wrote it does not merely produce an effect upon the audience, if any, but also on the poet himself'. His work will so be brought back towards a closer relationship with music and the spoken word, having the potential to reconcile 'poetry and the common man'.³⁵ Several articles printed in the *BBC Quarterly* in the early 1950s elaborated similar positions: Bridson suggested the microphone might have an influence on poetry as profound as 'the invention of writing and the invention of the printing press', in promoting a return to a poetry of the ear rather than the page; Day Lewis thought the medium would encourage the poet to 'extend his technique upon less purely subjective material', such as through writing narrative and dramatic poetry.[36] Such hopes proved difficult to realise, not least because the BBC's administrators struggled to find ways to coordinate the commissioning of poetry.[37] Nevertheless, many individuals at the corporation did manage to broadcast an impressive body of work from poets in a variety of new formats that exploited the medium's radiophonic possibilities. Bridson picked out Douglas Cleverdon's productions as going 'a long way to establishing the canon of the best creative work written for radio':

> Dylan Thomas's incomparable *Under Milk Wood*, David Jones's *In Parenthesis*, the satirical *A Very Great Man Indeed* sequence of Henry Reed, his *Streets of Pompeii* and his strangely neglected *Vicenzo*, J. Bronowski's *The Face of Violence*, George Barker's verse plays, and Ted Hughes's *The Wound* were only a few of Cleverdon's more memorable productions.[38]

Murphy might have come to view his early epic ambitions as an 'immense mistake', but by the late 1950s and early 1960s he was managing to write narrative poems and have them broadcast.[39] In 1962, Cleverdon produced a reading of 'The Cleggan Disaster' by the actor Denys Hawthorne with an introduction by the poet.[40] The poem recounts at some length (the recorded version lasted just over twenty-one minutes) the ordeal of the Inishbofin fisherman Pat Concannon and his crew as they battled for survival in a small fishing boat during an infamous 1927 storm. The narrative and its manner in some respects seem to fulfil the rubric of Murphy's earlier critical prescriptions. He had praised Day Lewis' narrative poems not only for their 'brilliant observation and resourcefulness of language' but also for 'bringing the real world of the poet's experience fully into the picture'.[41] Striving objectively to describe Concannon's thoughts and actions in the third person, Murphy brings to the task his own 'practical experience of being at sea' off the west coast of Ireland.[42] This is apparent in the technical and physical specificity of his description of the boat ('her keel adzed out of oak'), the act of fishing ('warps were hitched / To the strong stems'), and the knowledge of the sea's workings that helps Concannon to battle his ship to safety:

> Over and over
> He heard in his heart,
>   'Keep her stem to the storm,
> And her nets will help her
>   to ride the water;
> Meet the force of the seas
>   with her bows,
> Each wave as it comes.'[43]

The extensive use of alliteration and assonance, within a line that clearly draws on Old English stress patterns, shows that this is a poem that 'thrives on poetic devices'.[44] Beyond an extensive metaphorical linking of the stormy sea to fire (owing something perhaps to Gerard Manley Hopkins' *The Wreck of the Deutschland*), though, the figurative aspects of the poem are mostly drawn from the community and environment in Connemara that the poem describes and to which the poet has tried to make himself belong. One epic simile, for instance, builds on likening the play of the wind to 'country fiddlers / In a crowded room', another extensively compares 'an upturned hull' to 'a black cow / In search of her calf'. The authorial-voice's language lies at a remove from the west-of-Ireland vernacular, in contrast to the later experiments with voice and dialect in some of the poems in *High Island* (1974). Nevertheless, the poem's combination of local terms of reference in its figurative aspects and the narrator's use of standard British-English usage might be viewed as communal in attempting to bridge the gap between the people the poem is written out of and the radio audience towards which it is broadcast. Moreover, the 'loaded, encrusted, stained-glass richness' that Seamus Heaney perceives in the poem's formality on the page might operate to somewhat different effect on the air.[45] In a poem written specifically for aural transmission, poetic devices might be read as rhetorical aids to the 'construction and movement of a large' work rather than a distraction from the narrative itself.[46] A measure of the success of the poem when broadcast can be gathered from a surviving letter in which Murphy thanks Cleverdon for 'the good news about the "Appreciation Index"' for the programme and also reveals that as a result 'of the favourable reception of the same broadcast in Dublin, I was recently asked by Irish Television to read The Cleggan Disaster myself on TV'.[47]

According to the markings on Cleverdon's script, the broadcasting of 'The Cleggan Disaster' looked to exploit something of radio's multi-temporal and polyvocal dramatic possibilities in having Murphy rather than Hawthorne read the final 'YEARS LATER' section of the poem. In most other respects, though, it was a fairly straightforward and traditional linear verse narrative written for oral performance, drawing on elements of the epic and the ballad. The same cannot be said of the poem and broadcast on which Murphy and Cleverdon were next to collaborate, Murphy's radiophonic masterpiece *The Battle of Aughrim* (1968). Almost straight after the recording of 'The Cleggan Disaster' on 30 March 1962, and before it had even been broadcast, Murphy and Cleverdon were discussing a new poem for the radio. Writing that May, Murphy already envisaged that 'its form will be narrative and require several voices to read, lasting up to an hour', that it would be set in 'the village of Aughrim in East Galway on Sunday the 12th. of July 1691' and that

> The battle will be sketched in personal episodes, some possibly in the present tense, to realise what it looked and felt like to be there. The issues of the war will be contained in these episodes, and the change from narrative to lyric or elegiac will come with the story.[48]

By July Cleverdon wrote with the good news that 'the Third have agreed to commission "The Battle of Aughrim"'.[49] Having met Cleverdon in London in the meantime, that October Murphy wrote about the production's music:

> If you are yet in touch with John Reedy [*sic*] [Seán Ó Riada] would you let me know what he says? My view at present is for single instruments – trumpet, bagpipe, drum, harpsichord and

flute – to play theme-tunes (which could be contemporary, such as Lilliburlero) between sections of the poem to make digestive pauses to the narrative, & to cover a lapse of time or a change of scene.[50]

In the same letter Murphy confidently predicted that a recording in a year's time 'could be planned with fairly high chances of being achieved', and also wrote to Newby (by then controller of the Third) thanking him for the commission that would enable him 'to get down to this work for the winter'.[51] Such a swift timescale was to prove optimistic and the poem was not to be broadcast until 1968.[52] Nevertheless, from its very origins Murphy seems to have conceived of *The Battle of Aughrim* as his most decisive engagement with the potential of radio as a medium for poetry.

In December 1967 Cleverdon wrote to say how 'delighted' he was to have finally received a complete script.[53] A revised version, together with an explanatory prose note, soon followed.[54] In the margins of this typescript Murphy can be seen allocating the various voices that will read the lyrics that make up the larger 'Now', 'Before', 'During' and 'After' sections of the poem, writing 'Irish voice A', 'Irish voice B', 'Irishwoman', 'Ulster voice', 'Anglo-Irish voice' and (the already specified) 'Ted Hughes'.[55] The other correspondence between poet and producer leading up to the recording on 31 May 1968 also accords with Murphy's later recollection of the considerable thought and effort that went into the casting of Hughes, Cyril Cusack, C. Day Lewis, Margaret Robertson (recruited when Siobhán McKenna became unavailable) and Niall Tóibín to speak these various voices (*K*, pp. 234–5). The music was no less carefully devised. Arranged by Ó Riada, it consisted mainly of interludes between the various sections and was only occasionally (though tellingly) interwoven with speech. The songs chosen resonated with the historical subject of the poem and the specifics of the preceding and succeeding sections: 'The White Cockade' was interposed between the 'Before' and 'During' sections, 'Limerick's Lamentation', which Ó Riada 'had found in a rare eighteenth-century copy', between the 'During' and 'After' (*K*, pp. 242–3). These pieces were performed under Ó Riada's direction by Ceoltóirí Chualann (several members of whom would soon find fame in the Chieftains) during separate recording sessions in the RTÉ studios in Dublin on 18 and 19 May, which both Murphy and Cleverdon attended.[56] Back in London and before the eventual first broadcast on 25 August, a BBC pianist also recorded, on a harpsichord, Henry Purcell's 'Sefauchi's Farewell' (Z656), which was evocatively edited in behind Day Lewis' distinctly Anglo-Irish voice.[57]

A sense of the broadcast's intricate 'oratorio-like' deployment of voices and music, within the performance of a sequence of poems that move between different viewpoints and temporalities, can be gathered from examining the shift in the opening 'Now' section of the broadcast from the second poem, 'Green Martyrs', to the third poem, 'Orange March'.[58] In the recording 'Green Martyrs' has Tóibín's male voice act as a framing narrator to Robertson's female voice bemoaning Ireland's wrong (inhabiting the stereotypical gendering of Ireland). A rare piece of background music starts up, as the tune 'Lilliburlero' is played on flutes accompanied by a drum, clearly to suggest an Orange marching band. Tóibín then starts to speak in an (it must be admitted not altogether convincing) Ulster accent the 'Orange March' section. The typescript Cleverdon used for the recording reads:

5. TOIBIN: I dream of a headless man
                      Sitting on a charger, chiselled stone.

                      A woman is reading from an old lesson:
6. ROBERTSON: ' ... who dies in the famine,

                      Royal bulls on my land,
                      I starved to feed the absentee with rent.

                      Aughrim's great disaster
                      Made him two hundred years my penal master.

                      Rapparees, whiteboys, volunteers, ribbonmen,
                      Where have they gone?

                      Coerced into exile, scattered
                      Leaving a burnt gable and a field of ragwort.'

7. TOIBIN: July the Twelfth, she takes up tongs
                    To strike me for a crop of calf-bound wrongs.

                    Her weekly half-crowns have built
                    A grey cathedral on the old gaol wall.

                                                              (contd.)

[page break]

8. TOIBIN   She brings me from Knock shrine
                    John Kennedy's head on a china dish.

                    (MUSIC: LILLIBURLERO)

9. ULSTER VOICE: In bowler hats and Sunday suits,
   (TOIBIN)   Orange sashes, polished boots,
                    Atavistic trainbands come
                    To blow the fife and beat the drum.

                    Apprentices uplift their banner
                    True blue-eyed with 'No Surrender!'
                    Claiming Aughrim as if they'd won
                    Last year, not 1691.[59]

Then the music ups and fades, as Cleverdon has written in by hand, before Tóibín reads the remaining eight lines of 'Orange March'.

A lot is going on in aural terms. 'Green Martyrs' evokes the subtle sound relationships of the Irish mode, as, for example, in its use of assonance between words at the end of one line and within the next ('man' / 'charger', 'land' / 'starved').[60] This is Murphy writing as Austin Clarke or F.R. Higgins. Then there is a shift into the altogether more blatant rhymes and rhythms of 'Orange March'. This point of prosodic difference is underlined as a difference in identity by the various accents and genders of the speakers, but also ironically commented upon by the music. The tune of 'Lilliburlero' is used for the Orange Order song 'The Protestant Boys' ('The Protestant Boys are loyal and true / Stout-hearted in battle and stout-handed too'), and its use in the broadcast evokes this association.[61] The original song, though, has its origins in the late seventeenth century (the tune being thought by some to have been written by Purcell) and its earlier lyrics bloodthirstily celebrate the appointment of the Catholic Richard Talbot as Lord Deputy of Ireland by James II:

> Ho, brother Teague, dost hear the decree
> Lillibulèro bullen a la
> Dat we shall have a new Debittie
> Lillibulèro bullen a la.
>
> Ho, by my soul, it is a Talbot;
> Lillibulèro bullen a la
> And he will cut all de English throat.
> Lillibulèro bullen a la.[62]

The assertive performance of an intransigent identity that is being described in 'Orange March' is undermined by the contrary historical origins of the tune to which the Orangemen are marching.

Furthermore, 'Lilliburlero' was also in widespread contemporary circulation (as Murphy above noted in first suggesting its possible inclusion) having, since the Second World War, been used by the BBC as an interval signal, especially on the World Service. This version would presumably have been more familiar to the majority of the BBC's listenership than the tune's Orange or Jacobite incarnations. The song, operating perhaps as a metonym for Ireland itself, was thus appropriated into a very different kind of transnational British modernity, post-empire and post-war. This complex associative chain in relation to the song corresponds to the international nature of the Williamite War itself, which the broadcast of *The Battle of Aughrim*, from its opening announcement onwards, carefully unpicks and highlights:

> The Irish army was a native force, equipped by Louis XIV, and commanded by the French Marquis of St. Ruth. Paid in brass, it fought in the name of King James II, an exile at St. Germain, and in the Catholic interest.
>
> The English army, aiding the planters in Ireland, was largely a force of foreigners, drawn from seven nations opposed to Louis, and commanded by a Dutch General, Baron Ginkel. Paid in silver and gold, it fought in the names of King William and

Queen Mary (nephew and daughter of James), in the Protestant interest.[63]

The broadcast might so be seen as enacting through its speech and music what Emily Bloom describes, in writing about Irish drama on the BBC in the 1950s, as 'the multivalent nature of Anglo-Irish cultural relations at midcentury'.[64] In relation to the complex interplay between the periphery and the metropolitan centre within the literary marketplace at this time, the availability of the BBC as an outlet for Irish writers could, of course, be a dangerous thing, with the stage Irishman becoming the radio Irishman – as is brilliantly satirised in Anthony Cronin's novel *The Life of Riley* (1964). This was a hazard to which the austerely self-conscious Murphy was unlikely to fall prey. Rather, a sense emerges, through his work, of a post-war period when the BBC not only offered a space for ambitious long-form poetry commissioned especially for radio, but also for an Irish poet to think about identity, politics and history in notably nuanced ways. Indeed, the poem seems evocative of a time when 'the hates engendered by Aughrim were finally to exhaust themselves' in the seeming 'new era of cooperation' between the Irish and Northern Irish governments of the mid-sixties.[65] In the context of Anglo-Irish cultural relations, though, it was not only the Third Programme that was about to change.

In relation to Murphy's earlier theories about narrative verse and the future of poetry more generally, the ambitious marshalling of radio's aural possibilities in *The Battle of Aughrim* constitutes a further attempt to achieve a poetry beyond 'journalism' and 'self-expression'.[66] Whereas 'The Cleggan Disaster' aspired to dispassionate objectivity through its stable, third-person-narrated epic and ballad-like modes, the multi-temporal and polyvocal nature of the later poem incorporates both subjective and objective viewpoints. A dispersed narrative voice (with Murphy's actual voice crucially left out of the broadcast) underlines a sense of a composite or divided self which the poem expands into a genealogical and historical feature, as Murphy has ancestors on both sides of the battle. Personal experience and observation, as well as the inclusion of found historical material, are also aligned to a more visionary kind of poetic authority. This allows Murphy to conjure up a visceral sense of the past while acknowledging his distance from it. Crucial in this respect is the deployment of Hughes. His distinctive Yorkshire accent in speaking the poems 'Mercenary' and 'Rapparees' – the Irish guerrilla half-pike men who were the Williamite army's most effective opposition – cuts across any too easy equation of nationality with class in relation to the battle. But these poems seem as well to take on something of the licence of Hughes' own lyrical investment in the force of the mystical and the animalistic:

> 38. HUGHES: Out of the earth, out of the air, out of the water
> And slinking nearer the fire, in groups they gather:
> Once he looked like a bird, but now a beggar.
> This fish rainbows out of a pool: 'Give me bread!'
> He fins along the lake-shore with the starved.
> Green eyes glow in the night from clumps of weed.
>
> The water is still. A rock or the nose of an otter
> Jars the surface. Whistle of rushes or bird?
> It steers to the bank, it lands as a pikeman armed.

The Audience Research Department's report on *The Battle of Aughrim* revealed a reaction index of 73, which it noted was above the 'current average for features on the Third Programme' of 65 and the average for 'poetry readings' of 60. Picked out for praise was Ó Riada's music in 'reinforcing the moods created by the poems' and evoking 'the period and the place' by its 'modal, simple and melodious style'. Welcomed, too, were the 'strong contrasts of the different voices', although 'a handful of listeners' felt that Hughes' 'English voice was not altogether apposite'.[67] The broadcast was repeated on 18 September, two days after Faber had published the poem in print. On 9 October RTÉ broadcast a filmed version produced by Jack Dowling, using about half the text read by Murphy and Siobhán McKenna.[68] A slightly edited version of the radio broadcast was also released the following year as an LP by the Dublin-based Claddagh Records. The poem was a veritable multimedia event and seemingly a successful one in those terms. Murphy's subsequent career followed different, less radiophonic, paths. The retirement of Cleverdon in 1969, the ending of the Third Programme in 1970, and Ó Riada's death in 1971 would in any case make this particular collaboration impossible to repeat. Nevertheless, the radio provided a crucial critical and creative impetus to much of the poet's early work. As he sought amid a post-war modernity to write a poetry that married classical restraint to romantic vision, he did so in part through writing for the radio and reaching for a radio poetics.

7

~

'Bygone canon, bygone spleen': Richard Murphy as a conflict poet in *The Battle of Aughrim*

SIOBHÁN CAMPBELL

Richard Murphy gives us a way towards making a reading of his long poem 'The Battle of Aughrim, 1691' with his riposte to aspects of Donald Davie's review in *The New York Review of Books*, 6 March 1975, of *High Island: new and selected poems*, a book in which this long poem appears.[1] He objects to Davie's assumption that all his forebears – and by implication, he – 'would have been on the other, the winning side' (i.e. the English Protestant side), adding:

> I suggest that the division of Ireland is not just in our country, but in every Irishman's blood; and has to be resolved individually, before the conflict can be settled as a whole. One should not falsify the ancient and current Irish equation with passionate simplicities, but try to clarify by defusing some of the explosive credal myths. Ultimately our divisive legends, some of which I explore in the long poem, turn out … to be grounded in error and ignorance.[2]

'The Battle of Aughrim, 1691' does indeed, as Murphy reminds Davie, state that 'our ancestors fought "in opposite camps" at the behest of "absent kings".[3] Murphy seems to suggest that it behoves a reader willing to go beyond the 'passionate simplicities' to make an interpretation of the work, which eschews exactly what Davie continues to do in his reply to Murphy's objections:

> Why does he bridle at it? I defined his Anglo-Irish stock as 'landed gentry, English by race, usually by religion and often enough by education ...'. And all he can say by way of proving this 'not true' is that his family was 'landed' only on his mother's side! What is all this about, anyway? I aimed at the refinement of our ignorance of his work: and I still think that the information I gave about him was helpful and necessary to that end.[4]

Davie resorts to the kind of literary criticism of birth, of upbringing and therefore of expected affiliation with which we are all too familiar in Irish letters. His description of Murphy's parentage points out that he is the son of Sir William Lindsay Murphy, one-time governor of the Bahamas, and that he was educated at Canterbury Cathedral Choir School, at King's School, Canterbury, at Wellington College, Berkshire, and at Magdalen College, Oxford: 'Will he deny that these facts fall into a pattern that may reasonably be called "Anglo-Irish," or even, in any previous generation, "Protestant Ascendancy"?'[5] With this retort, Davie proves that he has finally missed the point of the poem. Murphy may appear to be described here, but not his inclusivity of thought, nor his ambition for the work, and certainly not his ambition for an encounter with an adequate reader. His own use of the implied 'we' in 'our ancestors fought' shows how, in writing the public poem, he will undertake that most unfashionable of poetic tasks, and try to speak from within, and possibly for, a people. No wonder, then, that he bridles when it is assumed he can only apply his craft fully to one section of that people.

In a work where every word bears the mark of being carefully measured, it feels right to render the poem's title, 'The Battle of Aughrim, 1691', to include the date as it appears in Richard Murphy, *Poems 1952–2012*, published as *The Pleasure Ground: poems 1952–2012* in the UK. The subtitle also repays close reading: 'A meditation on colonial war and its consequence in Ireland written in Connemara between 1962 and 1967' (*P*, p. 59). Rereading the poem in 2016, it may be an aside, yet worth noting, that the date contains the numbers for

'1916' and, more seriously, that the fiftieth anniversary of the Easter Rising was 1966, within the period of writing, a time of rampant myth-making, and a time likely to augment Murphy's set of concerns. Here is a poem, then, in which the reader might expect violence and 'its consequence' to be taken on, a poem which took five years to write, a poem which may be one of those to which successive generations return, attempting to unpack its full set of meanings for our own time. This essay is one such attempt.

Murphy says in an interview with David Wheatley published in 2001 that while living in Cleggan, Galway he would drive through Aughrim:

> I felt I wanted to explore my background more in relation to the background of the country and the past as a whole ... Aughrim seemed a good focal point, because it was a kind of navel of Ireland and a watershed in history, and a far more important battle than the Boyne ...[6]

Murphy points out that, unlike in the earlier battle, neither monarch was present at Aughrim. James II had left Ireland after defeat at the Boyne in 1690 and William of Orange sent his Dutch commander Godart van Ginkel.[7] This was a battle fought by proxies, uneasy coalitions and mercenaries with, on the Jacobite, Catholic side, the French General Charles Chalmont, the Marquis de St Ruth, in charge. Elsewhere he says that his poem became 'an equation of all the forces that met and decided ... the future of the country at that time and place.'[8]

The development of the poem had support from Douglas Cleverdon of the BBC, who had produced *Under Milk Wood* for radio and had broadcast Murphy's 'The Cleggan Disaster' on 26 June 1962. His small commission, Murphy says, was important as 'Otherwise I'd have given up. Nobody was writing long poems and I often despaired of finishing it.'[9] Because of the radio commission, the work was written in a way that accommodates being presented by voices, though this reading posits that the actual 'voices' appearing in the poem have more in common than not.[10] It was broadcast on

BBC Radio 3 on 18 September 1968 accompanied by music by Seán Ó Riada and read by a group including Cyril Cusack, C. Day Lewis, Ted Hughes, Margaret Robertson and Niall Tóibín.[11]

The text opens with what may indeed be *the* 'Irish question': 'Who owns the land?'

> Who owns the land where musket-balls are buried
> In blackthorn roots on the esker, the drained bogs
> Where sheep browse, and credal war miscarried?
> Names in the rival churches are written on plaques.   (*P*, p. 61)

In an uneasy iambic with the opening of the line varied through the use of trochee and dactyl, Murphy sets the reader up for what may be an uncomfortable ride. We are primed to become aware of our expectations, and we will notice how these are upended and subverted throughout the poem.

The musket-balls 'buried' carries a resonance contemporary to this essay to anyone aware of the burying (and cementing in place) of arms as part of decommissioning – to put them 'beyond use'. The 'buried where they lie' of bullets (and of people, later epitomised by skulls) in an historical battleground is not, of course, actually linked to this particular prong of the peace process. But the fact that as a poet Murphy taps into our fascination with the actual and symbolic presence of weaponry and its accoutrements implies that he will show himself to be forensic in his exploration of human desires and human foibles. As a poet he has a knack for using the poem to delve to a point of no return, the point after which there is no appeal. In this lyric, for instance, in a knowing use of what is only an apparent detachment, he notices the Celtic cross that does not memorialise the battle dead, 'But someone killed in a car' (*P*, p. 61).

Here, too, he juxtaposes the continuing agricultural effort of draining bogs to create pasture against the futile nature of what the muskets may have achieved. Now 'sheep browse' in the aftermath of 'credal war'. In this poem the individuals killed in battle are seen as reduced to nothing more than lists of the dead in the 'rival churches', thus levelling their efforts to parallel sets of futility. Although we know that the battles at Aughrim and the Boyne effectively led to confirmation of the powers of the Protestant ruling class in Ireland and to the period of Penal Laws against Catholics, the tangible results, at least in this poem, will be seen to be more about augmenting the prevailing mythologies and acquiring the authority to do so.

This opening lyric, 'On Battle Hill', referring to Kilcommodon Hill above Aughrim, follows the speaker's visit there in the present of the 1960s and sets up the several strands that will weave through the entire poem. We meet individuals going about their daily lives as if unaware of the historical significance of the land they traverse. When 'summer hikers/Bathe' it is in a stream passed by the retreating cavalry, which was led by the traitor to the Jacobite side (*P*, p. 61) Henry Luttrell, who himself appears later in the work. And in a move which will become characteristic, a one-liner allows for the possibility of fleeting fulfilment: 'A girl cycles along the lane to meet her lover' (*P*, p. 61). In what will become part of Murphy's method, however, this momentary positive appears in the same stanza as the road death mentioned above as if to warn the reader against any lack of vigilance.

The juxtaposition of old and new, of tradition and progress, is flagged here by the thinning of turnips 'by hand' while earth movers are clawing out a highway nearby (*P*, p. 61). That this highway is the Dublin-to-Galway trunk road which was being laid as part of the efforts to modernise in the mid-sixties, as this poem was being written, is indicative of the commitment to concrete detail and the physical actuality of human presence throughout. Likewise, the 'Bullets under glass' of the National school denote the headmaster Martin Joyce's collection there of relics from the battlefield (*P*, p. 61). These bullets are not buried but, rather, on display. The implication may be that, thus, their significance as a deterrent can be more fully understood. While Murphy consistently refuses to create a symbolic register that would allow for any possible transcendent moment, he does manage to freight moments of actuality such as this with ongoing poetic resonance and his repetition of motifs appearing in different guises forms a large part of the poem's poetics.

Patrick Sarsfield, another recurring character, receives his first mention with his supposed death-bed phrase ('"Would to God this wound had been for Ireland"') here truncated to '*Would to God ...–*' (*P*, p. 61), with the ellipsis implying not only that the received story of this death scene may be historically suspect, but also acting to introduce 'God' as one of the 'characters', just as influential on misconstrued beliefs, who will reappear – later even receiving his own lyric (*P*, p. 80). The poet arrives at the 'death-cairn' of St Ruth, leader of the Jacobites at Aughrim, whose last words serve Murphy's ironic purposes exactly: '*Le jour est a nous, mes enfants*', he pronounces. This is followed by the final line: 'A cannonball beheaded him, and sowed a myth' (*P*, p. 61). The stark informational nature of the latter, added to the idea that St Ruth's death was just one more which created a 'myth', alerts a reader to Murphy's poetic methods. He will not shy away from the realities of violence, allowing it into the poem in a way which neither glorifies nor fetishises it. He will recount the facts of history in a way which shows them to continually reinhabit the present.

'On Battle Hill' is the first lyric in 'Now', the opening section of the four numbered sections: 'Now', 'Before', 'During', 'After'. Initially these appear to delineate respectively: the 1960s; the time just before the battle in 1691; action during the battle itself; and subsequent events, but time is seen to be traversed readily to match the poet's own ends. In the Bloodaxe edition, the 'Now' appears on the same page and above 'On Battle Hill', as if to begin the implication of the continuing presence of the past.

In this opening Murphy sets up a cluster of wary fascinations which, he implies, will lead a reader to look closely at inherited pieties and their origins. The final line brings together the key set of concerns: how violence 'sows' myth, even into the very land which is the object of conflict, and how it is not the myths of one 'credal' group or another that he will address, but rather the fact that wilful mythologising is both endemic and dangerous.

'Green Martyrs', the second lyric in the sequence, is written in couplets, some displaying full rhyme but more of them using consonance and assonance to build an uneasy sound chamber which offsets the yoking together of touchstone metaphors one might invoke if retelling an inherited tale of the 'green'. Indicative of the method is that end words 'land' and 'rent' don't rhyme, whereas 'great disaster' and 'penal master' make a clear connection (*P*, p. 62). Here are many tropes of lament: the 'disaster' of Aughrim as well as other disasters including the Famine, the absentee landlord, "'Rapparees, whiteboys, volunteers, ribbonmen'", and the "'Where have they gone?'", coerced "'exile'" (bringing to mind the Flight of the Earls as well as the migration of the 'wild geese'), and, via the word "'penal'", the Penal Laws themselves (*P*, p. 62).

The woman in this piece appears to be reading from what might almost be a primer on how to become (a certain kind of) Irish person, detailing, as Murphy has it, 'a crop of calf-bound wrongs' (*P*, p. 62). We learn that it is the half-crowns of the struggling poor which are collected to build the cathedral, and in exposing this as abusive Murphy cannot resist mention of the fact that this edifice is 'on the old gaol wall', thus implying another sort of imprisonment (*P*, p. 62). And in the final lines Murphy is at his most tongue-in-cheek. In place of those who have fulfilled the need for idealism in the past, he places instead the dishy JFK, here appearing on a souvenir bought at a religious shrine:

> She brings me from Knock shrine
> John Kennedy's head on a china dish.   (*P*, p. 62)

Linking this 'head' of another figure of mythological power in the Irish imagination with that of St Ruth is part of Murphy's characteristic forward and backward move in time. The motifs he deploys are both pertinent to their place in the poem and to his set of wider concerns. Here he begins to lay out the full ambition of the work, where each lyric will build on the last, creating a coherent whole, even as each looks askance at local and tribal myths. If 'green' has been dealt an ironic blow here, it is no surprise that the following piece is 'Orange March'.

In a satisfying, if somewhat stultifying, AABB rhyme scheme this four-stanza lyric is written in strong tetrameters that seem to 'beat the drum' mentioned in stanza one. The apprentice boys 'Claiming

Aughrim as if they'd won / Last year, not 1691' captures the atavistic
pleasures of the victor which carry on down the centuries as long as
upheld by credal or tribal belief (*P*, p. 63). The irony-seeking Murphy,
however, skewers the colonial interference and implied enslavement
of peoples by describing the banners on which

> … Victoria gives
> Bibles to kneeling Zulu chiefs.
> Read the moral, note the date:
> 'The secret that made Britain great.'   (*P*, p. 63)

An added irony in 'date' related to this lyric of course is that the Battle
of Aughrim was fought on 12 July in the old style (Julian) calendar
and was related to the Orange celebrations on that date subsequently,
later being replaced by the Battle of the Boyne as the central motif
of Williamite dominance celebrated on the Twelfth, even though the
latter's date of 1 July 1690 in the old-style calendar is equivalent to
11 July in the new-style (Gregorian) calendar. 'Orange March', then,
acknowledges the ongoing presence of the decisive Battle of Aughrim
in the current, often still divisive, commemorations.[12]

The final stanza uses both 'Derry' and 'Londonderry' as if to say it
actually *is* both, and the city walls, so iconic to the same Apprentice
Boys, have '*Fuck the Queen*' chalked on at night, something that tells
quite a different story (*P*, p. 63). But it is in the mocking tone of the
last line that Murphy asks the reader to contemplate whether these
deeply felt animosities can ever truly be considered 'bygone':

> Bygone canon, bygone spleen.   (*P*, p. 63)

In this line, striking in its aphoristic power, are implied questions,
already set up by the first three lyrics: How should a society actually
enact or interpret what is 'gone'? How can a culture speak of that
which was perpetrated in the past to render it actually 'bygone'?
Reading this as the institutions of Northern Ireland, set up under the
peace process, regularly stagger from crisis to crisis, and seeing these
pressures as part of an ongoing cycle of reworked but much-the-same

'spleen' is to encounter Murphy once more at his most prescient in this meditative poem.

Somewhat in contrast is the lyric 'Casement's Funeral', since, in its account of watching the funeral on television, it incorporates a sense of being written after a new Labour government agreed to finally allow Roger Casement's remains to be returned to Ireland. This political move can be seen in retrospect as having to do with a softening of relations between the two governments partly because of Irish support in Britain for Labour and possibly also because of imminent trade talks in the run-up to membership of the European Economic Community. At the same time, however, Murphy stays true to his wont, honing in on a mockery of what he calls 'Rebels in silk hats' who 'now / Exploit the grave' of the newly reburied Casement (*P*, p. 64). His awareness of the ambiguities of the Protestant patriot (and exposer of imperial corruption) being honoured by 'High Mass' in Dublin's Pro-Cathedral while being the object of discussion by some who were inclined to vilify him and by others who still considered him a true patriot, lends the piece a wry wit. But it is the fact that Casement now will 'tower in legend like Wolfe Tone' which makes the link to the exposure of shifting loyalties already pursued in this section.

One way to give an overall interpretation of 'Now' is to focus on 'History', the final lyric of the section, where, in case we have not understood this already, we are told that 'The past is happening today' (*P*, p. 69). Murphy could not be clearer about the fact that the Irish re-enact the past. But what can he mean by foregrounding physical detail and the sometimes brutal moments of power-mongering that he presents with an almost cool detachment? He gives a hint at the end of 'History':

> The battle cause, a hand grenade
> Lobbed in a playground, the king's viciousness
> With slaves succumbing to his rod and kiss,
> Has a beginning in my blood.   (*P*, p. 69)

In what is a heady pendulum motion, the reader swings from a 'cause' to a 'hand grenade', from a violent playground to aristocratic

viciousness, from a 'rod' to a 'kiss'. This maelstrom of passions mixed
with violence is characterised as having its 'beginning' in the blood.
And it is the set of assumptions around supposed blood-created
affiliations and limitations which may have affected the readings (or
lack thereof) of Murphy's work. John Goodby opines that 'the relative
neglect it has suffered stems in part from a perception of "Protestant"
in terms of stereotypes of Anglo-Irishness or Englishness'.[13] Maurice
Harmon and Roger McHugh say in their *Short History of Anglo-
Irish Literature* that Murphy's poetry 'springs from his Ascendancy
background and his attempts to bridge the gap between that and
the native Irish world'.[14] Edna Longley in her essay 'Searching the
Darkness' says that Murphy's concern with the 'external facts of
history', may be explained by an anxiety not only to digest Ireland but
that Ireland should digest him'.[15] Longley believes that 'In seeking a
"truly Irish" identity Murphy also seeks absolution from Ascendancy
guilts'.[16] This latter may well be the case with regard to the persona
adopted in other works, including the poems of *Sailing to an Island*,
but for *The Battle of Aughrim* I want to suggest that Murphy instead
is implying that we should, as readers, be able to address this material
in a different way. Could it be that 'Anglo-Irish' is seen here to outlive
its usefulness, at least as a term which retains any purchase within
literary criticism? Might it be that the import of this poem implies
that the mixed and mongrel 'Irish' of the island should acknowledge
that we carry all of the past within our 'blood' and that by continuing
to mythologise, rather than face up to consequences, we have
continued to enact the 'bygone spleen', ensuring it is anything but
bygone? *The Battle of Aughrim* shows Murphy attempting to upend
the exceptionalism that permeates both nationalism and loyalism,
the 'them not us' approach, in a work which builds a solid edifice of
lyrics that add up inexorably to saying that our present situation is
all *us*, and we are the direct consequence of both our actions and our
failures to act.

Having been trained by the first section, 'Now', to appreciate the
way the lyric as a form can seem to privilege both past and present
at once, my reading of 'Before' shows up a deepening clarification of
the themes in play. Almost as if daring the reader to identify with one

or other 'side', Murphy presents traitors and supposed heroes alike as flawed, self-aggrandising and misled. In an almost cinematic group of lyrics, these portraits are animated by images of violence, including those of soldiers lynching innocents ('Martial Law', *P*, p. 74), of the testicles of a 'shorn heretic' ('Dragoon', *P*, p. 79), and of 'ice on the axe / When it hacked the king's head' ('Planter', *P*, p. 81). It is as if Murphy asks us to look closely enough to see that what drives all of these characters is a capacity for violence in the service of ignorance, the potential for which, he seems to imply, we should recognise within ourselves.

In this section the theme of communication and lack thereof, of translation and mistranslation, is starkly rendered. 'Legend', the opening lyric, begins with what could be a warning about the danger of always interpreting inherited stories in the same way. 'The story I have to tell', says the speaker in the poem, was apparently told by a teacher, who – at another remove – read it in a poem – which was written in a 'dying language' (*P*, p. 70). This story, told supposedly of Aughrim but actually one of much wider remit, concerns 'our ancestors', who are the same people, separated only by 'Ten marriages', and who 'In opposite camps' dispute the division over the status of the Eucharist which has animated Catholic/Protestant doctrinal divides for centuries (*P*, p. 70). As Murphy puts it, they were 'Gambling to settle verbal things', a phrase which does the job of making their march into battle at the end of the piece seem both incongruous and grossly misguided (*P*, p. 70).

In a prose rendering of 'St Ruth's Address to the Irish Army', Murphy makes use of the work of George Story, whose *An Impartial History of the Wars of Ireland* is one of the texts he studied to create this poem.[17] The general's 'address' of course had to be translated from French at the time of being delivered, and here is being 're-translated' by the poet, as it were, partly to show up the moral turpitude of those who urge the sacrifice of others. Its place is earned due to the use of all-too-familiar promises, 'God will make you all Saints' (*P*, p. 72), and the contemporary reader shudders at the resonance with rhetoric being used to spur on religiously motivated fighters of our present moment.

Translation and utterance is brought to the fore in another story from Aughrim told in 'The Sheepfold', where, in this poem of taut terza rima, farmer Kelly and his shepherd Mullen are rebuffed when asking for compensation for their flock commandeered by 'the Frenchman' (*P*, p. 76). They take 'the bog path to the richer camp' with a traitor's 'limp', where, not being able to speak to the Danish mercenaries, they are assumed to be spies, until the Dutch commander 'who serves England's Orange king' gives them each a purse (*P*, p. 77). The price of such 'translation' will be that they can point out St Ruth the following day in battle, an act which leads to his death. Murphy seems to be asking us to contemplate who exactly is 'foreign', and by implication who then might be termed 'native' or 'loyal' when the driving force for these and other actions is greed and self-preservation.

The relentlessness with which Murphy pursues his themes can threaten to make his plangent pessimism about human nature become the main aftertaste of this poem. And some readers might agree with Seamus Deane when he says that in Murphy, 'The energy of his language is not matched by an answering rhythmical variation in his music.'[18] However, in *The Battle of Aughrim* at least, the variation of approach to the material and the mordant humour that pervades the whole combine to strengthen the poem, enlivened by internal jokes like 'king' rhymed with 'dung' ('Mercenary', *P*, p. 78) and by semi-surreal moments when it may seem as if concrete realities are being modified, until one remembers the notion that the rebel 'rapparees' would hide in streams:

> A fish rainbows out of a pool – 'Give me bread!'
> ('Rapparees', *P*, p. 83)

The almost brutal realisation of violence within the poem continues in the third section, 'During', which contains six lyrics. Murphy opens with 'St Ruth', portrayed in his finery in the present tense, almost as if in a painted portrait. He speaks only 'French and Italian' while his officers know just English and 'Their men only Irish' (*P*, p. 84). The complexities of credal cause are mirrored again here in the clash of tongues. In a reprise of the opening of the work, St Ruth is soundly given his ironic ending after deciding 'victory is sure' when 'His head is shot off' (*P*, p. 85). 'Patrick Sarsfield' is also portrayed as he 'rides' at the head of his regiment, but here he has been relegated to the 'reserve', and he sees the rout of fleeing Jacobites, hearing 'cries, groans, shrieks' from the sidelines (*P*, p. 87). Murphy follows this with lines that carry particular resonance:

> Nothing he will do, or has done
> Can stop this happening.   (*P*, p. 87)

The use of the present tense brings a reader back to the import of 'The past is happening today' (from 'History' in the first section, 'Now'). Writing this poem in the mid-sixties, before the 'Troubles' began, but nonetheless aware of the tribal and sectarian divides inscribed in Irish society, Murphy shows himself to be the subtlest of moralists. He will not describe what should or could be done but is finding ways to portray what has been and is being done in lyrics of stark, visceral imagery. He puts it up to the reader to achieve that 'individually' wrought accommodation that he mentions in his *New York Review of Books* riposte to Davie. This must be done, he says, 'before the conflict can be settled as a whole'.

Section 4 of *The Battle of Aughrim* is 'After' – though given all that is said above, a reader might wonder what kind of 'after' might be inscribed. The first lyric, titled 'The Wolfhound', notes 'The wild geese have flown' (*P*, p. 91), referring to the departure of what was left of the Jacobite army under Sarsfield for France as part of the terms of the Treaty of Limerick in October 1691, though, given Murphy's methods, it may also refer to Irish mercenary soldiers fighting abroad in the sixteenth, seventeenth and eighteenth centuries. The more memorable 'after' here is in the form of a couplet lodged in the actual battlefield, where the death toll is shocking:

> Vermin by moonlight pick
> The tongues and sockets of six thousand skulls.
>
>   (*P*, p. 91)

Given Murphy's emphasis on 'tongue' and 'skulls' already noted, I take this most realistic of images as also metaphoric as the generations to come (me, you) pick over language suitable to navigate the continuing divides on the island.

Having had St Ruth's death early on, Murphy follows two of the other main characters of the poem into this section. Henry Luttrell, traitor of the battlefield, meets his death twenty-six years afterwards at the hand of an assassin who would have answered 'no' to the real import of the question 'Had they not buried Aughrim's dead?' ('Henry Luttrell's Death', *P*, p. 95). Here, though many of the people in this poem have been shown to waver in their loyalties, 'No one betrayed his assassin', even though there was 'three hundred pounds reward' on offer (*P*, p. 95).

Sarsfield is treated with a narrative poem in rhymed, rather plodding quatrains, 'Patrick Sarsfield's Portrait'. True to form for Murphy, there is a horrible image of women clutching the boats as the Jacobites left, hoping to be taken aboard. They drown in what is apparently an incident of record and Sarsfield is treated with a decided ambivalence by Murphy here: 'it was too late when you looked back' (*P*, p. 98). In this poem Murphy characterises his subject as a loyal fighter on the Continent, and credits him with having 'saved the city' (*P*, p. 97). He uses the full '"Would to God / This wound had been for Ireland"' – the supposed last words – followed by

> Cavalier,
> You feathered with the wild geese our despair.   (*P*, p. 98)

to capture both an aspect of the respect for Sarsfield which still continues today along with a sense that he was also capable of being 'cavalier'.

The final lyric of *The Battle of Aughrim* is 'Battle Hill Revisited', bringing the reader back to the opening section of the work. The piece is about contemporary visitors, who 'seek out ancestors' and 'know little about God' (*P*, p. 99), suggesting a certain remoteness of the religious conflicts of the seventeenth century for the modern-day tourist. Now there is a 'new signpost to the credal slaughter', Murphy writes, in a kind of ironic swipe at war tourism (*P*, p. 99). These visitors from Europe may indeed be 'Called after wild geese' but they, too, 'may hear / Rival prayers of their warring ancestors' (*P*, p. 99). Murphy will not allow any group he portrays to think themselves the pure inheritors of one side's predilections. The visitors 'locate the dun' where St Ruth planned the battle and there, he allows,

> They try to imagine
> Exactly what took place, what it could mean,   (*P*, p. 100)

but with customary faithfulness to the actual world, Murphy notes that even these visitors seem doomed to fail as they 'turn in time to catch a plane for France' (*P*, p. 100).

The Battle of Aughrim, with its clear-eyed depictions of violence, an almost mesmeric classical cadence, and the formality of its prosody demonstrates what Frank Bidart calls 'the severity and ferocity at the root of classic art, addicted to mimesis'.[19] As Ted Hughes said,

> Richard Murphy's verse is classical in a way that demonstrates what the classical strengths really are. It combines a high music with simplicity, force and directness in dealing with the world of action. He has the gift of epic objectivity: behind his poems we feel not the assertion of his personality, but the actuality of events, the facts and sufferings of history.[20]

It is that actuality of events which remains with a reader after time spent with the poem. The skulls, the futility, the self-deceptions remain, as well as a sense, pessimistic but true, that there may be no easy saving of ourselves, but that we should be judged by our very action or inaction. This is applicable in broad terms to our violent present when the threat of terror is global, and it also applies to the particular terms of the Irish condition, as referred to by Murphy in his riposte to Davie, which is why this poem seems to speak directly to our *now*.

Although partly written initially for voices and to be read on radio, the point is not that this poem encapsulates different voices, but that it shows us many shades of what could be the same voice. If human nature is a cauldron of primal desires driven by greed and self-preservation, then Murphy has devised a poetics to match that realisation. *The Battle of Aughrim* is an exemplary kind of 'war' poetry or poetry of conflict, which is as prescient in its significance to our contemporary moment as it has been to the times between its publication and the present. Where artists working in violent times or their aftermath must be wary of poetic strategies which re-encode what Murphy calls 'the explosive credal myths', his poetic strategy has been to use his innate sense of formality as a vehicle to convey the altogether more risky import of his content. While positing that human nature is treacherous and often wilfully misguided, he provides a poetic antidote of sorts, by applying a distinctive poetic orderliness while positing that the radical power of poetry is to mirror us to ourselves. His very reliance on the power of the poem ensures that *The Battle of Aughrim, 1691* continues to ask us today whether we are ready to see clearly.

8

Richard Murphy's Poetry of
Aftermath

JOSEPH SENDRY

In 2013, at the age of eighty-six, Richard Murphy published *The Pleasure Ground: poems 1952–2012*, a selection spanning his entire career, unmistakably presented as a guide to how he wishes it (and himself) to be interpreted and remembered. Since biographical references, complex and sometimes obscure, characterise much of Murphy's work, factual data about his life are often needed to elucidate the poems. To uncover their multiple layers of significance, however, other data are required. His work must also be placed within several interlocking matrices: genealogical, social, national historical, even world historical. To provide such background the 2013 volume includes prose pieces running to thirty-five pages. The most salient is 'The Pleasure Ground', a reminiscence carefully revised from a 1963 BBC broadcast.[1] Placed first in the volume (*P*, pp. 13–16), the essay furnishes not only its title but also, as its Preface, a concentrated statement of underlying themes in the entire canon. The small but significant changes that Murphy has made to the BBC broadcast, and other earlier writings, evince a concerted effort to locate himself within the stream of history. My aim in this essay is to articulate Murphy's sense of history as it is encapsulated in *aftermath*, a linguistic, metaphorical and conceptual complex that manifests itself repeatedly throughout his career.

Beyond the prose selections included in the 2013 collected poems, establishing multilevelled autobiographical documentation has been

a major project of Murphy's later years. It began with publication
of his memoir *The Kick* in 2002, reissued in a new edition by Cork
University Press in 2017. It continued with the shaping of chapter-like
notes, each on a selected sonnet from *The Price of Stone* (1985) based
on journals he kept 'between April 1981 and November, 1983' which
contain abundant detail on the creative process that generated the
sonnets.[2] Notes on twelve of the fifty sonnets comprising the sequence
were published in *Poetry Ireland Review* in three instalments from
2011 to 2013.[3] A total of thirty-seven are now collected in *In Search of
Poetry* (Clutag Press, 2017).

In *The Kick* Murphy reconstructs the moment when he came to
full imaginative realisation of how his personal and family history
was enmeshed in the conflicted history of Ireland. The moment
occurred in Cleggan on 12 July 1962, the anniversary of the Battle of
Aughrim.

> I remembered driving through the village of Aughrim, right
> in the centre of Ireland, and feeling a sense of desolation in
> the place. The battle fought there on Sunday 12 July 1691 was
> the last and bloodiest in a war that established the Protestant
> ownership of land in Ireland for almost the next two centuries.
> The Famine of 1845–47, the partitioning of Ireland in 1922, and
> the long ebb tide of emigration that was, we hoped, about to
> turn, were remote consequences of the battle. And I recalled that
> one of my mother's ancestors, Robert Miller, had acquired from
> a dispossessed Catholic the land and house he called Milford.
>
> A question uppermost in all Irish minds in our agricultural
> past – *Who owns the land?* – occurred to me so strongly that
> I took an envelope from the pocket of my donkey jacket and
> wrote those words … (*K*, p. 196, emphasis added)

Murphy used 'those words' to open his long historical poem *The Battle
of Aughrim*. By singling out later developments – famine, partition
and emigration – as 'remote consequences of the battle', he presents
a layered view of history as a succession of problematic conditions
unfolding in discernible stages. His summary formulation of the

battle's significance – '*Who owns the land?*' – lays down a theme that persists not only in his work but, indeed, in Irish historiography. In his review of *The Princeton History of Modern Ireland*, R.F. Foster called special attention to the frequency with which the contributors returned on many levels to this theme.[4]

Murphy's clarifying moment of insight on 12 July 1962 began more than a year of creativity arising from his preoccupation with the issues it raised. Before the end of 1962 he wrote 'some of the best parts of *The Battle of Aughrim*'.[5] In summer and autumn of 1963 he made his father's problematic situation as a landowner in the British colony of Rhodesia the major concern of another long poem, 'The God Who Eats Corn'. At the midpoint of this creative period, January 1963, he was asked to contribute to a BBC radio series, *Writers on Themselves*, and in February he retired to Cleggan to compose 'The Pleasure Ground'. In that seminal autobiographical essay, Milford became the arena for tenacious grappling with the question he has never laid to rest. When, as an appendix to the 2013 collected poems he excerpted from *The Kick* the account (in part quoted above) of how he wrote *The Battle of Aughrim*, Murphy quietly emphasised Milford's centrality in his own life by inserting the clause 'where I was born' to the name of the estate that his ancestor acquired in 1691 (*P*, p. 255).

The passage from *The Kick* appends to the starkly worded question of land ownership a phrase brimming with implication: it was 'uppermost in all Irish minds *in our agricultural past*' (emphasis added). In the original edition of the *Oxford English Dictionary* the definition of 'aftermath' derives from agricultural practice: 'a second or later mowing ...'.[6] This meaning has been largely supplanted by a darker, figurative one absent from the *OED* until its second edition originally published in 1989: 'a state or condition left by a (usually unpleasant) event, or some occurrence arising from it'.[7] Since each sense implies two successive states, the term lends itself readily to historical application.

In the poet's scheme of things, 'mowing', the key term in the agricultural definition of 'aftermath', is itself highly charged. It makes a notable appearance in 'Sailing to an Island', the title poem of Murphy's breakthrough volume, where it was strategically placed first, as it is, regardless of chronology, in his *Collected Poems* (Gallery Press, 2000) and in his latest collection (*P*, pp. 19–21). The author's note on an excursion he and his party undertook on a late summer's day in 1952 signals the poem's pivotal importance: 'We were planning to go to Clare Island, a place renowned for legends... Contrary winds brought us instead to an island I had never heard of, called Inishbofin.' The resulting poem 'about our rough passage and change of course ... led to a change in my life' (*P*, p. 245) and, it should be added, a decisive change in his poetry. Prior to the voyage Murphy's creative energy had been consumed by a never-published epic on the myth of Diarmuid and Gráinne. The legend for which Clare Island is known centres on another Gráinne (Granuaile in 'Sailing to an Island', *P*, p. 19), the sixteenth-century pirate queen Grace O'Malley. The navigational turn from Clare to Inishbofin represents Murphy's turn from a poetry of myth to one of engagement with the Ireland of history. Inishbofin is 'the land where the men are mowing' (*P*, p. 20).

Given his acute sensitivity to the meaning of words in both current and past usage, Murphy's choice of the word 'mowing' merits special attention. The fee he asked for *The Battle of Aughrim* was 'the price of *The Oxford English Dictionary* in its original twelve volumes' (*P*, p. 255). His poem 'Bookcase for *The Oxford English Dictionary*' characterises those volumes as a garner of future creative harvest: 'All the words I need / Stored like seed' (*P*, p. 162). Where 'mowing' is concerned, the *OED* reveals unsuspected complexity, in both the word and the activity. The entry for 'mowth', 'a mowing', gives 'math' as an alternate term; the entry for 'aftermath' gives 'aftermowth' as its alternative. The second part of the *OED* definition of 'aftermath' is '... The crop of grass which springs up after the mowing in early summer'. Though he does not employ the word 'aftermath' itself, Murphy introduces its synonym 'aftergrass' in two poems, the closing portion of 'The Woman of the House' (1959) and the opening section of *The Battle of Aughrim* (1968). In both contexts second growth entails debasement.

Murphy discerns far-reaching cultural significance in mowing as a human activity. For the first definition of 'mow' as a verb, the *OED* offers: 'to cut down (grass, corn, etc.) with a scythe, or (in recent use) with a machine that operates like a scythe'. His poem entitled 'Scythe' (*P*, pp. 153–4) invokes mowing as the defining characteristic of a major phase of civilisation. Skill in wielding the instrument becomes paradigmatic; its blade, 'primordial'. An ordinary event illustrates. '[O]n Omey Island / An old farmer / … is teaching / … A tinker / … how to hold and handle / a scythe'. The attempt is futile because the pupil's 'tribe has never owned land', and this 'tinker' would have to change his way of life and 'quit travelling' if he ever did (*P*, p. 153). Like 'aftermath', 'mow' carries a darker ulterior signification. In one transferred use 'mow' means 'sweep down on men in battle' (*OED*, 2c) and in a transferred and figurative use followed by 'off' or 'down' '… to destroy or kill indiscriminately or in great numbers' (*OED*, 1c). Even in 'Scythe' mowing is metaphorically transformed into a military activity, its cutting blade 'Advancing swathe by swathe over warrior grasses, / … their plumes laid low' (*P*, p. 154). For lack of standard ordnance, the scythe served by default as a weapon in the Williamite Wars.[8] In *The Battle of Aughrim* Murphy pictures 'scythe-armed yokels' (*P*, p. 97).

Within a larger cultural framework, the human effort to make things grow that begins in planting and eventuates in mowing requires land where crops can be replanted and mowed again. In historical contexts the noun 'planter' also takes on troubled meanings. In Ireland it can mean 'One of the English or Scotch settlers planted on forfeited lands in the 17th c.' (*OED*, 3a), and 'in [the] 19th c., A person settled in the holding of an evicted tenant' (*OED*, 3b). Given more global extension, the word can be applied to 'the proprietor or occupier of a plantation or cultivated estate … now used generally of such persons in tropical or subtropical countries' (*OED*, 4). In this last sense, 'planter' would be interchangeable with 'colonist' in the Rhodesia of 'The God Who Eats Corn' and the Sri Lanka of Murphy's later writing.

As 'Scythe' implies, agriculture entails deep-seated consequences for the way society is organised. On the issues involved, Karen Armstrong outlines a useful model in the Introduction to *Fields of Blood: religion and the history of violence*.[9] She argues that in pre-modern societies, when growing food crops replaced hunting and gathering as the means of subsistence, land – and often, sad to say, those who tilled it – became the primary form of wealth. Increased food supplies enabled population growth and that required an increasing amount of arable land, along with the force needed to acquire, defend and exploit it. In Armstrong's précis, 'With agriculture came civilization; and with civilization, warfare.'[10]

As Murphy views Irish history, the causative moments of greatest significance, those pertaining to who owned the land, can be readily identified, though he does not always refer to them directly. The first is Cromwell's Irish campaign of 1649–59, which resulted in wholesale confiscation and redistribution. Next is the victory of William III's forces at Aughrim in 1691, which, by removing effective military and political opposition, enabled systematic expropriation, thereby 'establish[ing] the Protestant ownership of land in Ireland for almost the next two centuries', to requote the poet's words (*K*, p. 196). In the aftermath, severe restrictions on Catholics, well beyond land ownership, reached their apogee with the Penal Laws enacted from 1695 to 1728. Two developments reversed the historical current in favour of Catholics: with regard to possession of land, the series of Land Acts from the later nineteenth century to the outbreak of the First World War; with regard to political power, the Treaty creating the Irish Free State in 1921, the civil strife that eventuated from it, and the establishment of the Republic in 1949.

Three poems from *Sailing to an Island* touch on the link between past violence and present ownership, early instances of the aftermath motif that Murphy brought to full development in his reflections on Aughrim. The 2013 collection prints the three in sequence; the first edition of *Sailing to an Island* did not. In the former, two bear dates of composition: 'Epitaph on a Douglas Fir' (1956), 'Woman of the House' (1958) and 'Droit de Seigneur'.

'Epitaph on a Douglas Fir' deals with an event soon after the poet and his wife became landowners by purchasing a house and 180 adjoining acres in County Wicklow (*K*, pp. 148–51). Felling a massive ninety-year-old evergreen becomes matter for social comment as the poet imagines its ceremonial installation by members of the Ascendancy class:

> At a wedding breakfast bridesmaids *planted*
> With trowel and gloves this imported fir.
>
> (*P*, p. 28, emphasis added)

Because trees outlive human generations, planting them is a way of affirming possession of land for one's posterity. In the 2013 collection Murphy identified the tree as a North American species by inserting 'Douglas' into the title, refining a point made in the phrase 'imported fir' and offering a subtle reminder that the land lodging the tree was acquired by outsiders through expropriation. Murphy makes his generation participants in that dispossession: 'They ... *planted* well, so that we might do better' (*P*, p. 28, emphasis added). A reminder of what was required to keep possession intrudes in a not-so-subtle allusion to British imperial history, the Second Battle of Burma in 1852 where 'an officer patched with a crude trepan / ... fought in Rangoon for these quiet acres'. But land tenure does not last indefinitely: 'How soon, measured by trees, the party ended' (*P*, p. 28).

The question of land ownership occupies the foreground of 'Droit de Seigneur'. Its 1820 setting evokes a period when secret agrarian societies, here the Ribbonmen, rose up against Ascendancy landowners, 'Refusing to pay tithes or rent' (*P*, p. 33). A landlord's portrait of Cromwell, hastily concealed in anticipation of violence, moves the situation into the territory of aftermath. As a Protestant the landlord is beneficiary of Cromwell's scheme for land apportionment; as rector, the Lord's local representative in the Established Church, he claims divine sanction for his acts ('droit de seigneur'); as land owner he can muster British soldiers to safeguard his holdings. Though the Ribbonmen challenge at its foundation the system that supports him, the expedition of the landlord and 'a few soldiers' becomes a mere skirmish where the only culprit apprehended and executed is 'a young simpleton' lacking the wits to escape (*P*, p. 33). Like Cromwell's portrait the incriminating green ribbon found in the boy's pocket provides a tangible marker of its bearer's loyalties in the continuing conflict over land.

Murphy wrote 'The Woman of the House', an elegy for his maternal grandmother, soon after her death. In the 2013 collection he emphasises her ties with the house by joining its name to hers in an italicised caption inserted below the title, '*In memory of my grandmother Lucy Mary Ormsby of Milford, Kilmaine, County Mayo, 1873–1958*' (*P*, p. 29). Moments from the dwelling's past pinpoint stages in Irish history. It was a 'house that famine labourers built' (*P*, p. 30). Her connection with it through marriage bestowed on Lucy advantages that accrue from past transfers of land: 'Gardeners polite, governesses plenty' (*P*, p. 30). Nineteenth-century 'Rangoon prints', a medal from the Crimean War (1853–56), mention of an uncle who survived cholera in India only to 'slaughter a few sepoys' before 'retir[ing] to Galway in search of sport' all testify to Milford's links with imperial power (*P*, p. 30). And the man of the house, Murphy's grandfather, as 'Colonel Rector' (*P*, p. 31), held ranking posts in both the empire and the Established Church.

Lucy, however, discounted her status as 'Mistress of mossy acres and unpaid rent' by venturing beyond the walls that traditionally enclosed demesnes like Milford 'on foot to feed the sick' (*P*, p. 29) and by inviting the neighbouring poor into the house, where she 'bandaged the wounds that poverty caused' (*P*, p. 30). Though her striving 'to cure impossible wrong' from the past won her no place in the historical record, her elegist grandson sees her invalidating the order enshrined there:

> At last, her warmth made ashes of the trees
> Ancestors planted, …   (*P*, p. 31)

Widening its outlook to embrace current conditions, at a key point the elegy plays on the agricultural sense of 'aftermath' to judge the poet's generation:

> The children overseas no longer need her,
> They are like after-grass to her harvest.   (*P*, p. 32)

The Land Acts and Irish independence have changed the system governing ownership of land. Tractors have replaced horses. Emigration has taken a different form, where the progeny of the land-rich have joined the land-poor to find better lives elsewhere. The prestige of the hereditary demesne has dissipated. Milford itself has fallen into disrepair. The poet duly acknowledges this dismantling of the order established by Aughrim and the inauguration of another stage of aftermath in Irish society, but most of all he mourns the capacity for love that passed with his grandmother: 'Her house, but not her kindness, has found heirs' (*P*, p. 31).

In 'The Woman of the House' Lucy Mary Ormsby, by sheer magnanimity, flouts the adverse outcomes of history. In 'The Pleasure Ground' her grandson effectively concedes that he is powerless to escape them, and with that coming to awareness his sense of aftermath reaches full development. Milford is again the nexus. When converting the text of the 1963 broadcast into the 2013 Preface, Murphy highlighted the mansion's aristocratic past by specifying it as an 'old demesne house in south County Mayo' (*P*, p. 13). Appropriately, it was through his grandmother that Murphy came to know the side of Irish history belonging to 'those whose ancestors had lost the struggle for the land which ours had won' (*P*, p. 15). 'The Woman of the House' barely mentions his childhood visits to Salruck, County Galway, where Lucy was raised and to which those divested of land had been relegated ('We'd motor west where salmon boats tossed', *P*, p. 29). 'The Pleasure Ground' dwells on the area at some length, highlighting the bleakness of 'this land of the dead ... stark, desolate, uncultivated, storm-bound and profoundly mournful' (*P*, p. 15).

Writing of Milford the poet carefully distinguishes between the West Wing, the patriarchal domicile 'built in William and Mary style shortly after the battles of Aughrim and the Boyne' (*P*, p. 14) and the East Wing, the servants' quarters. The poet was born in the West Wing. At his own expense his father refitted the East Wing for his family. Adjacent to it was Milford's neglected garden, the 'Pleasure Ground' where at ages twelve and thirteen Murphy spent what he calls 'the happiest time of [his] life' (*P*, p. 14). There he became a planter, but instead of new saplings meant to last for generations, he assiduously cultivated and successfully revived 'a very old fig tree', surrounding it with flowers, along with 'carrots, parsnips, onions, lettuce and cress for us to eat' (*P*, p. 14). The BBC broadcast mentioned only carrots.

Since vegetables are native-grown, everyday plants that require no mowing, the extended list in the Preface acts as counterpoint to the acquisitive, aristocratic aura of 'demesne'.

This account of the Pleasure Ground invites Edenic interpretation. And although the 2013 Preface does style the garden a 'paradise', it flanks the term with qualifiers that consign it to the maelstrom of history, 'a seedy paradise of impoverished Anglo-Irish pride' (*P*, p. 13). To perform this demythologising manoeuvre, Murphy activates figures from agriculture. 'Seedy' enmeshes the garden in the process of growth, fruition, decay and aftermath. In its positive sense the word means 'abounding in seed' (*OED*, 1a), promising increase. Its negative sense, 'shabby, ill-looking' (*OED*, 1b), calls to mind the expression 'gone to seed', in decline, a note reinforced by the past tense of 'impoverished', which implies a prior condition of wealth, now lost. Murphy drives this reversal home through the starkness of numbers. Late seventeenth-century Milford had 70,000 acres. By mid-twentieth century, 'famine, revolution and land reform had cut [it] to 350' (*P*, p. 15). Even during the 'happiest time' when Murphy tended his idealised plot (May 1940 to September 1941), news of war brought the west of Ireland into the currents of world history. The vegetables raised in the Pleasure Ground 'became part of [the boy's] "war effort" against de Valera's neutrality' (*P*, p. 14). After the war the immersion in history continued. The Pleasure Ground sank into decay because the energy needed to maintain it, along with the culture it represented, dispersed: 'the old people died and the young left the country' (*P*, p. 16).

Milford and its environs figure at specific points in *The Battle of Aughrim*: the deterioration of the estate under its heirs in 'Inheritance' (*P*, p. 67), Murphy's baptism in 'Christening in Kilmaine, 1927' (*P*, p. 68), and the original acquisition of the estate by an ancestor in 'Planter' (*P*, pp. 81–2). Inevitably, however, Aughrim itself is the locus for this poem commemorating the momentous encounter that took place there. Accordingly, the historical perspective expands well beyond the personal to include developments from the time of the battle to the poem's present at multiple levels of society in Ireland and the world beyond. By playing past and present against one another and differentiating specific moments within a larger temporal frame, the poem's four-part structure is well suited to demonstrate the dynamics of history.[11] Part I, 'Now', is set at the time of writing, to which the poem loops back in the concluding twenty-six-line section of Part IV. The point of reference for Parts II, III and IV – 'Before', 'During' and 'After' – is 12 July 1691, the date of the battle, the aftermaths of which Murphy is at pains to identify. A plural is required because the consequences of Aughrim take multiple forms not only in the 'Now' of the 1960s when Murphy wrote but also at intervals in the centuries following the battle.

Differentiation of cultural epochs organises the first section of Part I, 'On Battle Hill' (*P*, p. 61), where a contemporary landscape reflects the tensions metaphorically implicit in 'aftermath'. Agriculture goes on where a decisive conflict once raged to determine 'who owns the land' where cultivation takes place. Well versed in the battle's history, the poet-speaker identifies features of the terrain that governed tactical decisions: a 'ditch, defended with pikes', 'a stream passed by cavalry traitors'. Agricultural activity that has obliterated evidence of combat manifests itself in stages running from the primal ('a tinker woman / ... thinning turnips by hand', 'a rook tied by the leg to scare flocks of birds'), through the timeless ('sheep browse'), to the modern ('A tractor sprays a rood of flowering potatoes'). Even mechanised agriculture makes way for more advanced technology, evidenced by 'Dairy lorries on the fast trunk-route' and 'giant earth-movers / Shovel[ling] and claw[ing] a highway'.

The poet's visit to Aughrim is in the nature of a quest. His immediate object is the memorial to the battle's Jacobite commander, the Marquis St Ruth. A Celtic cross commemorating – no accident – a minister for agriculture 'killed in a car' commands notice (*P*, p. 61). St Ruth's cairn does not. Later sections of Part I ponder where the sought-for meaning might be found. In 'History', the ninth and final section (*P*, p. 69), the poet rejects conventional written records, 'dog-eared inventories of death', and affirms that 'Touch unearths military history'. The poet insists that only when we have tactile evidence connected directly with human individuals who took part in events or who transmitted them do we arrive at an authentic historical account. Thus, through direct contact with the battlefield, the 'Bones and bullets' of individual narratives can be felt 'fingering [the] mind' (*P*, p. 69) and may be said to truly lodge '"in a skull"', as is suggested also in the fifth section of Part I, 'Historical Society' (*P*, p. 65).

This discussion of *The Battle of Aughrim* will focus simultaneously on two interrelated issues: first, what is buried on the battlefield, literally or metaphorically, and what springs from those remains – aftermath in its multiple forms; second, the physical violence of war and the moral violence of betrayal that produced this havoc and finally determined who owns the land. As a prelude to considering these issues in Parts II, III and IV, Murphy addresses in Part I the spurious historical constructions, themselves a form of aftermath, generated after the fact to account for the battle's outcomes. The speaker invokes a telling metaphor ('Starlings worm the aftergrass') as he approaches 'the death-cairn of St Ruth' in the opening section, then follows it with a veritable programme note for the rest of Part I: 'A cannonball beheaded him, and *sowed a myth*' (*P*, p. 61; emphasis added).

In 'Green Martyrs' and 'Orange March', the second and third sections of Part I, the opposing sides deliver their justifying myths. In 'Green Martyrs' (*P*, p. 62) a Catholic woman personifying her oppressed people rehearses the effects of Aughrim in a telescoped version of history: Penal Laws, seizure of land, starvation at the hands of absentee landlords, emigration of fighters for the cause. Her listing of its generational cohorts amounts to an historical roll-call of the Catholic insurgency: rapparees (seventeenth century), Whiteboys (earlier eighteenth century), Volunteers (later eighteenth century) and Ribbonmen (into the nineteenth century). In 'Orange March' (*P*, p. 63) middle-class Protestants, donning 'Orange sashes' on 12 July, transpose myth into ritual re-enactment by annually staging the siege of Derry, where their forebears successfully withstood a months-long assault by Jacobite forces the year before Aughrim.

Mythic patterns of advocacy rearrange themselves kaleidoscopically in the following sections, among which the fourth, 'Casement's Funeral' (*P*, p. 64), stands out. The disposition of Casement's corpse establishes burial as a pre-eminent component of the aftermath motif.

Buried bones do not rest dormant in the earth but return as myths that set off chains of retaliatory action. As for Casement, 'the traitor's dock / Hurt him to tower in legend like Wolfe Tone', the archetypal case of a patriot whose execution fired generations of Irish rebels. Murphy couches Casement's mythic transfiguration in agricultural terms: 'his fame roots in prison lime: / … a revolution *seeds*' (emphasis added).

The most resonant treatment of burial and its metaphorical aftermath occurs in Part IV, an account of Aughrim's devastation culled by Murphy from his source, in the section entitled 'The Reverend George Story Concludes *An Impartial History of the Wars in Ireland*':

> Seen from the top of the hill, the unburied dead
> Covered four miles, like a great flock of sheep.   (*P*, p. 93)

With that simile Murphy integrates the fallen dead into his thematic network linking war and agriculture. Earlier, he devoted an entire section, 'Mercenary', to a metaphorical elaboration of this linkage. A foreign hireling, who could have fought on either side, protests that whoever wins, his body and those of his comrades will simply 'manure the grass / Where we wouldn't be let trespass / Alive,' (*P*, p. 78). Earlier yet, in 'Inheritance' an advertisement for fertiliser defaces a field of death: 'On ancient battleground neat painted signs / Announce "Gouldings Grows"' (*P*, p. 67).

Multifarious issues at stake in land ownership come together in a second case of disinterment, that of Henry Luttrell, a Jacobite cavalry leader at Aughrim. Luttrell makes a brief but notable appearance in Part III when, hearing of St Ruth's death, he turns traitor by withdrawing his regiment, depriving foot soldiers of vital support ('Henry Luttrell', *P*, p. 89). Having capitalised handsomely on his betrayal in succeeding years, in Part IV ('Henry Luttrell's Death', *P*, pp. 95–6) he is challenged in a coffee-house toast: '"It's time to bury Aughrim's dead."' Whereupon he goes into denial:

> … that was done
> Twenty-six years ago, he said,
> Had they not buried Aughrim's dead?   (*P*, p. 95)

In fact they buried only some of them. After the battle the Dutch General Godart van Ginkel, commander of the Williamite forces, ordered that his fallen troops be buried but that the corpses of the Irish defenders be dispersed over miles of surrounding terrain.[12]

Unburied, 'Aughrim's dead' produced abundant after-growth from Irish soil. That night in 1717 an assassin's bullet took down Luttrell on his way home from the coffee house. During the twenty-six years after the battle, Penal Laws suppressing the practice of their religion and ownership of land had been imposed on Catholics, compounding rancour that continued to generate aftermath in the form of insurgent groups like those tallied by the Irish woman in 'Green Martyrs'. Resistance came to a head with Wolfe Tone's rebellion and defiant death in 1798. 'Masked men, inspired by Wolfe Tone', broke into Luttrell's tomb that year and 'smashed the skull with a pickaxe' (*P*, p. 96).

As presented by Murphy the Catholic defeat at Aughrim turned on two further betrayals motivated by ambition to own land or the products of its husbandry. One involved common folk who worked the land, the other a landlord. In the former, sheep became the issue when Jacobite forces commandeered the flocks of two commoners, Kelly and Mullen ('The Sheepfold', *P*, pp. 75–7). When St Ruth summarily dismissed their plea for recompense, the pair went to the enemy general, Ginkel, who handsomely complied with their request. The two then showed the way to St Ruth's position, where a cannonball handily dispatched him ('The Winning Shot', *P*, p. 86).

The remaining betrayal unfolds at midpoint in the poem in a section aptly entitled 'Planter' (*P*, pp. 81–2). The culprit, Robert Miller, acknowledged by Murphy as 'one of my mother's ancestors', was already a prosperous landowner on the eve of the battle (*K*, p. 196). A portrait adorning his well-appointed household bespoke Cromwell's Irish conquest four decades earlier as the source of Miller's wealth. '[G]arden ycws / Forty years planted' testify that he intended, from the start, to maintain permanent possession of his windfall. For the local populace the long-term consequences of Cromwell's victory were less benign: 'Food at a famine price, / Cattle raided, corn trod', and signs of an ongoing insurgency. As the battle approaches, Miller gloats over his success in enticing his Jacobite house guest 'Red-mouthed O'Donnell' away from the battle. The section leaves no ambiguity as to his motives:

> May the God of battle
> Give us this day our land
> And the papists be trampled.   (*P*, p. 81)

For his efforts Miller gained the estate he named Milford and forged the first link in a chain of inheritance that connected the poet to Aughrim.

If other key agents at Aughrim betrayed their cause for material gain, Patrick Sarsfield, 'native of Ireland', distinguished himself both for loyalty as a military leader and for probity as a steward of landed holdings:

> Landlord who never racked, you gave your rent
> To travel with your mounted regiment.   (*P*, p. 97)

The third section of Part III, 'Patrick Sarsfield' (*P*, p. 87), reviews his military accomplishments before Aughrim, where St Ruth shunted him to the sidelines, powerless to affect the battle's outcome. After their defeat Sarsfield evacuated the Irish forces, the 'wild geese', to France. Two years later, fighting under French colours, he fell and was buried in what is now Belgium. To the extent that the poem, and the battle, have a hero, it is Sarsfield. Murphy elevates him by giving him the poem's penultimate section, 'Patrick Sarsfield's Portrait' (*P*, pp. 97–8), the last on the battle itself, where perhaps with a nod to Wagner the work reaches at least provisional closure. The overture to *Tristan and Isolde* famously introduces a chord left unresolved until the final scene of the opera. In the overture section of *The Battle of Aughrim* ('On Battle Hill') Murphy quotes the first three words of the Irish general's dying wish, '*Would to God* ...–' (*P*, p. 61, italics in original). He completes the utterance only in the final stanza of Sarsfield's section: '"Would to God / This wound had been for Ireland"' (*P*, p. 98).

In *The Iliad* the gods would not be satisfied, nor could that primordial narrative of warfare conclude, until Achilles handed over the body of Hector, his defeated rival, for proper funeral rites and burial. In *The Battle of Aughrim* the dead left unburied on contested land keep sprouting conflict over successive generations of Irish history. Rounding back to its opening, the poem's closing section ('Battle Hill Revisited') introduces tourists of Irish ancestry who, like the poet, seek out St Ruth's memorial and what meaning it may hold: 'Seed, there should be seed, buried in a cairn' (*P*, p. 99). But St Ruth's remains are not to be found at Aughrim. His corpse was taken from the battle site for burial at Loughrea.[13] Hence the quest, like the poem, must end in irresolution. The best message the tourists can hope for, 'If they listen', is 'Rival prayers of their warring ancestors' (*P*, p. 99). Defeated in their aspiration to find meaning in history, these modern versions of the 'wild geese' leave Ireland 'to catch a plane for France' (*P*, p. 100).

Colonialism, which hovers steadily in the background of *The Battle of Aughrim* and intrudes at points in 'The Pleasure Ground', moves to the foreground in 'The God Who Eats Corn', the third composition that followed upon Murphy's insight of 12 July 1962. The two former works uncover roots of troubling historical involvement in his mother's family line; 'The God Who Eats Corn' turns to his father's. Whereas his mother's ancestors held Milford for more than two centuries, 'Neither [his father] nor his Murphy forbears [*sic*] had ever owned a house or an acre of land' (*P*, p. 13). That situation changed after his father retired in 1949 (now Sir William Lindsay Murphy) to what was then Rhodesia, where he 'bought fifteen hundred acres of virgin land with no house in a farming area unjustly restricted to whites' (*K*, p. 102) and 'at the age of 63' built a house on it.[14]

The process by which Sir William established 'the young plantation of his old age' (*P*, p. 104) in an explicitly colonial setting recapitulates the narrative tracing expropriation of land in Ireland. In 'The God Who Eats Corn' Cecil Rhodes plays a role analogous to Cromwell's as the one who initiated its seizure from the native population. Left unnamed, Rhodes is referred to as 'a childless millionaire', by his familiar epithet 'the Founder', and by allusion to the stratagems he employed to wrest control. For 'gold and diamonds', Rhodes and his associates prevailed on Lobengula, king of the leading regional tribe, to grant mineral rights to the 'Pioneer Column', 200 carefully selected miners, each of whom was assured – a detail recorded in the poem – 'three thousand [acres] of grass', as against 'ten acres for millet' 'To each black' (*P*, p. 105). The depth of the deceit can be gauged by the fact that, for the Africans, the very notion of land ownership was alien.[15]

In the historic aftermath of Rhodes' massive expropriation of land, Murphy's father acts, both literally and figuratively, as planter. Like the owners of Milford he sets out to create what amounts to a pleasure ground. It is trees that he plants, pledges for enduring possession, and it is foreign dignitaries ('A chairman of mines', 'a Governor', 'great names / Written on tags') who preside at the planting of each (*P*, p. 103). Even with diligent care from native workers, the imported species barely survive in the African climate.

The foundering of Sir William's arboretum emerges as an emblem of the 'planting' of Rhodesia itself. Even though he and Lady Murphy conscientiously dispensed education along with European social and religious values to the Africans who worked their land, the harmony they sought to create was not forthcoming. The waters channelled to irrigate the garden 'cannot cool the racist fever', nor does the cultivated grove give needed shade where 'indaba / Could heal the blood feud' (*P*, p. 103). *Indaba*, a Zulu derivative defined in the *OED* as 'a conference or consultation between or with South African natives', cannot take root in this alien environment. The word appears twice again in the poem (*P*, pp. 105, 108), associated each time with the tree under which the defrauded king, Lobengula, traditionally held counsel.

The works discussed above show Murphy articulating, in increasingly determinate ways, his stratified sense of the past and the personal predicaments in which history has placed him. Two decades after the first conception of *Aughrim* in 1962, he brought that accumulated insight to bear in devising a form that captures his historical vision in multiple facets. The vehicle was *The Price of Stone*, a volume that includes a fifty-sonnet sequence written from

1981 to 1983. The concision of the sonnet enabled him to concentrate on selected issues at selected moments. The expansiveness of the sequence freed him to engage an array of subjects not possible in a unitary poem. And the singular device of making the speaker of each sonnet (except the last) a building or place from his personal or communal past provided tactile objects of the kind he used in *The Battle of Aughrim* to bring history to life.

The sonnets engage with historical matters in varying degrees. The recently published (2017) notes derived from journals kept during their composition have enabled Murphy to add considerable depth and range, emotional and ideational, to his probing of cultural dilemmas. From the twelve notes published in *Poetry Ireland Review*, along with the sonnets they comment on, 'Carlow Village Schoolhouse' and 'Gate Lodge' are of special interest here.

'Carlow Village Schoolhouse' (*P*, p. 186) warrants attention for what it says about the poet's paternal ancestors, the part of his heritage about which 'The Pleasure Ground' is mostly silent. Since his paternal antecedents were landless, no counterpart to Milford existed on that side of the family. Diligent searching, however, led the poet to the site of a structure that marked a turning point in the Murphy fortunes, a 'Church of Ireland parish school' in County Carlow, where his great-grandfather, Richard William Murphy, was master. The notes report his ancestor's signature 'as a witness in a marriage register dated July 1845 … when the blight was beginning to blacken the potato fields across Ireland'.[16] The sonnet euphemistically records that the senior Richard Murphy 'sip[ped] / The cauldron soup', the price exacted from Catholics for deliverance from starvation during the Famine. Having thereby embraced Protestantism, he was eligible to serve as schoolmaster and so, again in the words of the sonnet, 'to be freed from bog-dens and sod-huts'.

For the junior Richard Murphy the crucial aftermath of his relative's conversion was a matter of language. Through local inquiry he learned that as schoolmaster his namesake stringently enforced the prohibition against use of the Irish language (an aftermath of the Penal Laws) and required pupils to memorise passages of the King James Bible. Education in English opened the way for subsequent generations of Murphys to advance in post-Famine Ireland and for the poet to matriculate at Oxford. '[T]hat change of language', he declares, 'ultimately gave me the voice with which I speak and write.'[17]

'Gate Lodge' (*P*, p. 202) also turns, in a significant way, on language and education. It finds the poet arriving at Milford on holiday from Canterbury Choir School, where he was a boarding student from age ten to twelve. Six other sonnets in *The Price of Stone* personify aspects of the estate, depicting it as the congenial site of his birth, boyhood memories and childhood mishaps.[18] 'Gate Lodge' stands out for its radically different perspective on Milford, giving voice to descendants of those who, dispossessed of the land, maintain it by their labour. The narrative of Milford's outbuildings is that of humans reduced to their function in a system of land ownership. Their utterance is cryptic, its suppressed resentment rivalling that of the mercenary in *The Battle of Aughrim* who saw himself and his cohorts as manure for the enrichment of others' land.

Physically, the gate lodge looks onto an earlier version of itself:

> I face my forebear's relic, a neat sty
> That hovelled with his brogue some grateful clod
> Unearthed by famine; …

'Sty' commingles humans and animals by virtue of their dwelling place. The *OED* gives two meanings for the term: a literal one, 'a place where swine are kept', and a transferred and figurative sense, 'a human habitation … no better than a pigsty'. As a noun, 'hovel' carries the same two meanings. The adjective 'neat' specifies this sty as a place where cattle, not pigs, are kept, but more to the point it comments with bitter irony on its squalor. Like the gate lodge the sty is humanised by its power of speech – a rustic Irish 'brogue' far removed from Murphy's 'souper choir school' English. At the same time the sty dehumanises its occupants by merging them with the land as 'grateful clod[s]'. 'Clod' familiarly denotes both a crude, unlettered person and a lump of earth. 'Grateful' in an unfamiliar sense means fertile when applied to land (*OED*, 2b). Here, then, fertility applies both to the soil and to the labourer who tills it and has been deprived of it, or 'Unearthed'. We learn from the notes that the barefoot girl who welcomes the young Murphy in the sonnet is one of seven children.

Murphy admonishes himself in the notes that in writing the sonnet he should 'let a voice of conscience address you with a sense of history from an ironical critical view …'.[19] The poet who writes the notes puts irony aside to deal with the problematic relations he bore to the tenants who greeted him on his boyhood arrivals at Milford. The father of the children who live in the gate lodge 'work[ed] day and night in the yard as cowherd and swineherd …'.[20] The 'obsequious' deference he, as member of the landlord's family, received on entering the grounds may well have been given 'to ward off the evil eye of possible eviction …'.[21] Like a guilty party he sifts through evidence in this case of land ownership, hazarding a particularity about Milford exceeding that of earlier published writing. The Millers were 'a Cromwellian family … of humble English origin' who took possession from 'an Irish Catholic family called French … in 1691'. His kinship with the Millers is from his 'mother's father's mother's side'. '[R]ising from upstart gentry', they annexed 'an estate that would grow to seventy thousand acres in Ireland's poorest county … one of the Millers holding for a few early eighteenth-century years the office of High Sheriff'.[22]

Simultaneously, however, the notes to 'Gate Lodge' develop a counterpoint, the excitement Murphy felt on returning home as he moved from the estate's entrance, passed one landmark after another, and arrived at 'my mother's wing of the house'.[23] He ends by articulating a new dimension in his relation to Milford, declaring 'a crux of the sequence … the transfer of love from a person into a place where the person used to be loved …'.[24] The emotion he expresses for his boyhood home rises to a pitch rarely found in his writing. 'There at the entrance to the demesne my love for my mother merged on our homecomings with my love of Milford *in a feeling of ecstasy*' (emphasis added).[25]

The contentment that Murphy evoked in earlier reminiscences of Milford's Pleasure Ground was like the garden itself, set apart, a retreat from history. Together with one strain in the notes, the 'Gate Lodge' sonnet makes Milford the point of entry for a tormented engagement with history. Its buildings and outbuildings and the people who inhabited them summon up stinging remorse over the societal wrongs that delivered ownership of the estate to his family. At the same time, as the locus of overwhelming personal affection, Milford provides an exit point from history's ordeals surpassing in degree and in kind the Pleasure Ground's satisfactions. The notes record a longing for something to transcend this dichotomous relation to history, 'to all of which the "Gate Lodge" speaking as a sonnet might give me access if I listen for a voice that will not have a brogue or a trace of blarney but speak from my conscience and heart'.[26] But that reconciling voice remains, as it did for him and the tourists at Aughrim, unheard. Reminding us that he writes from Knockbrack, the house on Killiney Hill outside Dublin where he lived in the early 1980s, he ends this chapter of notes by acknowledging that events are always producing new aftermaths: 'when the gate lodge keepers' children left Milford, their golden age lay in the future ... after my family lost the East Wing, our golden age lay in reinventing the past'.[27]

The current of aftermath that runs strong in Murphy's poetry would suggest a view of history that is not so much cyclic as regressive. Second growth is inferior to the first; 'progress' becomes deterioration or displacement by things of lesser value. Nearing the conclusion of a lecture at the Yeats International Summer School in Sligo in 2007, Murphy looked back to his own beginnings as a poet, 'at school in England during the war', and enunciated the sense of purpose he formed then: 'to make something that would last about the lives of people I loved'.[28] In closing the 1964 BBC broadcast of 'The Pleasure Ground' he used a characteristic agricultural metaphor to describe his initiation into the art of poetry.[29] By adding a phrase in the 2013 Preface he narrowed the metaphor to one of aftermath and thus assimilated his creativity as a poet into the troubled process of growth and regrowth that he discerned in history. 'I didn't imagine it would take so long and be so difficult to produce a first crop *or a last*' (*P*, p. 16, emphasis added).

9

'In a paradise for white gods he grows old': The instability of pastoral space in Richard Murphy's 'The God Who Eats Corn'

MICHAEL A. MOIR, JR

In the early 1960s the British Empire folded up shop in most of south-eastern Africa, leaving behind a number of fledgling nations that struggled to forge a new identity for themselves in the wake of the departure of the long-time colonial presence that had determined the borders of their countries and managed their affairs, sometimes humanely (if paternalistically), sometimes savagely, for seventy years. The poet Richard Murphy's father, William Lindsay Murphy, was a colonial servant of the former type, dedicated to what he perceived as the civilising humanitarian mission of the empire. He spent the last years of his life on a plantation in what was then Southern Rhodesia (now Zimbabwe), where he ran a school for local children. The poem Richard Murphy wrote in 1963 to commemorate his father, 'The God Who Eats Corn', is deeply ambivalent about its subject's participation in the larger colonial project. While the poem makes it clear that William Lindsay Murphy acts from pure and noble motives and does not share the vicious political opinions of his more aggressively racist white neighbours, it also takes him to task for creating a pastoral zone of 'empire in miniature', where the values of the conqueror are allowed to propagate unchallenged. The larger problem for the elder Murphy, though, is the ephemeral nature of pastoral retreats; the safety of a pastoral zone is created by artificial conditions that must eventually fail, and by the end of the poem it is clear that the 'Imperial Pastoral' in which W.L. Murphy lives is not only threatened but dying.

Murphy's work has received little critical attention of late, and most of this has been devoted to the poem with which 'The God Who Eats Corn' was first published, *The Battle of Aughrim* (1968). 'The God Who Eats Corn' was originally commissioned by *The Sunday Times* in 1963 to mark the break-up of the Central African Federation of Rhodesia and the birth of Zambia and Malawi as independent states. Murphy's fee was a round-trip ticket to Rhodesia, and while *The Sunday Times* did pay, it elected not to publish the poem, which was subsequently picked up by the BBC for broadcast (see *K*, pp. 212–15). The two poems appeared together in *The Battle of Aughrim*, then again in the 1975 US edition of Murphy's collection *High Island: new and selected poems*. Both are concerned with the poet's heritage; *The Battle of Aughrim* is about his distant forebears (he claims ancestors on both the Jacobite and Williamite sides), while 'The God Who Eats Corn' is about his own father's retirement to a plantation in Southern Rhodesia. Though Murphy himself was born in County Mayo, his father spent a lifetime serving the empire in its colonies. Murphy is, as James D. Brophy reminds us, the 'grandson of two Church of Ireland bishops, the son of the Mayor of Colombo (Ceylon) and Governor General of the Bahamas ...'.[1] Indeed, Murphy's Anglo-Irish background is sometimes used to explain away the relative lack of critical attention his work receives; in the *Cambridge History of Irish Literature*, Dillon Johnston and Guinn Batten note that

> his poems reinforce the sense that he is an isolated figure, the last Anglo-Irish poet of the planter caste whose poems focus from a controlled distance on the lives of Galway fishermen, tinkers, colonial subjects in Rhodesia or Ceylon or other participants in Ireland's colonial history.[2]

It is this critical distance from his subjects that makes his treatment of colonial spaces particularly interesting.

In the case of 'The God Who Eats Corn' this critical distance comes at the expense of the approval of the father whom the poem was intended to honour. For William Lindsay Murphy, as his son records in *The Kick*, the colonial service had not simply been a job, but a lifelong calling in keeping with his status as a gentleman:

> he had gained first-class honours in classics at Trinity College, Dublin, and had joined the Ceylon Civil Service in 1910, believing that Britain ruled her colonies for the benefit of the natives and set an example to the world. For this reason he had expected the British Empire to last longer than the Roman. (*K*, p. 213)

The elder Murphy is presented by his son as a true believer in the superiority of British civilisation and the benefits (and responsibilities) that British citizenship confers. He was apparently deeply offended by 'The God Who Eats Corn', which seemed to him to mock his years of labour as ultimately pointless and counterproductive; Murphy writes that

> his pride in the British colonial service would not allow him to tolerate what he perceived as criticism of its injustice by one of his sons .... In a tone of injury, he said: 'I think the trouble with the poem is that you don't love Africa.' (*K*, p. 214)

The son's critical attitude, according to the father, is the result of an affected distance from his subject. Sir William equates imperialism in its more benevolent guise with 'love', itself an indication of the privileged bubble within which white settlers lived. The younger Murphy cannot believe in the fantasy because he does not 'love Africa' in the way that his father does.

Indeed, like many poets whose connection to Ireland is complicated by their ethnic or confessional origins, Murphy's account of his family background seeks to stress his territorial connection to Irish soil, not to his father's colonial posts. In a 1979 interview with Neal Bowers, Murphy stated that

> By birth I could be described as Anglo-Irish. My name implies
> my Murphy ancestors, most of whom were pure Irish. But my
> mother's side was ultimately of English descent. My mother's
> family were landlords in the [*sic*] County Mayo, and in the 18th
> century they had vast estates. On my father's side, on the other
> hand, at the time of the famine my great-grandfather was school
> master in a tiny village in County Carlow. So I am descended
> really from the two cultures of this country.[3]

This thumbnail sketch of family history is reminiscent of similar
proclamations by other Anglo-Irish poets whose Irishness is
considered somehow 'suspect', ranging from the facetious (MacNeice's
claim that he was descended from Conchubar mac Nessa) to the
defensive (Hewitt's 'Once Alien Here'). Such arguments suggest an
anxiety about *which* Irish people have a claim on the national space,
and that some Protestant writers of English descent attempt to stake out
territory largely by conforming to a definition of Irishness formulated
by Catholic nationalists rather than presenting an alternative way of
being 'Irish', as in the preceding examples of MacNeice and Hewitt,
whose claims to Irish identity are couched in conditions set by the
Catholic majority. The cosmopolitan internationalist MacNeice does
not seem much bothered by this dilemma, and Hewitt's socialism
aligns him as much with the working classes as with any ethnic or
sectarian identity. Murphy, though, is perhaps the most eloquent
contemporary representative of the Anglo-Irish landlords who have
now all but vanished, and the vexed history of his class intersects
with an attachment to homeland in a way that produces a unique
approach to the construction of space.

The world that the 'god' represents has, in fact, already disappeared,
and it is only the walls he has constructed around his plantation that
sustain his vision:

> Tall in his garden, shaded and brick-walled,
> He upholds the manners of a lost empire.   (*P*, p. 107)

The plantation, the school, the fields and the values of the empire are all artificial constructs placed in a spatial and cultural context that cannot and will not absorb them; the only way to keep them alive is to bar the door, keeping the destabilising forces of the 'real world' at bay. While Murphy's father has built something more like an Edenic imperial paradise (if a paternalistic one), most of his neighbours, clearly less well-intentioned, protect their own profit-making enterprises with guns and police rather than with brick walls and the Greek classics. This attempt to build a Rhodesian utopia is doubly doomed, as it ignores both the brutal realities of colonialism and the resentment of the native population.

The planter's attempt to create an 'island' of Western culture in the middle of Rhodesia is emblematic of what Brophy calls the central theme of Murphy's poetry from *Sailing to an Island* (1963) to *High Island* (1974), 'the need for a homeland or home and the requisite search for it'.[4] The problem for the Anglo-Irish colonial servant is, perhaps, that he is not really 'at home' anywhere. Irish by birth, English by heritage, spending most of his adult life in service abroad, Sir William can only make a 'home' for himself by imposing his will upon his surroundings, a process Edward W. Soja outlines in *Postmodern Geographies*:

> Territoriality ... refers to the production and reproduction of spatial enclosures that not only concentrate interaction ... but also intensify and enforce its boundedness ... Regional differentiation within and between locales is in turn the setting for a contingent regionalism, an active consciousness and assertive-ness of particular regions, *vis-à-vis* other regions, as territorial and social enclosures. As an expression of the territoriality of locales, regionalism is grounded in the geography of power.[5]

Planted in an unfamiliar region, the settler must demonstrate his power over the locale and over anyone who already happens to live there in order to set his own territorial boundaries. This display of power creates a 'micro-geography of human interaction hinging around the portable bubbles of personal space zonation and "proxemic" behavior', or 'portable ego'.[6] The integrity of the settler's territory is dependent upon his ability to project his own authority outward from his person, or its symbolic equivalent – a plantation, for example.

Such symbolic enclosures seem to be a central feature of Murphy's conception of Anglo-Irish life. In a 1963 essay, 'The Pleasure Ground', Murphy describes his grandfather's garden as a pastoral space, walled off from the troubles of the outside world to allow its inhabitants to experience a sense of freedom through separation:

> The whole garden was surrounded by an Anglo-Irish wall, a great wall of pride and oppression, liberally overgrown with romantic ivy. For years the place had been neglected. Many things had improved in Ireland, but this garden of the ascendancy had declined like the family fortune. A laurel forest now covered the lawn except for a patch kept trimmed by rabbits round the trunk of the beech tree. The yew hedge, where the daughters of high sheriffs had decorously flirted, was now a dark row of trees, and the walks were impassable with briars. My mother devoted herself to restoring this pleasure ground.[7]

It is especially telling that Murphy refers to the garden's boundary as an 'Anglo-Irish' wall, as if there is something peculiarly Anglo-Irish about the very practice of building walls. The garden itself is clearly a kind of fairy-tale demesne, full of beauty and a hint of sexuality while housing within its borders hints of 'danger' – the 'dark row of trees' and the 'walks … impassable with briars'. Indeed, these demonstrate that not only is movement into and out of the garden restricted by the presence of a wall covered by the 'romantic ivy' of nostalgia, but that movement *within* the garden is also impaired. The sense of 'freedom' that it imparts is illusory; however much the generation that inherits the garden may want to rehabilitate it, it is a 'portable ego' that decays and breaks up the further it is removed in time from the builder who first shaped it.

Pastoral has traditionally been connected to nostalgia for a lost time and place – the Alexandrian Greek poet Theocritus, who invented the form, wrote about his birthplace on the remote, rural island of Cos (one of the trees in the planter's garden, a plane tree which he planted himself, comes from Cos in what is probably not mere coincidence), and Andrew V. Ettin notes in *Literature and the Pastoral* that the golden age of English pastoral occurs in the 'Augustan and Renaissance periods', which 'were ... eras of the villa, the comfortably rural home in which society and nature, elegance and simplicity, can be joined'.[8] The 'god' in this poem aims for just such a kind of nostalgic simplicity, intellectually connecting his plantation in Africa with the 'Big House' in Ireland where he was born:

> Last thing at night he checks the rain-gauge
> Remembering his father on a rectory lawn.   (*P*, p. 108)

It is this combination of nostalgia and ignorance of developments in the world outside of the plantation walls that makes this a version of pastoral, in addition to the instability of the idyll; as Ettin argues, 'The pastoral realm takes its meaning from its vulnerable borders',[9] and the colonist who builds a westernised paradise in the middle of Rhodesia and fails to acknowledge the violence at the heart of the colonial enterprise is, in the end, defenceless against the historical forces that will destroy the Rhodesian colony.

Murphy has earned for himself a reputation among critics as a 'builder' of unique poetic spaces, and Terence Brown connects this tendency to Murphy's Anglo-Irish background:

> ... Anglo-Ireland was a splendid colonial caste which built heroically, amidst a somewhat dishevelled landscape, monuments to its own magnificence. Clearing a demesne and building a great house were claims to possession and permanence.[10]

Murphy demonstrates his awareness of the mentality of the colonist in a note dated 1 April 1969, just after he purchased High Island:

> Buying an island, even with the intention of creating a wild life sanctuary, is a predatory act among predators, much easier than writing a book. Once you become the owner, your view

of the island alters: you turn possessive and protective. People regard you as a different person – a man who owns an island and therefore must be rich. But I know that High Island can never be possessed because it will always remain in the possession of the sea. Its virtue will grow from its contemplation not its use, from feelings and ideas evoked by its wild life and its end of the world terrain.   (*K*, p. 250)

Murphy acquires this land through a legal purchase, not through conquest, but he still shows that he is tempted by the idea of 'possessing' a parcel of land and shaping it to his own ends. He tries to short-circuit the colonialist fantasy by turning the island into a wildlife sanctuary, allowing it to return to the condition of unclaimed wild space, yet using the island as a protected refuge for animals requires the construction of another kind of pastoral space. Outside forces that might threaten the wildlife on the island must be held at bay artificially. The island is no longer the 'possession of the sea', much as Murphy might wish that it was.

In the case of 'The God Who Eats Corn', meanwhile, the demesne clearing and house building occur not in Ireland but in the colony of Rhodesia. The colonist in this case is a planter, twice removed from his national inheritance and planting himself in a life-world to which he has no organic connection. Indeed, however kind the colonist's intentions may be, the space on which he builds is cleared and ordered for him by violence, the space of Western European imperialist history, as described by Henri Lefebvre in *The Production of Space*:

> Violence is in fact the very lifeblood of this space, of this strange body. A violence sometimes latent, or preparing to explode; sometimes unleashed, and directed now against itself, now against the world; and a violence everywhere glorified in triumphal arches … gates, squares and prospects.[11]

The apparently benign spaces built by Murphy's father – his garden, his school, his farm – are legacies of this violence, and as such present only an illusory safety against the anti-colonial violence that lurks just outside the plantation.

It is to violence and disorder that, ultimately, these spaces will return. Murphy's note on the poem describes his father's project and his efforts to leave the land better than he found it, but the practices of his white neighbours and the simmering resentment of the dispossessed conspire to tear the idyll apart:

> He [Murphy's father] … settled in Southern Rhodesia in 1950 on virgin land, where he and [his wife] established a farm, and built a school to educate 250 children of farm workers through seven grades. There were no schools in the area, and the policy of white settlers was to keep Africans ignorant in order to ensure a supply of cheap, submissive, manual labourers …. The poem was written in Ireland in the second half of 1963, when direct colonial rule by Britain ended in central Africa with the emergence of Zambia and Malawi, which [Sir William] approved.[12]

Murphy's description of the land as 'virgin' elides any guilt by association with more violent settlement practices, implying that the land was unoccupied and unused before his father arrived. Indeed, he goes to great lengths to show that his father was not complicit in colonialist culture, despite his history as an imperial official, by noting that decolonisation had Sir William's blessing. In the final section of the poem,[13] however, it becomes clear that the private world he has carefully built up will not survive without him:

> They say, when the god goes, the rain falls,
> Contour ridges burst, sweeping off crops,
> The rafters crumble, trees shoot through floors,
> And wind carves the fields into smooth dust-heaps.[14]

The presence of the 'god' – that is, the white colonist – seems to be the only thing that prevents natural forces – the rain, the trees, the wind – from obliterating the built environment and turning it into a wasteland. When the 'god' disappears, the 'virgin' land will not be returned to its unspoiled splendour, but will instead be despoiled and rendered useless.

Meanwhile, the 'god' ignores both the aggressive chatter of the other settlers and the pent-up rage of his own employees – 'Thunder is pent in the drums of the compound' (*P*, p. 108) – preferring instead his own scholarly and philanthropic endeavours, pursued even as his world threatens to come apart around him:

> The trees that fail are soon devoured by ants.
> Sundowners bind together a white crowd:
> Some preach of partners, more sneer at the Munts
> Getting cheeky, lazier than ever. He's bored.

> While he prepares to fly to Ithaca,
> The BSA police hold rifle drill,
> Pyres kindle under *Pax Britannica*.
> He stays to build a club-room for the school.[15]

There is a lot of denial in the 'god's' attitude here. His response to his neighbours' racism is mere boredom; while he may not share their views, he does nothing to correct them, and is just as bound 'together' as everyone else by their shared predicament being part of 'a white crowd' in an African country. As he improves his school and reflects on his own classical education, the police are preparing for violence as the unstable peace provided by the might of the empire is laid in its grave.

The poem provides us with frequent reminders that it is only the waning might of the empire that props up this plantation and the pastoral space it represents. Few of the trees in the 'god's' garden are native to Africa, and all have been planted by visitors – the Queen Mother, a fellow governor, important missionaries. The majority of the trees come from other parts of the world, many of them erstwhile British colonial possessions: 'cypress' from Asia, 'copper beech' from Europe and 'silver oak' (*P*, p. 103) from Australia (the beech donated by 'a chairman of mines', the 'silver oak … trowelled by a Governor', and both reminders of the reasons the British were in Rhodesia in the first place); there is also a plane tree planted by the settler himself, 'brought as a seed from Cos', the Greek Island where Theocritus, inventor of the pastoral idyll in verse, was born. While the trees are planted by foreigners, it is the native population that must care for them and ensure that they thrive:

> In honour among watersprays that spin
> Rainbows to keep alive old English roses
> Hand-weeded by a docile piccanin
> The Queen Mother's cypress nods in a straw hood.   (*P*, p. 103)

Murphy writes in his accompanying note that the poem 'deploys with irony the diction of the period to voice the mindsets and politics of the period, whether racist, revolutionary, multicultural or democratic';[16] that the racist term 'piccanin' appears in this context demonstrates the subservience to colonial authority and colonial labelling that the maintenance of the plantation requires. While working within dominated space, the African gardener is a 'piccanin' or a 'kaffir' (*P*, p. 104) or a 'munt' – that is, he or she is called by names chosen by the colonist when in the colonist's space. 'Munt' is a word of unknown provenance used in Zimbabwe by white people to refer to black people; 'piccanin' is derived from Portuguese, and usually refers to a black child. 'Kaffir', meanwhile, is a corruption of an Arabic word that means 'stranger' or 'unbeliever'. Through this process of renaming, the native population of Rhodesia is reduced to a band of childlike strangers in their own land.

These three phases of spatial practice – 'virgin land', dominated/colonised space, and the 'wasteland' that will replace the 'god's' plantation – align with the varieties of spatial practice defined by Lefebvre in *The Production of Space*. The 'virgin land' on which the colonist settles is presented here as what Lefebvre calls 'absolute space', or 'natural space … populated by political forces. Typically, architecture picked a site in nature and transferred it to the political realm by means of a symbolic mediation …',[17] usually a statue or some other such artificial representation of the power to whom the space is now consecrated. In this case the 'symbolic mediation'[18] is provided by the foreign trees and flowers provided by important and powerful visitors, which must now be tended by native workers.

This '*Absolute space*' is thus transformed into the spatial practice that Lefebvre calls '*representations of space*' (italics in original), which tends to view space as something to be tamed and controlled through a system of signs. This is the tightly managed space of authority; Lefebvre defines it as

> conceptualized space, the space of scientists, planners, urbanists, technocratic subdividers and social engineers, as of a certain type of artist with a scientific bent – all of whom identify what is lived and what is perceived with what is conceived ... This is the dominant space in any society (or mode of production). Conceptions of space tend, with certain exceptions ... towards a system of verbal (and therefore intellectually worked out) signs.[19]

The racist terms used to describe the African workers are one example of a verbal sign used to dominate the planned-out spaces of the plantations; the 'labelled' trees are another (*P*, p. 103). The white settlers also seek more aggressive symbols of their ascendancy – 'a gunboat', 'silk flags and showers of assegais'.[20] The 'god's' school is another such symbol of cultural imperialism; it is labelled with a symbol of Britain's fading authority – 'A Union Jack droops on the school flag-pole' (*P*, p. 104) – and the texts taught in the school are Western classics – Homer, Horace, the Bible. The promise of Western learning is described as something akin to magic which entices the Africans out of their accustomed environment:

> Children are chanting hymns, their lean bodies
> Tropically sensual behind puritan desks,
> From mealie plot and swamp of tsetse flies
> Lured by the power of the god's mechanics.   (*P*, p. 107)

The 'Tropically sensual' bodies are naturally at odds with the 'puritan desks' and the singing of hymns; while the 'power' of the school is attractive to the students, it is clear that it is also an alien imposition, a collection of imperial symbols that rubs uncomfortably against their everyday experience.

The last stanza of each section typically reminds the reader of the disjunction between the intended meaning of a particular space and what it actually means to those who make use of it. Lefebvre characterises these disjunctions '*Representational spaces*' [his italics], or

> space as directly *lived* [Lefebvre's emphasis] through its associated images and symbols, and hence the space of 'inhabitants' and 'users', but also of some artists and perhaps of those, such as a few writers and philosophers, who *describe* [Lefebvre's emphasis] and aspire to do no more than describe. This is the dominated – and hence passively experienced – space which the imagination seeks to change and appropriate. It overlays physical space, making symbolic use of its objects. Thus representational spaces may be said, though again with certain exceptions, to tend towards more or less coherent systems of non-verbal symbols and signs.[21]

'*Representational spaces*' are symbolic spaces as interpreted by, and filtered through, the perceptions of ordinary people. The students in the schoolroom, for example, do not experience the space in the way the planner/teacher expects them to, largely because the planner has constructed a space that reinforces and validates cultural constructs that are alien to them. When 'representations of space' and 'representational space' are mismatched in such a way, the most likely outcome is a kind of misprision. The students in the 'god's' school may very well absorb what he is trying to teach them, but it will not be expressed in a way that replicates the white-man's culture. Rather, they will form a reading of space that combines what they are taught here with what experience and tradition have already taught them.

The schooling these children receive serves as kindling for the revolutionary impulse that will erase the protected private space of the plantation from existence. Murphy describes this process in the fourth section,[22] drawing attention to the inflammability of the space and of the Africans who are taught in the school:

> A red-hot poker flowers in the playground,
> A viper sleeps on the sand. The dry slate
> Under the sweating palm is rubbed and scrawled.
> They wait like logs, ready for fire and wind.   (*P*, p. 107)

The conditions are set for conflagration. All they require is something to light a spark – something like the friction produced by writing on their slates, which are 'dry' like kindling. The school ends up sharpening the students' sense of dispossession and resentment rather than reinforcing their loyalty to any imperial ideal, or even to Western cultural models.

By the poem's conclusion we see that the attempts of the settlers to 'plant' (*P*, p. 106) themselves in African soil is a failure, that their clearance of plants and wildlife is fruitless – 'drought followed flooding' (*P*, p. 106) – and their attempts to alter the fundamental nature of '*Absolute space*' have come to nothing:

> On the game-cleared plateau the settlers say
> 'This is our home: this is white man's country.'
> Dust-storms gather to hide their traces
> Under boulders balanced in a smouldering sky.[23]

The alliteration that balances the final line ('boulders balanced' paired with 'smouldering sky') indicates that the natural world responds to radical change by restoring space to a kind of stasis. The 'game-cleared plateau' can't be restored, but the footprints of the invader can be obliterated. Nothing built or planted by the colonising culture is here regarded as permanent; everything they do contributes to their own expulsion from the artificial Eden they have constructed. This idyll, like all idylls, is at best temporary.

'The God Who Eats Corn' reminds us that, however humane the intent of the individual colonist, colonialism is always founded on the violent seizure of territory and the imposition of an alien character upon it. It is only the will of the colonist that holds together the idyll against both natural cycles and the hostility of the dispossessed natives. The colonist rules through symbolic projections of power which attain a new force and a new meaning when they are taught to the colonised. These symbols, no longer exclusive, cease to protect the colonist and hasten the downfall of the empire he serves and the pastoral freedom he constructs for himself. The title of the poem plays up the vulnerability of the colonist, despite his power; as Murphy explains in his notes on the poem, the Bantu people of Central Africa called the white man '"the gods who eat corn"' because although 'These gods ... could kill from far off, they ... were subject as humans to hunger, desire, disease and death' (*P*, p. 102). His dominion ends as his body ages and weakens; once shaped by a 'god', the pastoral space he carved out will vanish and return to a state of nature once he is gone. Like all pastoral spaces, this colonial idyll exists but for a short time.

10

~

'Like fish under poetry's beaks': Richard Murphy and Ted Hughes

MARK WORMALD

In August 1987 Richard Murphy wrote to Anne Stevenson a letter containing six single-spaced typewritten pages containing memories of Sylvia Plath and Ted Hughes.[1] It would be published, with slight but as we shall see significant amendments, as the final appendix to *Bitter Fame*, Stevenson's biography of Plath (1989). Earlier in 1987 Hughes' sister and literary agent Olwyn 'had begged [Murphy] to put the Plath myth into perspective by writing with authority about Sylvia and Ted's visit to Connemara' (*K*, p. 208) in September 1962, their last trip together in what was to prove the last autumn of Plath's life. Murphy had demurred, until Hughes himself 'rang and asked' for 'a simple record of the facts' (*K*, p. 208): there were, he said, wild stories circulating among American champions of Plath. Murphy was uniquely placed to scotch those rumours.

Murphy's letter has the precise authority Olwyn had hoped for, drawing on the detailed dated notes he had always taken but had not yet begun to mine for published prose. The version of the text published as memoir two years later still has great power.[2] Indeed, it proved a powerful influence on Murphy himself. It demonstrated to him his skill and appetite for judiciously selective, but revealing literary memoir: little wonder that *The Kick* (2002/2017) absorbs much of this first foray into the genre, returning to it and retouching it with extraordinary care.

This essay traces the remarkable literary fruits of the close and complex friendship and literary relationship between Murphy and

163

Hughes that developed between 1962 and 1987. For all its early traumas, this friendship returned to, and in large part turned on, the scene of this remarkable first visit to Connemara. As well as involving the regular exchange and encouragement of each other's work, it marked at least two major collections of poems, Murphy's *High Island* (1974) and Hughes' *Gaudete* (1977). Perhaps because of the circumstances and tragic aftermath of that visit, the conduct of that friendship needed to rely on discretion, or at least on a succession of private codes, only now detectable among this record of plain fact.

I want to use this memoir, and in particular two moments in it, to expose the larger rhythms of their relationship, which shaped its emphases and its omissions. Without Hughes' friendship, Murphy would never have been approached to write in the first place; he would not have written as he did, or agreed to amend his text under acute and uncomfortable pressure; nor would it have taken its place at the heart of Murphy's *The Kick: a life among writers* or enabled that book's conclusion. Throughout, to borrow Murphy's description of another visitor to Connemara, 'Words began weirdly to take off inwards' (*P*, p. 43).

For all that, though, Ted Hughes was inevitably a secondary focus of Murphy's first short and precisely titled 'Memoir of Sylvia Plath and Ted Hughes on a Visit to the West of Ireland in 1962'. Murphy had watched and long been pained by the growth of what Hughes came to call 'the Plath fantasia'.[3] Murphy's papers at Tulsa include fascinating detailed notes of an interview he gave in New York in April 1974 to the journalist Harriet Rosenstein. Eighteen months after Robin Morgan had published *Monster*, in which her poem 'Arraignment' accused Hughes of mind-rape and murder, and six months after an English edition began to circulate, Murphy was determined to place on record his sense of the occlusion of Hughes by Plath during that same visit, and to re-establish what he saw as a sense of literary perspective: 'Ted wrote much better than Sylvia did.' He also spoke more sense, if fewer words:

> Her conversation was really much more violent than his. And there was much more of it; he could hardly get a word in

edgeways; she would take the words out of his mouth. Answer questions for him. [During the Cleggan visit] I was hoping to hear Ted more and he was very silent.⁴

Murphy went on to celebrate the controlled energy of Hughes' poetry, and his 'marvellous tenderness, love, love of children, and kindness'. But the interview was never published. Olwyn Hughes' approach in 1987 gave Murphy a second chance firmly to establish how, in those days in Connemara, Plath had, in her conversations with those locals she met in Cleggan and on Inishbofin and in her actions, 'sowed in [their minds] a few seeds of the future myth of her martyrdom'.⁵ Their marriage in crisis, its creative energy drained, and with Hughes contemplating a stay in Spain, Plath told Murphy she was looking for independence and creative space in a place which 'she seemed to have fallen in love with ... at first sight'.⁶ But 'alarmed' by her suggestion that she might rent the Old Forge, relegating him to the status of lodger in his own home, Murphy had found Plath a local house to rent for six months where she might write and live, and that same evening he summoned his friend Thomas Kinsella to come and help defuse the tension. Plath pressed on, on what turned out to be the last night of their abbreviated stay, in a move which Murphy had decided not to share with Rosenstein in 1974, when he had alluded only to Sylvia's intimacy with him as 'conversational', but which he now decided to expose: 'in the presence of Ted and Tom, though not noticed by them, Sylvia rubbed her leg against mine under the table, provocatively. It made me inwardly recoil.'⁷ Sylvia's 'secret sign', as Murphy described it, evoked an altogether too familiar friction.⁸ Murphy had himself endured the dire consequences of a literary guest overstepping the mark in 1957 on a visit and, in seducing Patricia Avis, prompting the break-up of their marriage. This was much more than the invasion of the literary territory which, in subsequent angry letters, Plath claimed Murphy feared; it was a more intimate violation of his hospitality, his past, his own deepest affiliations.

And that is perhaps why Murphy later felt able to use it for his own purposes. In *The Kick* he made this moment fit another larger pattern: the pattern suggested by his title. Murphy's second version of what happened during that dinner on 15 September reads: 'Sometime during the meal, Sylvia gave me a gentle kick under the table' (*K*, p. 205). Readers of *The Kick* who know what this instance of its central trope replaced are well placed to see how the invasion of self has become Murphy's to realign. We may begin to understand the ambivalence in the comment with which, in *The Kick*, he reflects once more on the aftermath of that night: his discovery, on his return from a day's sailing, that Hughes had left suddenly to go south to find trout or salmon fishing with Barrie Cooke in County Clare, and his own decision to tell Sylvia that she would therefore need to return to Dublin with Thomas Kinsella fuelled by a suspicion that Sylvia 'might have encouraged [Hughes] to go'.[9] 'For a long time afterwards, guilt haunted me for not having given Sylvia the haven she felt she needed in Connemara; and sometimes I felt angry at being made to feel guilty' (*K*, p. 208).

Comparing *The Kick* with Murphy's first published 'Memoir' provides another reason for Murphy's guilt. In his letter to Olwyn Hughes, Murphy had recalled the visit they had paid with fifteen-year-old Seamus Coyne to Yeats' tower at Ballylee, then in disrepair, on the first full day of their visit. As Murphy explained to Anne Stevenson in a letter from August 1987, and as he recalls in *The Kick*, Yeats delivered unexpected fruit. Plath and Hughes insisted that they get Seamus to climb an old apple tree and shake free its apples for a winter's worth of apple pie; Murphy 'protested', but his own 'objections were brushed aside. Ted said, very quietly and firmly: "The only thing to do, when you come to a place like this, is to violate it".[10] When Olwyn read Ted this draft, both agreed that it would clearly be disastrous to provide one more reason, amid the ongoing Plath fantasia, to regard him as desecrator. So Hughes wrote to Murphy, in a letter of 7 October 1987 not yet found among the extensive correspondence at Tulsa, explaining that his remark had been nothing more than a facetious joke; according to Murphy he 'regretted not having spoken about the golden apples of the sun, the silver apples of the moon' (*K*, p. 208). Murphy took note, though declining to give Hughes all the credit for the allusion. Rather than risk losing that friendship for the sake of a sentence, he instead took six months to find his own way to 'gloss the gap', as he put it in *The Kick* (*K*, p. 208). The text of the revised memoir dated February 1988 reads:

> my objections were brushed aside by Ted very firmly, as if these were not mere cookers but
>> The silver apples of the moon.
>> The golden apples of the sun.[11]

Scrumping had become an act of licensed poetic homage; but in an unkempt garden of apple trees and rhubarb bushes from which 'The rhetoric of the owners had disappeared', as Murphy wrote in a review of Yeats' 'Explorations' published in *The Observer* within a month of their visit;[12] 'The Song of Wandering Aengus' had still been flourished to provide appropriate rhetorical cover for wandering Ted.

Over the next fifteen years Hughes and Murphy overcame the trauma of that first visit to Cleggan, and forged a strong poetic friendship. Murphy was careful to reveal the origins of that friendship in his account of their first meeting. In July 1961 Plath and Hughes were within six weeks of their own move from London to the country, to North Tawton, Devon. For Hughes that meant the country of the two rivers, the Taw and the Torridge, which had furnished his imagination ever since he read Henry Williamson's *Tarka the Otter* at school in Mexborough. Murphy's recollection of their first conversation that month, in a restaurant near the Mermaid Theatre in London, was that 'Our talk was more about living in the country, fishing and the sea, than about poetry.'[13] But for neither poet were the poles of these exchanges mutually exclusive. On the contrary. Hughes had published *The Hawk in the Rain* (1957) and, in *Lupercal* (1960), 'Pike', a poem which made vividly present his teenage fishing. Though Murphy had not yet settled on a definitive text of 'Sailing to an Island', that poem had already appeared in at least three earlier versions since 1953, and a fourth would appear in *The Listener* the following month.[14] And he was already living his own version of a life exposed to poetry and rural landscapes and communities on which Hughes and Plath were themselves only just embarking, in their move to Court Green and Tarka country. Hughes' essay on 'Tarka the

Otter' appeared in September 1962 in *The Sunday Times*, the weekend after his flight from Connemara for Clare. 'Once you are wandering about in the open, hunted, the countryside reveals itself as the place from which we in the city are hiding.'[15] Murphy cited his own 'desire to … stay away from big cities' as one reason for his own move to Cleggan in 1959 (*K*, p. 108).

They had something more particular in common, as an apparently contingent detail Murphy supplies makes clear. He explains that it was his next contact with Plath that led to his offering the invitation to visit Cleggan that she and Ted eventually took up, and that this contact came about as a result of the Cheltenham literature festival, for whose poetry prize she was one of the judges that same year, 1961. Murphy had entered 'The Cleggan Disaster' under the pseudonym 'Fisherman'. 'The poem celebrates a fisherman who survived by holding on to his nets instead of giving up the struggle', Murphy's 'Memoir' records.[16] Those consecutive details are deliberate choices, not just poetic self-representation but also a quiet mark of his affiliation with a poet whose work Murphy recognised, in a review of Hughes' *Season Songs* (1976), as blessed with the kind of vision that enabled him to see salmon in a river when others saw none.[17] A similar nod towards an imaginative sympathy with Hughes is the detail Murphy also supplies of the conversation in the van on the way to Coole Park and then Thoor Ballylee, to which he was at least as attentive as he was to the talk of 'marriage and divorce' with which Plath was occupying Murphy as he drove: in the back 'Ted talked about poachers and guns and fishing to Seamus [Coyne], who was fifteen years old.'[18] And then, of course, after an evening of ouija poetry, and while Richard was out with his own boats, Ted left, after having told Murphy rather more privately about the loss of creativity in their marriage, for an alternative source of inspiration, the detail of which is worth repeating: he 'had gone to stay with Barrie Cooke, the painter, in County Clare, where he was hoping to do some trout or salmon fishing'.[19] A quarter of a century on, Murphy had come to realise that, in acting as he did, Hughes was following an imperative, a path, with which he could and should sympathise; so when Hughes suggested, after hearing Murphy read him his memoir over the telephone, that at Yeats' tower he should have mentioned Yeats' golden and silver apples as justification of his violation of this territory, he was himself responding entirely appropriately to Murphy's coded signals in that memoir about the importance of this imaginative territory and way of thinking for Hughes. For of course if 'The Song of Wandering Aengus' ends with those 'golden' and 'silver apples', it begins with 'a fire in my head' that sent him fishing.

Now, Hughes, of course, is not Yeats, and Yeats, of course, is not Aengus. But Yeats' hero goes fishing with a desperate if slightly implausible ingenuity, in the context of an Irish mythography in which the salmon of knowledge feeds on a hazel nut that has fallen into his pool so that the little silver trout he catches is always going to be more than just a trout. The girl Aengus' trout became when he turned his back on it to kindle the flames to cook it is never named, but wasted no time calling to him, and is still calling him on, as an old man; he resolves to

> ... find out where she has gone,
> And kiss her lips and take her hands;

Only then, after that semi-colon – though the poem leaves tantalisingly unclear whether what follows is success or continuing frustration   will he walk among the long grass 'and pluck till time and times are done'.[20] In writing this memoir in 1987, Murphy was careful to record, in his own account of Hughes' comments on the change his marriage had undergone, who else the girl beyond his fishing trip in County Clare might have become: 'Assia's name was not mentioned, but her role was implied.'[21] Her power did not remain implicit for long. As *The Kick* makes clear, Assia's 'Babylonian beauty' made a deep impression on him, in 1963, when she, too, visited Cleggan a few months after Sylvia's death, with her husband David Wevill (*K*, p. 208). This visit may well have had another, albeit subsidiary, role in easing the next and, certainly for Hughes, the most fruitful phase of the two poets' relationship.

By then Murphy had moved their friendship onto a more practical and intimate basis. In 1965 he sent Hughes' children Frieda and Nicholas two sweaters knitted by Mrs Coyne in what Hughes appreciated as 'that wild heath-grass green!', and successive versions of a poem he had written 'For Sylvia Plath'.[22] Hughes' response to this generosity was swift, and heartfelt, recognising and responding to Murphy's attempts at the poetry of aftermath. Hughes had been experimenting, too, struggling to escape, express or transmute aspects of his personal experience. Alongside some 'Journalism' he dismissed as a 'waste of application', his letter mentions two radio plays: one, *The Wound*, was a surreal return to the terrain of his own father's war experience; the other, *Difficulties of a Bridegroom*, was 'a highly poetical & theatrical work' which 'began as a grand demolishing of in-laws'. Hughes could sympathise with the ethical as well as aesthetic 'difficulties' which Murphy had evidently shared with him in struggling to write a poem in her memory, and was grateful for his friend's tact: 'I was going to ask you to delete the mention of the way she died – though it's common enough knowledge, it's not actually publicised', citing, as he did so, the children's vulnerability to discussion of a mother who was already 'such a spectacularly public figure'.[23] This was, of course, six years before Al Alvarez's decision to publish his own memoir of Plath's death and the even more difficult period of often hostile public scrutiny, which Hughes endured in dignified reticence until, in the 1980s, he began to publish the poems collected in *Birthday Letters* (1998).

But it is Hughes' response to the latest poetic meditation on surviving aftermath that provides the clearest indication that these two emphatically different poets would soon once more tread the same poetic territory. The night before, Thom Gunn's long poem 'Misanthropos' had been performed on the Third Programme of the BBC; its producer, Douglas Cleverdon, had already commissioned *The Battle of Aughrim*.[24] Gunn's poem, in four parts, was, Hughes says, 'about the last man – after a war. A quite simple schema', but one which strikingly anticipates that of Hughes' own *Crow*, which Hughes later revealed began life that same year, 1965: 'he first of all wants to destroy his consciousness, the vile human machine of sophistical errors', while honouring 'the minimal virtues – to keep control, to guide one's actions with a modest balance, surrendering

to no mystery or ideology etc. He becomes an animal.'[25] Lines in
'Misanthropos' echo Hughes' own 'Wodwo'; so, strikingly, would
Murphy's 'Rapparees', one of the sections Hughes would read from
The Battle of Aughrim when it was broadcast in 1968. The lovely lines
Seamus Heaney criticised for Murphy's recourse to 'indelibly English',
that is, unforgivably un-Irish choice of avian imagery[26] – those wild
mercenaries could shift shape and element, from bird to beggar, otter
to pikeman coming to land, and then again 'mingle like a nightjar /
Into the earth, into the air, into the water' (*P*, p. 83) – sound, when read
by Hughes, like Murphy's knowingly exact response to the elements
his friend's creature of earth and air had slipped between. And that
spirit of unexpected close comradeship and collaboration is present
in Hughes' description of the unexpected common cause that Gunn's
last man comes to discover. 'He finally meets other men – & by a
spontaneous act of sympathy for one of them (who is slightly hurt)
recognises his own instinct for community with them.' Gunn's last
man discovers, at last, 'his total commitment to mankind, in a spirit
of friendship – a solidarity against the nothingness & the merely
bestial & the irrational etc. Roughly that.' Formally, too, Hughes
admires the 'strength and virtue' of Gunn's conceptual schema as it
finds linguistic expression:

> it's [*sic*] theoretical procedure goes on in very pure language,
> interesting verse, & certain pure, clear, lovely pattern, sane poise,
> & some sort of personal authenticity in the ideas put forward.
> The verse is the mode of the sanity he advocates …[27]

Between nothingness and destructive bestiality, the verse demonstrates that 'it's possible to live balanced & alert'. It is tempting to
compare this high praise with the tribute Hughes would pay three
years later to Murphy's own 'classical strengths' and 'epic objectivity'
on the sleeve notes of Claddagh Records' *The Battle of Aughrim*.

By then they had come to share more than poetic territory.
And the final significance of Hughes' long letter is that he sets
this in motion. Hughes ends by hoping that they might meet, and
by asking Murphy to pass on his good wishes to Mrs Coyne. Five

months after this exchange, at the beginning of September 1965, Hughes wrote to Murphy asking for help in finding somewhere to live in Ireland, and by the sea. A fellowship from the University of Vienna had one stipulation, that 'I simply exercise my poetic talent', and the need for an escape from Court Green, as well as Murphy's recent gesture of friendship, made Connemara the ideal solution.[28] And Murphy obliged by finding a cottage he remembers as Doon Lodge, since significantly extended as Doonreagan,[29] at Cashel on the inlet-wrinkled southern coast of Connemara, where Ted, Assia, Frieda, Nicholas and Shura moved to in early February 1966. From there, at the end of March, again with Murphy's help, they moved to a converted cowshed at Cleggan Farm, and consolidated the rhythm of uninterrupted work established at Doonreagan.

And work he did. Notebooks in the British Library indicate that his long, vividly rising and falling, distinctly unShelleyan 'Skylarks' emerged from it;[30] he was also preparing an expanded version of the most substantial legacy of his earlier period of 'Journalism', the marvellous series of broadcasts on listening and writing for the BBC Schools Education Unit, for publication the following year as *Poetry in the Making*. The adjustments he made to the text incorporated two acknowledgements to Murphy's role in twice offering him a haven. The first might seem something other than a tribute. 'Writing about Landscape' adds a note of local lack of colour not in the original talk as broadcast on 1 May 1964, illustrating the baffling prices people will pay 'to hang very ordinary landscapes, even very dull landscapes, on their living-room walls': now he added, 'like an extra window onto some desolate Connemara landscape'.[31] A change to that chapter's end showed he had done more than look at the view. His concern was now to offer different means to young writers of feeling themselves into landscapes. The broadcast had ended with Plath's own 'Wuthering Heights', which he introduced as 'Not a description of the moors … but of what it feels like to be walking over them'.[32] A new note, addressed to teachers, concedes that children should not be expected 'to write excitedly about landscape in a style as impersonal'. He proposes, first, that pupils need 'release … in some special setting', where they can 'write the monologue of their journey', and then gives seven subjects 'from which at different times I get results'.[33]

But the most powerful contributions to each other's lives and work were those that Murphy and Hughes made in the wake of a new collapse. On 14 May 1969, the day after his mother Edith's death and in the aftermath of the deaths of Assia Wevill and Shura, Hughes invited Murphy, then lecturing at Hull University, to west Yorkshire: Murphy was once more instrumental in helping him find a creative territory. On a walk past Lumb Bank, the farmhouse in the valley below his parents' house at Heptonstall which he had contemplated buying six years before, Murphy prompted him to 'knock on the door and ask the owners if they'd care to sell their house and land' (*K*, p. 252). They named their price and, after being drenched in a thunderstorm, Hughes, regarding the lightning as propitious, took the decision to buy it. That October Hughes wrote to Murphy 'ensconced' at Lumb Bank, and reporting that 'for the first time in my life since that brief spell in Galway I can work for 12 hours a day. So now I'll groom & curry Crow'.[34] He praised Murphy's own new work, reflecting once more on the significance of *The Battle of Aughrim*. It 'was clearly a great thing to have done, for your relationship with modern Ireland'.[35]

Perhaps most significantly he also responded to the latest development in Murphy's life, which must have filled one side of their conversation that May day in west Yorkshire, when he announced his own recent purchase of High Island, concluded on the day of Assia and Shura's funeral, attended by Tony White, on 31 March 1969.

In a note written on his first day as owner of High Island, Murphy had, with uncanny prescience, compared the act of purchase to an act of predation, that would be much easier than writing a book; he also wondered about the distinctly qualified possession it would become, for

> it will always remain in the possession of the sea. Its virtue will grow from its contemplation not its use, from feelings and ideas evoked by its wild life and its end of the world terrain.
>
> (*K*, p. 250)

And Hughes himself responded to the imaginative and specifically poetic potential of this place for Murphy. In an unpublished letter, postmarked 21 July, Hughes declared his intention to buy something, preferably wildlife, for High Island. His first suggestion was 'musk oxen'; in October he wondered about St Kilda mice or foxes.[36] As he put it in that letter in July, 'We would have to be careful just what.'[37] That 'we' is notable: already, vicariously, Hughes was a participant, an investor, in this enterprise, this place, the potential of which he at once saw in relation to Cleggan and Murphy's larger movement to integrate Ireland's past and present:

> ... what will really justify the island is that it's the apotheosis of the poetic world you've been creating, it will let you into the past and spirit of it as nothing else would. It's as if Cleggan, the boats and the house were a reconnaissance for this real conquest. I'm sure it will show up pretty soon.[38]

This extraordinary, visionary statement of imaginative sympathy with Murphy's poetic project was, however, optimistic in one regard, and his encouragement could have felt like pressure. Instinctively generous, Hughes embodied spontaneous and intuitive creativity. And that neo-Romantic bravura must have daunted as much as it impressed a poet we prize for his craft and classicism, who built poems as he had built the Old Forge at Cleggan, from granite recovered from abandoned cottages. As we have seen, the power of what Hughes had told him, in Cleggan in 1966, endured, marking out that letter thirty years later and subsequently finding its way into *The Kick*. Rather than bombard poem with technique, and so threaten to demolish the edifices he was trying to construct, Hughes embodied intense, shamanic, shape-shifting concentration, memorably:

> He'd sit on the edge of a bed and focus his mind on the coccyx or cuckoo bone at the base of his spine, blanking out all other thoughts, until he'd start to feel himself falling and falling as if from a great height through the bed and the floor and the ground, deeper and deeper into the underground, till he'd fall

into a wide-awake trance in which he'd assume the body of
a bird, a beast, a fish, a tree or a stone. The poem from that
depth might take off in ways he could never have consciously
conceived.   (*K*, p. 253)

Even in *The Kick* the contrast between this placed memory and
Murphy's own carefully practical route to High Island – needing
a boat, he said, he bought the 'decaying hull of the boat in which
Pat Concannon … survived the Cleggan Disaster' from Pete Burke,
son of a local boatwright, and asked him to 'build a pookaun on the
model of Pete's relic' – seems loaded, coded: a mark of the distinctive
differences between their two characters as writers (*K*, p. 253). Mark
Kilroy's 1980 essay on Murphy's Connemara locale compared Hughes'
own confident self-myth-making with Murphy's laborious and slow
movement towards an order it took him years to find, in a gradual
process of weighing his own individuality against and through the
past and present of Connemara. Hughes entered animated dialogues
with creatures, became the wildlife and the elements of a landscape
he entered. Murphy's relationship with the elements of his locale
always depended on, and incorporated his interactions with, and
imaginative distance from, the locales and the elements of their life
and work.[39]

At any rate Murphy's own 'real conquest' of High Island, according
to Hughes' criterion, that is, in poetry, did not 'show up soon'. While
Murphy did occupy, as well as find himself possessed by, the island,
making use of its single room in the deserted nineteenth-century
miners' hut and writing vivid and precise journal entries of the ballet
of birds, the night sounds, the flora and fauna, it is inaccurate to
imply, as Eamonn Wall has done, that the poems of *High Island* sprang
immediately from that place, that inspiration implied immediate
composition.[40] The landscape of Murphy's imagination depends on
a combination of immersion and distancing; construction of new
walls, or lines, from reclaimed materials can take a long time. And
some defeated him altogether, requiring him to put an elegant gloss
on his inability to bring verse from the experience. The summer he

spent as a river watcher keeping poachers off the Erriff in 1952 had, he recorded in *The Kick*, long evaded his attempts to bring poems from its pools or flow:

> It was like living in a poem there was no need to write, rich in local memory conserved in the pools' names ... So strong was the river's influence on my senses in the night, and so great the tedium of killing the hours of weariness until dawn, that I never wrote a line that did justice to the river.   (*K*, p. 125)

Though he had spent time on the island, working hard and writing diary entries, *The Kick* suggests that the poems which lend the 1974 volume *High Island* its significance had not yet emerged by the time Hughes brought his new wife Carol and the two children back to Cleggan. This visit followed a reading tour, in March 1971, the two poets had made to the US, to coincide with the American publication of *Crow*.[41] Tony White managed the tour, and during it he and Hughes had witnessed Murphy's pain at not being able to write: so they collaborated to devise an ingenious, as well as amusing, method of helping Murphy with what, even for such a lapidary writer, had become the wrong kind of writer's block. Hughes and White both gave him lists of themes, Hughes' containing fifteen subjects, White's ten, along with advice designed to challenge the craftsman's lapidary care, and to exchange it for flow. Write fast, they urged, not stopping to search for the right word; and take care, also, to mine the rich darkness of the night, by praying to the goddess of the night last thing before the next morning's plunge into words on the theme assigned for the day. For any theme not tackled, any failure to keep to this schedule of compelled fluency, forfeits were to be paid in champagne. In *The Kick* Murphy credits this method as being 'helpful', as he had done in that letter to Hughes of 1996; he followed it, and completed the course of themes once back at Cleggan that spring of 1971. But he also claims that 'none of the twenty-five themes resulted in a publishable poem' (*K*, p. 269).

Readers who first encountered *High Island* as I did, after the publication of the letter containing Hughes' list of suggestions in

Christopher Reid's edition of his letters, might raise an eyebrow at that claim of Murphy's. A number of these 'starting points' are resonant. The second in the list is 'A congregation of gulls, storm petrels, seals – the text, the service'. The third is 'The voice in the well'. High Island is named in seven of these exercises, which ask Murphy to consider it as a woman, as a man, as the tenor of 'Fifty metaphors', and as both orchestra and choir. The island becomes the subject of a litany, and those who threaten it: one exercise contemplates St Feicín's 'curse on desecrators'. Some themes accommodate this while clearly responding to concerns of Murphy's: Christ's journey with the cross is adapted to fit 'the stations in the decline and fall of Inishboffin' [*sic*].[42]

Does the published text of *High Island* incorporate these suggestions? In one sense, of course: they embrace its spirit, its history, as well as its wildlife. Two of its finest poems, notable in Murphy's *oeuvre* for their explicit focus on the animal, the creaturely, 'Seals at High Island' and 'Stormpetrel', bookend the collection as first published, but echo the language of religious music as well as a Hughesian frankness of engagement with their subjects' sexuality. I would echo Patrick Crotty's view of 'Seals at High Island' as 'an extraordinary meditation on sexuality, the voraciousness of the natural world and (arguably, at least) the marginalization of the Anglo-Irish'.[43] But it may be more than that: it may also be a response to Hughes' invitation to rhapsody. The seals' flower-like mouths that had first gaped at a sexual ecstasy at nightfall play another part:

> … mourn the drowned,
> Playing to the sea sadly their last quartet,
> An improvised requiem that ravishes
> Reason, … (*P*, p. 144)

Hughes' letter had asked Murphy to remember the composer of his own favourite late quartets, and 'Beethoven's dictum to pupils: "Never mind the wrong notes – go through to the end."'[44] But we also note, in turning from these seals to the next poem in the collection,

'Little Hunger', a turn of this poetic tide that the reordering of the poems for *The Pleasure Ground* loses: the reassertion and defence of Murphy's method in taking pink stone from roofless houses on the promontory for 'the granite house I planned':

> Once mine, I'd work on their dismemberment,
>   Threshold, lintel, wall;
> And pick a hearthstone from a rubble fragment
>   To make it integral.   (*P*, p. 111)[45]

This seems like a knowing and determined rejoinder to Hughes' criticism that too much technique might reduce poems themselves to rubble.

The collection finds other ways of meditating on the darkness Hughes had found so fecund, and the question of an appropriate local response to it. Here, Murphy's own commitment to the social ecology of the place was exemplary for Hughes, whose own work approached a similarly exact, if so far unacknowledged, dedication to particular locations and friendships a decade later, in the poems of *River* (1983). Is it tenderness for its subject, an assertion of his own knowledge of the terrain to which it still clings,[46] or self-directed irony that leads Murphy's 'Song for a Corncrake' to ask:

> Why draft an epic on a myth of doom
> In staunchly nailed iambics
> Launched nightly near my room?
> …
> Give us lyrics,
> Little bridegroom.
> …
> Quicken your tune, O improvise, …   (*P*, p. 121)

But there are times when a tune needs to wait. *High Island*'s third poem, 'Lullaby', is in 1974 for a young girl whose mother takes her with her to an early death. In 2000, two years after the death of its closest reader, Murphy's *Collected Poems* added a dedication, 'For Shura'; *The Pleasure Ground* (2013) makes this lullaby an inscription named as 'Epitaph for Shura' (*P*, p. 122). An early version of another poem, 'Gallows Riddle', provoked by the final exercise Hughes suggested in 1971, 'rogues gallery' [*sic*], was first inscribed as a dedicatory verse in a copy of *Sailing to an Island* Murphy gave to Hughes during a stay at Court Green in February 1968.[47]

By the time Murphy first collected his poems in 2000, it had become clear and admissible that, as the sections of that volume put it, poems had a way of 'arising from the years' – generally, spans of a decade – like mist from a sea or a headland, slowly clearing.[48] Sometimes it took much longer, quite properly. Only in 1982 were memories of that summer on the Erriff sublimated in 'Waterkeeper's Bothy', and even then his sonnet (republished in 2017 in *In Search of Poetry* as 'Waterkeeper's Lodge') did not exhaust the practical use to which, in the right circumstances, for the right friends, Murphy was prepared to put his recognition that 'the river is in you all the time ... the salmon, the watchers, the poachers, and the muse'.[49] In 1984, mindful still of his old employer's attitude to poachers, hating those who 'disturb her fish by using nets or lime or bombs', while she 'tolerates, almost admires, a poacher who leaves no trace of his theft on the bank', Murphy advised Hughes, Barrie Cooke and their friend Paul Cullen interested in fishing the Erriff to concentrate their efforts (not entirely within the regulations on a fly-only fishery and not necessarily licensed) on Dead Man's Pool, out of sight of the road and bailiffs.[50] Hughes' unpublished fishing diaries record this visit; his friends told me of the 4lb fish he caught on a worm from the margins of the pool.[51]

But for all the pleasure both writers would have taken in that illicit salmon of local knowledge, Hughes' published writing bears more lasting and significant marks of his friendship with Richard Murphy, and of his profound sympathy with Murphy's Connemara. That brief return visit to Aughrusbeg Lough in June 1971 was 'worthwhile' not least because it inspired the eighth and distinctly Irish section of 'Skylarks', which he added to the poem the following year when including it in his *Selected Poems*. It also gave him 'A Violet at Lough Aughrisburg [*sic*]',[52] which would appear fifteen years later in *Flowers and Insects* (1986). Finally, a knowledge of Cleggan and the journey to and from it, along with the years of conversations about fishing, the countryside and poetry that he and Murphy enjoyed there, inform the work of Hughes that itself comes closest to embodying that account he gave to Murphy in 1966 of his rapt journey into the underworld of the poem, and the transformations that befell him there.

Like many of Murphy's poems, Hughes' *Gaudete*, published in 1977, had a long gestation, first developed as a treatment for a film script in 1964; it also has a complex structure and an ambitious if mysterious and troubling theme. It opens with a brief prose 'Argument' summarising its narrative, of the abduction by spirits of an Anglican clergyman '*into the other world*'.[53] The spirits put in his place a changeling, who '*interprets the role of minister in his own way*'[54] until a final day of events, which occupy the bulk of the volume, and consist of the changeling Lumb's sexual adventures with the women of the 'Southern English village'[55] in which he finds himself deposited, and the furious reactions of their outraged husbands to this 'interpretation' of Christian love. These events:

> *lead to his cancellation by the powers of both worlds.*
> *The original man reappears in this world, but changed.*[56]

This is not the place for a full discussion of a text that has only recently begun to attract serious and sustained attention from scholars. But a reader aware of Hughes' friendship with Murphy, from literary London to Cleggan to Gunn's 'Misanthropos' to Lumb Bank and beyond, cannot help but be arrested by the horrific opening. Hughes' poem describes Lumb striding, aghast, as last man in 'an empty town, in the North of England',[57] through streets piled high with dead bodies, until he meets the figure who will lure him to his abduction:

> A small aged face, wild as a berry – the scorched, bristly, collapsed face of a tinker.

And with:

> A rough-snagged shillelagh of voice, hard and Irish. But
> courteous, apologetic, almost affectionate. Lumb will have to
> accompany him for some little distance.[58]

Such a reader may recognise – I did – the location of the scene that,
halfway through the poem, after the changeling Lumb has beaten a
bloodied retreat to the river and recognised in its waters 'voices out
of his past', the narrative opens suddenly upon:[59]

> He sees a fish rise
> Off the point of the long broken finger of boulders
> Which pokes out into the lake, from the island.
> The lake is oil-still
> …
> The tops of the blue pyramid mountains, in the afterlight
> Tangle with ragged, stilled, pink-lit clouds
> That hang above themselves in the lake's stillness.[60]

It is here, as his terrified young companion Felicity first sees, that
fishing brings up not just a fish but Lumb's double; once Lumb is
persuaded to abandon a rising trout to defend her, the two versions
of himself wrestle in an extraordinary scene of tragicomedy.
And it is, finally, not far from here – perhaps also not so far from
Aughrusbeg Lough, where Hughes aroused that dormant passion
for the art in his young son, and returned with his children and his
new young wife in 1971 – 'In a straggly sparse village on the West
Coast of Ireland, on a morning in May', that three small girls come
to their own priest with stories of a man they had met on the sea
lough, who had summoned an otter from the waters and left them a
notebook full of verses.[61]

Hughes' choice of stage for the revelation of that literary harvest is
a fitting tribute not just to the landscape and nature of Connemara,
but also to the man who introduced him to it, as friend and as poet.

In a 2002 review of Murphy's *Collected Poems* and *The Kick* – which Murphy chose to end with an account of a meeting with Hughes in London, arranged to seal and celebrate the persistence of their memories, thirty-six years after the summer in which he and Sylvia first visited Connemara – Patrick Crotty observes: 'Each of the books under review needs and profoundly enhances the other. Together they form a unitary achievement, a life's work truer, broader and deeper than criticism has suspected.'[62] The same may be said of the friendship of Richard Murphy and Ted Hughes.

11

⁓

'The lyric barrier': Richard Murphy's America

EVE COBAIN

Richard Murphy's relationship with America throughout his career has been a continuous and engaging, though hardly simple, matter. As we know from his autobiography *The Kick* (2002/2017), the Irish poet played host to a number of significant American writers while in Connemara, and crossed paths with many more while teaching in the US during the 1970s and '80s. Murphy's writings, in *The Kick* and elsewhere, shed valuable light on American poetry during the second half of the twentieth century, confirming some essential differences between poetry happening on either side of the Atlantic. In this essay I discuss Murphy's perception of contemporary American poetics, with particular attention to the barriers facing comprehension, before moving on to consider the ways in which his poetry may have been variously resistant, and porous, to American experience.

During the early to mid-1950s, Murphy was continually seeking to muster a transatlantic conversation through his criticism and radio work. The Irish poet had expressed an interest in a number of twentieth-century American poets and was becoming increasingly engaged with contemporary verse. Robert Lowell, in particular, had caught the Irish poet's attention, and Murphy reviewed his *Poems: 1938–1949* for *The Spectator* in 1950 (10 November), heading the piece with the bold title 'A New American Poet'. 'There cannot be any doubt that Robert Lowell has a new and striking talent as a poet', wrote Murphy:

It is not just that his poems are published in England for the first
time in a year of mostly spiritless and spineless poetry, when
anything that is slightly good is likely to receive more praise than
it is worth, but such vigorous and determined originality as his,
which has spoken with the sure independence of an individual
rather than as one of the assenting voices in a group, would in
any age be remarkable.[1]

Yet the Irish poet's praise for the American was not unmixed. While
convinced of Lowell's originality, and the value of his work in a
European context, Murphy considered the American's verse still
juvenile, lacking in control and continuity: 'To say that this young
American poet is completely a master of his own half-realised art
would be to anticipate the culmination of his ability which has by
no means been reached', he wrote.[2] Thus, while he praised Lowell for
'the brightness of the particular image, the celerity of the phrase', he
felt his work to be equally possessed of 'phrases, and occasionally
moods, which are objectionably distasteful', and accused him of
stylistic 'excess'.[3]

Yet for all his 'untrained enthusiasm', Lowell had clearly piqued
Murphy's interest, especially with regard to his narrative verse, an
emerging preoccupation of Murphy's own. In a letter to the BBC's
P.H. Newby dated 28 November 1950, Murphy wrote to suggest he do
a further review of Lowell, noting:

> there are a few things I should like to say about him over and
> above my recent review in *The Spectator*. One reason is, I am
> particularly interested in narrative verse. He is working on a
> narrative poem at present, and he already has developed a strong
> narrative style.[4]

Indeed, Murphy had a good deal to say on the state of narrative
poetry in Ireland and America, and it is clear he regarded America
as a nation boasting many of the form's chief historical proponents.
'Narrative Poetry Today' was broadcast by the BBC Third Programme
on Saturday 28 July 1951, a talk that Murphy had proposed, and

which was followed with extracts by a number of other Americans, including Robert Frost and Ezra Pound.[5] The following month the polemic 'Why Has Narrative Poetry Failed?' was published in *The Listener*, and in it Murphy championed Lowell, along with Archibald MacLeish, as one of the only contemporary writers who had succeeded with the form.[6] Such discussion must have been a catalyst in Murphy's own poetic pursuits; in fact he was engaged, during this period, in his own narrative work. In April 1951 Murphy had signed a lease agreement with Myles Drury on the Quay House at Rosroe where he lived simply and for 'seven or eight hours a day' sat 'at a deal table typing ten or twenty lines of a narrative poem called "Voyage to an Island"' (*K*, pp. 119–20).

In August 1955 Murphy chaired another show for the BBC Third Programme, this time featuring the American poet Theodore Roethke, alongside Philip Larkin and Valentin Iremonger. More than the 1951 broadcast, this programme set out to draw some general lines of contrast between poetry happening in the US and on Murphy's own side of the Atlantic. And if Murphy had some concerns over the stylistic excess in Lowell's poetry, this quality he found to be yet more pronounced in Roethke. The commentary that surrounds the poems is illuminating, confirming Murphy's perception of a clear division between American and European verse forms. Where Larkin and Iremonger are upheld as rational, even cerebral poets, Roethke is pure emotion. Larkin, comments Murphy, 'wants 100 per cent precision, and is prepared on occasions to sacrifice feeling', while Roethke, 'On the other side of the Atlantic … seems unconcerned with things as they are, but very much concerned with the new universe of feeling he can create with words'.[7] Roethke's poetry is concerned with atmospheres – it is musical, full of subterfuge, and operates on the frontiers of consciousness. The Irish poet's sympathies are relatively unconcealed here, and his difficulty with the kind of emotionalism he attributes to Roethke is evident as early as his 1954 presentation 'The Future of Poetry', which was broadcast on the literary opinion show of the BBC's Third Programme. 'Unlike his elders during the war', asserts the young Murphy, the modern poet is not going to swell the page with his emotion … He will disdain excess, and will pay no attention to the cult of the incomprehensible heart. If he is a good poet, his poems will be rich in feeling, but they will be the feelings of the poem, something which the man has cast into poetic existence because he must reject it from his own.[8]

Seen from this perspective, Roethke appears the very antithesis of the modern poet. Indeed, what Murphy rejects here, in this early broadcast, is what he later comes to regard as intrinsic to the American poetic tradition.

Murphy's demarcation of the imaginative boundaries between Europe and America would come into sharper relief when the two poets finally met in the summer of 1960. Murphy had begun a correspondence with Roethke as early as 1955, writing to him in Washington with a request for some new poems for the BBC and with an invitation to visit him on Inishbofin.[9] The Pulitzer Prize winner responded in June 1955 enclosing a number of poems and concluding: 'Western Ireland I have always longed to see.'[10] He wrote again in July 1960, finally accepting the welcome: 'I have one wife, aged 34, part Irish. It would be wonderful to come to your island – both of them.'[11]

This disastrously high-jinks encounter receives extensive documentation in *The Kick* as well as in various interviews in which Murphy identified it as one of the most significant literary exchanges of his career.[12] If the Irish poet had appeared, in his 1955 appraisal, as somewhat suspicious of the excess at the heart of Roethke's poetry, his prose accounts, particularly in *The Kick*, dwell on a gross instability in the man himself. Indeed, it hardly helped moderate Murphy's preconceptions of the American poet – and the generation of poets to which he belonged – when after a bout of mania, which involved Roethke's holding a knife to hotelier Margaret Day's throat, the poet had to be ferried off the island and committed to Ballinasloe psychiatric hospital for treatment. 'Margaret Day remembered "the extreme peace after he'd gone"', Murphy would subsequently recall (*K*, p. 185). Six weeks later, after his treatment was complete, Roethke returned – this time without his wife, Beatrice – for a more productive stay.

Full of scathing perspicacity, Murphy's account consistently places the American within a 'confessional' framework – a category first posited by M.L. Rosenthal in his famous review of Lowell's *Life Studies* (1959), entitled 'Poetry as Confession'.[13] Roethke's voraciousness, his alcoholism, his emotional instability and thirst 'for praise' all come under the microscope where they show themselves as generational strains (*K*, p. 183). In what he sees as Roethke's insatiable quest for recognition, Murphy picks up on one of the major preoccupations of the contemporary American poet: the battle to be number one. This was a battle fought predominantly between a few young American males, most notably Robert Lowell, John Berryman and Delmore Schwartz. 'The most conspicuous feature of Berryman's personality', writes Vernon Young, paraphrasing Berryman's biographer John Haffenden, 'was not his devotion to life for the sake of art but to art as a road to prestige. And his appetite increased by what it fed upon.'[14] The accusation is not unjust, for when Robert Frost died in 1963, Berryman's initial response was to redraw the hierarchy: 'It's scarey [*sic*]. Who's number one? Who's number one? Cal [Lowell] is number one, isn't he?'[15] This attitude of fierce competition is one that Murphy perceives in Roethke, who shares Berryman's anxiety over the status of Lowell. 'When I mentioned a poem by Robert Lowell favourably', Murphy recalls, Roethke 'banged the counter in the pub with two fists and snarled, "Why are you always praising Lowell? I'm as mad as he is!"' (*K*, p. 183). Later, in the same account, Murphy writes of a suspicion that Roethke:

> was deploying madness ... as part of a grand strategy to win fame as the greatest poet on earth – America's answer to William Blake ... Insanity was the stinking wound that went with his talent.   (*K*, p. 183).

Yet for all its intensity, the 1960 encounter – particularly in its second phase – was a productive one, with the two workshopping poems and drawing upon existing connections to assist the other poet in

publishing his work abroad. Murphy, who was also eager for a degree
of recognition, notes Roethke's creative input in helping him get
a poem accepted by *The Yale Review*.[16] 'He read the poem aloud',
recalls Murphy, 'praising passages he liked, exposing the hollowness
of turgid, vague sonorities' (*K*, p. 186). In fact, the island encounter
was the basis for a number of poems on both sides. Roethke's most
significant offering was 'The Shy Man', a love poem in imitation of
Yeats, which he composed in honour of Beatrice and finally published
in *The Dubliner* in July/August 1962 alongside another, much cruder
'Bofin' poem, entitled 'Gob Music'.[17] 'The Shy Man', which is an
'evocation by song of a state of love', fits perfectly the description of
a typical Roethke poem as set out by Murphy in his 1955 broadcast.[18]
Moreover, while Roethke saw these poems as a great achievement
– boasting that he had 'Yeats licked' – Murphy considered them an
embarrassment, and was less than convinced that his friend would
'acquire an Irish reputation, rivaling Yeats's' (*K*, p. 186). Perhaps in
response to Roethke, Murphy also looked to *The Dubliner* to publish
his version of events, 'The Poet on the Island', which appeared a few
issues later in January 1963.[19] The poem was later printed in *Sailing to
an Island* (1963), then subsequently under the revised title 'Theodore
Roethke at Inishbofin, 1960' in *Collected Poems* (2000), and, finally,
in *The Pleasure Ground: poems 1952–2012* (*P*, pp. 43–4). That the piece
saw various revisions through Murphy's career is testament not only
to the poem's importance within his *oeuvre*, but also his changing
attitudes towards the American poet. In fact the poem, through each
of its incarnations, offers a much more ambivalent (even sympathetic)
account of Roethke's sojourn on Inishbofin than does *The Kick*.

The original title, 'The Poet on the Island', suggests an amount
of reverence on Murphy's part for the Pulitzer Prize winner while
conceding, at the same time, to Roethke's intolerable theatricality.
Indeed, while the lyric is often generous, taking stock of Roethke's
kindness and appeal to the children of Inishbofin, who Roethke was
said to have 'fathered in words', it quickly establishes his separateness
from the islanders as poet and American citizen: 'lonely they
left him, "one of the Yanks"' (*P*, p. 43). Roethke is presented as an
isolated figure, wrapped up in himself and his work, and Murphy

puts forward an image of the poet as a self-contained structure, faced with increasing pressure from both inner and outer forces. At the poem's outset Roethke – who is being ferried towards the island on the *Ave Maria* – is himself a vessel of poetic thought: 'Safety on water, he rocked with a new theme' (*P*, p. 43). While the rocking-boat image creates a sense of threat, there is not yet enough suggested turbulence to capsize the poet, who possesses a harnessed bardic energy that might any moment become song. In the third stanza Murphy switches the exterior/interior metaphor to that of a 'greenhouse' in which poems are 'nurtured'.[20] The allusion here is to Roethke's 'greenhouse poems', a series that relates to the poet's father, who ran a twenty-five-acre greenhouse in Saginaw, Michigan. As such, while the imagery through the poem becomes more personal to Roethke, in becoming more transparent and brittle it also comes to mirror his increasingly uneasy disposition throughout the duration of his stay on Inishbofin. By the end of the lyric, Roethke's exterior has 'cracked in a gale' (*P*, p. 44), an apt metaphor for psychic combustion. Of course, the concept of the house as a resonant psychic and poetic space was to become an enduring motif for Murphy, which culminates in the later sonnet sequence *The Price of Stone* (1985).

In 'The Poet on the Island' Murphy tailors his grammar and syntax to reflect Roethke's mental collapse:

> His fate was like fish under poetry's beaks:
> Words began weirdly to take off inwards.   (*P*, p. 43)

The Irish poet's phrasing possesses an atypical tonality here, being more akin to the songlike utterance he ascribed to the American in his 1955 broadcast. The poem's final incarnation, 'Theodore Roethke at Inishbofin, 1960', further accentuates these songlike or 'maternal' traits in Roethke. While the first three printings use martial imagery to present the American as a classical and heroic figure –

> His forehead, a Prussian helmet, moody, domed,
> Relaxed in the sun: a lyric was his lance.[21]

– the final version presents his poetic gift as much more vatic and mysterious in nature:

> The deep trough of his depression was becalmed
> In the womb of the harbour. Lyrics came in a trance.   (*P*, p. 43)

The masculine is replaced with the feminine, the decidedly aggressive with the somnambulistic; this transmutation places the poet, Roethke, more firmly within a confessional framework. The womb-harbour of this version, together with the poetic trance, serves, further, to imply that the poet's method is based more on suggestion or dream than on conscious craft. Arguably, the revelation of the poet's name in the revised title reduces the whiff of grandiosity and posturing in the original version, while the alterations in the fourth stanza serve to lessen the poet's stature and to lance him down to size.

The decision to excise martial imagery is a pointed one, especially since Murphy, in various critical essays, has pitted the classical, Apollonian mind against the romantic, Dionysian spirit. Murphy's work displays a preoccupation with these two opposing forces, which the lyric must hold in balance. In 'The Future of Poetry' Murphy argues for the necessity of 'a style which is controlled and cool, because it has exhausted madness and passion'.[22] Likewise, in his preface to *The Pleasure Ground: poems 1952–2012*, such tensions are communicated in the poet's discussion of his attempts, at nineteen, to rediscover the unfettered joys of childhood – 'that older earlier unfenced romantic pleasure ground in the treeless hills of Connemara on the edge of the sea' (*P*, p. 16). There, Murphy claims, he

> abandoned [himself] to mountains, lakes and waterfalls; stretched without clothes on the ground on summer nights; and once rolled naked in snow. I wanted to write poetry, and believed that someday, like the ripening of the figs, I might taste the fruit and it would not be poisonous.   (*P*, p. 16)

The older poet's account shatters the younger's illusion: 'I didn't imagine it would take so long and be so difficult to produce a first crop or a last' (*P*, p. 16). A similar, and also cautionary, narrative is given in Murphy's essay on Yeats, 'Rejoice', where, inspired by the elder poet, Murphy seeks refuge in the wilds of Connemara under the delusion that if he 'were to listen and look and live and love with enough devotion, the words that would flow from my pen in that solitary land would be poetry'.[23] The result, Murphy emphasises, was an 'ecstasy bordering on madness' that made him 'incapable of writing' when he finally returned to his undergraduate studies at Magdalen College, Oxford.[24]

In Murphy's poem for Roethke the sheer force of the Dionysian impulse prostrates the American poet. Speaking of his father's feelings on Roethke, Murphy comments that 'In his classical opinion, Roethke's trouble came from lack of moderation' (*K*, p. 184). Through every printing of the poem, Roethke is presented as unable to maintain a balance between 'the romantic impulse' and the 'mind which is classical',[25] and the final stanza (unwaveringly) sees him as having 'burst the lyric barrier' to arrive at a point where 'logic ended' and 'he agreed to sail' to the harbour of a psychiatric institution (*P*, p. 44). Yet the swapping of key imagery in 'The Poet on the Island' remains significant since it takes the temperature not only of Murphy's relationship with Roethke but also the American lyrical tradition more broadly. The poem was no doubt revised partly in the light of the period that Murphy spent teaching in the US between its first publication and its final reprinting in 2013. This experience would also account for the tonal shift that occurs between the original poem and the more pointed critique of Roethke in *The Kick*, published in 2002. Indeed, while the version of 'Theodore Roethke at Inishbofin' printed in *Collected Poems* (2000) remains partly sympathetic towards the poet, Murphy's attitude towards him appears to have hardened over time.

Murphy's first trip to America was at the invitation of Richard Eberhart to give 'forty readings from coast to coast beginning in October' (*K*, p. 219) in promotion of the Chilmark Press publication of *Sailing to an Island* in the autumn of 1964. In his memoir Murphy comments on how during this period he quickly 'learnt with trepidation of a college culture admiringly amused by the self-destruction of poets who drank themselves into the madhouse or the grave' (*K*, pp. 219–20). The concerns that his experience with Roethke had planted regarding the American lyric tradition appeared to be confirmed by Murphy's own sojourn in America. His experience of teaching at these colleges was to be another formative one, cementing the lyric barrier that he sensed between Ireland and the US.

In 1965 the Irish poet took up a position as visiting writer at the University of Virginia, where his predecessor had been William Faulkner, and in 1971 he was invited by Bruce Berlind to take up the O'Connor Chair at Colgate University, a position he held for two semesters, teaching courses in creative writing and modern British and Irish poetry. At Colgate Murphy quickly realised that any form of 'classical' poetry – as mapped out in the 1954 essay – was in short supply, and as a teacher he felt himself the necessary evangelist of 'form' in poetry. 'In my creative writing course, I stressed the value of mastering metre and rhyme before attempting to write free verse', (*K*, p. 267) writes Murphy:

> But my theories that the iamb derives from the heartbeat and the structure of a poem needs a body's or a building's symmetry put me out of key with the time. Metrical rhymed poetry had never come easily to me, nor did I expect it to be easy for students who equated poetry with self-expression.   (*K*, p. 267)

In 1972 the poet spent a term at Bard College where he had fewer complaints, yet returning in 1974 – this time to Princeton – Murphy again found difficulty in relating to his students, and struggled to instil in them an appreciation for 'rhythm and verse form, the technique of writing, which requires effort and still more effort'.[26] His students, even at Princeton, seemed to follow the same cultish principles as a poet like Roethke, who allowed his (unregulated) emotions to dictate the shape of his verse.

Murphy's struggle with the free-verse tradition emerges in numerous accounts of his time in the US. In another letter, to his daughter Emily Riordan dated 25 September 1974, he comments on his frustration at the institutional promotion and perpetuation of this kind of poetry. Speaking of his failure to secure a job for Tony White as his successor at Bard, he complains:

> the fat poet Robert Kelly, who writes only in free verse, put up a free-verse-writing American poet as <u>their</u> candidate for the job, he was interviewed, & his election was arranged.[27]

According to Murphy, then, Tony's status as a non-American writer of formal verse was sufficient to rule him out of the contest.

At the University of Iowa, too, where he taught for two semesters in the autumn of 1976, Murphy found his attitudes to be discomfortingly un-American. Yet in his capacity as workshop coordinator, Murphy took it upon himself to instil in his American students a proper regard for poetic form by introducing a course entitled 'Form of Poetry'. The curriculum included a list of books by mostly British and Irish writers, including Seamus Heaney, Philip Larkin and Ted Hughes, as well as the Anglo-American Thom Gunn. The course outline reads as follows:

> The purpose of this course is to give people who want to wrestle with the problems of writing in meter and rhyme a chance to improve their technique. Six or seven of the principal verse forms, which poets still find useful, will be practised in turn. A poem or some verse written in a different form every two weeks during the semester will be required.[28]

It would appear that Murphy's students, however, remained interested in more open forms, and he was unable to provoke them into writing the kind of forms that he desired. Instead, the writing was loose and driven by emotion. At Iowa, writes Murphy, 'the average … graduate student's attitude to the workshop was epitomised in my class by a woman who defended an obscure line written by a friend "I think I feel I know what she's trying to say"' (*K*, p. 294). Murphy's witty retort was to recognise the statement as '"a line of blank verse with five regular stresses"', and he considered, perhaps a little smugly, that it proved him 'as out of key as [he] felt' (*K*, p. 294). When it came to putting feeling into words, Murphy found himself continually faced with what he perceived to be a uniquely transatlantic barrier to expression.

Princeton in particular proved itself a lonely frontier for the poet, both psychically and creatively. His unhappiness during this time is best understood through the searingly honest letters that he wrote to his daughter from Jamesburg, where he lived during his first term teaching. Writing on 28 September 1974 he admits to his deepening isolation:

> It's not a good moment to write to you, because I'm feeling depressed by America, the humidity, the senseless waste of all the world's goods by the richest people on earth, the loneliness, the boredom. Making money but killing time in a terrible way, unable to write, because I feel like a plant uprooted and dried out.[29]

A subsequent letter finds him 'miserable in America, lonely and bored', confiding that he'd 'much rather be near London than New York'.[30] Murphy's prose, as he addresses this uniquely American environment, is shot through with an unusual and noticeably blues-like idiom. Yet while writers of the blues traditionally found themselves enabled by their blue feelings, the Irish poet was hardly even negatively inspired by his sociocultural environs. Murphy's suburban America is luridly pictured: 'a dark pit at nightfall when I get home from work in Princeton; and the gangs of sunburnt children leaning on the handlebars of bikes, scowl at me with curiosity'.[31] Full of vague and less than vague threats of violence, the poet's letters during this period are attuned to the atmospheres of vacuity and consumerism that he perceived at the core of American social experience: 'The houses in the street, each different to the next, are all the same fundamentally in being boxes full of gadgets rather than places in which to live' (14 September 1974).[32] For a poet so alive to the aesthetic and psychic significance of structures of dwelling, this was an irremediable criticism that bespeaks his inability to connect with an American aesthetic consciousness.

In Murphy's encounters with American writers during the 1960s and '70s, it often appears that the most striking were still the ones he had in Ireland.[33] In the summer of 1975 he was finally introduced to Robert Lowell at the Kilkenny Festival. 'My impressions of Robert Lowell began at Jerpoint', he recalls, 'with a man wrapped up in himself' (K, p. 284). Yet Murphy's initial impressions had clearly begun somewhat earlier, in his review of *Poems: 1938–1949* for *The Spectator* in 1950, which had praised Lowell for his 'traditional language' and criticised his bent towards the blatantly emotional.[34] Upon meeting the poet, however, Murphy found himself quickly renouncing his earlier claims about the poems, resolving that he had 'found them difficult, but instead of admitting this, handed out praise and blame in a strictly judgmental tone, to cover my ignorance' (K, p. 282). In fact, Murphy's impressions of Lowell, as a man 'wrapped up in himself', are consonant with his first commentary on Roethke, who becomes the standard against which the Bostonian is measured through the succeeding paragraphs. Yet if Murphy was critical of Roethke, his depiction of Lowell is almost equally exuberant in its praise. A drama unfolds in which Lowell plays Apollo to Roethke's Dionysus:

> Sure of his reputation, unlike Theodore Roethke, he didn't bang the table and boast of madness to put down rivals. He was courteous and diffident, without pomp or pretentiousness. At all hours of the day or night, even after two or three bottles of wine, his mind, if not his voice, kept its clarity and exaltation.
>
> (K, pp. 284–5)

While Murphy's early review of Lowell worried over the excess in Lowell's style, his later account in *The Kick* demonstrates no such concern. The prose becomes excitedly purple as Murphy registers the dissimilarities between one American and the other. If Murphy's discourse surrounding poetry in the US previous to this encounter suggested a number of initial fears, his encounter with Lowell appears to have led him to re-evaluate his impressions. Lowell's New Critical background comes through, for Murphy, in his general demeanour and attitude. His reading style is described as understated, even anti-poetic:

He read not quite well enough for one to accuse him of acting, though his act of occasionally mumbling or stumbling over a word, or asking for a window to be opened to let in some air, was that of a poet who had been persuaded against his inclination to perform.   (*K*, p. 288)

Murphy's analysis here suggests a deliberate effort on the part of Lowell to define his reading style against an ever-increasing number of poet-performers. This was a discussion in which Lowell had long been engaged, as indicated by his essay on William Carlos Williams, published in 1961, where he claims that

A seemingly unending war has been going on now as long as I can remember ... The beats are on one side, the university poets are on the other. Lately [in the 1960s] the gunfire has been hot. With such unlikely Williams recruits as Karl Shapiro blasting away, it has become unpleasant to stand in the middle in a position of impartiality.[35]

For Murphy, Lowell actively occupied this middle ground, and a large part of his appeal was to be found in his difference from the self-dramatising and volatile Roethke. Lowell's Apollonian attitudes are borne out in his performance as well as in his criticism. 'My own group' – 'that of Tate and Ransom' – writes Lowell,

was all for high discipline, for putting on the full armor of the past, for making poetry something that would take a man's full weight and that would bear his complete intelligence, passion, and subtlety ... The struggle perhaps centered on making the old metrical forms usable again to express the depths of one's experience.[36]

Such an achieved balance between form and emotion was something to which Murphy also clearly aspired. Thus, while his early review of *Poems: 1938–1949* expressed some concern over the force of the emotion in Lowell's poetry, Murphy's 1975 encounter with the poet himself was sufficient to convince him of Lowell's control and lyric prowess; the Irish poet had now discovered an American model whose practice he could admire, if not emulate.

In 1977, under unprecedented emotional duress, Murphy found himself writing in a new verse form. Two nights after his terminal phone call from his ex-wife Patricia Avis, and his last alcoholic drink, the poet describes how he was 'missing severely' his 'regular pint of stout'. Instead of going to the Pier Bar or Oliver's, relates Murphy, 'I went upstairs and sat on my bed under a skylight and took out a Parisian notebook' (K, p. 296). Here, thinking of his deceased friend Tony White, as he would 'every day of [his] life', he 'wrote a sentence that extended in half an hour to twenty-four long lines of free verse, not a word crossed out or needing to be changed' (K, p. 296). Murphy now had recourse to a form that he had previously lambasted as phoney and excessive and one he associated directly with the American tradition. 'The Price of Stone', which laments the loss of his friend and worries over the cost of building houses or poems, was published in 1979 by Peter Fallon and Dennis O'Driscoll in The First Ten Years: Dublin Arts Festival poetry,[37] and under the revised title of 'Stone Mania' in Poems 1952–2012. 'How much it hurts me', writes Murphy,

> … to have neglected all this summer
>   the friends whom I might have seen,
> But for my mad obsession of building more rooms
>   to entertain them in time to come: (P, p. 157)

The loss of conventional form speaks of his will to find a direct voice, to rediscover a poetics of temporality and emotion:

> How much it hurts to see the destruction that all good
>   building, even the best, must cause,   (P, p. 157)

Yet Murphy would find his way back into formal verse, and the selfsame title was to be adopted for his 1985 sonnet sequence in his fifth Faber volume, *The Price of Stone*. Alongside this sequence Murphy was compiling an associated collection of prose, or free-verse fragments, which documented his creative thoughts and processes; this he considered equally 'a work in progress, amounting to thirty-three chapters, "Transgressing into Poetry".[38] A selection of the sketches have since been printed in *Poetry Ireland Review* (nos 104, 107, 111), *Archipelago* (no. 11, 2016) and subsequently, in book form, as *In Search of Poetry* (2017).

The concept of transgression has long been synonymous with the American literary tradition, and the sonnets, along with their related commentary, represent a widening in Murphy's perspective, if not a translocation. Crucially, in the notebook project Murphy appears to be engaging with a contemporary American genre. As David Perkins notes in *A History of Modern Poetry*, 'in the 1960s the notebook genre flourished in the United States'[39] – a period in which Murphy was both present in America and active as a poet. Murphy recalls that

> Between April 1981 and November 1983, at an isolated house on Mullen's Hill in Killiney I wrote a sequence of sonnets called 'The Price of Stone', each with a different persona emanating from a building associated with my life – an indirect or ventriloquized autobiography compressed into fourteen lines of rhyming or off-rhyming verse. This allowed me, I felt at the time, to avoid the embarrassment, for myself and for my readers, of overtly confessional poetry. The process involved continuous writing of notes evoking more and more memories. I wrote with a fountain pen on the centimetre squared pages of a small French notebook, which seemed to provide a better-than-blank worksheet for metrical poetry. While examining my life, I often tried to circumvent inhibition by addressing 'myself' as 'you'. So came the different voices speaking from the sonnet houses.[40]

As in the account of his earlier experiment with free verse in 'Stone Mania', Murphy gives especial attention to the materiality of the notebook into which he transcribes his thoughts; yet here the description is not only romantic, it is also classical. In emphasising the self-imposed restrictions on his material, Murphy reminds us of his need for structural limitations. 'The wattle tent may have something to say', he tells us, 'but why should you want to fit a thing so loose into a form so tight as a sonnet? An emblem of my state of mind, loose within its constraints?'[41] Murphy answers this question in verse – his transgression *into* poetry. Meanwhile, his fear surrounding the 'confessional' is telling, for if the poet insists on the squared worksheet as a kind of scaffolding, it is only because he is at least as concerned with interior life as these American poets were. While these poems are 'replete with past complaints and future anxieties, in the ever present tense', Murphy's notes instruct the poet, 'do not let the poem break into a shard of anthropology, but use the shards you have found to make a poem …'.[42]

Such a balance – between order and emotion – was something he had detected earlier in the work of Robert Lowell, a poet who was also one of the chief exponents of the serial-notebook form. Now, as he sought to give shape to raw personal experience, Murphy looked to Lowell in the hope that he might find some direction for his notebook poems. Lowell's own engagement with the notebook form can be seen as early as *Life Studies* (1959), which concerns itself with a journey from the classically restrained to a more personal form of expression, moving, as it does so, in and out of verse.[43] Like Murphy, Lowell continually draws connections between architectural and psycho-poetic space. This is seen particularly in the collection's second section, the prose poem '91 Revere Street', as well as in its introspective third section, 'Life Studies', which deals almost exclusively with resonant familial spaces. Here, Lowell muses on the significance of various architectural spaces ('My Last Afternoon with Uncle Devereux Winslow', 'For Sale') as well as boats ('Commander Lowell', 'Sailing Home from Rapallo', 'Father's Bedroom'). Indeed, *Life Studies* was only the beginning of Lowell's work in the notebook form, and his 1969 sonnet sequence *Notebook 1967–1968* (revised and expanded as *Notebook* in 1970) bears nearer structural comparison to Murphy's *The Price of Stone*.[44] These notebook sonnets must surely have provided the poet with a model for examining his life without displaying a surfeit of emotion.

Yet in his engagements with Lowell, Murphy, as suggested earlier, was playing into a larger notebook tradition. Such an attitude of self-examination had also been integral to the work of the American poet John Berryman, whose Dream Songs (385 of which were published in 1969 as *The Dream Songs*) are often considered to have inspired and propelled Lowell into his lengthy sonnet project.[45] *The Dream Songs* also bears comparison to the notebook form, though it is governed and regulated by an (almost) unyielding adherence to Berryman's chosen form: an eighteen-line structure composed of three even and variously rhyming stanzas. Berryman, too, uses a character device in order to avoid the poem's slipping into simple confession: *The Dream Songs* is 'essentially about an imaginary character (not the poet, not me) named Henry, [who] has suffered an irreversible loss and talks about himself sometimes in the first person, sometimes in the third, sometimes even in the second'.[46] Yet more strikingly, this character – who bears hazardous comparison to the poet himself – is a number of times referred to as 'Henry House'.[47]

While Murphy's early discussion of contemporary American poetic practices is littered with scepticism, his later poetry demonstrates a more nuanced understanding and acceptance (or even assimilation) of American modes of expression. Murphy's early experience with Roethke left a considerable impression on him, and became a lens through which he surveyed the American poetic scene more generally. The Irish poet was right to have some concerns over the cult of emotion particular to American poetry during this period, and his comments – as an outsider looking in – offer a valuable European perspective on North American poetry during the middle and latter half of the twentieth century. Through the figure of Roethke, in particular, Murphy challenges what he regarded as an often performative and dangerous yoking of madness with brilliance. Still, in many ways, Murphy's early American encounters could be said to have stunted his understanding; there is a tendency towards judgement in his discourse surrounding free verse and confessionalism – a prejudice which, as he discovered in his Lowell review, might sometimes emerge from a lack of comprehension, or as

a cover for his 'ignorance' (*K*, p. 282). The Irish poet's own predilection
for formal verse, to a large degree, accounts for his various distastes
and helps to explain his discomfort with raw and untutored feeling
in verse, something he grew to regard as an unappealingly American
trait. Yet Lowell provided something of a bridge for Murphy and was
felt increasingly to speak as 'heir of both traditions', as Murphy initially
perceived in his 1950 review in *The Spectator*.[48] Lowell's emotionally
engaged, yet formalist, poetry – from the narratives to the sonnets –
appealed to the Irish poet as something adequately other, though not
radically different – an American paradigm he could slip into.

Murphy appears finally to have drawn out two distinct strains
in the American tradition. While he lauded Lowell, the Irish poet
continued to dislike and criticise poets who bore near comparison
to Roethke; his aversion to the performative and neurotic impulses
he detected in that volatile figure continued to colour his view of
American poets long after the summer of 1960. Listening to the
performance poet James Dickey, in 1983, Murphy comments: 'In the
nineteen years between my reading with him at Dartmouth College in
1964 and his solo reading at the Folger Museum', Dickey had become

> a replica of the poet Roethke towards the end of Roethke's life –
> a huge old clumsy bear with a lecherous eye, drunk on liquor
> and fame, liable to collapse in tears or explode in anger but for
> the sustenance of our applause.   (*K*, p. 306)

For Murphy, Roethke eventually grew to be the summation of
all that was deficient in American poetry, and he continued to
preside over all of Murphy's subsequent American affairs. Still, his
connection with the Roethke family persisted late into the 1970s,
when Beatrice Lushington (Roethke) wrote to him requesting that
he read at 'Ted's birthday' memorial, with the appeal that 'you'd be
the first non-American' (23 August 1978).[49] Beatrice was right to
highlight Murphy's transatlantic difference, for more often than not
the Irish poet's work was cultivated against the American grain; in
his early career especially, Murphy's American experiences served
to sharpen his sense of an Irish tradition. Yet Beatrice's request

also singles Murphy out as poetically transgressive and adaptable. Indeed, throughout his career Murphy was intent on establishing a transnational conversation, and while his early work suggests a certain resistance, his later projects grew to accommodate America. Finally, in *The Price of Stone*, Murphy was pressing beyond the close shores of home, agreeing to sail.

NOTE

Thanks are due to Benjamin Keatinge and Tom Walker for their generosity in sharing invaluable archival resources.

12

~

What Price Stone? The shaping of inheritance into form in Richard Murphy's *The Price of Stone* sonnet sequence

TARA STUBBS

In a chapter on Murphy written some years before the publication of *The Price of Stone*, Seamus Heaney worried that Murphy's preoccupation with the 'shaping of his inheritance into a poetic theme' betrayed a 'symptomatic unease between the manner and the matter of the poetry'.[1] To elaborate his point Heaney quotes Edna Longley's comment on Murphy's *The Battle of Aughrim* (1968) that 'something programmatic' in the 'design and designs' of Murphy's poetry 'stands in the way of total subjection of the offered experience'.[2] For both writers Murphy's perceived irresolution between the content and form of his poetry comes, in an echo of Yeats' famous definition of poetry, from 'his quarrel with himself' as a poet straddling Anglo-Irish and 'native' Irish traditions.[3] But in *The Price of Stone* (1985)[4] Murphy offers another gloss on his poetic method. In the sonnet the challenge is to work a theme into a form that is freighted by its own traditions. And rarely is the monumental element of the sonnet dealt with so concretely, or so actively foregrounded, as in *The Price of Stone*. Indeed, for Murphy, as he put it in a 2013 interview with *The Spectator*, the writing of *The Price of Stone* was enabling. Here, he could 'transmute remembered experience into urns of poetry', inspired as he was by another 'mantra' of Yeats – 'hammer your thoughts into unity'.[5]

This chapter will play on the implications of the title of Murphy's sonnet sequence to consider whether the fears of Longley and Heaney are realised in *The Price of Stone*. Are the forms and motifs hammered home at the expense of 'total subjection of the offered experience' – inhibiting our ability to find an authentic 'voice' among the ruins? Or do these poems become as much about the structures themselves – as living monuments, but also as monuments of verse – that channel Murphy's own conflicting inheritances, so that each sonnet functions instead (as he put it himself) as a 'rock that gives shape to a waterfall'? (*K*, p. 305).

Where Edward Hirsh and Eavan Boland argue in *The Making of a Sonnet* (2008) that 'the sonnet is both the most traditional and the most experimental of forms', noting further that 'it is also highly controversial', they are attuned to the possible cultural and even political implications of the form.[6] Boland, as an Irish poet and a woman poet, too, first met the form with resistance. Recalling her first encounter with 'The sonnet', she notes:

> At seventeen, I was a freckle-faced know-it-all, certain of my views on almost everything. I was newly returned from a childhood away from Ireland. I was trying to put together some foundation for my hope of being a poet. I wanted to belong to Irish poetry; I wanted Irish poetry to belong to me. The sonnet, I believed, could have no role in that. I had read it at school and resisted writing it. I was sure it was un-Irish, un-local, too courtly for a new republic; too finished to ever find a new beginning in the literature I was trying to understand.[7]

Extending the analogy further, Boland claims: 'I was sure the flourishing, musical industry of British sonnet-making – as I saw it, a factory of epigram, couplet, summary – must have been a sideshow of empire.'[8] She adds, 'I was equally sure it could never come to Ireland – to a new country, tense at the memory of its struggle with a larger one. Let alone to an untried and doubting Irish poet.'[9] What is telling about Boland's language here is not just the passion of her initial resistance to a form that felt so alien to her, so dominant and imperial, but the language of that 'struggle', that 'resistance'. And it is at this place that Boland and Hirsch locate the sonnet more generally – a place between constraint and self-expression, between revision and rebellion. It is no accident that they describe their anthology, somewhat militaristically, as 'a close-up of a single form – the extraordinary history of which is best shown through the poets who encountered and deployed it over time'.[10]

Even where the poet in question is not Irish – as is the case with the American Edward Hirsch – the tackling of the sonnet form raises similar questions about expression and restraint. Through fashioning something of a poetic joke out of a figurative analogy, which couches the sonnet as something that 'thinks on its feet', Hirsch points nonetheless to the sonnet as something that might be solid, or concrete – an entity that enjoys an almost material existence. 'The sonnet', Hirsch argues, 'is an obsessive form – compact, expansive – that travels remarkably well.' Anthropomorphising the form, he notes:

> There must be something hardwired into its machinery – a heartbeat, a pulse – that keeps it breathing. How many times over the decades has it been pronounced dead and then somehow revitalised, deconstructed, and then constructed again, refashioned, remade? It darkens and then lightens again.[11]

In Hirsch's mind the sonnet functions almost as the poet's poem, so that only once one has mastered the form might one be able to declare oneself a 'proper' poet. And it is the poet's role to meet the form head-on – to rise to the challenge that it makes. For Hirsch the sonnet is something weasel-like, almost wily; 'it is conducive to calculation and experimentation – a closed form that keeps on opening up'.[12]

For Murphy, as a contemporary Anglo-Irish poet, and particularly in the case of *The Price of Stone*, these examples seem to offer particularly fecund metaphors; we do not have to look too far to see in his sonnet sequence both an apparent (British?) compliance with the 'imperial' form of the sonnet and a willed (perhaps Irish?) resistance to the more traditional expectations of the same form. At the same time we can perceive in Murphy's ventriloquising of his subjects both the wiliness in each of the sonnet characters as implied by Hirsch's comments, and the materiality of his architectural subjects referenced through hints at the 'obsessive form' and 'machinery' of Hirsch's descriptions. Peculiarly fitting, too, is Boland's comment, made elsewhere in her personal memoir of sonnet writing, that the form 'can offer its marvellous interior architecture to shelter the moment'.[13]

But surely this is too easy? Surely it is too convenient to assert that the political implications of the sonnet – its toing and froing in the modern Irish tradition between rebellion and restraint, between tradition and innovation – and its tantalising invitation to the ambitious poet render it an ideal theme for Murphy? What I want to suggest, instead, is that something more complex, shifting and ultimately subjective is happening here with Murphy's use and choice of the sonnet form for what Heaney describes as his 'shaping of his inheritance into a poetic theme'. And this reading also opens up space for thinking about 'subjectivity' in verse as something not necessarily negative, therefore challenging the implications of Longley's suggestion that Murphy fails to create 'total subjection' within the 'offered experience'. Of course, the political implications of the term 'subjection' need also to be considered. For example, writing with considerable fervour the contemporary Irish poet Greg Delanty justifies his choice of the sonnet form for many of his political poems in terms of what he calls 'appropriate appropriation': for him the sonnet is 'a statement of implied complicity, which is mostly concealed within the poem's construct, as it is mostly concealed within the construct of our lives'.[14] Therefore, something insidious, almost dangerously so, is implied through our use of, our submission (or even subjection) to the sonnet form whenever we encounter it passively or use it without thinking. In stating that Murphy's poetry subjects itself to the form (the 'design and designs') of poetry rather than to the 'offered experience', then, Longley might be making a larger political point.

But while Murphy's use of the form in *The Price of Stone* offers an at once distinct and delicate example of 'appropriate appropriation', I want to suggest that the reasons for this are far from Delanty's manifest and obstreperous examples. Murphy neither 'appropriates' his writing to an imperial form too readily, nor does he fail to question the implications of such appropriation. Rather, *The Price of Stone* uses what is concealed and what is revealed about the sonnet form as a way of considering how poetry enables us not only to encounter and reject inheritances, but also to mediate between them. In so doing he is able to create a poetic output that is fittingly modern in its refusal to subscribe to a narrow definition of a specific 'Irish' tradition, therefore challenging Longley's famous (and rather disapproving) statement made in 1975 that 'It may be that the twentieth-century poet in any country no longer needs to feel himself significantly in touch with a particular tradition'.[15] *The Price of Stone*, instead, appears to ask whether it is the partisan parsing of such a 'tradition' that is at fault here, rather than the idea of 'tradition' itself. At the same time the sequence acknowledges that if, as Delanty implies, our life might be a construct, then so, too, might the poetry that reflects it – and this constructed-ness might actually be apposite rather than inappropriate.

What we have seen in the case of Heaney's and Longley's critiques of Murphy's earlier work is a desire to evaluate poetry in terms of its 'success'. This is something that seems to persist within criticism of Irish poetry, whereby a poem is further evaluated on its ability to meet the (often unspecified) criteria of a 'tradition'. But Murphy's poetry, and particularly *The Price of Stone*, asks that it be taken on its own terms; it appears simultaneously to create its own tradition and to extend the parameters of the existing traditions out of which it writes. It is both subjective and transgressive through its decision to borrow from and hew together 'traditions', more conservatively conceived, which others might view as inherently opposed. Bernard O'Donoghue, in a generous and persuasive reading of Murphy's 'Pat Cloherty's Version of *The Maisie*', sees Murphy's yoking together of traditions as essential to his unique poetic voice, wherein (in the case of this poem in particular) 'The subject-matter of all this is Irish and local, but the language and the poetics belong to English' (*P*, p. 276).[16]

But other critics, perhaps unsurprisingly, remain confounded by Murphy's poetic and personal stance, his decisive anglicising of Irish subjects. They may take the high road of Heaney and Longley, deliberating over his poetry's fidelity (or otherwise) to a form or to a tradition, or they may underestimate its ambition. If we add to this the qualitative aspect that often accompanies critiques of sonnet-making, then we can begin to see why writing an 'Irish sonnet' might be so apparently divisive. Alan Gillis certainly underestimates Murphy's achievement in his overview of 'The Modern Irish Sonnet':

> Richard Murphy's sequence *The Price of Stone* is made up entirely of straight Shakespearean sonnets, and the measure of each poem's success, or otherwise, is bound up entirely with its concluding couplet. The best poems of the sequence are those in which the final two lines are integral to the sonnet's development, providing both its narrative and musical culmination. More precisely, the best poems are those in which the concluding couplet generates a final turn, a sense of surprise, which simultaneously segues into a sense of ritualistic finish.[17]

I cite Gillis at length not to agree or otherwise with his preference for certain of the sonnets over others, but to remark upon his use of airy qualitative assessments ('best', 'success') within what extends to a one-paragraph summary of Murphy's sonnet sequence. It seems here that, through his use of 'straight Shakespearean sonnets', Murphy is regarded as being somewhat derivative, and therefore everything must ride on the 'concluding couplet', the 'final turn' and the 'ritualistic finish' (in this context, that 'success, or otherwise' is pointed, implying that certain of Murphy's poems fail to do this and therefore are unsuccessful). Like Longley's idea of 'Irish' poetry, then, wherein writers are treated cautiously if they are not 'in touch with a particular tradition', we again encounter a narrowness of viewpoint – but instead in relation to the parameters of the sonnet form. What strikes a cautious critical reader, too, is the use of terms such as 'success' and 'best' in relation to how faithfully Murphy's poems answer their Shakespearean predecessors – as if this is the main measure of their achievement both as sonnets and as poems. The double-edged term

'Irish sonnet' will lead readers and critics to come armed with their own preconceptions. And so a double assault confronts Murphy, as a sonnet-maker and as a poet writing out of an Irish tradition.

Yet Murphy's notes for *The Price of Stone*, published in *Poetry Ireland Review* under the titles 'Notes for Sonnets' (*Poetry Ireland Review*, no. 104) and 'Transgressing into Poetry' (*Poetry Ireland Review*, nos 107, 111), as well as in *In Search of Poetry* (2017), are (self-)exposing of the pitfalls and pratfalls concerned with writing a sonnet sequence, and particularly with writing an (Anglo-)Irish one. Murphy is aware, sometimes painfully so, of the paradoxes inherent in creating something for oneself when writing out of two traditions that each encompass their own practices, rules and customs. But there is a sense, too, in which the ambiguities and paradoxes of the sonnet form can mirror and reflect the experiences of the Anglo-Irish poet. Murphy notes himself on 'Writing *The Battle of Aughrim*' that 'As a renegade from a Protestant family that I loved, I wished the poem to unite my divided self in our divided country in a sequence faithful to the disunity of both' (*P*, p. 258). Murphy's convoluted syntax – similar to what Longley critiques in the poem itself as 'the labour-pangs of his syntax'[18] – bespeaks his awareness that this might be an impossible task. But a sonnet sequence, containing a unifying form that becomes unfaithful through its very insistence upon that unity, might (just) be up to the job.

In the collection of notes published in *Poetry Ireland Review* (nos 104, 107, 111) and in *In Search of Poetry*, Murphy explains the geneses of *The Price of Stone*, describing the poems as works which move 'from the flagellating Celtic hermits to the extortionate mine owner' while acknowledging the overreaching ambition of such an aim.[19] With a loftiness that is no less characteristic for being painfully self-aware, Murphy notes of his aims for his sonnets that 'With a split mind, part oratory, part miners' hut, I go from seeking salvation in words to breaking up the dedication which the art of eloquence demands'.[20] Though the specific sonnet 'Miners' Hut' is particularly in Murphy's mind here, this statement can be regarded more generally as one of intent, a commentary on his desire to shape into a poetic form something of the peculiarities and contrarieties of his complicated background. Throughout, however, is an awareness that while 'poetry can be creative archaeology that discovers and uses verbal roots', it is 'not above the risk of succumbing to fashion or linguistic vandalism'.[21] Poetry, in Murphy's mind, is fraught with its own hypocrisies. We are reminded, perhaps, of Marianne Moore's description of poems as 'imaginary gardens with real toads in them'.[22] The sonnet form, in all its contrived formality, is perhaps the most landscaped of these gardens, but there are still roots to be discovered, toads to be dug out.

As if extending Moore's analogy still further, the 'sonnet houses'[23] of *The Price of Stone* enable Murphy to contrive an imaginary landscape that enacts a complicated relationship with the outside world. The 'real toads' of Murphy's sonnets are, on one level, real things, but those real things are also refracted and remembered within his 'sonnet houses'. Moreover, the outside world consists not only of real structures, but also of memories and experiences that are filtered through Murphy's subjective responses. At the same time the apparent objectivity of the Shakespearean sonnet structure allows for mediation between the personal and the universal. Murphy tried to explain this process in an interview with *The Spectator* in 2013:

> By making the persona of each sonnet the spirit of that house or structure, I found I was better able to transmute the mud of remembered experience into urns of poetry, monuments, ruins, and lesser structures as ancient in design as a wattle tent, voices that had influenced my life – some of which were voices of my conscience arising from the past and admonishing me for my faults, while avoiding the hazards and avowals of confessional verse.[24]

This last phrase is telling, as throughout his notes for the sonnet sequence Murphy is preoccupied with producing something autobiographical that nevertheless avoids the expected solipsistic element; he wishes to move away from what Longley identifies in his poetry, as in that of Thomas Kinsella, John Montague and James Simmons, as 'the sense of isolated imaginations, seeking on various levels for structures in which to lodge themselves'.[25] On first reading, *The Price of Stone* seems to literalise Longley's metaphor, by providing both 'structures' and 'lodgings' for Murphy's conflicted thoughts and loyalties. James B. Kelley points out in his chapter on *The Price of Stone* in the present volume that even the 'confessional material' of Murphy's private notebooks 'has been transformed into the rigid, impersonal form of the sonnets in *The Price of Stone*, yielding a sequence that conceals as much as it reveals about the poet who produced it'.[26] Although I am less concerned with joining the dots between real lived and relived experience within the sequence, I do wish to show how the structural hypocrisies of the sonnets themselves complicate further the relationship between 'confessional material' and their 'rigid, impersonal form'.

In 'Transgressing into Poetry' Murphy tells us that the 'sonnet houses' function as metonyms for actual buildings that predate his own concerns, as if it is the buildings themselves that are seeking him out. The poems each have a 'different persona emanating from a building associated with my life', as Murphy explains, so that it is the building which comes before the 'persona' and the poem.[27] But the set-up is still more complicated, as at the moment that the poem and the building converge, they immediately and necessarily diverge because 'the poem, unlike the monument from which it speaks, must, of course, have an inner life'.[28] The sonnet houses, telling their own stories, are separate from those of the poet himself, as they are also separate from the actual buildings from which they emanate – with the buildings continuing to live lives that are separate from their parallel poem-personas. The poems, then, enact their own confessions – but of course these double back on the poet.

To investigate further how the sonnet houses function as confessionals separate from, but doubling back on, the poet, and to show how the architectural structures seek out the 'isolated' poetic imagination as much as answering it, I wish to turn to those two sonnets that Murphy refers to as the 'Wellington sonnets' in his 'Notes for Sonnets' – 'Wellington Testimonial' and 'Wellington College' – and their linked sonnet, 'Nelson's Pillar'.[29] It is in these poems in particular that the problems of Anglo-Irish inheritance, the literalising of the structural desire identified by Longley, and the politicised issue of 'subjection' are all brought to the fore. Each sonnet recalls, too, that most brilliantly constructed sonnet of monumental failure, P.B. Shelley's 'Ozymandias'.[30] Writing on 'Ozymandias' Albert Labriola notes the ironies inherent in its architectural make-up while conferring praise upon an 'artist' who may be Shelley, but may also be the sculptor within the story as well as the king whose 'works' we are asked to survey: 'The resulting ironies and ambiguities enable the reader of the sonnet not only to animate the sculpture but also to enliven the artist'.[31] Of course, as is true in the case of both 'Ozymandias' and the sonnet houses of *The Price of Stone*, this 'sculpture' refers at once to the building within the poetic narrative and to the structure of the sonnet itself.

Murphy is aware, sometimes painfully, sometimes playfully, of all of these complexities and more in his preparatory notes to the 'Wellington sonnets':

> Have all possible cadences been tried and exhausted in the sonnet? … ask this question in the Wellington sonnets … are you square-bashing in rhymed metrical verse … constrained by the left right left right of the metre and the rhyme, the platoons of polished boots on parade?
>
> Trace the connection, if there is one, between the sonnet as a love poem perfected by Petrarch and Shakespeare immortalising the beloved … and the Wellington Testimonial, constructed to immortalise the saviour of the nation, the victor of Waterloo, the Iron Duke … so precise, well-proportioned and banal … but from some angles epical … cold calculation put it there … to stand high and indifferent over the Phoenix Park … where Thomas Henry Burke and Lord Frederick Cavendish were murdered by the Invincibles in 1882 … and where, last summer, a nurse who had gone to the park to sunbathe was tortured and murdered by a man later found to be staying in a Dalkey penthouse belonging to the Attorney General.[32]

We can see the notes unravelling as Murphy muses further on the layers of hypocrisy generated from just one structural creation, the 'Wellington Testimonial'. Similarly, the 'Wellington sonnets' and

'Nelson's Pillar' give voice to the 'cold calculation' of the colonial project and the 'epical' possibilities of monumental verse – this despite Murphy's concern that perhaps 'all possible cadences' have been 'tried and exhausted in the sonnet'.

A similar suspicion is expressed in the opening lines of 'Wellington College', where the poem unfurls almost despite itself:

> Fear makes you lock out more than you include
> By tackling my red brick with Shakespeare's form
> Of love poem, barracked here and ridiculed
> By hearty boys, drilled to my square-toed norm.   (*P*, p. 205)

The voice seems to ask whether a 'love poem' should be appropriated – 'barracked' and bashed around in the schoolroom – to an environment that rules more by fear than by love. But again, Murphy shelters a moment just as he leaves it exposed; we are reading this story in a sonnet, after all, and a sonnet that is not (or is not obviously) about love. We are left wondering whether the 'square-toed norm' belongs to the parading boots of the student soldiers on parade in their militaristic college, or to the defiant angles of the red-brick school, or whether it refers to the versifying of the knowing poet himself – the fearful 'you' who has been institutionalised to create forever rhymed and metred sonnets.

Elsewhere in his notes to the 'Wellington sonnets', with echoes of the ridiculous bragging cry of Ozymandias – 'Look on my works, ye mighty, and despair!'[33]   Murphy muses how 'a sonnet in the Duke's laconic tone of voice might send up the absurd illusion of immortality in verse or in stone'.[34] Indeed, Murphy confesses in *The Kick* to taking 'refuge' while at Wellington College 'in the Renaissance conceit that a poem, if well made, could last longer than its maker, giving life after death to himself and his loved ones in the minds of his readers', a youthful illusion Murphy now ironises (*K*, p. 77). These considerations, of course, feed through to the concluding couplet of 'Wellington Testimonial', in which the monument half brags, half despairs:

> My sole point in this evergreen oak aisle
> Is to maintain a clean laconic style.   (*P*, p. 181)

Of course, the last line is a sort of joke, in that it cleanly answers its preceding line with a perfect rhyme and in a perfect iambic pentameter. But at the same time something is not quite right. Throughout the poem words seem misused as if, like the 'Testimonial' itself, things are out of place: here we get 'aisle' instead of 'isle' (and 'evergreen ... aisle' rather than 'Emerald Isle'). Perhaps this 'Anglo-Irish' voice does not know any better? Likewise, the phallic monument is characterised as 'Needling my native sky over Phoenix Park', 'obelis[ing] the victory of wit' (*P*, p. 181), so that nouns used usually for aggressive structures (needle and obelisk) are turned into verbs in an assertion of imperial power that is slightly misplaced. Murphy talks about this himself in his notes: 'The poem might develop the ambiguity implied by the verb "obelize" [*sic*] ... the critical mark must grow into self-criticism ... which is also a reflection on where and how I stand ... with an English voice in Ireland now'.[35] So it is not the unabashed self-aggrandising of Ozymandias with which we are presented, but something much more ambiguous, in which the 'Testimonial' itself becomes an uncertain and self-critical witness. Unfortunately for the Anglo-Irish Murphy, this leads to a fear that, like Wellington, perhaps he should not be speaking at all.

Yet Murphy and Shelley, like Petrarch and Shakespeare before them, have taken the time to construct such monuments of verse: ones that might outlive, or might have outlived already, the erections and characters they describe. And in Murphy's case this is despite the fact that, as his notes attest, he fears that he writes 'with an English voice in Ireland now'. Indeed, this kind of situation generates its own stories that, in their complexities and contrarieties, are ripe for poetry. Standing side by side within *The Price of Stone*, 'Nelson's Pillar' and 'Wellington Testimonial' contain within their titles an inscribed social and political history. Joseph Sendry sees these two sonnets as forming part of an opening to the sequence that 'communicates sterility, mainly through phallic structures ineffectually flaunted'.[36] Within these poems 'ineffectual flaunting' is performed by out-of-place British structures tethered to Dublin in order to give voice to a now diminished past.

'Nelson's Pillar' contains a further irony. By the time of composition the monument had, like Ozymandias' statue, been blown up by Irish republicans in 1966, around the fiftieth anniversary of the Easter Rising. So the poem becomes a remembering and re-rendering of the pillar and of Nelson before it, as the closing couplet opines:

> Dismasted and dismissed, without much choice,
> Having lost my touch, I'll raise my chiselled voice.   (*P*, p. 180)

The poem, like 'Ozymandias', contains the echoes and relics of the sculptors' (and builders') work, resounding through the 'chiselled voice' of Nelson atop his 'Pillar' and also through the 'good masons' who 'carved my four / Sea victories in granite' (*P*, p. 180). Of course, it is not merely the 'Pillar' that is talking here, but instead a kind of double ventriloquising is taking place, whereby the 'Pillar' conveys Nelson's thoughts at the same time as the poem-persona is giving voice to some of Murphy's own concerns about the legacy of British imperialism in Dublin (as further expressed, as we have seen, in his notes on the 'cold calculation' of the 'high and indifferent' architects and colonisers in 'Transgressing into Poetry').

In 'Nelson's Pillar' Admiral Nelson appears to have been reincarnated as the pillar itself; but Murphy's characterisation adds further complications to Nelson's narrative. Rather than being proud of his achievement, 'Nelson' wonders at his own displacement, and at the potentially cruel ramifications of erecting this monument for him:

> My duty done, I rose as a Doric column
> Far from at home, planted to reach the sky;
> A huge stake in the crossed heart of a glum
> Garrison city overlooked by my blind eye.   (*P*, p. 180)

The story that is being told here is not as simple as Sendry's suggestion that these particular sonnets 'proclaim the lost potency of imperial power now spent'.[37] This 'lost potency' is felt, certainly, in the flattening answering rhyme of 'glum' to 'column', which swiftly dispenses Nelson's erection. Yet Nelson, sitting atop his pillar, is aware of this, too, commenting on both the cruelty and the ridiculousness of the endeavour, and expressing dissatisfaction at having to spend his days in this 'glum / Garrison city'. Indeed, his self-aware mocking of his own inadequacies ('overlooked by my blind eye') is continued in the following lines, which deflate the overblown assertions of 'Rule Britannia', offering a bathetic portrayal of Nelson's figure as 'One-armed on a cold square abacus to rule / The waves, …' (*P*, p. 180).

But while Murphy does not ask us to mock so blindly Nelson's aggrandisements, thanks to his own pillar's embarrassments, neither does he want us to forget Nelson's achievements. For in almost the same breath in which we are asked to wonder 'Who cares, now, …[?]' (*P*, p. 180), we are also reminded of the naval 'victories' commemorated in inscriptions on the pillar. For a brief moment Nelson might be 'Ozymandias', but he is given none of that king's swagger: instead he is 'Dismasted', and the reader feels some sympathy for him (*P*, p. 180). It leads us to ask whether, when in the poem the destruction of the pillar is enacted – 'the blast wore / Red, white and blue in a flash of puerile skill' (*P*, p. 180) – this latter adjective refers to Nelson's own self-analysis. He knows, and has known all along, that his is a pillar of salt.

Reading the 'Wellington sonnets' and 'Nelson's Pillar' together usefully elucidates thematic and formal overlaps that contribute to the overall architecture of the sonnet sequence. The idea of returning themes suits not only the common idea of the 'turn' in the sonnet but also the circularity of the sonnet sequence. In 'Nelson's Pillar' and 'Wellington College', for example, the returning subject of schooling is used to suggest at first divergence and then convergence between students. The 'drilled' and 'hearty boys' (*P*, p. 205) of Wellington College seem initially far from the 'Poor beggars' of 'Nelson's Pillar' who are 'round my plinth, schooled to rebel' (*P*, p. 180). But straightaway we see how both groups are schooled according to tradition, custom and rules – and the circularity of the sonnet form and the larger sequence facilitate this understanding. On a micro-level Murphy's use of the sonnet form, and his manipulation of rhyme in particular, reveals an exploration of the competing ironies of his subject matter in these three sonnets. Quoted above, the closing rhyme of 'Nelson's Pillar' – 'choice / voice' – is as resounding as it is false, the clear ringing rhyme showing up Nelson's inability to 'raise' his 'chiselled voice' any longer, not least because the pillar itself no longer exists. Nelson attempts to raise his voice here despite the fact that the odds are stacked against him – he is 'without much choice', and he has 'lost' his 'touch' (*P*, p. 180) – with a bathetic result. He might try and cry out, but, again like Ozymandias, who will hear him? Again, we feel these questions resounding with Murphy's own 'self-criticism' of his poetic ambition.

To think more closely about Murphy's use of bathetic rhyme within these sonnets, and to suggest something about his overall approach to rhyme in *The Price of Stone*, I want to return to Gillis' assertion that within the sequence 'the best poems are those in which the concluding couplet generates a final turn, a sense of surprise, which simultaneously segues into a sense of ritualistic finish'. Of course, rhyme plays a large part in the 'finish' of 'concluding couplet'. Moving on from Gillis' evaluative judgement, however, I wish to question instead the assumption that something formulaic, and even 'ritualistic', is at play within the sonnets. Instead, I think that something more complicated, self-questioning and self-aware is taking place, which involves a manipulation of the expectations of rhyme and so moves a reader away from surprise, instead providing us with endings that are often contrived and often bathetic. In 'Nelson's Pillar', for example, 'voice' is an obvious rhyme with 'choice', but Nelson's deflation is more resounding as a result.

Significantly, the same rhyme is employed in 'Wellington College' – but the use of this rhyme allows us to view a similar subject from a different perspective:

> Yet ushered in, through my roll of honour voice,
> Cold baths in winter, field days on Bagshot Heath,
> Poetry gives you unconscripted choice
> Of strategies, renaissance air to breathe.   (*P*, p. 205)

Here, in contrast with 'Nelson's Pillar', the authoritative voice of another building constructed for another imperial war hero becomes a possible voice for good, enabling the conditions whereby the 'you' can discover the 'unconscripted choice / Of strategies' offered by learning poetry. Important, too, is that the enforced exercise of 'Bagshot Heath' literally gives the poet 'air to breathe', at the same time that 'Poetry' is imaginatively sustaining. The clear rhyme of 'voice' and 'choice', rendered less contrived through an ABAB model not possible within a rhyming couplet, complicates the bathetic model offered earlier in 'Nelson's Pillar'. In correspondence, then, the repeated rhymes of 'voice' and 'choice' ask challenging questions about the relationship between imperial might and learning. Had Wellington not succeeded, had he not been honoured, would the poet have found his own 'voice'? Was Murphy's militaristic schooling necessary, to throw into sharp relief the 'unconscripted' 'renaissance' offered by poetry? But then again, if Nelson is silenced on his 'Pillar', and perhaps rightly so, should the poet, educated from the spoils of his glories, be silenced, too?

The closing couplet of 'Wellington College' leads to further questioning, as we are provided with a conclusion that is nagging in tone, sounding as much like a mother scorning a naughty child as a school scorning either a future poet or a dead army hero:

> Weren't you born to command a regiment?
> How selfishly you serve your own heart's bent.   (*P*, p. 205)

Here, the rhyme is again bathetic: it feels forced, awkward, clunky even. But then surely this is the point. That concluding line, forced, too, in its determined iambic pentameter, castigates at the same moment as we sense the poet's self-scorn; the idea is being 'bent' to the line as if the 'you' – the schoolboy poet, now older – is unsure whether it is his 'heart's bent' to break free or to subscribe to preconditioned rules. Therefore, the concluding couplet offers at least two readings. The first sees the school scorning the boy for not achieving more in later life than writing poetry: for moving away from what he has been schooled in, and what he has been brought up as, in order to settle in Ireland and write. But the possibility of self-scorning opens up another reading: that this is the poet, talking through the college back to himself, asking why he serves his 'own heart's bent' in bending to a form which leads him back to where he started – a place where 'Fear makes you lock out more than you include' (*P*, p. 205). This could be a commentary on writing as much as on living. Here, then, the bathetic rhyme may come at the expense of apparent poetic 'success'; but it does not come at the expense of honesty.

Through the writing and construction of *The Price of Stone*, Murphy is able to bring apparent hypocrisies to bear on the poems, to see how they play out both within the overall structure of the sonnet sequence and within the autobiographical ventriloquising of the 'sonnet houses' themselves. Critics have often levelled at *The Price of Stone* the criticism that there is no overarching, consistent narrative to bring all the poems together, but the fact that the sequence nearly buckles under its own shaky foundations is surely the point. And this structural near-buckling reflects Murphy's own personal doubts and self-concealments as an Anglo-Irish poet trying to come to terms with his past by setting up home in rural Ireland. When Murphy tells us that he wrote *The Price of Stone* between April 1981 and 1983 'at an isolated house on Mullen's Hill in Killiney',[38] he is (painfully) aware of the irony that he is able to buy houses in order to write about other ones, or indeed to have the leisure time to write at all. There is contrivance in this process and he knows it. In Murphy's notes on 'Writing *The Battle of Aughrim*', which was first published in 1968, he comments on the 'absurdity of pretentious ancestral claims' of Irish people from all backgrounds, as if predicting his preoccupation in *The Price of Stone* with the pretentious absurdity of putting down one's roots in a country whose very soil is contested (*P*, p. 257). Thus, while Murphy stakes his claim on the land he loves, he is also aware of the attendant ironies that are raised by his doing so. At the same time, he needs to work out where he fits within the broader scheme of things:

> A question uppermost in all Irish minds in our agricultural past – *who owns the land?* – occurred to me so strongly that I took an envelope from the pocket of my donkey jacket and wrote those words, in case I might forget them during a day of chatting to tourists while trying to navigate safely to and from Inishbofin on the *Ave Maria*. (*P*, p. 255)

In this scene Murphy casts himself as slightly absurd – not only because of his status as part tourist, part observer, part Irishman, but also because of his status as poet. For what is most clear from this scene is his awareness of the poetic posture: he remakes the scene as he recounts it, while his taking down of notes tells us that he needs to work this stuff out into poetry. By virtue of being a poet, then, he is always a little apart.

In the same notes to writing *The Battle of Aughrim* Murphy discusses 'guilt' as a drive for writing the poem – in 1968, he tells us, he 'was trying to examine my army heritage and my guilt in not having served in the war that was brought to an end by the bomb on Hiroshima on my 18th birthday' (*P*, p. 257). By 1983, in *The Price of Stone*, this 'guilt' has become connected to an uneasy inheritance of land, places and buildings that Murphy both celebrates and ironises; yet, as we have seen in his manipulation of the sonnet form, these complexities are channelled into a highly self-aware, both painful and playful, verse. It is not quite the case, then, that as Longley puts it, 'In seeking a "truly Irish" identity Murphy also seeks absolution from Ascendancy guilts', but rather that his sequence acts as an acknowledgement that the atonement that all poets seek, and particularly poets who (like Murphy) carry a burden of guilt, is sometimes contrived, often circuitous, and even occasionally hypocritical.

But perhaps all poetry is to some extent hypocritical. To cite Christopher Ricks, although poetry seeks to indulge in an 'evocation of atonement as a finality', the form can never really answer the desire to atone, or to be at one: the two 'are finally irreconcilable, tonally and totally', because ultimately 'there can be no atonement of atonement and at-one-ment'.[39] The poem that places this acknowledgement at its centre, the sonnet that results from such self-aware seeking, can in turn seem contrived, circuitous and hypocritical. But it can also do other things, can take us into new directions of reading and thinking. Sendry includes in this new model an acknowledgement that in *The Price of Stone* sequence we have to imagine the poet as being an additional reader of, or listener to, his poems. He listens to his 'sonnet houses' as if their voices are separate from his. As if to counter Longley's earlier accusation, levelled at Murphy, as well as at other young poets, that their work manifests 'the sense of isolated imaginations, seeking on various levels for structures in which to lodge themselves', Sendry sees Murphy's structures as seeking him out and speaking to him:

> By organizing his sequence around a series of sonnets that speak to the poet instead of his speaking to them Murphy creates possibilities for extending the range of expressible meaning. As the one who is spoken to, the poet in a literal sense objectifies himself, though he deals with states of intense subjectivity.[40]

So where Longley suggests that Murphy's poetry 'stands in the way of total subjection of the offered experience', she is basing her reading on an assumption that the ultimate aspiration of a poet is 'total subjection'. But what happens when, as in the case of the sonnets of *The Price of Stone*, the objectification of the thing observed and the self-objectification of the poet himself combine to generate an 'intense subjectivity' of method?

In the sonnets of *The Price of Stone* 'intense subjectivity' becomes a creative substitute for the 'total subjection' that Longley and Heaney search for. But for a poet who places an awareness of the hypocrisies of poetry at the centre of things, and who relies on the sonnet, that most hypocritical of forms, to hammer his ideas home, it perhaps comes as no surprise that Murphy creates a poetic model that is sometimes shamefully, sometimes proudly aware of its profound subjectivity. This approach requires us to reconsider our critical language, to reinterpret the 'success' or 'otherwise' of his poems through their self-reflexivity and self-awareness rather than through their ability to subscribe to prescribed expectations. Heaney's accusation of Murphy's 'symptomatic unease',[41] then, is upturned by *The Price of Stone* because Murphy places his unease at the centre of things. The ventriloquised 'unease' of Murphy's self-acknowledged 'split mind'[42] becomes instead the bastion of the sequence – at once its cause, its symptom and possibly, also, its cure.

13

~

Exposure and Obscurity: The cruising sonnets in Richard Murphy's *The Price of Stone*

JAMES B. KELLEY

Writing in his notebooks about an emerging sequence that would be published in 1985 as *The Price of Stone*, Richard Murphy describes the various houses that he has acquired and lived in as 'objects and artifacts into which the spirit of friends … has permanently gone'. 'Some of the spirit', he continues,

> can be recovered by total strangers who can appreciate the beauty of random stonework, but much of it can only be recovered if I reveal the story that lives within the dead objects, the movement within the immobility of granite, and bring to life the persons whose love lies immured there. This requires words at the heat of blood. It requires narrative, telling of events in time.[1]

Like the houses described here, Murphy's rich, yet cryptically autobiographical sonnets require explanatory narrative if they are to be appreciated as much more than random, beautiful stonework and if their full significance is to be understood. However, few critics have had the opportunity to examine Murphy's extensive notebooks, which offer unflinching, detailed reflections on the life events and observations that have provided the building materials for his sonnets and which depict in equally extensive detail the process of composition of the poems themselves. Murphy himself had gradually

222

been completing a public narrative that reveals the half-concealed meanings in the sonnets of *The Price of Stone*, a narrative begun as early as 1984 in an extended radio programme by the Australian Broadcasting Commission (ABC) and developed most fully in *The Kick*, a volume of his memoirs published in 2002 and republished by Cork University Press in 2017. *The Kick* makes a number of brief references to the notebooks, including how they are the only place in which he wrote freely, without fear of criticism (*K*, p. 260), and reproduces substantial passages from one section of the notebooks (*K*, pp. 261–5), but it offers little that sheds light on the composition of the sonnets themselves. His work in progress, 'Transgressing into Poetry' – appearing in *Poetry Ireland Review* nos 104, 107 and 111 – offers selective but still substantial and fascinating glimpses into the notebook entries that would be reworked into some of the poems in *The Price of Stone*.[2] Most recently *In Search of Poetry* has provided the fullest insight to date of the compositional process behind the fifty sonnets included in *The Price of Stone*.[3]

The notebooks are small, bound volumes of grid paper started by Murphy in 1954, and these many volumes are now housed in Special Collections in the University of Tulsa's McFarlin Library. The notebooks were often kept at his bedside and were meant, Murphy writes in *The Kick*, to give order to his experiences and to record his thoughts in strictly honest and uncensored terms (*K*, pp. 139–40). Murphy's brief account in his memoir of finding and purchasing his first notebooks establishes a fascinating link between his poetic production and his sexual desires for other men; he writes that at the time that he purchased the first stack of notebooks, he had been pursuing 'two deviously related desires: to write poetry that might be accepted by T.S. Eliot at Faber; and to meet among strangers on the Left Bank a young soldier, sailor or gypsy who would give my poetry the passion and inspiration it lacked' (*K*, p. 139). Given the unflinching frankness with which he recorded his thoughts and experiences, he observes in his memoirs that 'from the start I knew the notebook would have to be kept secret' (*K*, p. 140).[4] To this day the contents have largely been kept secret in order to protect the privacy of some individuals still living.

As perhaps the first and only critic to publish an examination of *The Price of Stone* through the notebook entries that led to the production of the sonnets, Rand Brandes has observed:

> The composition and arrangement of the sonnets themselves is elaborate – seasonal, biological, sexual, musical, mathematical, mythical, historical, and topographical. Perhaps the most important organizational principle, however, was Murphy's own journey from isolation and barrenness to a rebirth of the poetic self, a rebirth manifested in the actual birth of his son in January 1982.[5]

Brandes develops this characterisation of the architectonics of the sonnet sequence – this development of the poet in heterosexual and procreative terms – by examining the first and the final two sonnets in the sequence of fifty poems: 'Folly', 'Beehive Cell' and 'Natural Son'.

Benjamin Keatinge has subsequently identified a similar pattern within the sonnets even as he argues that the sequence as a whole, particularly when read in light of Murphy's subsequent memoir, shows not so much a clear development towards fully heterosexual identity and procreativity, but rather presents a wide range of identities and affiliations that are complex, conflicted and challenging to classify, including the question of sexual identity. Keatinge writes that poems in the first half of *The Price of Stone* sonnet sequence (which forms Part II of Murphy's 1985 collection *The Price of Stone*) 'examine the furtive world of casual homosexual encounter using a series of phallic monuments to emphasize sterility and lack of issue'.[6] In his analysis he continues to emphasise their sterility – 'these are sterile poems' and 'these sexual meeting places represent an unproductive sterility' – and contrasts these poems in the first half with other poems in the sequence that focus on heterosexuality and childbirth: 'But there is another side to Murphy that celebrates heterosexual love and rejoices in sensuality'.[7]

These oppositions echo Richard Murphy's own division of the poems. In a set of short commentaries on the poems in *The Price of Stone* for the ABC broadcast in 1984, Murphy divides the sonnet sequence into four groups, placing the sonnets 'Beehive Cell' and

'Natural Son' in the grouping that he calls 'birth poems', and placing the two queer cruising sonnets 'Portico' and 'Gym' in the grouping that he calls more generally, even euphemistically, 'a sequence set in the Dublin area'.[8] The final sonnet to be examined here, 'Convenience', is grouped, surprisingly, with the poems that Murphy, in the ABC broadcast, characterises as those 'spoken in the many voices of my English and Irish education'; this poem is all about the tension and negotiations between extremes, among them the public and the private, the sense of innocence and of guilt, and the competing goals of exposure and concealment, self-expression and self-restraint. It records what Murphy would call in the ABC broadcast, using protectively generalised language, one of life's 'harsh … lessons'.[9]

My approach to the sequence builds on, but deviates from, Brandes' work by pairing the sonnets from the end of the sequence that extol heterosexual reproductivity – 'Beehive Cell' and 'Natural Son' – with two sonnets focusing on the marginal spaces in which men cruise for anonymous sex with other men and appearing much earlier in the sequence – 'Portico' and 'Gym'. In briefly uncovering the connections as well as tensions among these sets of poems – the 'birth poems' and those 'set in the Dublin area' – this approach problematises our attempt to read the sequence as tracing the development of the poetic self from sterility to fertility and from isolation to intimacy. The discussion closes with an extended look at a fifth sonnet, 'Convenience', that appears near the middle of the sequence.

If *The Price of Stone* is to be understood through architectural metaphors and if the sonnets, as a whole, indeed build a sort of arc or arch – whether it be one of development towards exclusive heterosexuality and biological fatherhood or one that spans a wide range of sexual desires and identities – then the sonnet 'Convenience', which appears near the middle of the sequence, serves as a sort of keystone. Indeed, in his early notebook entries for 'Convenience', Murphy calls this poem 'one of the most difficult and important and crucial in the sequence'.[10] 'Convenience' serves as a point of transition in the sonnet sequence and in the poet's life; the poems following it are set in western Ireland where Murphy moved after the break-up of his marriage to Patricia Avis in 1959. The poem alludes to the poet's traumatic experience in London in 1950 as recorded in *The Kick* (*K*, pp. 104–8). Murphy candidly describes in his memoir the same material alluded to in the poem: accusations of gross indecency in a public toilet, extortion by an undercover policeman or conman, and further humiliation by law-enforcement officials when the offence against his person is reported. This incident had lasting consequences for Murphy's life and work, leading him to avoid large cities for many years and, no less importantly, prompting him to engage in unflinching self-examination and to record his thoughts and experiences with absolute candour within his private notebooks. This confessional material has then been transformed into the rigid, impersonal form of the sonnets in *The Price of Stone*, yielding a sequence that conceals as much as it reveals about the poet who produced it.

In 'Beehive Cell' and 'Portico', as in all but one of the sonnets, there is no conventional speaker; the building itself is made to speak in what might be seen as a strategic displacement of authorial voice and identity. Murphy explains in his printed notes prepared for the ABC broadcast: 'The freedom I got from letting a building or structure speak in the first person released me into writing all the rest.'[11]

In his examination of 'Beehive Cell', Brandes quotes from some of the notebook entries that led to the development of the poem:

> Built for monks – women barred – men beating themselves – …
> in all my life of decay since that holy beginning – only one really
> sensational/miraculous/thing has happened to me […] and on
> her own, in my clochan, this woman knelt and gave birth to a son
>   For a thousand years I had nothing to remember but the
> sanctity and flagellation of dead monks.[12]

Brandes observes that only a few words from Murphy's extensive notes on 'the infertility of the monastic tradition' and 'the sterile spirituality of the monks'[13] find their way into the poem's final form, such as the words 'barren' and 'miracle'. The notebooks show that Murphy was equally methodical in his choice of words for 'Portico'.

Here, one finds listings of etymologically related words and their associations, including many terms of religion and churches, such as 'cloistered', 'ambulatory' and 'succursal aisles', only a few of which find their way into the finished sonnet.

These seemingly contrasting poems are similar in more than the method of composition. The men seeking out one another for anonymous sex in 'Portico' are likened to monks or priests, and this detail helps reveal the subtle homosexual imagery (not discussed by Brandes) in the early drafts of 'Beehive Cell': 'women barred – men beating themselves'. The settings of the two poems appear similarly connected; the barren island and the womblike stone structure of 'Beehive Cell', in which a pregnant woman finds shelter and gives birth, is prefigured in the 'concrete cloister' and the barren, even toxic landscape of 'Portico', with its 'mercury vapour across a bay of mud', 'black hole' and 'spumy grotto' that suggest a sperm-filled rectum rather than a fertilised womb (*P*, p. 179).

In the ABC broadcast on *The Price of Stone*, Murphy prefaces his reading of 'Portico' by offering some help with the difficult vocabulary of the poem, making a quick reference to 'the cult of the phallus' and quoting briefly from the philosopher Stuart Hampshire on the virtue of 'deviation on all sides of the norm'[14] (the quotation reappears as the epigraph to *The Kick*, *K*, p. xxiii). After reading the poem Murphy mentions having 'avoid[ed] big cities most of my life' and having been married to Patricia Avis in the 1950s. His public discussion of the poem drops few to no hints about his familiarity with the subject of the poem and provides no clear connection between the male poet and the poem's setting, a section of the docks frequented by men looking for anonymous sex with other men.

Murphy's introduction to the poem 'Gym' in the ABC broadcast is even briefer – only two sentences that do quite a lot: he identifies the title building as 'a men's sauna or bathhouse', gives a general sense of how to get there, shows his interest in etymologies, and makes a reference to the early AIDS crisis:

> There is a failure of loftiness in the underworld of a men's sauna or bathhouse known as 'The Gym', an appropriate name derived

from the Greek word for naked. 'Gym' is located in an alley in the heart of the city close to Dublin Castle, and by August 1983, when this poem was written, the freedom of the sexual revolution had been tainted by the tyranny of AIDS.[15]

The impersonal nature of those comments, like the cool, distanced, perhaps even derisive language of the sonnet itself, belies the poet's intensely personal connection with the subject of the poem. The notebook entries for 'Gym', written in a characteristically fragmented and elliptical style, suggest the poet's familiarity with the building's inner workings and, towards the end of the section quoted here, express his fear of contracting HIV by engaging in unsafe sex with other men while there:

> What next in the sequence? Something about deprivation ... emotional, physical, economic, sexual, mental, spiritual ... exemplified in the SAUNA ... where men meet stripped of everything ... strip off everything ... but this is a luxury ... you have to pay to enter ... the heat is dear ... the steam is a drug ... the dark room ... here you take your chance ... this is the apotheosis of exclusiveness ... excluding women, children, conversation, friendship, marriage, birth and, at least for the moment, death ... but as the seed is wasted on the ground, washed away in the shower, fertility liquidated (?), so other invisible seeds, bacteria, viruses are planted in your membranous tissues, implanted, causing your death ...[16]

This privately recorded fear of contracting HIV and dying from AIDS in the very early 1980s is confirmed publicly only much later, in a 2013 interview for *The Spectator* in which Murphy is asked what he was trying to express in 'Gym'. In a manner consistent with the treatment of sexuality in his private notebooks and in his public memoir *The Kick*, he answers frankly and with self-knowledge:

> That poem describes my deliberate fall, at different times and places, into what I regarded as a homosexual underworld of anonymous, illicit, promiscuous, risky and loveless sex. Each from a different angle speaks of the failure, denial or absence of

love in pursuit of sex and the misery for me of this. Not because the pursuit was queer but because it was without a spoken word. In many of these poems the speaker, a voice of my conscience, admonishes me for utterly different faults: in this particularly poem [*sic*] it was for exposing myself to the risk of acquiring AIDS by entering the temptingly repellent atmosphere of a gay sauna in a lane under the wall of Dublin Castle called 'the Gym', an apt word that derives from the Greek for nakedness. 'Absolute liberty', as I once heard Isaiah Berlin say in a lecture, 'leads to absolute tyranny'. In this case the tyranny that came in 1983 after the absolute liberty of the sexual revolution of the '60s and '70s was a deadly virus, unknown in those days, with no cure, spreading great fear.[17]

Building on the characterisation in the notebooks of the gay bathhouse as 'excluding women, children, … marriage, birth' – a characterisation that applies equally well to the monk's shelter in 'Beehive Cell', the cruising area in 'Portico', and the patrons of the gay bathhouse, who are 'immune from women' in 'Gym' (*P*, p. 183) – the notebook entry goes on to identify the community of the gay sauna as 'the very antithesis of family life' and finds fault, above all, with the lack of communication among the men who gather there.[18] In the published poem, 'Gym', the patrons are described as 'enter[ing] in retreat / From words that shame' and 'taking no verbal risk' (*P*, p. 183); the only named sound in the poem is the 'musak' – piped, anodyne, and lyric-free – that seems partly to cause the intoxication or lethargy that rules the patrons:

> Discreetly couched, taking no verbal risk,
> Ingled in clutches masked by sauna steam,
> Nude club members, immune from women, bask
> In tableaux mixed with musak, cocaine, jism.   (*P*, p. 183)

In 'Gym', as in all but one of the sonnets in *The Price of Stone*, Murphy uses the technique of speaking through the building. 'Portico' is equally free of human speech; the men cruising for sex perform only 'mute melodies' (*P*, p. 179), and the sounds in the closing couplet are animal-like grunts or are provided by the environment, not by the men gathered there:

> My hymns are hog-snorts, squealing bottle-glass
> Screwed underfoot, a wave's foghorn caress.   (*P*, p. 179)

The final poem, 'Natural Son', is the only one in the sequence not to speak through a building. In contrast to the earlier poems, the sonnet is filled with human sounds, from the child's 'birth-cry' near its beginning to the parents' 'vocal skill' near its end, and the speaker here is taken by some critics and close friends to be the poet finding himself at the end of a long journey (*P*, p. 226). For Brandes, as quoted earlier in this essay, this final sonnet illustrates 'Murphy's own journey from isolation and barrenness to a return of the poetic self',[19] and, as recorded by Murphy in a notebook entry of 1 February 1982, Dennis O'Driscoll characterises 'Natural Son' as 'a master key to the sonnet houses … a statement by the poet speaking in his own voice instead of ventriloquizing'.[20] The third stanza of 'Natural Son', however, may be read as calling into question the speaker's movement from isolation to intimacy as well as the certainty, power and complete authenticity of the poetic voice:

> No house we build could hope to satisfy
> Every small need, now that you've made this move
> To share our loneliness, much as we try
> Our vocal skill to wall you round with love.   (*P*, p. 226)

What is shared in this relationship is, paradoxically, not intimacy but 'loneliness', and spoken language seems inadequate to fully bridge the gap between persons. The *Oxford English Dictionary* lists multiple definitions for the verb 'try', among them: to make an attempt, to test the strength or to verify the guilt of something, but also to experiment or, more archaically, to sift, strain or separate: 'To separate the good part of a thing from the rest'. This final meaning seems reinforced by the phrase 'to wall you round', to build a barrier around a person that, to paraphrase Robert Frost's 'Mending Wall', keeps something in as much as it keeps something out.

Two substantial notebook entries published by Murphy in the section 'Family Seat' in *Poetry Ireland Review* no. 111 further suggest a lingering uncertainty in the poetic voice – the entry for '*Tues 26 Jan 1982*' meditates on 'the voice of a once powerful house-cum-family in terminal decline' and 'the failure to marry and have children'[21] – as well as a powerful division, a split, within the poet himself. The entry for '*Sat 30 Jan 1982*' reveals some of the narrative, including the conflicts, that has been sifted and strained from the notebooks into the sonnet 'Natural Son': 'In helping my friend to have the child she wanted, a son born yesterday in the Rotunda under the sign of Aquarius, in all the difficulties of our unmarried situation and what she loathes about my split-level life, we have had to endure the disapproval of our families.'[22]

Reading *The Price of Stone* sonnets as a narrative of the poet's development might require a separation of one part of the poet from the rest of him, a walling off of the lower half of the poet's 'split-level' self, in order for a change to be made evident in the final sonnet. However, reading the notebook entries alongside the 'birth poems' and the poems from 'sequence set in the Dublin area' underscores several sets of seemingly irreconcilable differences – intimacy and anonymity, speech and silence, fertility and sterility, heterosexuality and homosexuality, among others – even as it calls attention to powerful connections and interdependencies among the poems. Reading these materials alongside one another reminds us that they are all profoundly part of the speaking subject's complex experiences and complex identity.

Judging by the frequency with which Murphy revisits the traumatic experience immortalised within the sonnet 'Convenience' – the accusations of being queer, the extortion, and the failed attempt to resolve the matter by consulting with law-enforcement officials – one should not overlook its importance to *The Price of Stone* sonnet sequence and to Murphy's poetic career as a whole. Indeed, the experience is recounted in *The Kick* at length and in extensive detail, employing an uncharacteristically large degree of direct dialogue and written in a manner that makes it stand out from the general narrative voice of the memoirs (*K*, pp. 104–8). This account is fascinating in itself, with the twenty-one-year-old Murphy asserting his superiority if only in his mind: he is taller, better dressed, and has a loftier accent than both the man whom he observes in the toilet and the man who subsequently accosts, extorts and renders him immensely vulnerable.[23] The experience also maintains a subtle presence throughout the memoir. A few pages after the initial recounting Murphy writes:

> Around this time I read in a newspaper that a man of my age had taken a room on the seventh floor of the Dorchester Hotel, climbed out on to the windowsill and shot himself in the head. I pitied him, whoever he was, as it looked as if he might have got into the kind of trouble with the police or a blackmailer that I had narrowly escaped.   (*K*, p. 110)

Murphy realises that the suicide victim had indeed been a friend from his school years with whom he had had frank talks about their mutual same-sex attraction, just as he realises that this tragedy could have been his fate as well (recalling, perhaps, for the reader that in the initial account he had fleetingly thought of suicide on the spot). Some 200 pages later in *The Kick*, Murphy again briefly but tellingly revisits one of the lasting effects of the experience, writing: 'I had not lived in a city since I had left London, fearful of cities, in 1951' (*K*, p. 304). Long before publishing his memoirs Murphy made multiple attempts to process the experience in the private spaces of his notebooks as well as, increasingly but always with some caution, in public arenas. One early account in a notebook entry from 29 October 1967 ends: 'Took eighteen years to clarify the muck.'[24]

The entries that trace the composition of 'Convenience' take up some thirty-six pages in one notebook, across multiple entries dated from 28 April to 4 May 1982. The earliest entries are in prose, followed by a few stray lines of poetry, more prose, some quatrains, the opening stanza (in an entry dated 3 May), followed by more prose, multiple drafts of the poem, and then the completed poem as published in *The Price of Stone*. Among these extensive notebook entries on the poem is a singularly profound statement that connects the illegality of male homosexual acts in England and in Ireland, the commitment to brutal honesty in his notebooks, and the purposeful caution that shapes his writing and his statements intended for public consumption: 'your fear of the awful power of the law made your poetry obscure'.[25]

Murphy's prefatory comments to 'Convenience' in the 1984 ABC broadcast illustrate how this obscurity is maintained even in his public statements about the poem. Before reading the poem aloud he offers a highly cautious explanation of what the poem is about:

> The persona of 'Convenience' is a 'profane oracle' who speaks through a crack in a mental block about a traumatic incident that occurred one afternoon in the autumn of 1949 when I was twenty-one, in the Piccadilly Circus Underground in the heart of London, the 'omphalos' of the British Empire and the English language.[26] In England the word 'convenience' was then a euphemism equivalent to the American 'rest room', though its root meaning, ironically, is 'coming together'.[27]

He further explains that this 'traumatic incident' made him wish to live far from large cities for most of his life, but the precise nature of the incident – and, indeed, even the person to whom the incident had occurred – remains unspecified in these introductory comments: the poem is 'about a traumatic incident that occurred'; there is no clear sense of involvement, no '… to me' or 'I experienced …', in the explanation that he provides. The poem is left to speak for itself, and it does so only in a hesitant and ultimately cryptic manner.

The second stanza of 'Convenience' – formed of a single, complex sentence – suggests the conflicting desires to reveal and to conceal the full truth, to speak as the prized articulator of truth but also to 'speak through a crack' about an unnamed event that occurred 'far back' in time and that has had lasting, traumatic effects:

> Your profane oracle, I speak through a crack
> In a mental block, going far back to the year
> You stood here, epicentred on the shock
> Of gross accusation, quaking at words like queer.   (*P*, p. 207)

The enjambment of the lines – with one line flowing into the next, propelling the poem forward – suggests uninterrupted movement towards a revelation, yet both the insistent internal rhyming and the comma that divides each poetic line down the centre (techniques that, admittedly, are used elsewhere in the sonnet sequence) interrupt that flow, suggesting a hesitation, a reluctance to fully confront, make sense of, and speak openly about exactly what had occurred. At the end of the poem the reader can be certain that something occurred that causes the person addressed within the poem to feel immensely vulnerable for a long period afterwards but cannot be certain of what that something actually was. The final lines of the sonnet:

> A life sentence, ambiguously imposed,
> Props you behind all kinds of bars, exposed.   (*P*, p. 207)

suggest that the poem itself or perhaps even the profession of poet might serve as a prison. Autobiographical writing (the 'life sentence') and autobiographical poetry, in particular – the word 'bars' in the final line of 'Convenience' suggests the measured lines and the rigid, cage-like form of the sonnet – once published, does not simply liberate the speaking subject. Even as it elevates this poet and garners him justified recognition (it 'Props you'), the published work equally places him in a position of continued vulnerability (leaving you 'exposed').

Murphy's notebook entries, poetry and commentaries all attest to his interest in etymology and connotation, and he frequently uses terms that suggest two or more meanings at once. The phrase 'gross accusation' in the sonnet 'Convenience' expresses a sense of strong repugnance, of course, but it also echoes the language of the Labouchere Amendment (Section 11 of the Criminal Law Amendment Act, 1885), which made 'any act of gross indecency with another male person' punishable by up to two years in prison, with or without hard labour. That conveniently vague language of the Labouchere Amendment – what, exactly, is an act of gross indecency? – is woven into Murphy's account in *The Kick*, in which the man with the trenchcoat and Brylcreemed hair – whether undercover policeman or conman – accuses the young poet, whom he claims to have identified earlier as 'one of those homosexuals', as having been 'engaged in a criminal act of gross indecency in a public place – masturbating' (*K*, p. 105).

Homosexual acts between men at or over the age of consent were decriminalised in England by the Sexual Offences Act 1967 (Ireland did not remove its Victorian-era laws from the statute book until 1993). As might be expected, full transparency in the realm of high literature did not immediately follow this formal change in the law, and literary landmarks such as J.R. Ackerley's *My Father and Myself* (1968) and E.M. Forster's *Maurice* (1971) saw print only posthumously. Yet Murphy attributes the obscurity of his poetry not simply to 'the awful power of the law', which must have eased considerably between late 1949, when the traumatic experience occurred, and the early 1980s, when he began to work in earnest on the sonnet 'Convenience', but rather he attributes the obscurity to 'your fear of the awful power of the law'. The poems in *The Price of Stone* and Murphy's public narrative surrounding the poems may indeed strike one as strategically, if not fearfully, obscure well into the mid-1980s, particularly when compared to works and statements by his openly queer contemporaries Thom Gunn and Allen Ginsberg.

Writing before the publication of *The Kick*, Jill Siddall recognises this obscure treatment of queer identity and desire in Murphy's poetry, calling it 'subterfuge through necessity'.[28] In the penultimate paragraph of her review essay on *Collected Poems* (Gallery Press, 2000), Siddall writes:

> There is the suggestion here, that ... Murphy's sense of dislocation from a recognisable social or cultural milieu springs not only from his ancestry but from a more deep rooted sense of subterfuge through necessity. In his review of *The Price of Stone* for the *TLS*, Bernard O'Donoghue suggests that the poem 'Convenience' conveys the 'embarrassment, ludicrousness and seriousness of sexual consciousness'. From my reading, I suggest that 'Convenience' and a second sonnet, 'Gym', express an even deeper anxiety, that of sexual difference in a society as rigid as that of Murphy's childhood which always chose rule, order and conformity over freedom of life, limb and longing.[29]

This anxiety and subterfuge were likely exacerbated by Murphy's avoidance of large cities and his distance from the emerging urban gay subculture of the 1960s and 1970s that was so openly embraced by Gunn and Ginsberg, and are also suggested in the sense of extreme vulnerability connected to engaging in sex acts with other men. In one of his notebook entries for 'Convenience' from the early 1980s, for example, Murphy writes a paragraph-long string of free associations on the penis, listing words and phrases in one such paragraph that move from sexual aggression, violence and prowess to the possibility of impotence, and that end with the possibility of entrapment and castration:

> it is all one … it's just a prick … a weapon … a cock … a penis … a phallus … a tool … which can be used to assault, rape, ride, poke, fuck, bugger, fellate (in reverse), tantalize, tempt, thrust, withdraw, fail, collapse, shrivel … it can be caught or cut off … it can get you into trouble …[30]

This essay does not aim to indecently expose or otherwise embarrass the poet's legacy or to appropriate his identity in order to make him fit easily within a contemporary Western gay sensibility – or, as Murphy's close friend J.R. Ackerley once wrote about his own father, 'Hoping still to drag him captive into the homosexual fold'[31] – for such a fit would certainly not be easy. In a notebook entry written in the period in which 'Convenience' was being drafted, Murphy reflects on his dissatisfaction in applying to himself (or having someone else apply to him) the term 'homosexual':

> he, for the first time in your life, a stranger, a detective, had identified you as a homosexual, an identity you had not dreamed of accepting for yourself … you still don't like the identification, still feel it's a falsifying abstraction of who or what you are[32]

Rather, this essay hopes to contribute to Brandes' preliminary analysis of the ways in which material from the private space of Murphy's notebooks is transformed as it is brought into the public space of his published works even as this essay challenges Brandes' reading of the sequence as the development of the subject from isolation to intimacy, from silence to speech, from barrenness to fertility, and, ultimately, from cruising queer to paterfamilias. The sequence as a whole might be read equally well as an extended meditation – anxious and yet insightful, guarded and yet revealing – on the tensions and negotiations of a self between multiple, conflicting needs, desires and ideals. This approach may reveal more of the complexities within both the poems and the poet who produced them, presenting us with a writer who, among other things, grappled with dealing honestly with complex questions of sexuality and identity even as he operated under the threat of severe legal and social censure.

Concern about the privacy of individuals named in the notebooks is no doubt the primary reason that this resource is not readily available to researchers, and the delayed access is unfortunate. The notebooks present a methodical process of composition, often moving from concise prose reflections of life events to word associations and only loosely connected phrases and images to early drafts of the poems themselves, and the notebook entries for any one poem offer a much fuller understanding of how a poet might proceed than what we find, for example, in Edgar Allan Poe's widely republished essay 'The Philosophy of Composition', as can readily be seen from a comparison with Murphy's *In Search of Poetry* (2017) and other published extracts from his notebooks. The notebooks will be of great interest to scholars in a number of areas, from biography to queer history to poetic theory, and as they become more accessible to scholars they will allow the narratives within and behind the poems in *The Price of Stone* to be told more fully, bringing yet more life into Murphy's work.

NOTE

A much earlier version of this essay was presented, while I was a graduate student at the University of Tulsa, at the 1998 American Conference for Irish Studies Ninth Annual Southern Regional Conference at the University of South Carolina at Columbia. I am indebted to Richard Murphy for his willingness to share his experiences and writings with me.

14

~

'To seem a white king's gem': Richard Murphy's Sri Lankan poems and Irish postcolonial studies

BENJAMIN KEATINGE

Richard Murphy is unusual among Irish poets in having first-hand experience of (post)colonial circumstances in three distinct geographical areas – Ireland, Africa and Sri Lanka – and in writing searchingly about the injustices of colonialism in each case. In the opening pages of *The Kick*, Murphy dwells on his early memories of colonial Ceylon, where his father was a high-ranking member of the British colonial administration, and he foregrounds the injustices he perceived as a child and now understands more fully in adulthood:

> Nanny pitied the rickshaw coolies, who died young because they had to run like horses between the shafts all day barefoot on the hot red laterite roads in the sweltering heat. But when she was in a hurry, and the man pulling the rickshaw slowed to a walk, she would call him a lazy devil.   (*K*, p. 32)

Later in *The Kick* Murphy demonstrates the same awareness of colonial circumstances in Africa where the poet's parents had retired to Kiltullagh Farm in Southern Rhodesia. On a visit in 1959 Murphy notes that 'our table talk … was about multiracialism' but these ideals seemed 'doomed to extinction' (*K*, p. 172) in the postcolonial struggles in progress or shortly to be ignited in the 'demise of the Central African Federation of Rhodesia and Nyasaland and the independence of Zambia and Malawi' at the end of 1963 (*K*, p. 213) and in the struggle between 'the Mau Mau in Kenya' and 'white settlers' (*K*, p. 214). 'The God Who Eats Corn' was written to mark these transitions, but it led to a heated argument between Richard Murphy and his father, whose 'pride in the British colonial service would not allow him to tolerate what he perceived as criticism of its injustice by one of his sons' (*K*, p. 214). One of the great virtues of Richard Murphy's poetry is the connections made between these conflicts and those endured in Ireland so that much of Murphy's *oeuvre* may be read in terms of the subtitle of *The Battle of Aughrim* in *Poems 1952–2012*: 'A meditation on colonial war and its consequence[s] …' (*P*, p. 59). Indeed, as we shall see, Antoinette Quinn is not wide of the mark when she describes Murphy's 1989 volume *The Mirror Wall* as 'a Sri Lankan Aughrim'.[1] What is surprising, rather, is 'the total absence of reference to Murphy in current critical debates on postcolonialism', as John Goodby justly remarks.[2]

Based on his first-hand experience, Murphy's early Sri Lankan poems offer an extremely tactile and sensory account of colonial life from a child's perspective. The poems first published in *High Island* (1974) from Murphy's 'Childhood in Ceylon, *c*.1933' (*P*, p. 128) are full of unfamiliar sights and sounds unique to the 'resplendent freedom' ('Sri Lanka', *P*, p. 233) of this childhood before boarding school and Oxford would interrupt. A flavour of these memories is provided both in *The Kick* and in the poet's earliest correspondence with his mother and his elder sister Mary and brother Chris in 1933–34:

> Ward Place, Colombo
> My dear Mummy,
>   you will get this letter at Port Said. I am so glad you are coming back soon. the parm cat [*sic*] came at 10 o'clock in the night and got shot about 1 o'clock in the morning. We are having a loving a lovely time [*sic*]. I like my lessons with nanny. I had my bisakel [*sic*, bicycle] this morning and the cat is [illegible

word]. We are having are [*sic*] chrismas list [*sic*]. My kitten has
come from hospital.

>Lots of love and ooo and xxx from,
>
>Richard[3]

Colombo
My dear Mary and Christopher,
Thank you very much for the letter you sent me. I am sending
you each a bit of the guli guli man's leaf from the mango tree he
made grow. We have got tame baby squirrel he feeds out of are
[*sic*] hands.

>Lots of love from,
>
>Richard[4]

Such memories would form the poetic content of the Sri Lankan
poems in *High Island*. For example, 'The Fall' recalls a childhood
dare in which the poet dropped the family's cat Marmalade from the
'upstairs verandah of the Chief Secretary's Lodge in Kandy' (*K*, p. 31):

>Thunder in the patanas. He's falling off a cliff.
>Every branch he catches breaks.
>Down he hurtles, counting … one … two … then wakes
>In the nick of time. His heart pounds with relief.
>It's Nanny's afternoon off.
>He untucks his mosquito net
>And shakes the fear of scorpions from his shoes.
>
>Hours to go, nothing to do but wait.
>A tom-tom roars at the Temple of the Tooth.
>He peeps at the bathroom coolie rinsing a pot,
>Picks up his cat
>And saunters out on the upstairs nursery verandah.
>'Would Marmalade die if he fell from this height?'
>A bullock-bandy creaks past the compound gate.   (*P*, p. 131)

Fortunately, Marmalade survives the ordeal but the incident is
not without anxiety for the young poet. He has to confess his

misdemeanour – 'own[ing] up like a gentleman' (*P*, p. 132) – to his father and receives a severe scolding in consequence. Meanwhile, the cat disappears into the jungle where the Murphys' nanny surmises that 'a leopard or a monkey would be sure to kill him if he didn't die of his injuries' (*K*, p. 32). The incident has a comic aspect as recounted in the poem and in *The Kick*, but there are real anxieties behind it, as indicated by the childhood nightmare of 'Thunder in the patanas' in the first stanza and the nightmare of falling which the poem enacts, in dream and in reality. As with 'Firebug', in which the poet describes setting alight the 'celluloid doll' of his 'younger sister Liz' (*K*, p. 31), a childhood prank conveys wider uneasiness and danger. Murphy recalls in a 2017 interview the feelings of vulnerability in an environment full of genuine life-threatening dangers: 'my memories were of fear: fear of being bitten by a mosquito and catching malaria and dying, or being bitten by a snake. And it was scary.'[5] In the same interview the poet relates his sense of the paradoxical mixture of 'carnival and terror' ('National Tree', *P*, p. 234) at the heart of Sri Lankan experience, especially in the violence which plagued the island nation in the 1980s up to the defeat of the 'Tamil Tigers' (as the Liberation Tigers of Tamil Eelam, or LTTE, are often referred to) by the Sri Lankan army which occurred at Mullaitivu in 2009 where Murphy's father had been appointed 'assistant government agent' in 'his first posting' back in 1913.[6] As Murphy explains, in relation to the 1980s violence:

> One of the wonderful things about Sri Lanka is the capacity of the people for joy and joy expressed in carnival. The carnival went on and on and on all through the terror – the terror, on the one hand, from these left-wing killer extremists, and on the other, from the death squads that were unleashed against them by the government. The carnival went on and on. And that's a wonderful thing, the spirit of people survived in those who outlived the terror.[7]

Murphy's mature Sri Lankan poems are informed by the poet's witnessing of this horrific violence and his testimony for its victims.

A late poem like 'Death in Kandy' dwells on these 'nameless victim[s]' of postcolonial wars in Sri Lanka; explicit images of 'smashed teeth', 'a skeleton / picked clean by dogs and crows' trouble the tourist-board reputation of the island as a pristine destination for Western visitors (*P*, p. 235). The poet was able to survive both the childhood dangers of colonial Ceylon and the political violence of independent Sri Lanka, and his responses to the island's social and political complexities are both rational and affective, a combination of observation, analysis and memory.

In November 1984 Murphy 'decided to go' back to Sri Lanka for the first time since his childhood, in order 'to examine [his] colonial past in the light of its legacy and to purge my fear' (*K*, p. 308). An incongruous juxtaposition of violence, reconciliation and celebration is traced in his account of that return. As his plane lands at Negombo airport, near the capital Colombo, a 'wave of euphoria' washes over the poet, 'submerging fearful expectations' leading him to resist an impulse 'to kiss the ground' (*K*, p. 308). But Murphy is also clear-eyed about the realities of violence, poverty and discrimination in postcolonial Sri Lanka so that the later Sri Lankan poems 'finished in the years 1985–2012' (*P*, p. 227) focus more on the identity and challenges of a nation still overcoming the mixed legacy of its colonial history. These later poems combine the poet's dual sense of an island 'Exalted' and 'flawed' as the sonnet 'Sri Lanka' describes it (*P*, p. 233). The shadowy subaltern figures of the 1970s *High Island* poems – 'the bathroom coolie' (*P*, p. 131), 'kitchen coolies' (*P*, p. 132) and 'rickshaw coolies' (*K*, p. 32), or the 'punkah' who 'fans them' in 'The Writing Lesson' (*P*, p. 129) – become less exotic and removed, but more substantial and troubling. In 'Mangoes', from the later period, the poet encounters:

> A colourful boy in a Star Wars tee-shirt
> and a saffron batik sarong
> tightrope walking along a mango tree's
> top branches ...   (*P*, p. 229)

But the backdrop of the boy's life is squalid:

... a tower-block on a tourist beach
Around a lake dyed bottle-green with garbage
Of a foetid shanty slum.   (*P*, p. 229)

The idea of 'smiling resplendent Sri Lanka' (*P*, p. 235) is thus ironised and undercut by an acute sense of social and political injustice.

At least two impulses are at work in these poems of the later phase. There is a documentary aspect evident in 'Mangoes' and 'Death in Kandy' which share in the outrage of a poem like 'Amazement' (about IRA violence) from *The Price of Stone* (1985). The painstaking 'objectivity' of *The Battle of Aughrim* is also in evidence, what Ted Hughes identified as Murphy's gift for depicting 'the facts and sufferings of history'.[8] But these 'facts and sufferings' are mediated through Murphy's own memories of his 'incredibly happy childhood in this beautiful country'.[9] What we find is a mixture of poems alert to the paradoxical combination of exaltation and horror in an island nation scarred by its colonial past. Thus, for example, the poem 'National Tree' combines beauty and violence in a disconcerting fashion. The 'ironwood' is the 'National Tree', and its 'flowers ... Last for a day':

Yesterday's petals
Lie beheaded on the ground.
There are buds in hiding:
Tomorrow these will explode.   (*P*, p. 234)

The explosions, we assume, are not exclusively botanical; rather, it is strongly implied that they are the result of terrorist violence. And as Murphy makes clear in an interview, the context and conception of the poem is very much a colonial one:

Several decades ago, the rulers decided that Sri Lanka must have a national tree and they chose the ironwood tree. And in 1989, at the height of the JVP crisis[10] ... there was chaos and mayhem ... And I wrote the poem 'National Tree' after a visit to a very interesting arboretum near Dambulla. It was donated by its owner Sam Popham to the University of Peradeniya because he wanted it to be maintained as an arboretum ... Sam had allowed the jungle to come up. Nature – the goddess – was allowed to grow. But Sam – the colonialist – decided which aspects of nature he liked and which he didn't. So any trees he didn't like, one of his five gardeners would be told to uproot it; and the trees he liked were allowed to thrive – like satinwood, and ironwood, and mahogany and teak, and so on.[11]

But if the inspiration for the poem derives from an example of rational imperial control, the poem transcends those boundaries quite consciously. The ironwood tree 'grows high / Exuding festivity' (*P*, p. 234). In the resplendence of the ironwood we can discern a continuity with the equally evocative sights and sounds of the earlier 1970s phase. Indeed, as Seamus Deane has pointed out, on such occasions Murphy shows an ability to 'burst the lyric barrier', as American poet Theodore Roethke is supposed to have done on Inishbofin, in 1960. Words begin 'weirdly to take off inwards' (*P*, pp. 43–4) and, in the Sri Lankan poem 'Coppersmith', language becomes sound and loses rational content, 'Exuding festivity':

> And there I began to repeat
> Out loud to myself an English word such as beat beat beat,
>
> Till hammering too hard I lost the meaning in the sound
> Which faded and left nothing behind,
> A blank mind,
> The compound spinning round,
> My brain melting, as if I'd stood in the sun
> Too long without a topee and was going blind,
> Till I and the bird, the word and the tree, were one.   (*P*, p. 130)

Seamus Deane's point here is crucial:

> Richard Murphy insists on the clarities of the world – its flowers, its animals, ships, people, food, pictures ... [but] it is not accurate to speak of Richard Murphy's verse as though it had all the chaste Palladian virtues one would expect of a cultivated and gifted scion of Anglo-Irish stock.[12]

Rather, there are important instances in Murphy's poetry where the contours of the physically defined world recede in importance; in Deane's words, 'reason and logic do end, without disappearing'.[13] But the balance is maintained and the merger of world and self, dream and reality, word and tree is perfectly measured. Reason and transcendence are aligned, as in the arboretum of Sam Popham, and the critique of colonialism retains some of the structure and order that Murphy inherited from his father's world, even as he rebels against it. Murphy seems to acknowledge the justice of such a view at the end of *The Kick* when he describes his sister Mary's suggestion that he title his memoir '"A Conventional Rebel" because that's what you've always been' (*K*, p. 344). Murphy's critique of colonialism is that of an insider whose consciousness has been structured by the very system he rebels against.

The Kick is, of course, punctuated by the image of the kick that the three-year-old Richard Murphy inflicted on his eighty-year-old Aunt Bella at the Royal Hibernian Hotel in youthful resentment towards the old lady's Victorian severity (*K*, p. 4). W.B. Yeats famously said that the poet makes poetry out of the quarrel with him/herself, and Seamus Heaney has suggested that Richard Murphy's poetry has taken its inspiration from a quarrel with his inheritance in what Heaney calls 'Murphy's shaping of his inheritance into a poetic theme: his quarrel with himself'.[14] Murphy's typecasting as a 'poet of two traditions', as the volume dedicated to his work in 1978 describes him, has its origin in his quarrel with himself. Arguably, the attempt to exculpate that inheritance motivated not only Murphy's impatriation of himself on the Connemara seaboard, but also his depictions of postcolonial circumstances in Africa and Sri Lanka. Murphy's own 'inheritance' is an instructive example of the rationale for approaching Irish literature from a postcolonial perspective, a logic that has been underlined by leading scholars. In an essay on 'Postcolonial Studies and Ireland', C.L. Innes reminds us that it is race that has sometimes misled us into excluding consideration of Ireland from a postcolonial paradigm:

> the inclusion of Ireland within postcolonial studies would encourage us to question some of the assumptions that have

become too quickly embedded ... that racial categories are given, and that there are clear divisions between 'white' imperialists and 'coloured' natives. The case of Ireland indicates how readily racial categories are 'constructed' and how fluid these may be ...[15]

Equally, Luke Gibbons underlines how the 'subjugation', by England, of the 'Celtic periphery' (Scotland, Ireland and Wales) was ineluctably linked to the wider project of British imperial expansion, historical developments which have directly impinged upon Richard Murphy's own family background and life history:

> race and empire begin at home ... both colonization and the animus against Catholicism were inherently bound up with the subjugation of the Celtic periphery – Gaelic Ireland and the Scottish Highlands – from the early modern period ... the forging of the unity of the 'Three Kingdoms' was not antecedent to colonial expansion but was intrinsic to it ...[16]

The burden of guilt and the internalised conflicts of a divided inheritance is strongly felt in Murphy's earliest published poems. His elegy to his maternal grandmother 'The Woman of the House' is as good an image as any of the impossible task of escaping fully the burdens of a colonial past:

> She bandaged the wounds that poverty caused
> In the house that famine labourers built,
> Gave her hands to cure impossible wrong
> In a useless way, and was loved for it.   (*P*, p. 30)

The poem implies that the colonial situation deforms both the coloniser and colonised even though their relationship is symbiotic, an insight which is, of course, writ large in postcolonial theory, in particular theories of 'ambivalence' and 'mimicry' advanced by Homi K. Bhabha, the pertinence of which for Murphy's Sri Lankan poems will become clear. One can readily see how Murphy situates himself as victim, as well as inheritor, of imperial values and distortions. He rebels against himself, even while still respecting the liberal idealism of his father who 'had advanced the cause of education, particularly of women, in all the outstations where he had served' and who 'approved of the ultimate aim of leading the colony [Ceylon] towards independence' (*K*, pp. 32–3). The intimate family dilemmas of living between Europe and the East, with all of the logistical, financial and cultural confusion that such an existence entailed, are thus an all-consuming agon for Murphy.

The poet's background must therefore be situated within a wider context of Irish connections to other locations within the British Empire. Indeed, the insistence that Irish literature be viewed through a postcolonial prism has entailed considerable scholarly focus on such parallels. One compelling example is provided by the figure of Irish revolutionary Roger Casement, whose ambiguous legacy Murphy seems fully alert to in the poem 'Casement's Funeral' from *The Battle of Aughrim* (*P*, p. 64). Murphy's presentation of Casement's funeral is deliberately deflationary:

> Rebels in silk hats now
> Exploit the grave with an old comrade's speech:
> White hair tossed, a black cape flecked with snow.   (*P*, p. 64)

The poet knowingly alludes to the 'diarist's flesh' and his 'skeleton' as the subject of continued controversy because of the 'black diary deeds', leading to a polarised view of Casement as nationalist martyr or sexual deviant in a very white or black view of a complex historical figure current in the 1960s of the poem. Murphy also underscores the very pertinent contrast of colours on the formal garb of the ex-republicans in attendance in the falling snow to allude to the racial background of Casement's career and the gulf it traversed in his heroic anti-colonial and humanitarian work in the Belgian Congo and in the Putumayo region of the Amazon basin and in his support for Irish nationalism and the Easter Rising. Thus, as well as being an astute 'updating and rewriting of Yeats's "Parnell's Funeral"', as Declan Kiberd observes, it is also an important meditation on the essential continuity of (post)colonial concerns between a 'white' Ireland and the mixed or 'black' race of other colonial subjects outside Ireland, in such countries as Sri Lanka or in the newly formed nation states of East Africa.[17]

Roger Casement is now recognised for his clear-sighted linkage of colonial exploitation in Ireland with other, even more flagrant abuses in Africa and South America. In the novel *The Dream of the Celt* by Peruvian Nobel Prize-winner Mario Vargas Llosa, Casement is imagined meditating on his native Ireland as he struggles to complete his work documenting abuses in the rubber plantations on the Putumayo in 1910, work which had been commissioned by the British Foreign Office based on Casement's credentials as 'a specialist in atrocities':[18]

> During the night Roger woke several times, in anguish, thinking about Ireland … Since he had seen first-hand the *via crucis* of other colonized peoples, Ireland's situation pained him more than ever. He felt an urgency to finish with all this, to complete the report on Putumayo, turn it in to the Foreign Office, and return to Ireland to work … with his idealistic compatriots devoted to the cause of emancipation. He would make up for lost time, become more involved in the nationalist movement, study, take action, write …[19]

Casement's life and work provides exemplary insight into the degrading conditions of colonialism close to home and further afield, at a time when the Irish situation may have superficially appeared less extreme. His insights are a prelude to wider comparative surveys of Irish writing by contemporary scholars which examine Irish literature in relation to other (post)colonial literatures, readings of the kind that Declan Kiberd pioneered in *Inventing Ireland: the literature of the modern nation* (1995). Kiberd reminds us, for example, of ways in which Irish Revival writers like Yeats and Lady Gregory had links with colonies overseas; indeed, Lady Gregory's husband, Sir William Gregory, was 'a former governor of Ceylon' before becoming 'a landlord at Coole'.[20] Richard Murphy, as an aspiring poet of the 1950s, was aware of some of these links, and in a letter of 5 May 1950 written from his sister's flat in London to his parents, he mentions that he has 'been reading a lot in the Anglo-Irish literary revival' and asks:

Did you ever meet Florence Farr, who recited Yeats to a psaltery; she died in a Buddhist monastery in Ceylon about 1914, and I would be very interested to hear if you ever saw her there, or heard of it.[21]

By virtue of recent scholarship in postcolonial studies, we have become more aware of the orientalist slant to the Irish Revival. Joseph Lennon has explored Irish orientalism extensively, and his work documents the long-standing allegiances between orientalism and Celticism:

> Although some pieces of Irish literary Orientalism merely extended the discourse of Orientalism to Ireland ... many worked against the dominant representations of Orientalism, exposing the Orient for its constructed and politicized nature ... these representations reveal the liminal position often occupied by Irish writers and cultural nationalists within the British Empire, who could at once belong to both the imperial metropole and the colonized periphery. The variety of strategies associated with such a position – both collusive and subversive – suggests the scope and inherent liminality of Irish Orientalism, particularly as it pertains to nationalism and decolonisation in Ireland.[22]

I want to suggest that Richard Murphy's 1989 collection *The Mirror Wall* is an excellent example of how an Irish poet, in choosing to focus on oriental material, follows on from the Revivalist tendency to blend elements of subversion and collusion in their negotiations with non-Western cultures. Here, we can even suggest that there is something akin to what Homi K. Bhabha defines as 'hybridity' which takes the form of a

> liminal space ... [a] process of symbolic interaction ... that constructs the difference between upper and lower, black and white ... [and] prevents identities ... from settling into primordial polarities ... [and] opens up the possibility of a cultural hybridity that entertains difference without an assumed or imposed hierarchy.[23]

The sonnet 'Sri Lanka', written in the mode of the sonnets in *The Price of Stone* (1985) and placed as a prefatory poem to *The Mirror Wall* (1989), evinces an intimate awareness of the congeries of elements in Sri Lankan culture. The island was discovered by 'navigators' on voyages connected with the 'early spice trade' and it subsequently acquired different names and identities in the eyes of various explorers, traders and adventurers: 'Taprobane' for the ancient Greeks, 'Serendip' for Arab traders, and 'Tenarisim' or 'land of delight' by Indians for whom Sri Lanka appears as 'A star sapphire teardrop India shed' (*P*, p. 233). Murphy thus alludes to the island's complex history, involving colonial settlement by Portuguese, Dutch and English, and its diverse population which includes 'the Sinhalese and the Tamils and the Muslim minority' as well as Burghers, descended from early Dutch, Portuguese and British settlers.[24]

One can thus see how the poet would view the island as 'a pluralist's dream', as he explained to Dennis O'Driscoll in a 1987 interview about the translations he was then undertaking for *The Mirror Wall*.[25] Indeed, questions of mediation, transcription and translation are central to that volume in which Murphy responds to the ventriloquistic possibilities of his source material in allowing the voices of the graffiti inscriptions on the rock face of Sigiriya to be heard through the *Mirror Wall* poems. These ancient Sinhalese inscriptions are themselves graffiti which eulogise the 'Rain Girls'[26] or 'Apsaras'[27] erotically painted on the rock face at Sigiriya, a huge stone fortress in central Sri Lanka which is now a UNESCO World Heritage Site and symbol of Sri Lankan culture and independence. The voices are many-faceted, contradictory, by turns adoring, moralistic or dismissive; it is a textual patchwork rather than a unified poem or poetic sequence. As Murphy comments:

> It's a pluralist's dream of different levels, ranging from light erotic witticism to heavy moralising, or from mystical devotion to mundane scorn. If lucky, I record the rebirth, after a thousand years, of a Sinhala song in English.[28]

The importance for Murphy of his return to Sri Lanka in the mid-1980s should not be underestimated. As he says in *The Kick*: 'I was astonished to feel the estrangement of half a century from a place I had never regarded as home dissolve into love' (*K*, p. 309). The rendering into English of the inscriptions on the Mirror Wall represents Richard Murphy's own contribution to the literature of the island nation, and they join a vibrant Sri Lankan poetry scene that can be explored in such recent anthologies as *Mirrored Images: an anthology of Sri Lankan poetry* (2013), which offers selections from poets writing in Sinhala, Tamil and English.[29] In fact, Murphy's *The Mirror Wall* is a conspicuously hybrid volume and is one of several texts by anglophone authors which are 'an integral part of both the local tradition … and the British tradition, a hybridized form of creativity', as Melanie A. Murray notes.[30] We should not be surprised, for example, that Leonard Woolf's novel *The Village in the Jungle* (1913) is taught in Sinhala translation in Sri Lankan schools as an indigenous text,[31] or that Richard Murphy helped to distribute copies of *The Mirror Wall* to bookshops, schools and libraries in Sri Lanka when it was originally published.[32] Prize-winning authors like Michael Ondaatje, whose eclectic family history is celebrated in his evocative memoir *Running in the Family* (1982), further illustrate the strength of these 'hybridized form[s] of creativity'. Indeed, all of this may prompt an extension of the use of postcolonial terms like 'hybridity', 'ambivalence' and 'mimicry' beyond the subaltern groups to whom they were originally applied. As Satoshi Mizutani suggests in 'A Critical Reflection on Homi K. Bhabha's Post-historical Thought', 'the colonial presence of Eurasians' and their contributions to indigenous traditions, should 'be viewed … as a topic highly pertinent to the current debate on "hybridity"', leading to a reassessment of 'colonial racial boundaries' and the cultural delineations thereof.[33] What Robert J.C. Young refers to as the 'doubleness' of hybridity, its capacity for 'creating new spaces, structures, scenes … intervening as a form of subversion, translation, transformation'[34] is important in this context since its 'interrogative effects'[35] help us to better understand the alignment between Richard Murphy's (post)colonial concerns in both a Sri Lankan and an Irish context.

In her review of Murphy's 'Aughrim in Sri Lanka', Antoinette Quinn underscores the fundamental continuity between *The Battle* of *Aughrim* and *The Mirror Wall* and Murphy's Irish and Sri Lankan backgrounds:

> Though it has taken him over fifty years to make his way there, the 'mirror wall' seems purpose-built with Murphy in mind. Historical site, cultural shrine, mythological locus, Sigiriya is a Sri Lankan Aughrim … the *Sigiri Graffiti* is the kind of poetry he approves: offering 'an accurate memory of the tribe … a way of preserving the truth about the past'. That the Old Sinhala versifiers should have expressed a range of diverse and conflicting views in a multitude of thematically related but discrete poems is peculiarly congenial to Murphy's talent for amassing lyric sequences from self-contained, individual units. And, of course, their 'chiselled' voices and 'granite style' were irresistible to a poet afflicted with 'stone mania'.[36]

Quinn's observations affirm the postcolonial leap made in Murphy's poetic career between Irish and Sri Lankan experience as well as the continuities in poetic method and material from Aughrim to Sigiriya. We observe the same engagement with a site of cultural and historical significance stimulated by autobiographical investment and a gift for poetic interrogation and reclamation of post-imperial spaces.

In January 2018 Richard Murphy died peacefully at his home near Kandy, Central Province, Sri Lanka, where he lived for the final ten years of his life. By returning to the land of his 'incredibly happy childhood', in a certain sense the poet had chosen to return home.[37]

15

~

Richard Murphy's *The Kick*: The making of memoir

BARBARA BROWN

I met Richard Murphy at a dinner party in October 1994 at the home of Professor Maurice Harmon and his wife, Mrs Maura Harmon. After more than thirty years of teaching, I had retired as Professor of English literature at Marshall University, Huntington, West Virginia, and had come to live in Dublin. In addition to other undergraduate and graduate classes, I had introduced and taught an upper-division course in life-writing/autobiography, biography and memoir. I was well acquainted with Richard Murphy's poetry and his status, with John Montague and Thomas Kinsella, as one of the three foremost poets of the new generation publishing in the 1950s and '60s, in succession to Austin Clarke and Patrick Kavanagh. But I did not expect to have dinner with him in my first month in Ireland. As I entered the Harmons' sitting room, there, in a wing-backed chair beside an open fire sat Richard Murphy, the recognisable, chiselled features, shock of black hair and tall figure. That evening I was content to observe, to listen to his rich Oxbridge accent and to the wit and charm of the conversations around me. Then, in June 1995, Richard invited me to a garden party at Knockbrack ('speckled hill'), his stunning home in the hills of Killiney, twelve miles from Dublin city with views of the Irish Sea and the Sugar Loaf Mountain. Still a novice in Dublin literary society, again I observed and listened. Not until years later did I realise what a gathering was assembled: celebrated poets, writers, academics, musicians, editors, artists, publishers. As

I was saying goodbye and thanking Richard, he asked me to have luncheon with him at Knockbrack the following Thursday. Forced to communicate with him then as we ate the enormous salad he had prepared, I realised that, in the nicest way, he was interviewing me. As an experienced academic, would I be interested in reading and transcribing his family letters for possible publication in the future? Of course I would. Thus our collaboration began.

From 1995 onward, in addition to other projects, I transcribed Richard's and other family members' letters, then, after gaining his approval, was graduated to selected notebooks, the private notebooks he began writing in Paris in 1954. I was familiar with his characteristic use of language and his minuscule penmanship, his habits and manner of working. Richard had sold his papers, including the notebooks, to the University of Tulsa in Oklahoma in 1987 and had agreed to teach one semester a year for five years. While he was in America he asked me to live at Knockbrack and work full-time transcribing family letters and papers and notebooks. With the conclusion of the Tulsa commitment, in 1997, Richard sold Knockbrack to live in Durban, South Africa, to where his daughter, Emily, with her children, Theodora and Caspar, had emigrated.

We had talked about his using the notebooks as a primary source for a book, not an autobiography, but a memoir, an account of his complicated life and times and of persons and places of significance to him. Was there enough varied material to interest readers, he asked? I knew there were volumes of material: an exotic childhood in Ceylon (now Sri Lanka); idyllic years growing up in Milford, his birthplace on the Mayo–Galway border, with humorous and touching vignettes of childhood with his brothers and sisters; at Oxford cycling through the Quantock Hills, Somerset and dreaming of becoming a poet; punting on the River Cherwell, Oxfordshire; descriptions of teaching in the mountains of Crete and falling in love with a proud young shepherd from the White Mountains or luxuriating in high society in the Bahamas. There were accounts of his desire to escape from the restrictive life of the Big House to the wild and more imaginative life of the west of Ireland, finding inspiration and his subject matter there: memorable descriptions of the many friends he made there, such as that of the Inishbofin fishermen Pateen (meaning little Pat) Cloherty, whose account of the sinking of the Galway hooker the *Maisie* is the source for Richard's poem 'Pat Cloherty's Version of *The Maisie*',[1] and Pat Concannon, whose tragic story is the centre for his poem 'The Cleggan Disaster'; lyrical passages of mysterious, haunting days and nights on Omey and High Island; travels in America, teaching, giving readings with Ted Hughes and American poets Donald Hall and James Dickey, of *Deliverance* fame. In the 1980s and '90s, a return to Ceylon, reports of the repressive government during those years and of the brutal torture and death of a young Sinhalese friend, but also inspiration for the poetry of *The Mirror Wall* (1989), which was to be his last single collection before the publication of *Collected Poems* (2000) by Gallery Press in Dublin. Copius material for at least four fat volumes.

By then we were immersed in the memoir. The narrative of *The Kick*, as yet unnamed, is based on Richard's extensive primary source material, the private notebooks he had continued writing for over five decades. Because he was collecting material from them and masses of family letters and papers totalling millions of words and hundreds of pages, the principal problem he faced in its composition was selecting and reducing this raw material to four hundred pages of polished text, as commissioned by Granta Books, London. In 1999 I spent nearly five months in Durban, South Africa with Richard in the preliminary tasks of reading and assembling material. The memoir was not to be the wide ranging four volumes I had envisioned after examining only a fraction of the notebooks, but a single volume.

Durban, lined with tall pines and tropical plants and flowers, a beautiful seaside city and waterfront on the Indian Ocean, stretches out over more than thirty miles. But it was a dangerous city, where crime was rampant, unemployment and taxes high; I heard horror stories about muggings, shootings and robberies from everyone I met. Richard lived in Morningside, a relatively safe residential area with wealthy homes, two lovely parks and a zoo nearby. He had booked me into a residential hotel about a ten-minute walk from his beautiful, spacious home. We settled quickly into a work schedule. I read and marked passages in the notebooks from early morning until

2.30 p.m., walked to Richard's house where we worked together until 6.00 p.m., stopping for a cup of Earl Grey tea and a Kit Kat, Richard's choice of snack at that time. March is the beginning of autumn in South Africa but the temperatures seemed like hot summertime; after the sun went down, it was dark, no twilight. At the end of our day Richard walked me to the hotel in darkness.

I read, read, read until stupefied. Next I divided sections of each notebook into four categories: first, for possible use in the memoir; second, in a prose book about rhetoric and writing from his experiences teaching in America and writing reviews; then, in a possible novel, a fiction about his private life and experiences in the west of Ireland; and finally, in a prose study of the creative relationship between the poet's life and his poetry, focusing on the sonnets in *The Price of Stone* (1985). This was done quickly. Next, I took the notebooks with passages marked for possible use in the memoir to Richard for consideration. Decisions on contents were determined by two basic principles: potential interest to the reader and the achievement of a prose style at its best. Often our sessions were pleasant. He wished me to mark and to comment on passages I liked; I did, he approved. But sometimes he wanted to know why I had not marked this or the other paragraph. I explained, thinking, 'Am I to mark them all?' Often, Richard was preoccupied with painters in the new house, muttering, 'You are ahead of me, I must get to work.' I said, 'When I get far enough ahead of you, I plan to take a bus tour to Cape Town.' He retorted, 'I think you're skipping pages.'

One afternoon Richard pointed out mistakes in my text and showed me the page set-up he wanted for the materials. We were making progress as the pile of possible pages to use in the memoir grew. I was amazed at how often we approved whole sequences. In general we agreed to order the whole of the selected material chronologically. In truth there is no other way in a piece of life-writing. Life is lived chronologically and a truthful account of a life must respect that sequence. Richard agreed. To begin, he will detail family history and survey his life from his earliest memories, perhaps introduce his mother, Lady Murphy, recorded in one of her typically acerbic conversations. We also had begun putting sections of material into chapter headings, a tentative but positive advancement. In the final text we eliminated the use of chapters for an uninterrupted flowing narrative.

Richard had an idea for the title: The Kick. It carries a variety of explicit and implicit meanings. The first is suggested by an amusing account of his behaviour at a tea party given by his Aunt Bella, when he was three years old. A grand figure of almost eighty, something of a martinet as an academic, Dr Isabella Mulvany had been among the first women, known as 'the Nine Muses', to graduate from Trinity College, Dublin and the first woman to receive an honorary degree from Trinity. Told to thank Aunt Bella for his tea, he ran across the room and kicked her. The word 'kick' as used in boarding-school dormitories also means a boy whom a senior monitor fancied. In writing about his sexual experiences – describing himself as 'androgynous' (*K*, p. 143) – from his years in boarding school at Baymount in Dublin and King's School in Cornwall, Murphy writes of an older boy who 'attacked me with fists before lights out and seduced me with whispers', then climbed into his bed in the dark 'for the sake of a spasm of mutual relief', and adds, 'The guilty kick I got at night made me hunger for purification through history, literature and music during the day' (*K*, p. 70). There is also the seductive kick he received under the table from Sylvia Plath, when she and Ted Hughes visited him in Cleggan in 1961. And, sadly, it could refer obliquely to the foul kick received by his great friend Tony White on an icy football pitch in London that indirectly resulted in his death in 1976.

Richard's deciding on the title encouraged me. After five weeks I had completed the work on the thirty-three notebooks Richard had given me to read – thirty-three of over a hundred. But I had not read the later notebooks safeguarded in the Special Collections of the McFarlin Library, University of Tulsa. We also had decided to continue the manuscript until Lady Murphy's death in 1996, the same year Charles Monteith, his long-time friend and Faber director, died. In its last pages the tone of the memoir darkens, recording these deaths and his last meeting, in the Connaught Hotel in London, with Ted Hughes in September 1998, the year of his death, and ending in elegy and loss.

This whole process of selecting material emphasises the unease between autobiography and memoir, both written in the first person, and between memoir and the first-person narrator of fiction. Unlike autobiography and biography, there is no acknowledged masterpiece in memoir. Part of the difficulty is focus; memoir requires no autobiographical introspection and self-analysis, no concentration on the inner and private life of its subject, but instead the primary focus is on personalities other than the writer. Memoir, like all life-writing, is prompted in part by commemoration, the desire to keep alive the memory of persons and events; and as the past can be relived only in memory, memoir rediscovers, reorganises and often reinvents past life and times. It requires convoluted technique and style. Richard understood the difficulties. In the notebook dated June 1982, written when he was composing the sonnets in *The Price of Stone*, he writes about this generic relationship between life-writing and poetry: 'the poem is not an autobiography. Autobiography is one of the building materials you need to construct the poem', and adds, 'Memory is a quarry you work with your own labour and tools .... Even then it may only provide a few good cornerstones – and the far more difficult problem of building remains.'² In addition to a range of lyric poems – elegies, sonnets – from early volumes to later, much of Richard's poetry also can be characterised as narrative, whether he writes about people, as in 'The God Who Eats Corn', which is about his father, or places or historical events in Ireland, as in *The Battle of Aughrim*, or even in the fifty sonnets of *The Price of Stone*, which form an autobiographical narrative, corresponding to that in *The Kick*. Of Richard's poetry, Ted Hughes has written, 'He has the gift of epic objectivity.' It is a gift that served Richard well writing *The Kick*.

After more than four months of daily sessions we had identical computer files with more material than we could use; the final selection and organisation would be made from them. For the next eighteen months we would work daily, I in Dublin, Richard in Durban, by means of emails and telephone discussions; but the method would remain the same: Richard would send pages for me to read and to review and we would discuss them. Descriptive passages were changed into dialogue, letters and diaries, and dated pieces from the notebooks were added. Writing memoir often entails gaps in chronology as the writer moves from one significant incident, location or period in his life to another, selects certain materials in order to illuminate what he wants to bring into focus, while obscuring or even omitting others which he does not regard as significant or relevant to his purposes. He may change tense and voice, alter the point of view, and employ different styles.

The prose in the High Island notebooks selected for use in *The Kick* has a classic grandeur. High Island (Ardoileán), wild, untameable, off the north-west coast of Connemara, is a small island which Richard bought in 1969. Days and nights on High Island inspired some of his best poems, 'Seals at High Island', 'Stormpetrel' and 'High Island', and his most lyrical prose.

> 4 August 1970, New Forge
> Everything on the island connects, that is its glory, connecting what appears to be disconnected … the only land you can clearly see from the hermitage is Shark Head to the north and Slyne Head to the south, two ultimate fragments broken off the landmass of Europe and almost uninhabitable, the one deserted ten years ago, the other occupied by lighthouse keepers … but on the eastern side of the hill in the centre of the island you can see a panorama of mountains, bays, villages, islands, and rocks that lie between Achill Island and Slyne Head … signs of human activity on the mainland with which you cannot connect can make you yearn to get home, but looking from the hermitage out to sea, you can feel connected to the universe sublimely.
>
> (*K*, pp. 262–3)

Selecting passages written about or on High Island was particularly difficult because all were deeply moving prose poems. The High Island notebooks in themselves exceeded the word limit of 160,000 or about 400 pages we had agreed as an optimum length for the book and which novelist and critic John Banville had advised.

Another aspect of Richard's varied style in *The Kick*, characterised by one reviewer as 'funny, quirky and lyrical' – specifically the 'quirky' – is illustrated by his recreation of his interview at seventeen with C.S. Lewis for an Oxford Demyship. 'Called to judgement', he remembers Lewis as 'a short plump man' with 'a bright jovial face ... sitting on a sofa smoking a pipe':

> 'Can you tell me, Mr. Murphy', he [Lewis] began, as the sofa started to rise off the floor, 'what is meant by the "divine right of kings", and what importance, if any, is given to belief in that right by characters in Shakespeare's *Richard II*?' While I was answering with fluency beyond my control, quoting passages learnt by heart, the sofa turned upside down in mid-air with the balding top of C.S. Lewis's head a foot above the floor till the end of my answer.   (*K*, pp. 79–80)

He adds, 'My Oxford was a better preparation for a memoirist than a poet' (*K*, p. 85). A prophetic comment, as our current undertaking was proving.

During the last year our telephone discussions could become argumentative, for we were scrutinising specific paragraphs and sentences line by line. I am suspicious of adverbs in a sentence, a sign that the verb is weak, not doing its job and equally suspicious of adjectives, a sign that the noun is too general, not specific enough. Richard was sometimes not convinced, and we had heated discussions about these matters, stimulating and challenging. Usually we compromised to the greater effectiveness of the specific sentence.

The Kick contains brilliant literary portraits of Richard's meetings and friendships with many prominent writers and actors in London, Dublin and New York, including C.S. Lewis (his tutor at Oxford), T.S. Eliot and W.H. Auden, Kenneth Tynan, Harold Nicolson, Sylvia Plath and Ted Hughes, Irish writers Patrick Kavanagh, John McGahern and Seamus Heaney, American poets Robert Lowell, James Dickey and Theodore Roethke, actors Tony White, Robert Shaw, Mary Ure and Peter O'Toole. A dinner and evening with W.H. Auden hosted by Barbara Epstein in New York is recounted with the dry wit and slightly acerbic tone appropriate to its subject:

… Barbara Epstein gave me dinner at her apartment in New York on 22 November 1971. The only other guest was W.H. Auden. It was several years since I had met him in Stratford-upon-Avon, where his poetry reading impressed me because he knew his poems by heart. When his memory lapsed in the middle of a longish poem, he didn't fuss and fumble for the book, but closed his eyes and looked up to Heaven as if he were asking God to remind him of what he had wanted to say when writing the poem. Then, recovering his speech, he seemed to be inspired with thoughts he was just now putting into words. It made the poem all the more interesting to hear.

Barbara told me that once, when he was coming to dine, he got out of the elevator on the wrong floor, rang the bell, was admitted by a couple, who did not protest when he came in, and, seating himself in an armchair, asked for a vodka Martini. With this in hand he kept up a monologue that amazed and silenced the couple until his glass was empty. Then noticing the rather strange absence of the Epsteins, Auden asked where they were. 'Barbara and Jason live in the apartment above us,' he was told.

Auden was there when I arrived. He was sixty-four years old, looking rather scruffy and neglected, slouching on a Chesterfield, his hair 'all over the place', his nails dirty, slippers for shoes. Conversation with him was daunting, because he interrupted everything Barbara or I said. He seemed to have made up his brilliant mind about every possible topic, and condensed his conclusions into unanswerable aphorisms. The great crusted oyster of his mouth would open, an artificial pearl of polished thought would pop out, and the mouth would clam shut again. The voice was that of an English prep-school swot who could answer every question, pronouncing the letter *R* with a hint of the sound of a *W*.

While Barbara was cooking the dinner I tried to coax him down off the platform from which he seemed to be addressing an anonymous representative of an audience whom he had no wish to meet socially. So I mentioned J.R. Ackerley, as a friend who had stayed with me in the west of Ireland, knowing that

Auden had liked him enough to invite him to stay in Ischia. I plunged into a topic that was very close to Joe's heart, hoping to touch Auden's. I told him that when Joe came back from a visit to Athens in the mid-1950s, where he was the guest of the young novelist Francis King, a charming epicurean host, he told me he was shocked at being given a choice of a sailor, airman or royal guardsman for dinner in a taverna night after night. The promiscuity of his host had seemed immoral. I had suggested to Joe that age had altered his judgement. Hadn't he pursued guardsmen and sailors when he was young enough to enjoy the pursuit? 'You don't seem to understand,' Joe had corrected me, 'I was never promiscuous: I was always looking for an ideal friend.' Then Auden opened his mouth and out popped this pearl: 'All promiscuity is a search for the ideal friend.' During dinner he said, 'I hope God will let me die at seventy. I don't want to live longer than my natural span.' He wanted all his letters burned at his death, as he had burned, without reading, his father's letters when he died; and he wanted his friends to burn his letters to them – he was asking for this in his will. By destroying all his papers he hoped to make it impossible for anyone to write his life. Like the doctors of long ago, whose medical discoveries were kept secret, he expected his secrets to die with him.

In spite of his face's celebrated corrugations of age, he looked strong. He was disturbed by not being able to communicate with the students who attended his seminars at Columbia. They had no knowledge of the past, or of form, and no interest in either, which made it impossible for them to understand what poetry, his kind of poetry, was about. Barbara had once told me that she felt he wasn't aware of her as a person, and probably gave his students the same feeling. He had refused to give the Charles Eliot Norton lectures at Harvard, for which he was offered $29,000, on the grounds that he had nothing to say. 'Of course I could have dug something up that I've said before, but that would be bad.' Barbara had told me that he really needed the money.

How did we get on to the subject of witches? 'My mother-in-law was a witch,' he said, referring to the mother of Erika Mann, Thomas Mann's daughter, whom Auden had married in 1935 purely to make her a British subject. Then he said, 'And Louis's first wife is a witch,' referring to MacNeice. 'I'll drink a bottle of champagne the day I hear she's dead.' He was glad that Louis in his last years had found in Mary Wimbush, 'the first non-violent woman in his life'. Barbara said she thought my mother was a witch, adding that she liked witches and liked my mother. I agreed that my mother had the power of bewitching people.

(*K*, pp. 272–4)

Brilliant. Not an adverb nor adjective out of place in this delightful portrait.

In March 2002 Irish libel lawyers consulted by Granta Books were delaying publication of *The Kick* because of possible legal difficulties. Richard was concerned, for example, that what he had written about his wife Patricia Avis and Conor Cruise O'Brien – Irish politician, writer, historian, academic – might be a problem. When Richard called O'Brien directly from Durban, he agreed to read the chapter relating to him and Patricia. I delivered the relevant chapter across Dublin to O'Brien's house on the Hill of Howth. He made one correction: it was of what he had said to Patricia about the renovation of Lake Park; she had told Richard that O'Brien had said, dismissively, 'It smells of money.' Richard made the correction in *The Kick*:

Finally, he turned to Patricia and said, 'As Bob Hope remarked, "Everything I like in an apartment: all done over in contrasting shades of money."'   (*K*, p. 161)

Richard thanked him for this 'brilliant, witty improvement' and for O'Brien's permission to publish the book's account of the affair with Patricia.

For me, working with Richard Murphy on *The Kick* was an exhilarating and educational experience. I treasure his generous acknowledgement:

I thank Dr Barbara Browning Brown, emeritus professor of English literature at Marshall University, Huntington, West Virginia, for devoting seven years of her life in Dublin, from 1996–2002, to giving me unstinting editorial and inspirational advice, mostly by email and phone, while I was abroad. With more than a hundred notebooks to be sourced for this memoir, I could never have managed without Barbara's help.

(*K*, p. xxi)

In June 2002, the month when *The Kick* was launched in Dublin, Granta's managing director decided that the paperback edition (published in 2003) should have a different subtitle and she suggested 'A Life Among Writers'. Reviewers wrote: a 'superb memoir', from Patrick Crotty in the *TLS*; written 'with dignity and candour', adds Karl Miller in *The Spectator*, while in *The New York Review of Books* John Banville concludes, 'The book is a fine, considered and fascinating memoir of a life lived as close to the full as possible.'

16

~

The Kick and the Genre of Anglo-Irish Autobiography

ELENA COTTA RAMUSINO

T*he Kick* is a detailed memoir published by Richard Murphy in 2002. In the acknowledgements, readers are informed that it is based on notebooks the poet has kept for four decades. Notebooks and the memories they contain are often referred to in the text and increasingly quoted towards its end. Richard Murphy even describes the material characteristics of the notebooks, explaining that once, in Paris, he wanted to buy a 'blank notebook ... to hold the scraps of verse, elusive images, dreams, desires and revelations that might otherwise be forgotten' (*K*, p. 139) if unrecorded. But, instead of the object he had in mind, he

> discovered and bought, from a pile of black, orange and green
> *cahiers*, a small notebook for mathematicians, the pages lined
> with little squares, bound in green boards, quite cheap. I
> imagined that as numbers underlie music, and a score is essential
> for composition, so the page might hold in its net the music of
> poetry, and prevent words from swimming into measureless
> prolixity.   (*K*, p. 139)

This pattern becomes 'a symbol of perfection', the score that 'might exert day by day a subtle influence not to lie' and which 'would have to be kept secret, under guard like a salmon river, in which I alone could fish in the future for poems that might be lured to the surface from the stream of my past' (*K*, p. 140). Murphy returns to this 'mesh of vertical and horizontal lines' (*K*, p. 140) as 'a better-than-blank worksheet for metrical poetry' (*P*, p. 176) in a brief introduction to *The Price of Stone*, the sequence of sonnets dedicated to Dennis O'Driscoll. Thus, 'the centimetre-squared pages' (*P*, p. 176) become the archetype of the pattern, the perfect structure both holding and enabling the flux of life and of being.[1] The square-lined notebooks from Paris surface throughout *The Kick*, as symbols of continuity – they are a lifelong accompaniment to Murphy's writing – and favourable support. The need for a form conducive to perfection is a constant preoccupation in Richard Murphy's aesthetics, as shown by his exploration of structured forms, like the sonnet, and in the symmetry he aimed at, even when it was not fashionable, and in his interest in architecture and the relation between architecture, music and writing.[2]

The narrative based on the use of the notebooks is fluid and seemingly unstructured, without division in chapters, with changes of scene simply signalled by blank spaces or asterisks at times, a fluidity which aims at recreating the fluidity of becoming. Nevertheless, the underlying structure is revealed by the symmetry of the beginning and of the conclusion: the text begins with a kick and rebellion when Richard Murphy was three, and ends with his three-year-old grandson rebelling against him, a rebellion capped by Murphy's sister Mary telling him he has always been a '*Conventional* Rebel' (*K*, p. 344, emphasis added). The uncomplimentary adjective 'conventional' is emphasised by its final position in this autobiographical account: if it completes the symmetry, by qualifying and diminishing the nature of his rebellion, it is, at the same time, yet another disclaimer, or accusation, of the subject of this life against himself; this adjective, though, is also something more. It addresses a pervasive sense of inadequacy which marked the poet's relationship with his parents: indeed, 'conventional' would have been more suited to qualify his satisfaction of his parents' expectations – which he never fulfilled – than to define his decidedly unconventional and unsupported choice of a life devoted to poetry; 'I know you were never meant to be a poet', (*K*, p. 97) his mother once told him! His family's unswerving disapproval is subtly emphasised by the position of this adjective: its use at the end of *The Kick* makes it a lifelong judgement. Apart from the legendary kick to his aunt, the title clearly refers to Murphy's ambiguous sexual identity, the understanding of which proved so painful and frightening, but also to the kick Murphy gave to his previous life in 1959 when, after the end of his marriage, he decided to live among the islanders on Inishbofin.

The notebooks are a testimony recording thoughts and events; they implicitly raise one of the main issues of life-writing: the relationship between truth and fiction, the truth of the life and the fiction inherent in the narrative. Autobiographical writing is neither simply a recounting of the past nor a recounting of the author's past self: it is, indeed, a recreation of both from the perspective of the present of writing; it is not just a recollection, but rather a fictive creation true to the present self, more than to 'facts'. As Mark Freeman argues, 'the process of self-understanding is itself fundamentally recollective',[3] but the memory at work does not only recount the subject's past, it is, rather, 'an interpretive act the end of which is an enlarged understanding of the self',[4] of 'how we came to be'.[5]

The Kick traces the development of the life of a member of a prominent Anglo-Irish family from early childhood to maturity, while also accounting for the complex and often divided nature of his heritage, as a Protestant with (important) British connections and deeply rooted Irish affections. Richard Murphy's Anglo-Irish heritage is crucial to his growth and to its narration. As an Anglo-Irish autobiography, *The Kick* shares some of the features of the genre, but it also differs in some respects from other examples of Anglo-Irish life-writing. While a topos of early twentieth-century Irish and Anglo-Irish autobiographies was the close identification of self and nation, with the shaping of the self running in parallel with the shaping of the nation, *The Kick* does not conform to this paradigm. Although the nation narrative has been a distinctive feature of the genre in Ireland, as Eamonn Hughes among others has convincingly argued, this narrative does not represent a model for Richard Murphy's autobiography.[6] Indeed, as Claire Lynch claims, this topic is 'only notable if absent' since 'autobiographies from across the century shape themselves around the history of the nation to such an extent that it has become a standard element of the genre'.[7] Richard Murphy's distance from the nation narrative might be due to his divided heritage: Irish in Britain and British in Ireland: 'regarded as an Englishman because of my British accent, and yet feeling more self-consciously Irish in England than I ever would at home'.[8] Chronology is also important here. *The Kick* was published just after the beginning of the twenty-first century, that is, after the boom of autobiographies in the last decade of the twentieth century, but it tells the story of a man who, born in 1927, spent most of his life in the twentieth, and so participates in both. Moreover, as Elizabeth Grubgeld points out, at the end of the century

> Irish writers experimented with new forms of narrative and new configurations of the self. With a handful of exceptions ... the Anglo-Irish autobiography ceases to exist as a distinct category within contemporary Irish literary autobiographies, sexual identity replaces national identity as a pressing question, and religion appears less an ongoing influence than a set of discarded behavioural restrictions and attitudes.[9]

The foregrounding of sexual identity in the definition of the self is notable, for example, in Nuala O'Faolain's two highly successful autobiographical volumes which came out in this period, *Are You Somebody?* (1996) and *Almost There* (2003). In *The Kick*, sexuality also plays a prominent role. Even though several of Richard Murphy's poems deal explicitly with sexual themes and his homo- and hetero-sexuality – 'My form is epicene' as he writes in 'Folly' (*P*, p. 177) – *The Kick* provides an even more candid and personal account of the dilemmas of bisexual experience. This duality resonates with another dualism explored in *The Kick* and inherent in Richard Murphy's identity: his in-betweenness between Anglo-Irish and Irish identities. Moreover, the feelings connected to his sexual ambiguities, namely uncertainty and guilt, reverberate with his youthful desire to become a poet, and the sense of guilt at disappointing his parents' expectations in his choice of career – 'the ways in which I had disappointed [my father], had left scars' (*K*, p. 214).

A distinctive feature of Anglo-Irish autobiographies, which is also a prominent aspect of *The Kick*, is the relationship of the author to his or her locality. As Elizabeth Grubgeld claims, in the 'autobiographies of Anglo-Ireland, landscapes take part in human emotion and participate in human consciousness',[10] a relationship between subject and place which Michael Kenneally has defined as 'an inordinate concern with place'.[11] The Anglo-Irish relationship to the land is often embodied by the enclosed demesne – 'Tall trees and high walls enclosed us in the Milford demesne' (*K*, p. 44) – and by the apartness of the Big House.

Another feature of Anglo-Irish autobiographies – which can more generally be connected to the increasing alienation and uneasy position occupied by the Protestant Ascendancy in post-1922 Ireland – is the impending decadence of this class which looms over the narrative:

> Telling most often a tale of depleted fortune and influence, Anglo-Irish writers query their national and class identity through a narrative structure patterned on patrilinear descent or the history and geography of the family properties.[12]

This decadence is mirrored in the ruins of the Big Houses and their status as remnants of the past; as Seamus Deane writes in *The Field Day Anthology of Irish Writing*: 'All those ruins dotting the Irish landscape also populate Irish writing. The great buildings destroyed … and the cultures they represented are the relics of both external and internal oppression.'[13] Richard Murphy seems to be aware in *The Kick* of the belatedness of his Anglo-Irish narrative. This belatedness forms part of a nexus of feelings of postcolonial guilt and responsibility which is a noteworthy feature of his writing channelled as it often is by meditations on the remnants of Anglo-Ireland. These ruins also appear in a letter from Richard Murphy to his parents in which he recalls his visit to Coole Park in June 1950, the Anglo-Irish demesne par excellence:

> I went to see … Lady Gregory's Coole Park, of which not a stone of the foundations remained, but, to elaborate on Isaiah, waving ash-trees and tall hay were in the place of it. The pleasure-ground

was improved for being twenty years neglected, the glass-house
smashed, the shrubs overgrown, trees half-fallen across paths…[14]

In another letter Richard Murphy returns to the relationship between
creativity and ruins; here, the ruins are brought to life thanks to the
agency of friends Barrie Cooke and Sonja Landmere, who organised
a gathering of poets: 'What active beauty you are making out of inert
demesne ruins, using old structures to say something new, turning
barns into studies, and opening it all to friends for such generous
festivity…'[15]

Richard Murphy's special relation to the land is revealed in 'The
Pleasure Ground', a piece he wrote in the early 1960s, and which he
chose as Preface to his 2013 collected poems *The Pleasure Ground:
poems 1952–2012*, thus confirming its centrality to his *oeuvre*. In
this essay Murphy remembers the grounds of the Milford demesne,
the ancestral home – the poet's birthplace – of his mother's family
in the west of Ireland, a place which markedly contributed to his
development. Richard Murphy returned there during school
holidays and for an extended period during the Second World War,
when, with his siblings and his mother, he spent slightly more than
a year at Milford. Murphy refers to that period, when he was again
within the family (apart from his father), together in a beloved place,
as an idyllic time, a period in which studying 'poetry, music and
painting, even mathematics [was] an effortless delight' (*P*, p. 16),
because 'it earned my mother's praise' (*P*, p. 14), something he
would seek throughout most of his life. The Milford garden assumes
a prelapsarian quality which equates it with order, pointing out a
dynamic of order as opposed to decay, a decay which over the years
finally gained the upper hand: 'There was no young energy with a
will and money to mend walls, plant trees, sow and cultivate and
labour. I felt guilty and lost' (*P*, p. 16). The family demesne, like its
fortune, finally decays: 'As I grew older the Pleasure Ground sank
through decay into oblivion, as the old people died and the young
left the country' (*P*, p. 16).

When his personal pleasure ground decayed, he expanded it to
include the Connemara coast and the sea, 'that greatest of all pleasure

grounds' (*P*, p. 15), so that after the end of his marriage, Richard Murphy decided to go and live in the west of Ireland, where he lived off and by the sea from 1959 to 1976, when his beloved friend Tony White died. The sea represented both a vision and a means of economic support, an opportunity to prove himself against its 'measureless prolixity' (*K*, p. 139), but also an easier challenge than poetry – 'Sailing gave me strong, immediate satisfaction. It was easier than imagining in poetry the kind of hero I was not' (*K*, p. 176) – and a consolation – 'The sea chastened my resentment' (*K*, p. 190).

This is yet another declension of the inescapable relationship between place and voice, the centrality of which is affirmed by the opening question of his 1968 long poem *The Battle of Aughrim*: 'Who owns the land…?' (*P*, p. 61). This key and resonating issue in Irish history has a personal, autobiographical urgency for Murphy, as *The Kick* illustrates. An instance of 'historicize[d] geography', according to Declan Kiberd,[16] this poem is reflected upon in *The Kick* where Richard Murphy emphasises his efforts to make it encompass the voices of the winners and of the defeated, 'to evoke the spirit of both sides in that conflict' (*K*, p. 198). He claims his right to remember history without resentment: 'My underlying wish was to unite my divided self, as a renegade from a family of Protestant imperialists, in our divided country in a sequence faithful to the disunity of both' (*K*, p. 199). This aspiration for unity represents, as Murphy confided in an interview, a way of 'making sense of the complexities of my origin, and divided loyalties to Britain and Ireland, to my family and to my friends.'[17]

The Kick shows a lifelong connection to the country, his love of the west, his affiliation with the sea, and a fondness for solitude, as well as his need to reconcile the adjectives on both sides of the hyphen in Anglo-Irish. As a child, on his visits to the Connemara mountains, he met Irish children with whom he felt an affinity, seeing them as different and freer when compared with the more cloistered environment of his own family. Murphy explains the origins of his fascination with words in terms which echo those of William Butler Yeats as described in *Reveries over Childhood and Youth* where the latter recalls the dynamics of his identification and juxtaposition, as a child, with other social groups. Remembering the children at school in England, Yeats writes:

> I was divided from all those boys, not merely by the anecdotes that are everywhere perhaps a chief expression of the distrust of races, but because our mental images were different. I read their boys' books and they excited me, but if I read of some English victory, I did not believe that I read of my own people. They thought of Cressy and Agincourt and the Union Jack and were all very patriotic, and I, without those memories of Limerick and the Yellow Ford that would have strengthened an Irish Catholic, thought of mountain and lake, of my grandfather and of ships.[18]

In his essay 'The Pleasure Ground' Murphy writes:

> They were truly Irish, and that's what my brother and I wanted to be. They seemed sharper, freer…Stones, salmon-falls, rain-clouds and drownings had entered their minds, loaded with ancestral bias. Their manners seemed more natural than ours…[19]

The Kick actually testifies to a deep-rooted, dual feeling of simultaneous connectedness and alienation, affinity and distance, to a perpetual condition of 'in-betweenness' peculiar to the Anglo-Irish ('cut off from Ireland by the sea, from parents by the ocean, from the hope of peace by the reality of war', *K*, p. 76), of original loss ('a verbal English paradise that might replace the Irish one I had lost', *K*, p. 76), as well as a lack of unity or wholeness ('my divided self', *K*, p. 199). His struggles to be recognised as Irish, both in England and in Ireland, are lifelong, from the years spent at boarding school, where he was 'Scared of bombs' and was 'excoriated' by his housemaster – 'a survivor of the Somme' – for his 'Irish lack of British patriotism' (*K*, p. 77), to the years spent in the west of Ireland, where his origins, his education and his accent always marked him out as different, and reminded him that his position in the community might be easily endangered: even after his move to the west and his new life among the islanders, he was always conscious that he was 'a Protestant who sounded British and was divorced' (*K*, p. 190).

These anxieties are reflected in his need to anchor himself, to control and fix the flux of being, which is reflected in his preoccupation with form, from mathematics to music, from poetry to architecture. As Murphy stresses in an interview with John Haffenden: 'I think forms are the nature of things ... I do see poems as buildings and as music, there's a strong element of architecture in my poetry.'[20]

Seamus Heaney deftly summarises Murphy's struggles for self-definition in his 1977 essay on Murphy's poetry. In Heaney's eyes the Anglo-Irish poet's

> participation can never be total. Murphy will not surrender his sense of caste, his manners, his educated consciousness, his willed individuality to this essentially communal fatalistic and half-literate culture, however attractively that culture presents itself to his imagination. The constricted space he moves in and writes out of is a march between his Anglo-Irish Protestant background and his Irish Catholic surroundings, a space at once as neutral and torn as the battlefield at Aughrim ... sometimes invaded by nostalgia for the imperial, patrician past, sometimes hospitable to deprivations and disasters which somehow rebuke that heritage.[21]

Not only is the relation to place central to Richard Murphy's worldview, he also seems to need, in order to gain wholeness or security, a safe home, another instance of his yearning for structure, be it in words or in buildings. Therefore, it does not come as a surprise that, after his father's death, he decides to build a house with pink granite, 'a new house out of the old' and to 'replace in stone the lost firmament' (*K*, p. 225). Again, this recalls Murphy's description of his notebooks quoted at the beginning of this essay where 'the mesh of vertical and horizontal lines' presents a necessary pattern, and 'a symbol of perfection' (*K*, p. 140). As the poet himself claims:

> I think I've always looked for that kind of security – a place to which I belong, a house which is well built – because of the insecurity of my life and parts of my upbringing: an insecurity brought about by the war, and by my own loss of faith in

Christianity, and by the fall of the British Empire in whose strength I was reared.[22]

The Kick shows Richard Murphy's various engagements in providing a shelter and a home: first, around the time of his daughter's birth, 'searching for a place to live within sound and sight of the sea' (*K*, p. 155), and looking for 'a big house, or the ruin thereof, on fifty acres of demesne land' (*K*, p. 148); in this search for security he hoped that the 'Regency hunting lodge' (*K*, p. 155) in the Wicklow Mountains he found, Lake Park, would become 'an antidote for our [his wife Patricia's and his own] restlessness' (*K*, p. 149). His 'nest-building' (*K*, p. 156) was laborious and extended over time, becoming a substitute for writing poetry: 'When I tried to write poetry, I found I had nothing to say .... When I felt the lyric dying, I started building on an epic scale' (*K*, p. 157). Some years later, after his divorce, and after having settled in Connemara, he decided to build a house of pink granite there, an endeavour he characterises as one in which 'the poet as builder wrote himself into a block', sentiments which found expression in some discarded lines for 'Little Hunger':

> Did I need stone to build a house
> or a house to build with stone?   (*K*, p. 248)

Terence Brown offers an interesting interpretive hint for Murphy's fascination with stone, emphasising its retrospective quality: 'For what the stones have to offer is retrospection; the life they possess is the life they have enshrined', an observation which underscores the retrospective nature of autobiography, which, of course, offers the narration of a life by looking back from the present moment.[23]

Later on, his need to connect to the land drives him to buy High Island: 'I got excited at the thought of buying this inaccessible holy island, restoring the beehive cells and oratory of its derelict hermitage, and preserving the place from destruction either by tourists or by sheep' (*K*, pp. 249–50). The island charms him, again, because it seems to counteract his constant inner feeling of division and alienation: 'Everything on the island connects', he writes, 'connecting what appears to be disconnected' (*K*, p. 262). In the spring of 1974 he buys some land on Omey Island, where 'I designed a hexagonal studio of Omey granite to look as if it had grown out of the rock' (*K*, p. 279). This 'hexagonal studio' becomes yet another centre:

> Whenever I entered, harassed by rain, wind and the anxieties of life on the mainland, the figure of the hexagon, repeated like a musical theme with variations in the walls, the table and the ceiling, calmed me with a sense of concentricity and gave me the centripetal energy I needed to sit down, take out a notebook and pen, and write.   (*K*, p. 280)

Cork University Press issued a new edition of *The Kick: a memoir of the poet Richard Murphy* in 2017; the original one was the 2002 Granta edition, with a slightly different subtitle: 'A Life among Writers'. By defining the environment in which this life had been lived, and by foregrounding its literary journey, which began very early, the subtitle also underlined the importance played by the web of personal relationships around the poet.

The Kick overflows with anecdotes about major figures in the literary and cultural world sketched with varying degrees of admiration and empathy, feelings which at times magnify other authors. Always, in the background, there is an implicit comparison with the I's own achievements and failures ('My poetic ambition, buried in shame, would lie dormant', *K*, p. 92): the other poets and writers are the 'other' against which the self is shaped. 'How could you tell if you were a born poet or not?' (*K*, p. 86) he wonders after having listened to Stephen Spender; while poetry seems to him a means of 'redemption' (*K*, p. 77), he seems to realise that 'poetry was not my birthright. To me poetry would never come naturally, as a gift. It would have to be made' (*K*, p. 86), again, like a building, one could say.

Other poets, through these pages, seem to naturally enjoy the gift that is so hard for him to harness: British and Irish poets, from Philip Larkin, whose work he admired 'enormously',[24] to his friend Ted Hughes, whose poetry he thinks 'wonderfully fertile and explosive, hot, passionate',[25] to Seamus Heaney, but also American poets, like Theodore Roethke, whose 'devotion to his craft' Murphy admires even as he recognises 'a stinking wound that went with his talent' (*K*, p. 183). *The Kick* also offers sketches of authors, major and minor ones, whose portraits are sometimes unflattering, as when he remembers Roethke's ravings and hard drinking, or James Dickey's dismissive superiority at a reading on Murphy's first American tour in late 1964. However, the most influential creative relationship, as it emerges in *The Kick*, is Richard Murphy's friendship with Tony White, a gifted London actor who had eschewed success and fame and had left London and was writing a play on Inishbofin when Murphy arrived there in June 1959. He was a man 'who wanted neither to possess nor be possessed' (*K*, p. 290). Over the years of their friendship he became Murphy's ideal reader, his sometime supplier of notebooks from Paris, the man who could help him improve his writing, his buildings and his life:

> 'All that I ever wrote in these notebooks since I began to use the square-lined page was written with an underlying assumption that Tony would be the one to read with complete understanding all I had written, that he would outlive me, that he would make sense of the confusions in my life ... now I must make whatever sense I can ... now I must clarify.'   (K, p. 290)

he writes after Tony's sudden death.

While his writer friends constitute a web of relationships, Murphy's recurrent feeling of not belonging also extends to his writing; as he recalls in *The Kick*, his belief that 'the structure of a poem needs a body's or a building's symmetry put me out of key with the time' (*K*, p. 267), extending Murphy's outsider status to the domain of his craft of poetry.

The Kick widens the range of life-writing in Ireland; it testifies to the shaping of a self against uncertainties, family expectations, against a pervasive sense of guilt in the context of the author's hyphenated identity. An essential part of this process concerns the shaping of his poetic voice against a deep sense of inadequacy, the looming risk of failure, and the daunting comparisons with fellow poets. The resultant self-portrait is of a poet who writes against poetic fashions but who, in doing so, exhibits a personal and poetic integrity throughout.

Notes

Introduction

1 'President Leads Tributes to Poet Richard Murphy', *Irish Times*, 31 January 2018, https://www.irishtimes.com/culture/books/president-leads-tributes-to-poet-richard-murphy-1.3375383 [accessed 21 June 2018].

2 Gerald Dawe, 'Richard Murphy at 90: a poet of other people', *Irish Times*, 23 October 2017, https://www.irishtimes.com/culture/books/richard-murphy-at-90-a-poet-of-other-people-1.3265705 [accessed 10 November 2017].

3 Terence Brown, 'Poets and Patrimony: Richard Murphy and James Simmons', in *Ireland's Literature* (Mullingar: The Lilliput Press, 1988), p. 189.

4 Patrick Crotty (ed.), *Modern Irish Poetry: an anthology* (Belfast: Blackstaff Press, 1995), p. 149.

5 Gerald Dawe, 'Anecdotes Over a Jar', *The Proper Word: collected criticism*, ed. Nicholas Allen (Omaha, NE: Creighton University Press, 2007), p. 114.

6 *Sailing to an Island: a poem* (Dublin: The Dolmen Press, 1955); *The Woman of the House: an elegy* (Dublin: The Dolmen Press, 1959); *The Last Galway Hooker: a poem* (Dublin: The Dolmen Press, 1961). These were published as books by the Dolmen Press but were absorbed into Richard Murphy's main collections later. For full details of the publication histories of these poems, see 'Richard Murphy: A bibliography' in this volume and discussion in the essays by Lucy Collins and Tom Walker.

7 Elgy Gillespie, 'Richard Murphy upon Omey', *Irish Times*, 21 November 1975.

8 Richard Murphy, 'The Continual Sea' (review of *The Nightfishing* by W.S. Graham), *Times Literary Supplement*, no. 2,784, 8 July 1955, p. 379.

9 'The Woman of the House' was broadcast on the BBC's Third Programme on 17 May 1959 having been published in *The Listener* on 23 April 1959. 'Sailing to an Island' and 'The Last Galway Hooker' were broadcast on 6 February 1961 and published in *The Listener* on 17 August 1961 and 9 February 1961 respectively. 'The Cleggan Disaster' was broadcast by the BBC on 26 June 1962 and on RTÉ on 27 December 1962 and was published in *The Dolmen Miscellany of Irish Writing*, ed. John Montague (Dublin/London: The Dolmen Press/Oxford University Press, 1962), pp. 46–61.

10 Edna Longley, 'Searching the Darkness: Richard Murphy, Thomas Kinsella, John Montague and James Simmons', in *Two Decades of Irish Writing: a critical survey*, ed. Douglas Dunn (Cheadle: Carcanet Press, 1975), p. 130.

11 John Haffenden, *Viewpoints: poets in conversation with John Haffenden* (London: Faber & Faber, 1981), p. 153.

12 J.R. Ackerley, letter to Richard Murphy, 2 December 1963, in *The Letters of J.R. Ackerley*, ed. Neville Braybrooke (London: Gerald Duckworth & Company Ltd, 1975), p. 235.

13   Dawe, 'Anecdotes Over a Jar', p. 113.
14   Michael Longley, 'The West', in *One Wide Expanse: writings from the Ireland Chair of Poetry* (Dublin: UCD Press, 2015), p. 48.
15   Seán Lysaght, 'Corncrake', in *Erris* (Oldcastle: The Gallery Press, 2002), p. 24; 'Storm Petrels', in *Carnival Masks* (Oldcastle: The Gallery Press, 2014), pp. 32–3.
16   Jody Allen Randolph, *Close to the Next Moment: interviews from a changing Ireland* (Manchester: Carcanet Press, 2010), p. 123.
17   Mary O'Malley, 'Tracing', in *Where the Rocks Float* (Cliffs of Moher: Salmon Poetry, 1993), p. 52.
18   Ibid., p. 53.
19   Mary O'Malley, 'The Foreigner', in *Where the Rocks Float*, p. 5.
20   Mary O'Malley, 'Rebuilding the St John', in *The Boning Hall: new and selected poems* (Manchester: Carcanet Press, 2002), p. 30.
21   Mary O'Malley, 'Craft', in *Asylum Road* (Cliffs of Moher: Salmon Poetry, 2001), p. 82.
22   *Voices at the World's Edge: Irish poets on Skellig Michael*, ed. Paddy Bushe (Dublin: Dedalus Press, 2013), pp. 40–1.

1.   Division and Distress in the Poetry of Richard Murphy

1   'Rebecca Schull Talks to the Poet Richard Murphy about His Recently Completed Additions to the W.B. Yeats Version of Sophocles' *King Oedipus* for the Abbey Theatre and about His Own Background', *Irish Times*, 17 May 1973.
2   Richard Murphy, 'Transgressing into Poetry', *Poetry Ireland Review*, no. 107, September 2012, p. 26.
3   Ibid.
4   Richard Murphy, 'Transgressing into Poetry', *Poetry Ireland Review*, no. 111, December 2013, p. 120; Richard Murphy, *In Search of Poetry* (Thame: Clutag Press, 2017), p. 39.
5   Richard Murphy, 'Notes for Sonnets', *Poetry Ireland Review*, no. 104, September 2011, p. 95; *In Search of Poetry*, p. 116.
6   Ibid.
7   Richard Murphy, 'Transgressing into Poetry', *Poetry Ireland Review*, no. 107, September 2012, p. 27; *In Search of Poetry*, p. 46.
8   Richard Murphy, 'Transgressing into Poetry', *Poetry Ireland Review*, no. 107, September 2012, p. 26.
9   Richard Murphy, 'Transgressing into Poetry', *Poetry Ireland Review*, no. 111, p. 129; Murphy, *In Search of Poetry*, p. 152.
10   Richard Murphy, 'Transgressing into Poetry', *Poetry Ireland Review*, no. 111, p. 133; *In Search of Poetry*, p. 155.

2.   Richard Murphy's Plainstyles

1   Bernard O'Donoghue, '"Pat Cloherty's Version of *The Maisie*", Richard Murphy', in 'Poems that Matter: 1950–2000', ed. Peter Denman, *Irish University Review*, vol. 39, no. 2, autumn/winter 2009, pp. 239–45. Reprinted as 'Critique of "Pat Cloherty's Version of *The Maisie*"', in Richard Murphy, *Poems 1952–2012* (Dublin: The Lilliput Press, 2013), pp. 273–9.

2 There are many affinities between Synge and Murphy: they both went to the west of Ireland to find subjects and language; both have separate styles: accomplished versions of standard English (Synge in *The Aran Islands*, for instance) or a kind of local pastoral (Synge's plays, but also poems like 'Corrymeela').

3 I am using the dubious compound term 'plainstyle' rather than 'plain style' because the two-word form has connotations and historical meanings – briefly defined in the fourth paragraph below – that I do not want to invoke.

4 A good example of this willing incomprehension is Murphy's brilliant 'Photographs from Inishbofin – May 1960. *A dialogue between two boatmen*' (variously published, *P*, pp. 249–50). For example, 'Up the mouth this time and into the hole we run.'

5 William Wordsworth and Samuel Coleridge, *Wordsworth and Coleridge: lyrical ballads* (1802), eds R.L. Brett and A.R. Jones (London: Routledge, 2005), p. 245.

6 See W.J. Ong, *Ramus: method and the decay of dialogue* (Cambridge, MA: Harvard University Press, 1958), especially pp. 283ff 'The Plain Style'.

7 Ibid., p. 283.

8 Ibid., p. 284.

9 Ibid.

10 Donald Davie, 'Cards of Identity', *New York Review of Books*, vol. 22, no. 3, 6 March 1975, pp. 10–11.

11 Patrick Kavanagh, *A Poet's Country: selected prose*, ed. Antoinette Quinn (Dublin: The Lilliput Press, 2003), p. 315.

12 James Randall and Seamus Heaney, 'An Interview with Seamus Heaney', *Ploughshares*, vol. 5, no. 3, 1979, p. 21.

13 In its view of the bearing of past history on the present day, the other Irish contemporary that Murphy's use of history recalls is Brian Friel, especially in the play *Making History* (1988), which employs narrators in a way that is reminiscent of Murphy's 1963 poem.

14 See Michael J. Sidnell, *Yeats's Poetry and Poetics* (London: Macmillan, 1996), pp. 19–38.

15 W.B. Yeats, *Autobiographies* (London: Macmillan, 1955), p. 455.

16 Lady Augusta Gregory, *Seventy Years: being the autobiography of Lady Gregory*, ed. Colin Smythe (Gerrards Cross: Colin Smythe, 1974), p. 392.

17 Yeats, *Autobiographies*, pp. 102–3.

18 Ibid.

19 Cf. *The Kick*, pp. 143–6.

20 This version in *The Pleasure Ground* has Murphy's imprimatur: there is a minor change in the punctuation from the version in *Sailing to an Island*, and the word 'hollowed' is corrected to 'hollered'.

21 Seamus Heaney, *New Selected Poems 1966–1987* (London: Faber & Faber, 1990), pp. 100, 228.

22 W.B. Yeats, 'A General Introduction for My Work' (1937), in *Essays and Introductions* (London: Macmillan, 1961), p. 521.

23 Ibid., p. 529.

24 Heaney, *New Selected Poems*, p. 57.

25 Richard Murphy, *The Mirror Wall* (Dublin: Wolfhound Press, 1989), p. 61.

3. **'As if the sun shone': Love and loss in Richard Murphy's poems**

1 The poem 'Grounds' was first published in Richard Murphy's *Collected Poems* (Oldcastle: The Gallery Press, 2000), p. 57.

2 Patricia Avis (1928–1977), having qualified in medicine at Oxford, was a gifted editor and writer. Her *roman-à-clef Playing the Harlot* was published posthumously by Virago in 1996.

3 James Booth, 'Single in Belfast', in *Philip Larkin: life, art and love* (London: Bloomsbury, 2014), pp. 168–86.

4 Richard Murphy, letter to Philip Larkin, 18 September 1977, Tulsa. Philip Larkin had also visited Murphy and his daughter Emily in Cleggan, County Galway in August 1969 with Monica Jones and Charles Monteith, their editor at Faber & Faber. A photograph of the gathering is included in Richard Bradford's *The Importance of Elsewhere: Philip Larkin's photographs* (London: Frances Lincoln, 2015), p. 229.

5 Richard Murphy, letter to Philip Larkin, 18 September 1977, Tulsa.

6 It may be worth noting that the poem 'Stone Mania', definitively published in both Murphy's *Collected Poems* (2000) and in *Poems 1952–2012* (2013), was also published with the title 'The Price of Stone' in at least two anthologies closer to the time of the poem's composition. See *The First Ten Years: Dublin Arts Festival poetry*, eds Peter Fallon and Dennis O'Driscoll (Dublin: Dublin Arts Festival, 1979), p. 51; *Soft Day: a miscellany of Irish writing*, eds Peter Fallon and Seán Golden (Dublin: Wolfhound Press, 1980), pp. 71–2.

7 First published as 'The Pleasure Ground', *Listener*, vol. 70, no. 1794, 15 August 1963, pp. 237–40.

8 Variants of 'Sailing to an Island' would be published on four separate occasions prior to Murphy's 1963 volume *Sailing to an Island* from Faber & Faber. See 'Voyage to an Island', *Bell*, vol. 18, no. 7, December 1952, pp. 396–400; 'Sailing to an Island', *Listen*, vol. 1, no. 3, winter 1954, pp. 39–40; *Sailing to an Island: a poem* (Dublin: The Dolmen Press, 1955); 'Sailing to an Island', *Listener*, vol. 66, no. 1690, August 1961, p. 250.

9 Philip Larkin, 'Sunny Prestatyn', in *Collected Poems* (London: Faber & Faber, 2003), p. 106.

10 Richard Murphy, 'The Art of Debunkery', *New York Review of Books*, vol. 22, no. 8, 15 May 1975, p. 31.

11 'Richard Murphy', *Viewpoints: poets in conversation with John Haffenden* (London: Faber & Faber, 1981), p. 146.

12 See J.G. Farrell's magnificent 'Empire' trilogy: *Troubles* (1970), *The Siege of Krishnapur* (1973) and *The Singapore Grip* (1978).

4. **Richard Murphy's Island Lives**

1 In a recent essay on the island poem in Irish and Scottish traditions, critic Edna Longley remarks on the range of such poems, which she divides into three types: the docu-poem, the 'holy island' poem and the 'parable island' poem. Edna Longley, 'Irish and Scottish "Island Poems"', in *Northern Lights, Northern Words: selected papers from the FRLSU conference, Kirkwall 2009*, ed. Robert

McColl Millar (Aberdeen: Forum for Research on the Languages of Scotland and Ireland), pp. 143–61.

2 Eiléan Ní Chuilleanáin's 'Vertigo' was written after a trip to Skellig Michael organised by fellow poet Paddy Bushe. Ní Chuilleanáin's poem was published alongside the work of several other leading Irish poets in the anthology *Voices at the World's Edge: Irish poets on Skellig Michael*, ed. Paddy Bushe (Dublin: Dedalus Press, 2013), p. 111. Jen Hadfield, who was born in Chester to Canadian and British parents, was awarded a residency with the Shetland Arts Trust and has since settled there.

3 Kim Cheng Boey, 'Sailing to an Island: contemporary Irish poetry visits the Western Islands', in *Shima: the international journal of research into island cultures*, vol. 2, no. 2, 2008, p. 21.

4 Yeats' version of events is questionable but he claims to have advised Synge, 'Go to the Aran Islands. Live there as if you were one of the people themselves; express a life that has never found expression.' W.B. Yeats, 'Preface to the First Edition of *The Well of the Saints*', in J.M. Synge, *Collected Works, Vol. 3: Plays book 1*, ed. Ann Saddlemyer (Gerrards Cross: Colin Smythe, 1982), p. 63.

5 Heather Clark, 'Leaving Barra, Leaving Inishmore: islands in the Irish Protestant imagination', *Canadian Journal of Irish Studies*, vol. 35, no. 2, fall 2009, p. 30.

6 Arthur Symons, *Cities and Seacoasts and Islands* (London: W. Collins & Sons, 1918), p. 306.

7 Gilles Deleuze, 'Desert Islands', in *Desert Islands and Other Texts 1953–74*, trans. Michael Taormina, ed. David Lapoujade (Los Angeles, CA: Semiotext(e), 2004), p. 10. Italics added.

8 Andrew Harwood, quoted in Elaine Stratford et al., 'Envisioning the Archipelago', *Island Studies Journal*, vol. 6, no. 2, November 2011, pp. 113–30.

9 Deleuze, 'Desert Islands', p. 11.

10 Jonathan Pugh, 'Island Movements: thinking with the archipelago', *Island Studies Journal*, vol. 8, no. 1, May 2013, p. 9.

11 Ibid., p. 10.

12 See John Brannigan, 'Folk Revivals and Island Utopias', in *Archipelagic Modernism: literature in the Irish and British Isles, 1890–1970* (Edinburgh: Edinburgh University Press, 2015), pp. 21–67.

13 See Brannigan, *Archipelagic Modernism*, pp. 33–49 and Nicholas Allen, 'Synge, Reading and Archipelago', in *Synge and Edwardian Ireland*, eds Brian Cliff and Nicholas Grene (Oxford: Oxford University Press, 2012), pp. 159–71.

14 J.P. O'Malley, 'A Rebellious Son of the Ascendancy Who Found His Voice in Connemara', *Irish Examiner*, 21 September 2013. John Goodby has argued, however, that Murphy's 'marginalised position, in terms of caste, culture and geography' complicates this stereotype.

15 The foremost publisher of poetry in the early decades of the twentieth century was Cuala Press. Maunsel Press, identified with late Revival printing, published the early work of key figures among mid-century poets, such as Austin Clarke and F.R. Higgins. Maunsel ceased trading in 1926.

16 Maurice Harmon, 'Biographical Note on Richard Murphy', *Irish University Review*, vol. 7, no. 1, spring 1977, p. 13.

17 For further detail on this first volume, see Liam Miller, *Dolmen XXV: an illustrated bibliography of the Dolmen Press 1951–76* (Dublin: The Dolmen Press, 1976), p. 24.

18 Charles Monteith, letter to Richard Murphy, 9 May 1962, Tulsa.

19 The following year the Dolmen Press reprinted *The Last Galway Hooker* in a slightly smaller format with a print run of 1,000 copies. Miller, *Dolmen XXV*, p. 33.

20 'Sailing to an Island' first appeared as 'Voyage to an Island' in *The Bell*, vol. 18, no. 7, December 1952, pp. 396–400; it was republished in *Listen*, vol. 1, no. 3, winter 1954, pp. 39–40. The following year it appeared as 'Sailing to an Island' in a private printing from the Dolmen Press and again under that title in *Three Irish Poets* (Dublin: The Dolmen Press, 1961), published to accompany a reading by John Montague, Thomas Kinsella and Richard Murphy in the Royal Hibernian Hotel, Dublin. 'Sailing to an Island' is the opening poem of *Sailing to an Island* (London: Faber & Faber, 1963) and of Murphy's first *Selected Poems* (London: Faber & Faber, 1979).

21 Richard Murphy, 'Author's Note on the Provenance of "Sailing to an Island"', in *The Pleasure Ground: poems 1952–2012* (Newcastle: Bloodaxe, 2013), p. 245. A version of the same passage appears in *The Kick*, p. 129.

22 J. Edward Chamberlin, *Island: how islands transform the world* (London: Elliott & Thompson, 2013), p. 44.

23 See William Boelhower, 'The Rise of the New Atlantic Studies Matrix', *American Literary History*, vol. 20, nos. 1–2, 2008, pp. 83–101.

24 An early typescript of 'Voyage to an Island and Other Poems' plays with a three-part structure and incorporates some of the poems that would later appear in *Sailing to an Island*. Tulsa.

25 Pearse Hutchinson's early work is shaped by his experience of living in Spain, just as John Montague's is by periods he spent in the US and in Paris. Thomas Kinsella is primarily identified with Dublin landscape and history.

26 The poem was first published in *The Listener*, vol. 65, no. 1,663, 9 February 1961, p. 274.

27 Bernard O'Donoghue, 'The Lost Link: Richard Murphy's early poetry', *Metre*, no. 10, autumn 2001, p. 139.

28 The 1963 version offers a more workmanlike description: 'With her brown barked sails, and her hull black tar, / Her forest of oak ribs and the larchwood planks, / The cavern-smelling hold bulked with costly gear', *Sailing to an Island* (London: Faber & Faber, 1963), p. 17.

29 In the 1963 version the sexual connotation is taken further: 'In this boat's bows he sheathed his life's harpoon', *Sailing to an Island*, p. 19.

30 Barry Cunliffe, *Facing the Ocean: the Atlantic and its peoples 8000 BC to AD 1500* (Oxford: Oxford University Press, 2001), p. 79.

31 Richard Murphy, *High Island* (London: Faber & Faber, 1974), p. 13.

32 Shin Yamashiro, *American Sea Literature: seascapes, beach narratives, and underwater explorations* (New York: Palgrave Macmillan, 2014), p. 95.

33 Eamon Grennan, 'Riddling Free: Richard Murphy's *The Price of Stone*', in *Facing the Music: Irish poetry in the twentieth century* (Omaha, NE: Creighton University Press, 1999), p. 235.

34 Richard Murphy, letter to Philip Larkin, 20 April 1969, Tulsa.
35 Tim Robinson, *Connemara: the last pool of darkness* (London: Penguin, 2008), p. 209.
36 Philip Conkling, 'On Islanders and Islandness', *Geographical Review*, vol. 97, no 2, April 2007, p. 191.
37 Wall refers to the distinction made by Seamus Heaney between pagan wilderness and spiritual principles. Eamonn Wall, 'Wings Beating on Stone: Richard Murphy's ecology', in *Out of the Earth: ecocritical readings of Irish texts*, ed. Christine Cusick (Cork: Cork University Press, 2010), p. 11.
38 Philip Hoare, *The Sea Inside* (London: Fourth Estate, 2013), p. 7.
39 Richard Murphy, 'The Pursuit of Islands', unpublished essay, Tulsa.

5. Fluid Geographies: Richard Murphy's poetics of place

1   Richard Murphy, 'Notes for Sonnets', *Poetry Ireland Review*, no. 104, September 2011, p. 98; Richard Murphy, *In Search of Poetry* (Thame: Clutag Press, 2017), p. 127.
2   Note from Tuesday 12 January 1982. Richard Murphy, 'Transgressing into Poetry', *Poetry Ireland Review*, no. 111, September 2013, p. 118.
3   'Transgress' (v.) Def. 2.b. *Oxford English Dictionary*.
4   Richard Murphy, 'Charm of Eire', *Listener*, vol. 59, no. 1503, 16 January 1958, p. 119.
5   Maurice Harmon, 'Introduction: the poet and his background', in *Richard Murphy: poet of two traditions*, ed. Maurice Harmon (Dublin: Wolfhound Press, 1978), p. 7.
6   Murphy, 'Transgressing into Poetry', p. 124; *In Search of Poetry*, p. 109.
7   Laurence J. Kirmayer, 'Landscapes of Memory: trauma, narrative, and dissociation', in *Tense Past: cultural essays in trauma and memory*, eds Paul Antze and Michael Lambek (London: Routledge, 1996), p. 182.
8   'The Pleasure Ground', *Listener*, vol. 70, no. 1,794, 15 August 1963, p. 240. A version of this essay that Murphy revised in January 2012 serves as a preface to *Poems 1952–2012* (pp. 13–16); however, this characterisation of his grandmother at Milford was excised. All subsequent references to 'The Pleasure Ground' are to the version printed in *Poems 1952–2012*.
9   'The Landscape of Three Irelands: Hewitt, Murphy and Montague', in *Contemporary Irish Poetry: a collection of critical essays*, ed. Elmer Andrews (London: Macmillan, 1992), p. 159.
10 Terence Brown, 'Poets and Patrimony: Richard Murphy and James Simmons', in *Ireland's Literature: selected essays* (Mullingar: The Lilliput Press, 1988), p. 192.
11 Mark Kilroy, 'Richard Murphy's Connemara Locale', *Éire-Ireland*, vol. 15, no. 3, autumn 1980, p. 127.
12 Ibid., p. 133.
13 Ibid.
14 Richard Murphy, 'Transcription of Introductory Notes for Four Broadcast Recordings from *The Price of Stone* Recorded in Dublin for the Australian

Broadcasting Commission by RM'. Original broadcast directed by Dennis O'Driscoll. Sydney: Australian Broadcasting Commission, 1984. Tulsa.

15 Kilroy, 'Richard Murphy's Connemara Locale', p. 127.

16 Ibid.

17 Norman Vance, *Irish Literature: a social history* (Oxford: Basil Blackwell, 1990), pp. 216–17.

18 Brown, 'Poets and Patrimony', p. 189.

19 Neal Bowers, 'Richard Murphy: the landscape of the mind', *Journal of Irish Literature*, vol. 11, no. 3, September 1982, pp. 40–1.

20 Brown, 'Poets and Patrimony', p. 194.

21 Julian Moynaghan, *Anglo-Irish: the literary imagination in a hyphenated culture* (Princeton, NJ: Princeton University Press, 1995), p. 204.

22 Richard Murphy, letter to his parents, 17 June 1950, Tulsa.

23 Richard Murphy, letter to his parents, 5 November 1949, Tulsa.

24 Bertrand Westphal, 'Foreword', in *Geocritical Explorations: space, place, and mapping in literary and cultural studies*, ed. Robert T. Tally, Jr (New York: Palgrave Macmillan, 2011), p. xv. Italics in original.

25 Westphal, *Geocritical Explorations*, p. xiv. The only departure I make from Westphal's is that he predicates this on a geo-centred rather than an ego-centred approach. In other words, we would treat a single place from a multiplicity of views rather than a single author's treatment of it. In Murphy's case, however, his empathetic ventriloquism aims to subsume the poet's ego in order to allow a multiplicity of voices to describe place.

26 Bertrand Westphal, *Geocriticism: real and fictional spaces*, trans. Robert T. Tally, Jr (New York: Palgrave Macmillan, 2011), p. 46.

27 Ibid., p. 49.

28 Richard Murphy, 'Afternoon at Home', *Listener*, vol. 49, no. 1258, 9 April 1953, p. 594.

29 John Goodby, *Irish Poetry Since 1950: from stillness into history* (Manchester: Manchester University Press, 2000), p. 82.

30 Roy F. Foster, *Paddy and Mr Punch: connections in Irish and English history* (Harmondsworth: Penguin, 1995), p. 107.

31 Charles Monteith, letter to Richard Murphy, 30 November 1960, Tulsa.

32 Michel Foucault, 'Of Other Spaces: utopias and heterotopias', trans. Jay Miskowiec, *Diacritics*, vol. 16, no. 1, spring 1986, p. 27.

33 Gilles Deleuze and Félix Guattari, *A Thousand Plateaus: capitalism and schizophrenia*, trans. Brian Massumi (London: Continuum, 2004), p. 401. Italics in original.

34 Ibid.

35 Ibid., p. 399.

36 Ibid., p. 427.

37 Ibid.

38 Ibid., p. 47.

39 Brown, 'Poets and Patrimony', p. 192.

40 Westphal, *Geocriticism*, p. 47.

41 W.B. Yeats, 'Coole Park and Ballylee, 1931', in *The Poems*, ed. Daniel Albright (London: Everyman, 1992), p. 293.

42 Ibid., p. 294.

43 Murphy, 'Transcription of Introductory Notes for Four Broadcast Recordings from *The Price of Stone*', Tulsa.

44 Foucault, 'Of Other Spaces', p. 24.

45 Murphy, 'Transgressing into Poetry', p. 124; *In Search of Poetry*, p. 109.

46 Ibid.

47 Foucault, 'Of Other Spaces', p. 25.

48 Ibid., p. 27.

49 Ibid., p. 26.

50 Murphy, 'Transgressing into Poetry', p. 124; *In Search of Poetry*, p. 110.

51 Murphy, 'Transgressing into Poetry', p. 125; *In Search of Poetry*, p. 111.

52 Murphy, 'Transgressing into Poetry', p. 121; *In Search of Poetry*, pp. 53–4.

6. Richard Murphy: Radio poet

1 Richard Murphy Talks File 1 1950–1962, BBC Written Archives.

2 Kate Whitehead, *The Third Programme: a literary history* (Oxford: Clarendon Press, 1989), p. 1.

3 Richard Murphy, talk on *The Collected Poems of W.B. Yeats*, broadcast 15 August 1950, BBC General Overseas Service, Radio Talks Scripts Pre-1970, MUL–MUR T351, BBC Written Archives. All BBC broadcast dates given have been cross-checked with *The Radio Times*, now available online as a searchable database: http://genome.ch.bbc.co.uk. Murphy had published a review of W.B. Yeats' *Collected Poems* in the column 'Books and Writers' in *The Spectator*, vol. 185, no. 6372, 11 August 1950, p. 183.

4 Richard Murphy, 'A New American Poet' (review of Robert Lowell, *Poems: 1938–1949*), *Spectator*, vol. 185, no. 6,385, 10 November 1950, p. 480.

5 Richard Murphy, 'The Cocktail Party', *Spectator*, 28 April 1950, p. 569. This letter was written in response to an earlier piece by Bonamy Dobrée in the magazine that had praised the play.

6 Richard Murphy, 'Books and Writers' (review of Peter Russell, ed., *Ezra Pound*), *Spectator*, vol. 185, no. 6,386, 17 November 1950, p. 516.

7 Richard Murphy, letter to P.H. Newby, 6 November 1950, Richard Murphy Talks File 1 1950–1962, BBC Written Archives.

8 Talks proposal form, 13 December 1950, Richard Murphy Talks File 1 1950–1962, BBC Written Archives.

9 Richard Murphy to P.H. Newby, 28 November 1950, Richard Murphy Talks File 1 1950–1962, BBC Written Archives.

10 Talks proposal form, 13 December 1950, Richard Murphy Talks File 1 1950–1962, BBC Written Archives.

11 Richard Murphy, 'Narrative Poetry Today', broadcast 28 July 1951, BBC Third Programme; a version was reprinted as 'Why Has Narrative Poetry Failed?', *Listener*, vol. 46, no. 1171, 9 August 1951, pp. 226–7.

12 'Why Has Narrative Poetry Failed?', *Listener*, p. 226.

13 Ibid., p. 227.

14 Ibid.

15 Richard Murphy, letters to P.H. Newby, 12 February 1951 and 6 March 1951, Richard Murphy Talks File 1 1950–1962, BBC Written Archives.

16 Richard Murphy, letter to Louis MacNeice, 2 September 1952, MacNeice Papers, Box 18, Bodleian Library.

17 Louis MacNeice, letter to Richard Murphy, 25 November 1952. *Letters of Louis MacNeice*, ed. Jonathan Allison (London: Faber & Faber, 2010), pp. 555–6.

18 *First Reading*, broadcast on 24 May 1953, BBC Third Programme, as listed in *The Radio Times*, no. 1,541, 22 May 1953, p. 13.

19 'Introduction', in *The Movement Reconsidered: essays on Larkin, Amis, Gunn, Davie and their contemporaries*, ed. Zachary Leader (Oxford: Oxford University Press, 2009), pp. 2–3.

20 [J.D. Scott], 'In the Movement', *Spectator*, vol. 193, no. 6,588, 1 October 1954, pp. 399–400.

21 Richard Murphy, 'The Future of Poetry', *Literary Opinion*, broadcast 15 September 1954, Third Programme, Radio Talk Scripts Pre-1970, LIS–LIV T296, BBC Written Archives.

22 *New Verse*, broadcast 17 August 1955, Third Programme, Radio Talk Scripts Pre-1970, MUL–MUR T321, BBC Written Archives.

23 Richard Murphy, letter in response to 'In the Movement', *Spectator*, vol. 193, no. 6,591, 21 October 1954, p. 491.

24 Clive Wilmer, 'In and Out of the Movement: Donald David and Thom Gunn', in *The Movement Reconsidered*, p. 214.

25 Donald Davie, letter to Richard Murphy, 29 October 1955, Tulsa.

26 Donald Davie, 'Cards of Identity', *New York Review of Books*, vol. 22, no. 3, 6 March 1975, p. 10.

27 Paul Long, '"Ephemeral Work": Louis MacNeice and the Moment of "Pure Radio"', *Key Words*, no. 7, 2009, p. 73.

28 'Introduction', in *Broadcasting Modernism*, eds Debra Rae Cohen, Michael Coyle and Jane Lewty (Gainesville, FL: University Press of Florida, 2009), pp. 3–5; 'Introduction', in *Broadcasting in the Modernist Era*, eds Matthew Feldman, Erik Tonning and Henry Mead (London: Bloomsbury, 2014), pp. 2–3.

29 Emilie Morin, '"I beg your pardon?": W.B. Yeats, Audibility and Sound Transmission', in *Yeats's Mask: Yeats annual no. 19*, eds Margaret Mills Harper and Warwick Gould (Cambridge: Open Book Publishers, 2013), pp. 192–3.

30 Robert Giddings, 'Radio in Peace and War', *Literature and Culture in Modern Britain Volume II: 1930–1955*, ed. Gary Day (London: Longman, 1997), p. 157.

31 Laurence Gilliam, 'Features', *Radio Times*, 30 September 1949, as quoted in Whitehead, *The Third Programme*, p. 86.

32 Whitehead, *The Third Programme*, pp. 2–3.

33 Louis MacNeice, general introduction to *The Dark Tower and Other Radio Scripts* (1947), as reprinted in *Selected Plays of Louis MacNeice*, eds Alan Heuser and Peter McDonald (Oxford: Oxford University Press, 1993), p. 406.

34 D.G. Bridson, *Prospero and Ariel: the rise and fall of radio. A personal recollection* (London: Victor Gollancz, 1971), p. 182.

35 George Orwell, 'Poetry and the Microphone' [written in autumn 1943], *New Saxon Pamphlet*, no. 3, March 1945, reprinted in *The Collected Essays, Journalism and Letters of George Orwell, II: my country right or left, 1940–1943*, eds Sonia Orwell and Ian Angus (Harmondsworth: Penguin, 1970), pp. 376, 378.

36 D.G. Bridson, 'Radio's Approach to Poetry', *BBC Quarterly*, autumn 1950, pp. 167–72, and C. Day Lewis, 'Broadcasting and Poetry', *BBC Quarterly* (spring 1950), pp. 1–7, as quoted in Whitehead, *The Third Programme*, pp. 159–60.

37 Whitehead, *The Third Programme*, p. 156.

38 Bridson, *Prospero and Ariel*, p. 200.

39 Richard Murphy, letter to John Wain, 27 October 1954, Tulsa.

40 Richard Murphy, *The Cleggan Disaster*, broadcast 26 June 1962, Third Programme. Prior to this, 'The Woman of the House' was read by Murphy and introduced by George MacBeth on *New Verse*, broadcast 17 May 1959, Third Programme. MacBeth (another central figure in the story of poetry and the post-war BBC) produced the programme *To the Island*, which included Murphy reading and introducing 'Sailing to an Island' and 'The Last Galway Hooker', broadcast 6 February 1961, Third Programme. (Richard Murphy Talks File 1 1950–1962, BBC Written Archives.)

41 Richard Murphy, 'Narrative Poetry Today'. 'Why Has Narrative Poetry Failed?', p. 227.

42 Richard Murphy, interview with John Haffenden, *Viewpoints: poets in conversation with John Haffenden* (London: Faber & Faber, 1981), p. 146.

43 The lineation, which highlights the heavy use of caesura in the poem and is different to printed versions of the poem, is taken from the copy of the script Cleverdon used for the broadcast: Cleverdon MSS II, Lilly Library, Indiana University. All subsequent quotations from the poem are taken from this typescript.

44 Bernard O'Donoghue, '"Pat Cloherty's Version of *The Maisie*", Richard Murphy', *Irish University Review*, vol. 39, no. 3, autumn/winter 2009, p. 241.

45 Seamus Heaney, 'The Poetry of Richard Murphy', *Irish University Review*, vol. 7, no. 1, spring 1977, p. 24.

46 Richard Murphy, 'Narrative Poetry Today'.

47 Richard Murphy, letter to Douglas Cleverdon, 15 December 1962, Cleverdon MSS II, Lilly Library, Indiana University. The BBC's Audience Research Department produced reports on broadcasts based on the responses of its listener research panel, including an appreciation index. The report and hence appreciation score for this broadcast have not been traced. Murphy read 'The Cleggan Disaster' on RTÉ on 27 December 1962: 'Reading of Cleggan Poem', *Irish Times*, 24 December 1962, p. 9.

48 Richard Murphy, letter to Douglas Cleverdon, 31 May 1962, Cleverdon MSS II, Lilly Library, Indiana University.

49 Douglas Cleverdon, letter to Richard Murphy, 13 July 1962, Cleverdon MSS II, Lilly Library, Indiana University.

50 Richard Murphy, letter to Douglas Cleverdon, 31 October 1962, Cleverdon MSS II, Lilly Library, Indiana University.

51 Richard Murphy, letter to Douglas Cleverdon, 31 October 1962; Richard Murphy, letter to P.H. Newby, 31 October 1962, Richard Murphy Talks File 1 1950–1962, BBC Written Archives.

52 Richard Murphy, letter to Douglas Cleverdon, 15 December 1962, Cleverdon MSS II, Lilly Library, Indiana University. In the meantime, Murphy was commissioned to give a talk, 'The Pleasure Ground' (which ended with a reading of 'The Woman of the House'), as part of a series called *Writers on Themselves*, broadcast 8 August 1963, Third Programme. After the failure to have 'The God Who Eats Corn' published in the *Sunday Times* (which had paid for Murphy's expensive air fare to Africa to write it), a reading was produced by MacBeth and broadcast on 5 August 1964, Third Programme: Richard Murphy Talks File 2 1963–1967, BBC Written Archives.

53 Douglas Cleverdon, letter to Richard Murphy, 15 December 1967, Cleverdon MSS II, Lilly Library, Indiana University.

54 Richard Murphy, letter to Douglas Cleverdon, 30 January 1968, Cleverdon MSS II, Lilly Library, Indiana University.

55 Richard Murphy, typescript of *The Battle of Aughrim* (*c.* January 1968), Cleverdon MSS II, Lilly Library, Indiana University.

56 Douglas Cleverdon, BBC internal memo, 2 April 1968, Cleverdon MSS II, Lilly Library, Indiana University. On the importance of Ó Riada's ideas and practice to many Irish poets of the period, see Damian Keane, 'Poetry, Music and Reproduced Sound', in *The Oxford Handbook of Modern Irish Poetry*, eds Fran Brearton and Alan Gillis, (Oxford: Oxford University Press, 2012), pp. 266–81.

57 Douglas Cleverdon, BBC internal memo, 6 August 1968, Cleverdon MSS II, Lilly Library, Indiana University. This memo states that the harpsichord was played by Cyril Gell, offering a minor correction to Keane's description of Ó Riada playing 'unaccompanied baroque music on the harpsichord' in the recording: Keane, 'Poetry, Music and Reproduced Sound', p. 269.

58 Julian Moynihan, 'The Battle of Aughrim: a commentary', *Irish University Review*, vol. 13, no. 1, spring 1983, p. 103. The original recording can be listened to in the British Library. This was subsequently released, with the opening radio announcement cut out, as an LP by Claddagh Records (CCT 7, 1969), which can currently be purchased in digital form online.

59 Cleverdon MSS II, Lilly Library, Indiana University. All subsequent quotations from the poem are taken from this typescript.

60 For an overview of the Irish mode, see Matthew Campbell, *Irish Poetry Under the Union, 1801–1924* (Cambridge: Cambridge University Press, 2013), pp. 21–47.

61 'The Protestant Boys', sung by Richard Hayward and accompanied by the Loyal Brethren [n.d.], Irish Traditional Music Archive, 1573-ITMA-EP.

62 Colm Ó Lochlainn (ed.), *Irish Street Ballads* (Dublin: The Three Candles, 1939), pp. 72–3.

63 Richard Murphy, typescript of *The Battle of Aughrim* (*c.* January 1968), Cleverdon MSS II, Lilly Library, Indiana University.

64 Emily C. Bloom, 'Channel Paddlers: 1950s Irish drama on the British airwaves', *Éire-Ireland*, vol. 50, nos 1–2, spring/summer 2015, p. 46.

65 Moynihan, '*The Battle of Aughrim*: a commentary', p. 103.

66 Murphy, 'The Future of Poetry'.

67 Audience Research Department Report on *The Battle of Aughrim*, 20 September 1968, Cleverdon MSS II, Lilly Library, Indiana University.

68 Irish Film & Television Index: http://www.tcd.ie/irishfilm [accessed 28 December 2018]; Murphy, *The Kick*, pp. 245–6.

7. 'Bygone canon, bygone spleen': Richard Murphy as a conflict poet in *The Battle of Aughrim*

1 *The Battle of Aughrim* first appeared alongside 'The God Who Eats Corn' in *The Battle of Aughrim and the God Who Eats Corn* by Richard Murphy (London: Faber & Faber; New York: Alfred A. Knopf, 1968). Davie's review is of the US publication *High Island: new and selected poems* (New York: Harper & Row, 1975). The edition of *High Island* from Faber (London: Faber & Faber, 1974) had no selected poems included and did not contain this poem.

2 Richard Murphy's letter to the editors published as 'The Irish Situation' in *The New York Review of Books*, vol. 22, no. 6, 17 April 1975, p. 38 was written in response to 'Cards of Identity', Donald Davie's review of *High Island: new and selected poems* (*New York Review of Books*, vol. 22, no. 3, 6 March 1975, pp. 10–11). Murphy's 'The Irish Situation' was followed by a reply by Donald Davie.

3 Ibid.

4 Ibid.

5 Ibid.

6 Richard Murphy, interview with David Wheatley, *Metre*, no. 10, autumn 2001, pp. 146–7.

7 In his 'Glossary to '*The Battle of Aughrim*', Jonathan Williams notes: 'Godart van Reede Ginkel (1630–1703) … followed William to England in 1688, commanded a body of horse at the Boyne and was active at the siege of Limerick. In September 1690 he was given sole charge of the [Williamite] forces in Ireland and remained in command for the rest of the war. He received the earldom of Athlone in 1692 and the barony of Aughrim.' A number of variations can be found of his name and title(s), but his military position at Aughrim was that of lieutenant general. Jonathan Williams, 'A Glossary to *The Battle of Aughrim* and *The God Who Eats Corn*', *Irish University Review: Richard Murphy special issue*, ed. Maurice Harmon, vol. 7, no. 1, spring 1977, p. 84.

8 Richard Murphy, 'The Use of History in Poetry', in *The Uses of the Past: essays on Irish culture*, eds Audrey S. Eyler and Robert F. Garratt (Newark: University of Delaware Press, 1988), p. 19.

9 Ibid.

10 See Tom Walker's essay 'Richard Murphy: radio poet' in this volume for more extensive discussion on *The Battle of Aughrim* as a poem for radio.

11 The recording of *The Battle of Aughrim* can now be purchased online in digital format: *The Battle of Aughrim* (Claddagh Records, 1969), Spoken Word LP series, CCT 7.

12 As noted above, *The Battle of Aughrim* was published alongside 'The God Who Eats Corn'. Though the kind of close reading undertaken in this essay precludes discussion of the work through an expressly postcolonial prism, it is worth noting that the latter poem mirrors some of the exploration of conflicting impulses that mark *The Battle of Aughrim*, combining what appears to be some admiration for what was achieved in Africa by 'colonisers' with a clear insight into the worst practices of the coercive regimes that some maintained. John Goodby, in the work cited below, notes the irony inherent in a situation in which there is a 'total absence of reference to Murphy in current critical debates on postcolonialism', and this, despite the fact that '"The God Who Eats Corn" is perhaps the only poem by an Irish writer to deal first hand with a post-war decolonization event'. In Goodby's view this state of affairs reveals 'the narrowness of the discussion' (p. 84).

13 John Goodby, *Irish Poetry since 1950: from stillness into history* (Manchester: Manchester University Press, 2000), p. 81.

14 Roger McHugh and Maurice Harmon, *Short History of Anglo Irish Literature from Its Origins to the Present Day* (Dublin: Wolfhound Press, 1982), p. 315.

15 Edna Longley, 'Searching the Darkness: the poetry of Richard Murphy, Thomas Kinsella, John Montague and James Simmons', in *Two Decades of Irish Writing: a critical survey*, ed. Douglas Dunn (Cheadle: Carcanet Press, 1975), p. 127.

16 Ibid.

17 George Warter Story, *An Impartial History of the Wars of Ireland: with a continuation thereof. In two parts* (London: Printed for R. Chiswell, 1693).

18 Seamus Deane, *A Short History of Irish Literature* (London: Hutchinson, 1986), p. 238.

19 Frank Bidart, in the poem 'Ulanova at Forty-six at Last Dances Before a Camera Giselle', *Poetry*, vol. 190, no. 3, June 2007, pp. 171–2.

20 Ted Hughes, quoted on the inside back flap of the dust jacket of *The Mirror Wall* (Dublin: Wolfhound Press, 1989).

8. Richard Murphy's Poetry of Aftermath

1   Richard Murphy, 'The Pleasure Ground', in *Writers on Themselves*, introduced by Herbert Read (London: BBC, 1964), pp. 62–6.

2   Richard Murphy, 'Transgressing into Poetry', *Poetry Ireland Review*, no. 107, September 2012, p. 26.

3   'Notes for Sonnets', *Poetry Ireland Review*, no. 104, September 2011, pp. 92–104; 'Extract: Transgressing into Poetry', *Poetry Ireland Review*, no. 107, September 2012, pp. 26–36; 'Essay: Transgressing into Poetry', *Poetry Ireland Review*, no. 111, September 2013, pp. 117–33.

4   R.F. Foster, 'Book of the Irish', *Times Literary Supplement*, no. 5,911, 15 July 2016, p. 10.

5   Maurice Harmon, 'Biographical Note on Richard Murphy', *Irish University Review*, vol. 7, no. 1, spring 1977, p. 15.

6   *The Compact Edition of the Oxford English Dictionary: complete text reproduced micrographically*, 2 vols (Oxford: Oxford University Press, 1971). Reference to

definitions from this source will be designated in the text (*OED*) and cited by the word being defined. Where necessary to differentiate among several definitions of a word, the *Dictionary*'s subdivisions will be given in parentheses. The 'text micrographically reproduced' is that of the first edition, published in ten volumes in 1928 and in twelve volumes with supplement in 1933. Except for the one immediately following, all citations are from this edition, the one Murphy used.

7 *The Compact Oxford English Dictionary*, 2nd edn (Oxford: Clarendon Press, 1994).
8 John Childs, *The Williamite Wars in Ireland* (London: Continuum, 2007), p. 46.
9 Karen Armstrong, *Fields of Blood: religion and the history of violence* (New York: Alfred A. Knopf, 2014), pp. 3–17.
10 Ibid., p. 12.
11 The four parts, herein designated by Roman numerals, are divided into unnumbered units referred to as sections and designated by Arabic numbers.
12 Childs, *The Williamite Wars*, p. 338.
13 Ibid., p. 336.
14 Murphy, 'Transgressing into Poetry', *Poetry Ireland Review*, no. 111, p. 117.
15 A.J. Wills, *An Introduction to the History of Central Africa: Zambia, Malawi, and Zimbabwe*, 4th edn (New York: Oxford University Press, 1985), p. 133.
16 Murphy, 'Transgressing into Poetry', *Poetry Ireland Review*, no. 111, pp. 117–18.
17 Ibid., p. 118.
18 Sonnets which explore the Milford estate in *The Price of Stone* include: 'Birth Place', 'Queen of the Castle', 'Planter Stock', 'Rectory', 'Suntrap' and 'Milford: East Wing'.
19 Murphy, 'Transgressing into Poetry', *Poetry Ireland Review*, no. 107, p. 30.
20 Ibid., p. 29.
21 Ibid., p. 31.
22 Ibid., p. 29.
23 Ibid., p. 31.
24 Ibid., p. 32.
25 Ibid., p. 31.
26 Ibid.
27 Ibid., p. 32.
28 Richard Murphy, 'Rejoice', *Poetry Ireland Review*, no. 116, September 2015, p. 9.
29 Murphy, 'The Pleasure Ground', in *Writers on Themselves*, p. 66.

9. 'In a paradise for white gods he grows old': The instability of pastoral space in Richard Murphy's 'The God Who Eats Corn'

1 James D. Brophy, 'Richard Murphy: poet of nostalgia or *pietas?*', in *Contemporary Irish Writing*, eds James D. Brophy and Raymond J. Porter (Boston: Twayne, 1983), p. 49.
2 Dillon Johnston and Guinn Batten, 'Contemporary Poetry in English: 1940–2000', in *The Cambridge History of Irish Literature, Vol. II: 1890–2000*, eds Margaret Kelleher and Philip O'Leary (Cambridge: Cambridge University Press, 2006), p. 373.

3   Neal Bowers, 'Richard Murphy: the landscape of the mind', *Journal of Irish Literature*, vol. 11, no. 3, September 1982, pp. 35–6.

4   Brophy, 'Richard Murphy', p. 54.

5   Edward W. Soja, *Postmodern Georgraphies: the reassertion of space in critical social theory* (London: Verso, 1989), pp. 150–1.

6   Ibid., p. 151.

7   Richard Murphy, 'The Pleasure Ground', *Listener*, vol. 70, no. 1,794, 15 August 1963, p. 237.

8   Andrew V. Ettin, *Literature and the Pastoral* (New Haven, CT: Yale University Press, 1984), p. 30.

9   Ibid., p. 98.

10 Terence Brown, 'Poets and Patrimony: Richard Murphy and James Simmons', in *Ireland's Literature: selected essays* (Mullingar: The Lilliput Press, 1988), p. 194.

11 Henri Lefebvre, *The Production of Space*, trans. Donald Nicholson-Smith (Oxford: Blackwell, 1991), p. 277.

12 Richard Murphy, *Collected Poems* (Oldcastle: The Gallery Press, 2000), p. 233.

13 It is worth noting that there are several important textual and organisational differences between 'The God Who Eats Corn' as published in *The Battle of Aughrim* (Faber & Faber, 1968), pp. 53–64; *High Island: new and selected poems* (Harper & Row, 1974), pp. 75–83; *Collected Poems* (The Gallery Press, 2000), pp. 90–5; and *Poems 1952–2012* (The Lilliput Press, 2013), pp. 101–8. The 2013 version omits a number of stanzas previously included and reduces the number of sections of the poem to five. The original version (1968) has six sections which are replicated in the US edition of *High Island: new and selected poems* (1974). The version in *Collected Poems* (2000) comprises of the same text in seven sections, while the definitive 2013 version is a significantly edited text compared to the previously published versions. Therefore, some citations in this essay refer to earlier versions of the poem and include lines and stanzas not published in *Poems 1952–2012* (The Lilliput Press, 2013).

14 Murphy, *Collected Poems*, p. 95.

15 Ibid.

16 Ibid., p. 233.

17 Lefebvre, *The Production of Space*, p. 48.

18 Ibid.

19 Ibid., pp. 38–9.

20 Murphy, *Collected Poems*, p. 95.

21 Lefebvre, *The Production of Space*, p. 39.

22 As printed in *Poems 1952–2012*, p. 107, and in *High Island: new and selected poems*, p. 82, and *The Battle of Aughrim*, p. 62. This stanza is printed as section five of the version of the poem published in *Collected Poems*, p. 94.

23 Murphy, *Collected Poems*, p. 94.

10. 'Like fish under poetry's beaks': Richard Murphy and Ted Hughes

1   Anne Stevenson Archive, Cambridge University Library. Add 9451, box 19, f.2.

2   Richard Murphy, 'A Memoir of Sylvia Plath and Ted Hughes on a Visit to the West of Ireland in 1962', in Anne Stevenson, *Bitter Fame: a life of Sylvia Plath,*

with additional material by Lucas Myers, Dido Merwin, and Richard Murphy (London: Viking, 1989), p. 358. See also Murphy's 'Sylvia Plath and Ted Hughes: a visit to the west of Ireland in 1962', *London Magazine*, vol. 29, nos 3–4 (June/ July 1989), pp. 31–43.

3 Ted Hughes to the editor of *The Guardian*, 30 April 1989, in *The Letters of Ted Hughes*, ed. Christopher Reid (London: Faber & Faber, 2007), pp. 551–2.

4 Richard Murphy Papers, 1951–1982. 1988.014. Department of Special Collections, McFarlin Library, University of Tulsa. I am indebted to Benjamin Keatinge for providing me with access to this material, reproduced with kind permission of the University of Tulsa and the estate of Richard Murphy.

5 Murphy, 'A Memoir', p. 352.

6 Ibid., p. 350.

7 Ibid., p. 351.

8 Ibid., p. 352.

9 Ibid.

10 Richard Murphy, letter to Anne Stevenson, 4 August 1987, Anne Stevenson Archive, Cambridge University Library: Add 9451, box 19, f.2. In *The Kick* (p. 202) Murphy rephrases Hughes' statement and omits Plath's endorsement of it.

11 Murphy, 'A Memoir', pp. 349–50.

12 Richard Murphy, 'The Empty Tower at Ballylee', *Observer*, 7 October 1962, Books section.

13 Murphy, 'A Memoir', p. 348.

14 The four early versions of the poem are as 'Voyage to an Island', in *The Bell*, ed. Peadar O'Donnell, vol. 18, no. 7, December 1952; in winter 1954 as 'Sailing to an Island' in *Listen*, vol. 1, no. 3, ed. George Hartley; in 1955 as *Sailing to an Island* (Dublin: The Dolmen Press); and as 'Sailing to an Island' in *The Listener* on 17 August 1961 (no. 1,690). I am indebted to Benjamin Keatinge for this information.

15 'Ted Hughes, the Poet, Introduces Another in His Series of Extracts from Great Books He Believes All Children Will Enjoy and Remember', *Sunday Times*, 16 September 1962, colour section, p. 18.

16 Murphy, 'A Memoir', p. 349.

17 Richard Murphy, 'To Celebrate Existence', *Hibernia*, 17 December 1976, p. 20. Strikingly, Murphy told me that he never fished with Hughes, nor saw him fish; but he recognised how much fishing meant to him.

18 Murphy, 'A Memoir', p. 349.

19 Ibid., p. 352.

20 W.B. Yeats, *Selected Poems*, ed. Timothy Webb (London: Penguin, 1991), p. 45.

21 Murphy, 'A Memoir', p. 350.

22 Reid (ed.), *The Letters of Ted Hughes*, p. 240.

23 Ibid. In fact, Murphy's poem was published, as 'For Sylvia Plath 1932–1963', first in *Cheltenham Festival of Literature: programme of the Cheltenham Arts Festival, 1965* (Cheltenham: Cheltenham Arts Festival, 1965), pp. 54–5, and subsequently in *A Prose and Verse Anthology of Modern Irish Writing*, ed. Grattan Freyer (Dublin: Irish Humanities Centre, 1978), p. 249. I am indebted to Benjamin Keatinge for this information.

24 See Tom Walker's essay 'Richard Murphy: Radio poet' in this volume for a detailed account of the commissioning of *The Battle of Aughrim* by the BBC and also for details of Hughes' role in the radio broadcast of the poem for the BBC Third Programme on 18 September 1968.

25 Reid (ed.), *The Letters of Ted Hughes*, p. 241.

26 Seamus Heaney, 'The Poetry of Richard Murphy', in *Richard Murphy: poet of two traditions*, ed. Maurice Harmon (Dublin: Wolfhound Press, 1978), p. 26.

27 Reid (ed.), *The Letters of Ted Hughes*, pp. 241–2.

28 Ibid., p. 254.

29 Richard Murphy, email of 24 April 2013; see also: https://doonreagan.wordpress.com/ [accessed 30 December 2018].

30 Ted Hughes Archive, British Library, Add MS 88918.7.2.

31 Ted Hughes, *Poetry in the Making* (London: Faber & Faber, 1967), p. 75.

32 Ibid., p. 81.

33 Ibid., pp. 82–3.

34 Reid (ed.), *The Letters of Ted Hughes*, p. 295.

35 Ibid.

36 Ted Hughes to Richard Murphy, postmarked 21 July 1969. Tulsa.

37 Ibid.

38 Ibid.

39 Mark Kilroy, 'Richard Murphy's Connemara Locale', *Éire-Ireland*, vol. 15, no. 3, autumn 1980, p. 132.

40 Eamonn Wall, 'Wings Beating on Stone: Richard Murphy's ecology', in *Out of the Earth: ecocritical readings of Irish texts*, ed. Christine Cusick (Cork: Cork University Press, 2010), p. 9.

41 The first American edition of *Crow: from the life and songs of the crow* was published by Harper & Row on 5 March 1971.

42 Reid (ed.), *The Letters of Ted Hughes*, p. 314.

43 Patrick Crotty, 'What a Strange Boy You Are', *Times Literary Supplement*, no. 5,192, 4 October 2002, p. 27.

44 Reid (ed.), *The Letters of Ted Hughes*, p. 314.

45 Richard Murphy, *High Island* (London: Faber & Faber, 1974), p. 11.

46 On the day of my visit to High Island, at Murphy's encouragement, in May 2013, its then owner Feicín Mulkerrin's inflatable launch also carried a surveyor of the chain of islands' population of corncrakes.

47 For the 'rogues gallery', see Reid (ed.), *The Letters of Ted Hughes*, p. 314. The copy of *High Island* is now with the rest of Hughes' library in the Manuscripts and Rare Books Library, Emory University. I am grateful to Kathleen Shoemaker for sending me a copy of the inscription.

48 Richard Murphy, *Collected Poems* (Oldcastle: The Gallery Press, 2000), contents pages: the phrase is used to introduce poems in Parts I, III and IV.

49 Richard Murphy, *In Search of Poetry* (Thame: Clutag Press, 2017), p. 107.

50 Ibid., p. 106. Conversation with Richard Murphy, 23 June 2017.

51 Ted Hughes Archive, British Library, Add MS 88918.122.4; conversation with Paul Cullen, 23 May 2013.

52 The title of Ted Hughes' poem 'A Violet at Lough Aughrisburg' is given as it appears in Ted Hughes, *Flowers and Insects* (London: Faber & Faber, 1986).

53 Ted Hughes, *Gaudete* (London: Faber & Faber, 1977), p. 9. Italics in original.

54 Ibid.

55 Reid (ed.), *The Letters of Ted Hughes*, p. 384.

56 Hughes, *Gaudete*, p. 9. Italics in original.

57 Ibid. p. 11.

58 Ibid., p. 13.

59 Ibid., p. 77

60 Ibid., pp. 77–8.

61 Ibid., p. 173.

62 Crotty, 'What a Strange Boy You Are', p. 27.

11. 'The lyric barrier': Richard Murphy's America

1   Richard Murphy, 'A New American Poet', *Spectator*, vol. 185, no. 6,385, 10 November 1950, p. 32.

2   Ibid.

3   Ibid.

4   Richard Murphy, letter to P.H. Newby, 28 November 1950. Richard Murphy Talks File 1 1950–1962, BBC Written Archives.

5   Richard Murphy, 'Narrative Poetry Today', broadcast 28 July 1951, BBC Third Programme. Radio Talks Scripts Pre-1970, MUL–MUR T351, BBC Written Archives.

6   Richard Murphy 'Why Has Narrative Poetry Failed?', *Listener*, vol. 46, no. 1,171, 9 August 1951, pp. 226–7.

7   Richard Murphy, 'New Verse', broadcast 17 August 1955, BBC Third Programme. Radio Talks Scripts Pre-1970, MUL–MUR T351, BBC Written Archives.

8   Richard Murphy, 'The Future of Poetry'. Tulsa. Broadcast as *Literary Opinion*, 15 September 1954, BBC Third Programme, Radio Talk Scripts Pre-1970, LIS-LIV T296, BBC Written Archives Centre, Reading.

9   This is made clear in Roethke's reply. Theodore Roethke, letter to Richard Murphy, 10 June 1955, Tulsa.

10 Ibid.

11 Theodore Roethke, letter to Richard Murphy, 12 July 1960, Tulsa.

12 See, for example, 'Richard Murphy at Sixty', *Poetry Ireland Review*, no. 21, spring 1988, pp. 14–18; 'An Interview with Richard Murphy on his Eightieth Birthday' (1 December 2007), Poetry International Web, http://www.poetry internationalweb.net/pi/site/cou_article/item/10647/An-interview-with-Richard-Murphy/en [accessed 30 December 2018].

13 Rosenthal's review was first published in *The Nation*, 19 September 1959, and was later reworked and extended as 'Robert Lowell and the Poetry of Confession' for *The Modern Poets: a critical introduction* (New York: Oxford University Press, 1965), pp. 225–44.

14 Quoted in Vernon Young, 'The Worst Possible Ordeal', rev. of *The Life of John Berryman* by John Haffenden', *New Criterion*, vol. 1, no. 6, 1 January 1983, p. 79.

15 Ibid.

16 'The Netting', *Yale Review*, vol. 50, no. 4, June 1961, pp. 567–8.

17 *Dubliner*, vol. 1, no. 4, July/August 1962, pp. 51–4.
18 Murphy, 'New Verse'.
19 *Dubliner*, vol. 1, no. 6, January/February 1963, pp. 51–2.
20 Ibid. The corresponding lines in 'Theodore Roethke at Inishbofin, 1960' revised for *Poems 1952–2012* read: '… he rocked to a new theme, / While a poem in his mind's greenhouse bloomed / On the model of a Saginaw chrysanthemum' (*P*, p. 43).
21 *Dubliner*, p. 51; *Sailing to an Island*, p. 53; *Collected Poems*, p. 44.
22 Murphy, 'The Future of Poetry'.
23 'Rejoice', *Poetry Ireland Review*, no. 116, September 2015, p. 8.
24 Ibid.
25 Murphy, 'The Future of Poetry'.
26 Richard Murphy, letter to Emily Riordan, 14 September 1974, Tulsa.
27 Richard Murphy, letter to Emily Riordan, 25 September 1974, Tulsa.
28 Richard Murphy, 'Form of Poetry' course outline, Tulsa.
29 Richard Murphy, letter to Emily Riordan, 28 September 1974, Tulsa.
30 Richard Murphy, letter to Emily Riordan, 6 October 1974, Tulsa.
31 Ibid.
32 Richard Murphy, letter to Emily Riordan, 14 September 1974, Tulsa.
33 On the 1964 tour Murphy lodged with Richard Eberhart, and found himself sharing the stage with such acclaimed poets as James Merrill (at Virginia), James Dickey and Donald Hall.
34 Murphy, 'A New American Poet', p. 32.
35 Robert Lowell, *Collected Prose* (New York: Farrar, Straus & Giroux, 1987), p. 42. The essay's various parts were published in a number of places between 1947 and 1962. The third section, from which this quotation is taken, was published as 'William Carlos Williams', *Hudson Review*, vol. 14, no. 4, winter 1961–62, pp. 530–6.
36 Lowell, *Collected Prose*, p. 43.
37 *The First Ten Years: Dublin Arts Festival poetry*, eds Peter Fallon and Dennis O'Driscoll (Dublin: Dublin Arts Festival, 1979), p. 51.
38 Richard Murphy, 'Notes for Sonnets', *Poetry Ireland Review*, no. 104, September 2011, p. 92.
39 David Perkins, *A History of Modern Poetry, Volume II: modernism and after* (Cambridge, MA: Belknap Press, 1989), p. 415.
40 Richard Murphy, 'Transgressing into Poetry', *Poetry Ireland Review*, no. 107, September 2012, p. 26.
41 Ibid., p. 27.
42 Ibid.
43 'In the last few years', writes Murphy, 'I have selected, edited and added to notes that suggest how the sonnets emerged from prose into verse – sometimes with a loss of poetry'. *Poetry Ireland Review*, no. 107, p. 26.
44 During the mid-1960s Lowell became a compulsive sonneteer and after his work on the *Notebook* poems he went on to publish, in 1973, a further three such collections: *History*, *For Lizzie and Harriet* and *The Dolphin*.
45 The work was published in two parts, appearing first as *77 Dream Songs* in 1964, with a second instalment, *His Toy, His Dream, His Rest*, in 1968. The two books,

which were envisaged as part of one long poem, were published as *The Dream Songs* by Farrar, Straus & Giroux in 1969.

46 Ibid., p. xx.

47 For example, Dream Songs 12 and 17. Ibid., pp. 14, 19.

48 Murphy, 'A New American Poet', p. 32.

49 Beatrice Lushington, letter to Richard Murphy, 23 August 1978. Tulsa.

12. What Price Stone? The shaping of inheritance into form in Richard Murphy's *The Price of Stone* sonnet sequence

1 Seamus Heaney, 'The Poetry of Richard Murphy', in *Richard Murphy: poet of two traditions*, ed. Maurice Harmon (Dublin: Wolfhound Press, 1978), pp. 25–6.

2 See Edna Longley, 'Searching the Darkness: Richard Murphy, Thomas Kinsella, John Montague and James Simmons', in *Two Decades of Irish Writing: a critical survey*, ed. Douglas Dunn (Cheadle: Carcanet Press, 1975), p. 130.

3 Heaney, 'The Poetry of Richard Murphy', p. 25.

4 For ease of discussion, for the rest of the chapter 'The Price of Stone' will refer to the sonnet sequence of fifty sonnets rather than to the original collection of 1985 in which the sonnets were contained.

5 J.P. O'Malley, 'Interview with a Poet: Richard Murphy, an old *Spectator* hand', *Spectator*, 10 September 2013, https://blogs.spectator.co.uk/2013/09/interview-with-a-poet-richard-murphy-an-old-spectator-hand/ [accessed 31 December 2018].

6 *The Making of a Sonnet*, eds Edward Hirsch and Eavan Boland (New York: W.W. Norton, 2008), p. 36.

7 Eavan Boland, 'Discovering the Sonnet', in *The Making of a Sonnet*, p. 43.

8 Ibid.

9 Ibid., p. 44.

10 Hirsch and Boland, *The Making of a Sonnet*, p. 35.

11 Edward Hirsch, 'My Own Acquaintance', in *The Making of a Sonnet*, p. 39.

12 Ibid., p. 40.

13 Boland, 'Discovering the Sonnet', p. 48.

14 Greg Delanty and Paul McLoughlin, 'An Interview with Greg Delanty', *Poetry Ireland Review*, no. 90, June 2007, p. 29.

15 Longley, 'Searching the Darkness', p. 118.

16 Bernard O'Donoghue, 'Critique of "Pat Cloherty's Version of *The Maisie*"', in Richard Murphy, *The Pleasure Ground: poems 1952–2012* (Tarset: Bloodaxe, 2013), p. 276.

17 Alan Gillis, 'The Modern Irish Sonnet', in *The Oxford Handbook of Modern Irish Poetry* (Oxford: Oxford University Press, 2012), p. 577.

18 Longley, 'Searching the Darkness', p. 131.

19 Richard Murphy, 'Excerpt: Notes for Sonnets', *Poetry Ireland Review*, no. 104, October 2011, p. 93. Richard Murphy, *In Search of Poetry* (Thame: Clutag Press, 2017), p. 113.

20 Ibid., p. 94; *In Search of Poetry*, p. 116.

21 Ibid., p. 93; *In Search of Poetry*, pp. 113–14.

22 See Marianne Moore, 'Poetry', longer version, in *Complete Poems* (London: Faber & Faber, 1987), p. 267.

23 I use the term according to Murphy's use of it in 'Extract: Transgressing into Poetry'. See, for example, his use of the term in *Poetry Ireland Review*, no. 107, September 2012, p. 26. In his introduction to *The Price of Stone* in *The Pleasure Ground*, Murphy hyphenates the term ('sonnet-houses'): see *The Pleasure Ground*, p. 176; but elsewhere in the sequence he uses it without. For consistency I have chosen to use it without a hyphen, as I am referring mainly to his 'Transgressing into Poetry' notes here.

24 O'Malley, 'Interview with a Poet'.

25 Longley, 'Searching the Darkness', p. 123.

26 James B. Kelley, 'Exposure and Obscurity: The cruising sonnets in Richard Murphy's *The Price of Stone*' in this volume.

27 Murphy, 'Extract: Transgressing into Poetry', p. 26.

28 Murphy, 'Excerpt: Notes for Sonnets', p. 102.

29 Ibid., p. 101.

30 See P.B. Shelley, 'Ozymandias', in *Romanticism: an anthology*, ed. Duncan Wu (Oxford: Blackwell, 2002), p. 1108.

31 Albert. C. Labriola, selections from 'Sculptural Poetry: the visual imagination of Michelangelo, Keats, and Shelley', *Comparative Literature Studies*, vol. 24. no. 4, 1987, p. 326. Reprinted in *Percy Bysshe Shelley*, ed. Harold Bloom (New York: Chelsea House, 2001), p. 25.

32 Murphy, 'Excerpt: Notes for Sonnets', p. 101. Ellipses in the original. *In Search of Poetry*, pp. 136–7.

33 Shelley, 'Ozymandias', p. 1108.

34 Murphy, 'Excerpt: Notes for Sonnets', p. 102; *In Search of Poetry*, p. 138.

35 Ibid., p. 103; *In Search of Poetry*, p. 140.

36 Joseph Sendry, 'The Poet as Builder: Richard Murphy's *The Price of Stone*, *Irish University Review*, vol. 15, no. 1, spring 1985, p. 41.

37 Ibid.

38 Murphy, 'Excerpt: Notes for Sonnets', p. 26.

39 Christopher Ricks, 'At-one-ment', in *The Force of Poetry* (Oxford: Oxford University Press, 1999), p. 321.

40 Sendry, 'The Poet as Builder', p. 48.

41 This is taken from the longer quotation that began this essay: see Heaney, 'The Poetry of Richard Murphy', p. 26.

42 See Murphy, 'Excerpt: Notes for Sonnets', p. 94, and discussion of the longer quotation earlier in the present essay.

13. Exposure and Obscurity: The cruising sonnets in Richard Murphy's *The Price of Stone*

1 Richard Murphy, unpublished Notebook, Richard Murphy papers, 1951–1982. 1988.014. Department of Special Collections, McFarlin Library, University of Tulsa. In *The Kick* he states that: 'To me poetry would never come naturally, as a gift. It would have to be made.' (*K*, p. 86)

2 Richard Murphy, 'Notes for Sonnets', *Poetry Ireland Review*, no. 104, September 2011, pp. 92–104; Richard Murphy, 'Transgressing into Poetry', *Poetry Ireland*

Review, no. 107, September 2012, pp. 26–36; Richard Murphy, 'Transgressing into Poetry', *Poetry Ireland Review*, no. 111, September 2013, pp. 117–33.

3   Richard Murphy, *In Search of Poetry* (Thame: Clutag Press, 2017).

4   Although extracts from the notebooks have been shared selectively among Richard Murphy's friends, it should be noted that the notebooks referred to are held in the Special Collections at the McFarlin Library, University of Tulsa and are under strict embargo until twenty-five years after the poet's death. Extracts quoted here are reproduced by kind permission of Richard Murphy and the Department of Special Collections, McFarlin Library, University of Tulsa.

5   Rand Brandes, 'Drafting *The Price of Stone*: Richard Murphy's manuscripts for "Beehive Cell"', in *The Snow Path: tracks 10* (Dublin: Dedalus Press, 1994), pp. 63–4.

6   Benjamin Keatinge, '"My form is epicene": sexual ambiguity in the poetry of Richard Murphy', in *Essays in Irish Literary Criticism: themes of gender, sexuality and corporeality*, eds Sharon Tighe-Mooney and Deirdre Quinn (Lampeter: Edwin Mellen Press, 2008), p. 24.

7   Ibid., p. 25.

8   Richard Murphy, 'Transcription of Introductory Notes for Four Broadcast Recordings from *The Price of Stone* Recorded in Dublin for the Australian Broadcasting Commission by RM', Richard Murphy Papers, 1951–1982. 1988.014. Department of Special Collections, McFarlin Library, University of Tulsa. Original broadcast directed by Dennis O'Driscoll. Sydney: Australian Broadcasting Commission, 1984.

9   Ibid.

10 Richard Murphy, unpublished Notebook [OK-17.125-26, dated 2 October 1977, Syracuse]. Others have recognised the central importance of 'Convenience'. Jill Siddall notes its centrality in her review of *Collected Poems* (The Gallery Press, 2000) in *Metre*, no. 10, autumn 2001, p. 134. It is also one of only four poems from the sequence to be included in Patrick Crotty's *Modern Irish Poetry: an anthology* (Belfast: Blackstaff Press, 1996), where the others included are: 'Roof-tree', 'Kylemore Castle' and 'Natural Son', pp. 156–8.

11 Murphy, 'Transcription of Introductory Notes for Four Broadcast Recordings from *The Price of Stone*'.

12 Brandes, 'Drafting *The Price of Stone*', p. 77.

13 Ibid.

14 Murphy, 'Transcription of Introductory Notes for Four Broadcast Recordings from *The Price of Stone*'.

15 Ibid.

16 Richard Murphy, unpublished Notebook, Richard Murphy Papers, 1951–1982. 1988.014. Department of Special Collections, McFarlin Library, University of Tulsa.

17 J.P. O'Malley, 'Interview with a Poet: Richard Murphy, an old *Spectator* hand', *Spectator*, http://blogs.spectator.co.uk/2013/09/interview-with-a-poet-richard-murphy-an-old-spectator-hand/ [accessed 12 November 2017].

18 Richard Murphy, unpublished Notebook, Richard Murphy Papers, 1951–1982. 1988.014. Department of Special Collections, McFarlin Library, University of Tulsa.

19 Brandes, 'Drafting *The Price of Stone*', p. 64.

20 Murphy, 'Transgressing into Poetry', *Poetry Ireland Review*, no. 111, p. 123.

21 Ibid., p. 121.

22 Ibid., p. 122.

23 A subtle but recurring theme in Murphy's notebook entries for 'Convenience' is the dissolution of social-class distinctions that occurs when men enter the public toilet and unzip. See, for example, these sections of one extended entry: 'the different kinds of men who use the place for different purposes … military, police, crooks, business men … universal … the whole world … foreigners, everybody, anybody, nobody, just male bodies or parts of them revealed through clothes …' and 'the little phallic image may be possessed by a thief or a murderer or a prime minister … or a minister of religion'. Richard Murphy, unpublished Notebook, Richard Murphy Papers, 1951–1982. 1988.014. Department of Special Collections, McFarlin Library, University of Tulsa.

24 Richard Murphy, unpublished Notebook, Richard Murphy Papers, 1951–1982. 1988.014. Department of Special Collections, McFarlin Library, University of Tulsa.

25 Ibid.

26 Murphy has stated in conversation that, in making sense of his traumatic experience in the Piccadilly Circus Underground, a passage in Virginia Woolf's *The Waves* came to mind, one in which Jinny's enthusiasm about being at the very centre of things – '"Here I stand" … "in the Tube station where everything that is desirable meets …"' – is tempered by sudden awareness of the aging of her own body and by an equally sudden realisation that the many commuters travelling down the stairs towards the Underground trains are equally on a metaphorical journey into the underworld. See Virginia Woolf, *The Waves* (London: Vintage, 2000), p. 128.

27 Murphy, 'Transcription of Introductory Notes for Four Broadcast Recordings from *The Price of Stone*'.

28 Jill Siddall, 'Grotesquely Free, Though Ruled by Symmetry', *Metre*, no. 10, autumn 2001, p. 134.

29 Ibid.

30 Richard Murphy, unpublished Notebook, Richard Murphy Papers, 1951–1982. 1988.014. Department of Special Collections, McFarlin Library, University of Tulsa.

31 J.R. Ackerley, *My Father and Myself* (London: Pimlico, 1992), p. 201.

32 Richard Murphy, unpublished Notebook, Richard Murphy Papers, 1951–1982. 1988.014. Department of Special Collections, McFarlin Library, University of Tulsa.

14. 'To seem a white king's gem': Richard Murphy's Sri Lankan poems and Irish postcolonial studies

1   Antoinette Quinn, 'Aughrim in Sri Lanka', *New Nation*, no. 7, 1989, p. 20.

2   John Goodby, 'Richard Murphy: last of the Anglo-Irish?', *Irish Poetry Since 1950: from stillness into history* (Manchester: Manchester University Press, 2000), p. 84.

3 Richard Murphy, letter to Elizabeth (Betty) Mary Murphy, the poet's mother, undated, *c.*1933. Tulsa.

4 Richard Murphy, letter to Mary Murphy and Christopher Murphy, the poet's sister and brother, undated, *c.*1933. Tulsa.

5 Benjamin Keatinge, 'Richard Murphy in Sri Lanka: an interview', *Poetry Ireland Review*, no. 122, August 2017, p. 86.

6 Ibid., p. 89.

7 Ibid., p. 93.

8 Ted Hughes, blurb for *High Island* (1974), reproduced on back covers of *Collected Poems* (The Gallery Press, 2000), *Poems 1952–2012* (The Lilliput Press, 2013) and *The Pleasure Ground: poems 1952–2013* (Bloodaxe, 2013).

9 Keatinge, 'Richard Murphy in Sri Lanka', p. 87.

10 JVP stands for Janatha Vimukthi Peramuna, which translates as People's Liberation Front. A Marxist-Leninist political grouping founded in the late 1960s, it led an often violent revolt against the Sri Lankan government. Although banned after a wave of violence in 1971, it was to reemerge in the early 1980s and its insurgency was especially intense in the period from 1987 to 1989.

11 Ibid., pp. 91–2.

12 Seamus Deane, 'The Long Ascendancy', *Honest Ulsterman*, no. 66, July–October 1980, pp. 68–9.

13 Ibid., p. 69.

14 Seamus Heaney, 'The Poetry of Richard Murphy', in *Richard Murphy: poet of two traditions*, ed. Maurice Harmon (Dublin: Wolfhound Press, 1978), p. 25.

15 C.L. Innes, 'Postcolonial Studies and Ireland', in *Comparing Postcolonial Literatures: dislocations*, eds Ashok Bery and Patricia Murray (Basingstoke: Macmillan, 2000), pp. 29–30.

16 Luke Gibbons, *Gaelic Gothic: race, colonization and Irish culture* (Galway: Arlen House, 2004), p. 11.

17 Declan Kiberd, 'Richard Murphy and Casement's Funeral', *Metre*, no. 10, autumn 2001, p. 136.

18 Mario Vargas Llosa, *The Dream of the Celt*, trans. Edith Grossman (London: Faber & Faber, 2012), p. 162.

19 Ibid., p. 260.

20 Declan Kiberd, *Inventing Ireland: the literature of the modern nation* (London: Vintage, 1996), p. 84.

21 Richard Murphy, letter to his parents, 5 May 1950. Tulsa.

22 Joseph Lennon, 'Irish Orientalism: an overview', in *Ireland and Postcolonial Theory*, eds Clare Carroll and Patricia King (Cork: Cork University Press, 2003), p. 130. See also Joseph Lennon, *Irish Orientalism: a literary and intellectual history* (New York: Syracuse University Press, 2004).

23 Homi K. Bhabha, *The Location of Culture* (London: Routledge, 1994), p. 5.

24 Keatinge, 'Richard Murphy in Sri Lanka', p. 87.

25 Dennis O'Driscoll, 'Richard Murphy at Sixty', *Poetry Ireland Review*, no. 21, spring 1988, p. 18.

26 Richard Murphy, *The Mirror Wall* (Dublin: Wolfhound Press, 1989), p. 1.
27 Keatinge, 'Richard Murphy in Sri Lanka', p. 88.
28 Dennis O'Driscoll, 'Richard Murphy at Sixty', p. 18.
29 Rajiva Wijesinha (ed.), *Mirrored Images: an anthology of Sri Lankan poetry* (New Delhi: National Book Trust, 2013).
30 Melanie A. Murray, *Island Paradise: the myth. An examination of contemporary Caribbean and Sri Lankan writing* (Amsterdam: Rodopi, 2009), p. 39.
31 As Christopher Ondaatje notes in his 'Afterword to the 2005 Edition' of *The Village in the Jungle*, 'It was later translated into Sinhalese, so that alongside the original English edition *The Village in the Jungle* has become an essential part of the literary culture of Sri Lanka.' Leonard Woolf, *The Village in the Jungle* (London: Eland, 2008), p. 208.
32 Neil Astley, email to the author, 26 July 2017.
33 Satoshi Mizutani, 'Hybridity and History: a critical reflection on Homi K. Bhabha's post-historical thoughts', *Ab Imperio*, no. 4, 2013, p. 29.
34 Robert J.C. Young, *Colonial Desire: hybridity in theory, culture and race* (London: Routledge, 1995), p. 25.
35 Ibid., p. 24.
36 Quinn, 'Aughrim in Sri Lanka', p. 20.
37 Keatinge, 'Richard Murphy in Sri Lanka', p. 87.

15. Richard Murphy's *The Kick*: The making of memoir

1   An account by Richard Murphy of his friendship with Pateen Cloherty and the source of the poem 'Pat Cloherty's Version of *The Maisie*' is given in 'A Footnote to "Pat Cloherty's Version of *The Maisie*"', in *The Mayo Anthology*, ed. Richard Murphy (Castlebar: Mayo County Council, 1990), p. 62.
2   Richard Murphy, unpublished Notebook, Richard Murphy Papers, 1951–1982. 1988.014. Department of Special Collections, McFarlin Library, University of Tulsa.

16. *The Kick* and the Genre of Anglo-Irish Autobiography

1   Murphy's short introduction to his *Price of Stone* sonnet sequence was first published in 'Transgressing into Poetry', *Poetry Ireland Review*, no. 107, September 2012, p. 26, and is reprinted, in a slightly different form, in *Poems 1952–2012*, p. 176.
2   For example, in an interview with John Haffenden, Murphy speaks of his 'love of the architecture of Canterbury Cathedral' where he sang as a chorister while attending the Cathedral School. These interests have carried over into his poetry, and Murphy says that he sees 'poems as buildings and as music'. Interview with John Haffenden, in *Viewpoints: poets in conversation with John Haffenden* (London: Faber & Faber, 1981), pp. 153–4.
3   Mark Freeman, *Rewriting the Self: history, memory, narrative* (London: Routledge, 1993), p. 29.
4   Ibid.
5   Ibid., p. 30.

6 Eamonn Hughes, '"The Fact of Me-ness": autobiographical writing in the Revival period', *Irish University Review*, vol. 33 no. 1, spring/summer 2003, pp. 28–45.

7 Claire Lynch, *Irish Autobiography: stories of self in the narrative of a nation* (Bern: Peter Lang, 2009), p. 24.

8 Haffenden, *Viewpoints*, p. 143.

9 Elizabeth Grubgeld, 'Life Writing in the Twentieth Century', in *The Cambridge Companion to the Irish Novel*, ed. J.W. Foster (Cambridge: Cambridge University Press, 2006), p. 233.

10 Elizabeth Grubgeld, *Anglo-Irish Autobiography: class, gender, and the forms of narrative* (Syracuse: Syracuse University Press, 2004), p. 24.

11 Michael Kenneally, 'The Autobiographical Imagination and Irish Literary Autobiographies', in *Critical Approaches to Anglo-Irish Literature*, eds Michael Allen and Angela Wilcox (Gerrards Cross: Colin Smythe, 1989), p. 126.

12 Grubgeld, 'Life Writing in the Twentieth Century', p. 224.

13 Seamus Deane, 'Autobiography and Memoirs 1890–1988', in *The Field Day Anthology of Irish Writing, Vol. III*, ed. Seamus Deane (Derry: Field Day, 1991), p. 381.

14 Richard Murphy, letter to his parents, 17 June 1950, Richard Murphy Papers, 1951–1982. 1988.014. Tulsa.

15 Richard Murphy, letter to Barrie Cooke, 11 September 1975. Tulsa.

16 Declan Kiberd, *Inventing Ireland* (London: Vintage, 1996), p. 599.

17 J.P. O'Malley, 'Interview with a Poet: Richard Murphy, an old *Spectator* hand', *Spectator*, http://blogs.spectator.co.uk/2013/09/interview-with-a-poet-richard-murphy-an-old-spectator-hand/ [accessed 10 August 2017].

18 W.B. Yeats, *Autobiographies*, eds William H. O'Donnell and Douglas N. Archibald (New York: Scribner, 1999), p. 61.

19 Richard Murphy, 'The Pleasure Ground', in *Writers on Themselves* (London: BBC, 1964), p. 65.

20 Haffenden, *Viewpoints*, p. 153.

21 Seamus Heaney, 'The Poetry of Richard Murphy', *Irish University Review: Richard Murphy special issue*, vol. 7, no. 1, spring 1977, p. 19.

22 Haffenden, *Viewpoints*, p. 143.

23 Terence Brown, 'Poets and Patrimony: Richard Murphy and James Simmons', in *Across a Roaring Hill: the Protestant imagination in modern Ireland*, eds Gerald Dawe and Edna Longley (Belfast: Blackstaff Press, 1985), p. 189.

24 Haffenden, *Viewpoints*, p. 148.

25 Ibid., p. 152.

Richard Murphy: A bibliography

~

BENJAMIN KEATINGE

From the early 1950s to 2018 Richard Murphy published a fascinating range of poetry, prose criticism and memoir. His poetry was published in all the major literary journals of the period and his work was represented in all major anthologies of Irish poetry. In addition, his poetry has stimulated debate and discussion among leading critical commentators in Ireland, Britain, the US and in the wider English-speaking world – South Africa and Australia, for example – as well as in Europe. It has been translated into at least ten European languages, including Dutch, German, French, Italian, Spanish and Scandinavian languages.

This bibliography endeavours to identify all of Richard Murphy's published work. It follows a chronological, rather than alphabetical order and it divides Richard Murphy's *oeuvre* into poetry volumes, poetry in journals, poetry in anthologies, translations, prose memoir and prose criticism, alongside listings of critical essays on his poetry and selected reviews of his work as well as some entries on works in other media. The bibliography thus extends from Richard Murphy's first published volume *The Archaeology of Love* (The Dolmen Press, 1955) and his first individual published poem 'Creragh' in *The Bell* (16 December 1950) to the many tributes published following the poet's death on 30 January 2018. Every effort has been made to establish precise bibliographical details for each publication and no effort has been spared in checking these details. Nevertheless, the bibliographer's aim of inclusivity is a receding horizon which he or she can never quite catch up with, and undoubtedly gaps will remain for future scholars to fill.

This bibliography has built on the pioneering work of Mary FitzGerald, whose 'A Richard Murphy Bibliography' – which was first published in the *Irish University Review: Richard Murphy special issue* of 1977 under the editorship of Professor Maurice Harmon – remains a valuable resource for students of Richard Murphy's earlier poetry and prose. In addition, the bibliography of Philip Keel Geheber in his MPhil thesis on Richard Murphy (Trinity College, Dublin, 2007) is also extremely useful as is the bibliography by Andrew McEwan in his MPhil thesis on Richard Murphy (Trinity College, Dublin, 2013). I am also indebted to several individual scholars without whose generous assistance many details would have remained doubtful. In particular, I would like to thank the following: Einat Adar (Charles University, Prague), Rebecca Barr (NUI Galway), Olga Bartosiewicz (Jagiellonian

University, Kraków), Elena Cotta Ramusino (University of Pavia), Gerald Dawe (Trinity College, Dublin), James Hazleton (Macquarie University, Australia) Dirk van Hulle (University of Antwerp), Thomas Korthals (Hamm-Lippstadt University of Applied Sciences, Germany), Joanna Kruczkowska (University of Łódź), Michael McAteer (Pázmány Péter University, Budapest), Ruben Moi (Arctic University of Norway), Tomasz Niedokos (University of Lublin), Laura Salisbury (University of Exeter), Tara Stubbs (University of Oxford), David Wheatley (University of Aberdeen) and Mark Wormald (University of Cambridge). Finally, I am immensely grateful to Richard Murphy himself who, in spite of declining health during 2016–17, provided me with invaluable support in the task of tracing his past publications.

PUBLISHED POETRY

(1) Books and Pamphlets

The Archaeology of Love (Dublin: The Dolmen Press, 1955), 28pp.

Contents: 'For Patricia' [Dedication]; 'Living with Animals'; 'The Philosopher and the Birds'; 'Auction'; 'Houses'; 'September on the Embankment'; 'Dépaysé'; 'Girl at the Seaside'; 'Samson's Secret'; 'Eclogue in the Louvre'; 'Letter from Babylone'; 'The Photographer'; 'Sappho to Anactoria'; 'A Picnic in Crete'; 'The Fall of Knossos'; 'To a Cretan Monk in Thanks for a Flask of Wine'; 'The Archaeology of Love'

Sailing to an Island: a poem (Dublin: The Dolmen Press, 1955), 8pp.

The Woman of the House: an elegy (Dublin: The Dolmen Press, 1959), 10pp.

The Last Galway Hooker: a poem (Dublin: The Dolmen Press, 1961), 15pp.

Sailing to an Island (London: Faber & Faber, 1963), 63pp.

Sailing to an Island (New York: Chilmark Press, 1963), 63pp.

Contents: Part I – 'Sailing to an Island'; 'The Last Galway Hooker'; 'The Cleggan Disaster'. Part II – 'The Woman of the House'; 'Auction'; 'Epitaph on a Fir-tree'; 'Girl at the Seaside'; 'To a Cretan Monk in Thanks for a Flask of Wine'; 'The Netting'. Part III – 'The Philosopher and the Birds'; 'The Poet on the Island'; 'The Progress of a Painter'; 'Connemara Marble'; 'Droit de Seigneur'; 'The Travelling Player'; 'The Drowning of a Novice'

The Battle of Aughrim and *The God Who Eats Corn* (London: Faber & Faber, 1968), 64pp.

The Battle of Aughrim (New York: Alfred A. Knopf, 1968), 74pp.

Contents: *The Battle of Aughrim*; *The God Who Eats Corn*

Largesse by Richard Murphy with 'Crow's Song About Prospero and Sycorax' by Ted Hughes (Washington DC: Folger Poetry Series, 17 March 1971), broadsheet, [2]pp.

High Island (London: Faber & Faber, 1974), 48pp.

Contents: 'Seals at High Island'; 'Little Hunger'; 'Lullaby'; 'Largesse'; 'Jurors'; 'Walking on Sunday'; 'Travelling Man'; 'Song for a Corncrake'; 'Ball's Cove'; 'The Writing Lesson'; 'Coppersmith'; 'Double Negative'; 'Pat Cloherty's Version of *The Maisie*'; 'Firebug'; 'Mullarkey'; 'Brian Boru's Well'; 'The Reading Lesson'; 'Nocturne'; 'Sunup'; 'The Fall'; 'Granite Globe'; 'Gallows Riddle'; 'The Glass Dump Road'; 'High Island'; 'Traveller's Palm'; 'Stormpetrel'

High Island: new and selected poems (New York: Harper & Row, 1974), 118pp.

Contents: (I) from *Sailing to an Island* (II) *The Battle of Aughrim* (III) 'The God Who Eats Corn' (IV) New Poems [identical to *High Island*, above, but with slightly different ordering of the poems and subtraction of 'Mullarkey' and addition of one new poem, 'Corncrake']

Niches (Old Deerfield, MA: The Deerfield Press; Oldcastle: The Gallery Press, 1978), illustrations by Timothy Engelland, 6pp.

Contents: 'Niches'; 'A Nest in a Wall'

Selected Poems (London: Faber & Faber, 1979), 63pp.

Contents: 'Sailing to an Island'; 'The Philosopher and the Birds'; 'Auction'; 'Girl at the Seaside'; 'Epitaph on a Fir-tree'; 'The Woman of the House'; 'Years Later'; '*From* The Last Galway Hooker'; 'The Poet on the Island'; 'Aughrim'; 'History'; 'Rapparees', 'Planter'; 'Wolfhound'; 'Luttrell's Death'; 'Patrick Sarsfield'; '*From* The God Who Eats Corn'; 'Little Hunger'; 'Lullaby'; 'Mary Ure'; 'Walking on Sunday'; 'Coppersmith'; 'Firebug'; 'Traveller's Palm'; 'Jurors'; 'Double Negative'; 'Pat Cloherty's Version of *The Maisie*'; 'Song for a Corncrake'; 'The Reading Lesson'; 'Care'; 'Shelter'; 'Granite Globe'; 'High Island'; 'Stormpetrel'; 'Nocturne'; 'Seals at High Island'

Care (Amsterdam: Cornamona Press, 1983), 44pp.

Contents: 'To Gerald and Mary Cookson on their Silver Wedding' [dedication]; 'Moonshine'; 'Trouvaille'; 'Mary Ure'; 'Swallows'; 'Shelter'; 'Enigma'; 'Care'; 'To Anya on New Year's Day 1977'; 'Stone Mania'; 'Niches'; 'The Glass Door'; 'Husbandry'; 'A Nest in a Wall'; 'Tranquillity'; 'Tony White at Inishbofin 1959'; 'Double Negative'; 'Bookcase for *The Oxford English Dictionary*'; 'Tony White'; 'Morning Call'; 'Arsonist'; 'Elixir'; 'Amsterdam'; 'Altar'; 'Displaced Person'; 'Vertigo'; 'Amazement'; 'Visiting Hour'; 'Natural Son'; 'Tourniquet'

Beehive Cell by Richard Murphy, printed at the Shadowy Waters Press, April 1985, 3pp. [150 copies distributed to participants in the 23rd Annual Meeting of the American Committee for Irish Studies, April 1985]

The Price of Stone (London: Faber & Faber, 1985), 92pp.

Contents: Part I – 'Moonshine'; 'Care'; 'Trouvaille'; 'Mary Ure'; 'Shelter'; 'Niches'; 'Swallows'; 'Stone Mania'; 'Husbandry'; 'A Nest in a Wall'; 'Tony White'; 'Tony White at Inishbofin'; 'Bookcase for *The Oxford English Dictionary*'; 'Morning Call'; 'Arsonist'; 'Elixir'; 'Amsterdam'; 'Altar'; 'Displaced Person'; 'Amazement'; 'Visiting Hour'; Part II, The Price of Stone – 'Folly'; 'Lead Mine Chimney';

'Portico'; 'Nelson's Pillar'; 'Wellington Testimonial'; 'Georgian Tenement', 'Gym'; 'Knockbrack'; 'Ice Rink'; 'Carlow Village Schoolhouse', 'Roof-tree'; 'Red Bank Restaurant'; 'Little Barn'; 'Connemara Quay'; 'Birth Place'; 'Queen of the Castle'; 'Liner'; 'Planter Stock'; 'Family Seat'; 'Rectory'; 'Letterfrack Industrial School'; 'Baymount'; 'Canterbury Cathedral'; 'Choir School'; 'Suntrap'; 'Gate Lodge'; 'Milford: East Wing'; 'Carlyon Bay Hotel'; 'Wellington College'; 'Oxford Staircase'; 'Convenience'; 'Lecknavarna'; 'Killary Hostel'; 'Waterkeeper's Bothy'; 'Kylemore Castle'; 'Tony White's Cottage'; 'Pier Bar'; 'Miners' Hut'; 'Hexagon'; 'New Forge'; 'Cottage for Sale'; 'Horse-drawn Caravan'; 'Old Dispensary'; 'Chalet'; 'Prison'; 'Wattle Tent'; 'Newgrange'; 'Friary'; 'Beehive Cell'; 'Natural Son'

The Price of Stone and Earlier Poems (Winston-Salem: Wake Forest University Press, 1985), 190pp.

Contents: Part I – from *Sailing to an Island*; Part II – *The Battle of Aughrim*; Part III – *High Island* [as for Faber edition of *High Island* with the following poems excluded: 'Travelling Man', 'Mullarkey', and with one new additional poem, 'Corncrake']; Part IV – *Care* [identical to Part I of *The Price of Stone*, above]; Part V – The Price of Stone [identical to Part II of *The Price of Stone*, above]

The Price of Stone (Madley, Hereford: Five Seasons Press, 1985), 56pp. [limited edition of the fifty sonnets in Part II of *The Price of Stone*, above].

New Selected Poems (London: Faber & Faber, 1989), 190pp.

Contents: [identical to *The Price of Stone and Earlier Poems*, above]

The Mirror Wall (Dublin: Wolfhound Press, 1989), 84pp.

The Mirror Wall (Tarset: Bloodaxe, 1989), 84pp.

The Mirror Wall (Winston-Salem: Wake Forest University Press, 1989), 84pp.

Contents: 'Sri Lanka' [a sonnet]; '*Preface*' [by Richard Murphy]; '*The Frescoes at Sigiriya*' [illustrations]; 'Invocation'; 'Kassapa'; 'Falling and falling'; 'Climbed up the Lion Rock'; 'Coming up the mountain track'; 'Look, my darling'; 'The king's palace rock'; 'All over the Lion Rock'; '"I'm dying"'; 'Who got angry?'; '*When spoken to*'; 'Longing to sing'; 'Her loose appearance'; 'They deck you'; 'Some of the figures'; '*Good Luck!*'; 'Adorable mountain girl'; 'You who remain'; 'With her hair tied up'; 'Women like you enable people'; 'Does the blue waterlily'; 'In your eyes the lustre'; 'Your eyes have turned'; 'Eyebrows midnight blue'; 'No, don't look at her!'; '*I am Friar ...*'; 'I'm Bati'; 'Beyond looking brilliant'; 'I was in paradise'; 'Her hand is given like water'; 'Superlative make-up artist'; 'Yes / She is beautiful'; 'She's planting'; 'From Hunagiri Temple'; 'No! You must not believe'; 'Just let me creep away'; 'Does a good lover'; 'She stopped me feeling sad'; 'Thinking endless thoughts'; '*The song of Lord Sirina*'; 'Pure as the hare with spots'; 'I looked'; 'The virtue of this breeze'; 'Doesn't the Sanskrit "apsaras"'; 'The moon rose'; 'The wet monsoon'; 'Wow!'; 'Oh no!'; 'If you examine the way'; 'A melon-pip smile'; 'Becoming attached'; 'How can that dancer'; 'As a woman'; 'He kept coming back to look'; 'Once he'd imagined them'; 'Crushed by ill treatment'; '*I am Kitala*'; 'His ploy'; 'This act of

his'; 'When I approach'; 'Women, please wave'; 'The subtle and ethereal'; 'The
message I received'; 'A nectar-soaked bee'; 'No, / We do not know'; '"Do we
know why?"'; 'The good luck and joy'; 'While swans are making'; 'Governor
Nakka's poem'; 'I don't believe'; *'Sigiriya, 11 January 1987'*; 'If happiness could
come'; '"*You won't remember*"'; 'Maybe when royalty had gone'; 'On our way';
'Entangle'; 'They came here'

Collected Poems (Oldcastle: The Gallery Press, 2000), 235pp.

Collected Poems (Winston-Salem: Wake Forest University Press, 2000), 235pp.

Contents: Part I – *Sailing to an Island* and poems arising from the years 1952–1962
[one new poem: 'Grounds, 1959' and a heavily revised version of 'Living with
Animals' published as 'Rosroe, 1955']; Part II – *The Battle of Aughrim* 1962–67
and *The God Who Eats Corn* 1963; Part III – *High Island* and poems arising
from the years 1968–74 [Three new poems: 'Ardilaun', 'Omey Island', 'Woman
Marooned'; 'Mullarkey' retitled 'Walled Up']; Part IV – *Care* and poems arising
from the years 1974–84 [five new poems: 'Scythe', 'Circles', 'The Afterlife', 'Sea
Holly', 'Quays']; Part V – *Sri Lanka* and poems of 1985–1992 [five new poems:
'Mangoes', 'Orphanage', 'National Hero', 'National Tree', 'Double Vision']; Part
VI – *The Price of Stone* 1981–84

Poems 1952–2012 (Dublin: The Lilliput Press, 2013), 288pp.

The Pleasure Ground: poems 1952–2012 (Tarset: Bloodaxe, 2013), 288pp.

Contents: Part One – *Sailing to an Island* and poems of the years 1952–62 [with
revised versions of 'The Cleggan Disaster' and 'The Last Galway Hooker']; Part
II – *The Battle of Aughrim* and poems of 1962–67 and *The God Who Eats Corn*
1963; Part III – *High Island* and poems of 1967–73 ['Lullaby' retitled 'Epitaph
for Shura', 'Traveller's Palm' retitled 'Kandy Perahera', 'Largesse' not included];
Part IV – *Care* and poems of 1974–84; Part V – *The Price of Stone*: a sequence of
fifty sonnets 1981–84; Part VI – *Sri Lanka* and poems finished the years 1985–
2012 [seven new poems: 'Sigiriya', 'Death in Kandy', 'A River of Notebooks',
'Rite of Passage', 'Waking from a Dream', 'Vagrant', 'Last Word']

(ii) Poems Published in Journals and Periodicals

'Creragh', *Bell*, vol. 16, no. 3, 16 December 1950, p. 16. Repr. *Archipelago*, no. 12,
spring 2019, p. 1

'My Three and Twentieth Year', *Envoy: a review of literature and art*, vol. 4, no. 13,
December 1950, p. 49

'Emigration', *Irish Times*, 3 February 1951, p. 6. Repr. *Archipelago*, no. 12, spring
2019, p. 2

'Snow', *Listener*, vol. 46, no. 1,178, 27 September 1951, p. 499

'A West Indian Village', *Irish Times*, 21 June 1952, p. 6

'The Restoration', *Irish Times*, 13 December 1952, p. 6

'Voyage to an Island', *Bell*, vol. 18, no. 7, December 1952, pp. 396–400

'Aasleagh in Autumn', *Irish Times*, 17 January 1953, p. 6

'The Repair of Albert Bridge', *Times Literary Supplement*, no. 2,665, 27 February 1953, p. 131

'Advice About Wind', *Bell*, vol. 18, no. 10, 18 March 1953, pp. 586–8

'The Return', *Bell*, vol. 18, no. 10, 18 March 1953, pp. 584–6

'Cove of Trains', *Listener*, vol. 49, no. 1255, 19 March 1953, p. 480

'Afternoon at Home', *Listener*, vol. 49, no. 1,258, 9 April 1953, p. 594

'Payday', *Irish Times*, 11 April 1953, p. 6

'The Dozing Woods', *Irish Times*, 20 June 1953, p. 6

'The Philosopher and the Birds', *Adelphi*, vol. 29, no. 4, August 1953, pp. 342–3

'Sun and Thorn', *Irish Times*, 5 September 1953, p. 6

'The Halcyon Days: Crete', *Listener*, vol. 51, no. 1,297, 7 January 1954, p. 14

'Sonnet on the Closing of a House', *Spectator*, vol. 192, no. 6,549, 1 January 1954, p. 25

'Sailing to an Island', *Listen*, vol. 1, no. 3, winter 1954, pp. 39–40

'The Exiled Fisherman', *Irish Times*, 24 April 1954, p. 8

'Letter to a Friend Leaving Ireland', *Irish Times*, 22 May 1954, p. 6

'The Singing Wood', *Irish Times*, 10 July 1954, p. 8

'Circumcision at the Temple', *Listener*, vol. 52, no. 1,333, 16 September 1954, p. 437

'September on the Embankment', *Listener*, vol. 52, no. 1,336, 7 October 1954, p. 558

'The Sisters', *Irish Times*, 16 October 1954, p. 6

'The Fall of Knossos', *New Statesman and Nation*, vol. 48, no. 1,241, 18 December 1954, p. 832

'Letter from Babylon', *Listener*, vol. 52, no. 1,347, 23 December 1954, p. 1113

'Eclogue in the Louvre', *Listener*, vol. 53, no. 1,349, 6 January 1955, p. 1113

'The Clown and the Garden', *Irish Times*, 26 March 1955, p. 6

'Houses', *Irish Times*, 9 July 1955, p. 6

'A Picnic in Crete', *New Statesman and Nation*, vol. 49, no. 1258, 16 April 1955, p. 546

'Girl at the Seaside', *Encounter*, vol. 5, no. 2, August 1955, p. 50

'Auction', *Encounter*, vol. 5, no. 2, August 1955, p. 50

'Samson's Secret', *Encounter*, vol. 5, no. 2, August 1955, p. 50

'Living with Animals', *Listener*, vol. 54, no. 1,390, 20 October 1955, p. 653

'To a Cretan Monk in Thanks for a Flask of Wine', *Irish Times*, 22 October 1955, p. 6

'The Lake at Carrahall', *Irish Times*, 19 November 1955, p. 6

'An Air-raid Siren in Peacetime', *Irish Times*, 4 February 1956, p. 6

'Epitaph on a Fir-tree', *Irish Times*, 9 June 1956, p. 6

'Around the World in Ninety Hours', *Listener*, vol. 59, no. 1,503, 16 January 1958, p. 132

'The Woman of the House', *Listener*, vol. 61, no. 1,569, 23 April 1959, p. 723

'Miscarriage', *Listen*, vol. 3, no. 2, spring 1959, p. 6

'A Fable for Lovers', *Listen*, vol. 3, no. 2, spring 1959, pp. 6–7

'Epitaph on a Fir-tree', *Listen*, vol. 3, no. 2, spring 1959, p. 7

'Wild Geese', *Irish Times*, 23 May 1959, p. 6

'The Island Girl', *Listen*, vol. 3, nos 3–4, spring 1960, pp. 3–4

'Graves at Inishbofin', *Irish Times*, 28 January 1961, p. 6. Repr. *Archipelago*, no. 12, spring 2019, p. 2

'The Last Galway Hooker', *Listener*, vol. 65, no. 1,663, 9 February 1961, p. 274

'The Poet on the Island', *Poetry*, vol. 98, no. 4, July 1961, pp. 224–5

'Sailing to an Island', *Listener*, vol. 66, no. 1,690, 17 August 1961, p. 250

'The Netting', *Yale Review*, vol. 50, no. 4, June 1961, pp. 567–8

'Droit de Seigneur', *Listener*, vol. 67, no. 1,717, 22 February 1962, p. 339

'Latch', *Listen*, vol. 4, no. 1, autumn 1962, p. 7

'The Travelling Player', *Irish Times*, 8 December 1962, p. 6

'Latch', *Dubliner*, vol. 1, no. 6, January/February 1963, p. 52

'The Poet on the Island', *Dubliner*, vol. 1, no. 6, January/February 1963, pp. 51–2

'Armada Anchor', *Irish Times*, 16 February 1963, p. 8. Repr. *Archipelago*, no. 12, spring 2019, pp. 3–4

'Elegy for a Battle' [Narrator – Woman of Ireland; Narrator – Brigit; A mercenary soldier; Narrator – Cromwellian settler; Narrator – Rapparees], *Massachusetts Review*, vol. 5, no. 2, winter 1964, pp. 250–5

'The God Who Eats Corn', *Reporter*, vol. 30, no. 10, 7 May 1964, pp. 34–6

'The God Who Eats Corn', *Listener*, vol. 72, no. 1,845, 6 August 1964, pp. 191–2

'Slate', *St. Stephen's*, vol. 2, no. 9, Trinity term 1966, p. 8

'Girl at the Seaside', *Observer*, 16 August 1966, p. 16 [colour magazine]

'Christening', *Hibernia*, vol. 31, no. 2, February 1967, p. 22

'From *The Battle of Aughrim*' ['Inheritance'], *New Statesman*, vol. 76, no. 1,956, 6 September 1968, p. 289

'Walking on Sunday', *Times Literary Supplement*, no. 3,509, 29 May 1969, p. 585

'Ray Wings', *Broadsheet No. 4: The Poetry Workshop UCD*, ed. Richard Ryan (1970), unpaginated. Repr. *Archipelago*, no. 12, spring 2019, p. 5

'Saint Gormgall's Well', *Poetry*, vol. 118, no. 6, September 1971, pp. 333–4

'Little Hunger', *Poetry*, vol. 118, no. 6, September 1971, p. 334

'Corncrake', *Poetry*, vol. 118, no. 6, September 1971, pp. 334–5

'Gallows Riddle', *Poetry*, vol. 118, no. 6, September 1971, p. 335

'The Reading Lesson', *New York Review of Books*, vol. 17, no. 6, 21 October 1971, p. 11

'Song for a Corncrake', *Times Literary Supplement*, no. 3,655, 17 March 1972, p. 314

'Little Hunger', *Irish Press*, 22 April 1972, p. 11

'The Reading Lesson', *Irish Press*, 22 April 1972, p. 11

'Saint Gormgall's Well', *Irish Press*, 22 April 1972, p. 11

'Firebug', *New York Review of Books*, vol. 19, no. 8, 16 November 1972, p. 6

'Seals at High Island', *New York Review of Books*, vol. 20, no. 2, 22 February, 1973, p. 24

'Ball's Cove', *Hibernia*, vol. 37, no. 5, 30 March 1973, p. 14

'The Reading Lesson', *London Magazine*, vol. 3, no. 1, April/May 1973, p. 20

'Brian Boru's Well', *London Magazine*, vol. 13, no. 1, April/May 1973, pp. 19–20

'Ball's Cove', *London Magazine*, vol. 13, no. 1, April/May 1973, p. 20

'Seals at High Island', *London Magazine*, vol. 13, no. 1, April/May 1973, pp. 21–2

'Overboard', *London Magazine*, vol. 13, no. 1, April/May 1973, p. 22. Repr. *Archipelago*, no. 12, spring 2019, p. 6

'The Glass Dump Road', *New York Review of Books*, vol. 20, no. 19, 29 November 1973, p. 25

'Pat Cloherty's Version of *The Maisie*', *Stand*, vol. 15, no. 4, 1974, pp. 8–9

'Sunup', *New Review*, vol. 1, no. 6, September 1974, p. 46

'Jurors', *New Review*, vol. 1, no. 6, September 1974, p. 46

'Double Negative', *New Review*, vol. 1, no. 6, September 1974, p. 47

'Granite Globe', *New Review*, vol. 1, no. 6, September 1974, p. 47

'Lullaby', *New Review*, vol. 1, no. 6, September 1974, p. 47

'Stormpetrel', *New Review*, vol. 1, no. 6, September 1974, p. 48

'Travelling Man', *New Review*, vol. 1, no. 6, September 1974, p. 48

'High Island', *American Review*, no. 21, October 1974, pp. 144–5

'Traveller's Palm' [also published as 'Kandy Perahera'], *New York Review of Books*, vol. 21, no. 17, 31 October 1974, p. 34

'Firebug', *London Magazine*, vol. 14, no. 4, October/November 1974, p. 47

'The Writing Lesson', *London Magazine*, vol. 14, no. 4, October/November 1974, pp. 47–8

'Coppersmith', *London Magazine*, vol. 14, no. 4, October/November 1974, pp. 48–9

'The Fall', *London Magazine*, vol. 14, no. 4, October/November 1974, pp. 49–50

'Traveller's Palm' [also published as 'Kandy Perahera'], *London Magazine*, vol. 14, no. 4, October/November 1974, pp. 50–2

'Brian Boru's Well', *Word-smith*, vol. 1, nos 1–2, summer/winter 1975, p. 9

'Gallows Riddle', *Word-smith*, vol. 1, nos 1–2, summer/winter 1975, p. 10

'Mary Ure', *Times Literary Supplement*, no. 3,827, 18 July 1975, p. 790

'Trouvaille', *Times Literary Supplement*, no. 3,828, 25 July 1975, p. 838

'Seals at High Island', *Austin Clarke Memorial Broadsheet*, October 1975, unpaginated

'The Glass Dump Road', *Austin Clarke Memorial Broadsheet*, October 1975, unpaginated

'Shelter', *Austin Clarke Broadsheet 2*, October 1975, unpaginated

'Swallows', *Austin Clarke Broadsheet 2*, October 1975, unpaginated

'Shelter', *Sewanee Review*, vol. 84, no. 1, winter 1976, p. 127

'Swallows', *Sewanee Review*, vol. 84, no. 1, winter 1976, pp. 127–8

'Care', *New York Review of Books*, vol. 24, no. 4, 17 March 1977, p. 20

'For Anya on New Year's Day 1977', *Irish University Review: Richard Murphy special issue*, vol. 7, no. 1, spring 1977, p. 31

'Care', *Irish University Review: Richard Murphy special issue*, vol. 7, no. 1, spring 1977, p. 32

'Shelter', *Irish University Review: Richard Murphy special issue*, vol. 7, no. 1, spring 1977, p. 33

'Mary Ure', *Irish University Review: Richard Murphy special issue*, vol. 7, no. 1, spring 1977, p. 34

'Trouvaille', *Irish University Review: Richard Murphy special issue*, vol. 7, no. 1, spring 1977, p. 34

'Enigma', *Irish University Review: Richard Murphy special issue*, vol. 7, no. 1, spring 1977, p. 35

'The Price of Stone' ['Stone Mania'], *Irish Press*, 29 April 1978, p. 13

'The Glass Door', *Hibernia*, vol. 43, no. 37, 20 September 1979, p. 21

'The Price of Stone' ['Stone Mania'], *Poetry Australia*, no. 72, October 1979, p. 9

'A Nest in a Wall', *Poetry Australia*, no. 72, October 1979, p. 10

'Niches', *Poetry Australia*, no. 72, October 1979, p. 10

'Tony White', *New York Review of Books*, vol. 26, no. 15, 11 October 1979, p. 12

'Bookcase for *The Oxford English Dictionary*', *London Review of Books*, vol. 2, no. 1, 24 January 1980, p. 24

'Arsonist', *Times Literary Supplement*, no. 4,012, 15 February 1980, p. 177

'Morning Call', *Helix*, nos 5–6, February–August 1980, p. 67 [Australian poetry journal]

'A Nest in a Wall', *London Magazine*, vol. 19, no. 12, March 1980, p. 5

'Morning Call', *London Magazine*, vol. 19, no. 12, March 1980, pp. 5–6

'The Glass Door', *London Magazine*, vol. 19, no. 12, March 1980, pp. 6–7

'Niches', *London Magazine*, vol. 19, no. 12, March 1980, p. 7

'Tranquillity', *London Magazine*, vol. 19, no. 12, March 1980, pp. 7–8

'The Price of Stone' [subsequently collected as 'Stone Mania'], *London Magazine*, vol. 19, no. 12, March 1980, p. 8

'Husbandry', *London Magazine*, vol. 19, no. 12, March 1980, p. 9

'Displaced Person', *Bananas: the literary magazine*, no. 26, April 1981, p. 35

'Visiting Hour', *New Statesman*, vol. 99, no. 2,564, 9 May 1980, p. 719

'Reflection', *Poetry Ireland Review*, no. 1, spring 1981, p. 14

'Elixir', *Poetry Ireland Review*, no. 1, spring 1981, pp. 13–14

'Pier Bar', *Poetry Ireland Review*, no. 1, spring 1981, p. 14 [different poem from 'Pier Bar' sonnet published in *The Price of Stone* (1985), p. 79]. Repr. *Archipelago*, no. 12, spring 2019, p. 7

'Amazement', *London Review of Books*, vol. 3, no. 19, 15 October 1981, p. 17

'Lead Mine Chimney', *Times Literary Supplement*, no. 4,099, 23 October 1981, p. 1224

'Elixir', *Times Literary Supplement*, no. 4,102, 13 November 1981, p. 1331

'Folly', *Times Literary Supplement*, no. 4,103, 20 November 1981, p. 1351

'Altar', *Times Literary Supplement*, no. 4,103, 27 November 1981, p. 1385

'Dry Stonework', *Concerning Poetry*, vol. 14, no. 2, 1981, p. 4

'Tony White at Inishbofin 1959', *Concerning Poetry*, vol. 14, no. 2, 1981, p. 58

'Moonshine', *Times Literary Supplement*, no. 4,111, 15 January 1982, p. 56

'Natural Son', *Irish Times*, 13 February 1982, p. 13

'Georgian House', *Times Literary Supplement*, no. 4,123, 9 April 1982, p. 400

'Tony White', *Connaught Tribune*, 30 April 1982, p. 20

'Amsterdam', *Times Literary Supplement*, no. 4,136, 9 July 1982, p. 738

'Nelson's Pillar', *Irish Times*, 9 July 1983, p. 12

'Letterfrack Industrial School', *New York Review of Books*, vol. 30, no. 9, 2 June 1983,
  p. 24

'Conolly's Folly', *Sunday Tribune*, 17 July 1983, p. 12 ['Inside *Tribune*' section]

'Birth Place', *Irish Literary Supplement*, vol. 2, no. 2, 1 September 1983, p. 26

'Old Dispensary', *Irish Literary Supplement*, vol. 2, no. 2, 1 September 1983, p. 26

'Carlow Village Schoolhouse', *Irish Literary Supplement*, vol. 2, no. 2, 1 September
  1983, p. 26

'Rectory', *Irish Literary Supplement*, vol. 2, no. 2, 1 September 1983, p. 26

'Suntrap', *Irish Literary Supplement*, vol. 2, no. 2, 1 September 1983, p. 26

'Connemara Quay', *Irish Literary Supplement*, vol. 2, no. 2, 1 September 1983, p. 26

'Killary Hostel', *Irish Literary Supplement*, vol. 2, no. 2, 1 September 1983, p. 27

'Horse-drawn Caravan', *Irish Literary Supplement*, vol. 2, no. 2, 1 September 1983,
  p. 27

'Hexagon', *Irish Literary Supplement*, vol. 2, no. 2, 1 September 1983, p. 27

'Miners' Hut', *Irish Literary Supplement*, vol. 2, no. 2, 1 September 1983, p. 27

'New Forge', *Irish Literary Supplement*, vol. 2, no. 2, 1 September 1983, p. 27

'Cottage for Sale', *Irish Literary Supplement*, vol. 2, no. 2, 1 September 1983, p. 27

'Friary', *Times Literary Supplement*, no. 4,199, 23 September 1983, p. 1017

'Lecknavarna', *Times Literary Supplement*, no. 4,199, 23 September 1983, p. 1017

'Wattle Tent', *Times Literary Supplement*, no. 4,199, 23 September 1983, p. 1017

'Beehive Cell', *Times Literary Supplement*, no. 4,199, 23 September 1983, p. 1017

'Baymount', *Times Literary Supplement*, no. 4,199, 23 September 1983, p. 1017

'Wellington Testimonial', *Times Literary Supplement*, no. 4,199, 23 September 1983,
  p. 1017

'Planter Stock', *Times Literary Supplement*, no. 4,208, 25 November 1983, p. 1306

'Convenience', *Times Literary Supplement*, no. 4,212, 23 December 1983, p. 1434

'Red Bank Restaurant', *Poetry Ireland Review*, no. 8, 1983, p. 7

'Portico', *Grand Street*, vol. 3, no. 2, winter 1984, p. 15

'Family Seat', *Grand Street*, vol. 3, no. 2, winter 1984, p. 16

'Milford: East Wing', *Grand Street*, vol. 3, no. 2, winter 1984, p. 17

'Wellington College', *Grand Street*, vol. 3, no. 2, winter 1984, p. 18

'Roof-tree', *Grand Street*, vol. 3, no. 2, winter 1984, p. 19

'Tony White's Cottage', *Grand Street*, vol. 3, no. 2, winter 1984, p. 20

'Canterbury Cathedral', *Oxford Poetry*, vol. 1, no. 3, spring 1984, p. 99

'Chalet', *Oxford Poetry*, vol. 1, no. 3, spring 1984, p. 99

'Carlyon Bay Hotel', *Times Literary Supplement*, no. 4,230, 27 April 1984, p. 475

'Gate Lodge', *Times Literary Supplement*, no. 4,267, 11 January 1985, p. 39

'Miners' Hut', *Poetry Review*, vol. 74, no. 4, January 1985, p. 20

'Carlow Village Schoolhouse', *Poetry Review*, vol. 74, no. 4, January 1985, p. 20

'Waterkeeper's Bothy', *Times Literary Supplement*, no. 4,267, 11 January 1985, p. 39

'Kylemore Castle', *Times Literary Supplement*, no. 4,270, 1 February 1985, p. 110

'Ice Rink', *London Review of Books*, vol. 7, no. 2, 7 February 1985, p. 4

'Knockbrack', *Times Literary Supplement*, no. 4,273, 22 February 1985, p. 193

'Little Barn', *Times Literary Supplement*, no. 4,273, 22 February 1985, p. 193

'Prison', *Times Literary Supplement*, no. 4,273, 22 February 1985, p. 193

'Choir School', *London Magazine*, vol. 25, nos 1–2, April/May 1985, p. 37

'Killary Hostel', *London Magazine*, vol. 25, nos 1–2, April/May 1985, pp. 37–8

'Rectory', *London Magazine*, vol. 25, nos 1–2, April/May 1985, p. 38

'Liner', *London Magazine*, vol. 25, nos 1–2, April/May 1985, pp. 38–9

'Newgrange', *Irish Times*, 25 May 1985, p. 12

'Orphanage', *Times Literary Supplement*, no. 4,309, 1 November 1985, p. 1232

'National Hero', *Poetry Ireland Review*, no. 15, winter 1985–6, p. 9

'Sri Lanka', *New York Review of Books*, vol. 33, no. 8, 8 May 1986, p. 8

'Sri Lanka', *Poetry Ireland Review*, no. 20, autumn 1987, p. 27

'Poems from the Mirror Wall', *Times Literary Supplement*, no. 4,479, 3 February 1989, p. 108

'The Mirror Wall', *Grand Street*, vol. 8, no. 3, spring 1989, pp. 18–25

'Double Vision', *Irish Times*, 18 January 1998, p. 30 [Weekend Supplement, p. 8]

'Omey Island', *Irish University Review*, vol. 22, no. 1, spring/summer 1992, p. 179

'The God Who Eats Corn', *The Snow Path: tracks*, no. 10, ed. John F. Deane (Dublin: Dedalus Press, 1994), pp. 109–15

'Legend', *The Snow Path: tracks*, no. 10, ed. John F. Deane (Dublin: Dedalus Press, 1994), p. 72. Repr. *Archipelago*, no. 12, spring 2019, p. 8

'Mangoes', *Poetry*, vol. 67, nos. 1–2, October/November 1995, p. 88

'Double Vision', *Agenda*, vol. 33, nos 3–4, autumn–winter 1996, p. 83

'Grounds', *Times Literary Supplement*, no. 4,883, 1 November 1996, p. 4

'The Afterlife', *New York Review of Books*, vol. 44, no. 10, 12 June 1997, p. 8

'A River of Notebooks', *Irish Times*, 17 May 2003, p. 47 [Weekend Supplement, p. 11]

'Rite of Passage' *New York Review of Books*, vol. 51, no. 2, 12 February 2004, p. 8

'Waking from a Dream', *Poetry Ireland Review*, no. 93, March 2008, p. 5

'Vagrant', *Times Literary Supplement*, no. 5,516, 19 December 2008, p. 5

'Last Word', *Times Literary Supplement*, no. 5,487, 30 May 2008, p. 22

'Death in Kandy', *Times Literary Supplement*, no. 5,743, 26 April 2013, p. 11

'Travelling Man', *Bulletin of the Poetry Book Society*, summer 2013, p. 17
'Sailing to an Island', *Irish Times*, 17 August 2013, p. 45 [Weekend Supplement, p. 11]

(iii) Poems Published in Anthologies

'The Philosopher and the Birds'; 'The Archaeology of Love', in *Poetry Now: an anthology*, ed. G.S. Fraser (London: Faber & Faber, 1956), pp. 124–7

'The Archaeology of Love', in *English Love Poems*, eds John Betjeman and Geoffrey Taylor (London: Faber & Faber, 1957), pp. 192–4

'The Woman of the House', in *The Guinness Book of Poetry, 1958–59* (London: Putnam, 1960), pp. 100–2

'Sailing to an Island', in *Three Irish Poets: John Montague, Thomas Kinsella, Richard Murphy* (a poetry reading presented by the Dolmen Press at the Royal Hibernian Hotel, 3 February 1961), unpaginated

'The Progress of the Painter', in *Poetry at the Mermaid: souvenir programme* (London: Westerham Press, 1961), pp. 51–2

'The Cleggan Disaster', in *The Dolmen Miscellany of Irish Writing*, ed. John Montague (Dublin/London: The Dolmen Press/Oxford University Press, 1962), pp. 46–61

'Sailing to an Island'; 'The Last Galway Hooker'; epilogue to 'The Cleggan Disaster' ('Years Later'); 'Girl at the Seaside'; 'The Netting'; 'The Philosopher and the Birds'; 'The Poet on the Island'; 'The Progress of a Painter'; 'Epitaph on a Fir-tree'; 'The Woman of the House', in *Six Irish Poets*, ed. Robin Skelton (London: Oxford University Press, 1962), pp. 89–111

Epilogue to 'The Cleggan Disaster' ('Years Later'), in *Handbook of the Cheltenham Festival of Literature 1–6 October 1962* (Cheltenham: Cheltenham Arts Festival 1962), pp. 61–3

'Sailing to an Island'; 'The Last Galway Hooker', in *New Poems 1962: a P.E.N. anthology of contemporary poetry*, eds Patricia Beer, Ted Hughes and Vernon Scannell (London: Hutchinson, 1962), pp. 83–90

'Sailing to an Island'; 'The Philosopher and the Birds'; epilogue to 'The Cleggan Disaster' ('Years Later'), in *New Poets of Ireland*, ed. Donald Carroll (Denver, CO: Alan Swallow, 1963), pp. 92–6

'The Cleggan Disaster', in *Prose and Verse Readings: BBC broadcasts to schools* (London: BBC, 1963), pp. 24–33

'The Cleggan Disaster'; 'Epitaph on a Fir-tree'; 'The Philosopher and the Birds'; 'The Poet on the Island'; 'The Woman of the House'; 'Girl at the Seaside'; 'Connemara Marble'; 'Droit de Seigneur'; 'The God Who Eats Corn', in *Penguin Modern Poets 7: Richard Murphy, Jon Silkin, Nathaniel Tarn* (London: Penguin, 1965), pp. 11–39

'For Sylvia Plath 1932–1963', in *Cheltenham Festival of Literature: programme of the Cheltenham Arts Festival, 1965* (Cheltenham: Cheltenham Arts Festival, 1965), pp. 54–5

'Epitaph on a Fir-tree', in *The Faber Book of Twentieth Century Verse*, eds John
    Heath-Stubbs and David Wright (London: Faber & Faber, 1965), p. 228

'The Poet on the Island'; epilogue to 'The Cleggan Disaster' ('Years Later'), in *The
    Mentor Book of Irish Poetry*, ed. Devin A. Garrity (New York: Mentor Books,
    1965), pp. 290–2

'Military History' [an early variant of 'History' from *The Battle of Aughrim*], in
    Poems, ed. Eric W. White (London: Poetry Book Society, 1966), unpaginated

'The Netting' [also published as 'The Archaeology of Love'], in *Love Poems of the
    Irish*, ed. Seán Lucy (Cork: Mercier Press, 1967), pp. 142–3

'Sailing to an Island', in *Poetry in the Making* by Ted Hughes (London: Faber &
    Faber, 1967), pp. 83–6

'Girl at the Seaside'; excerpts from *The Battle of Aughrim* ('The Story I Have to Tell',
    'A Country Woman and a Country Man', 'Rapparees'), in *100 Postwar Poems:
    British and American*, ed. M.L. Rosenthal (New York: Macmillan, 1968), pp. 46–8

'Walking on Sunday', in *A Standard of Verse and Nine Poems*, ed. John Moat
    (Newbury: Phoenix Press, 1969), p. 41

'The Poet on the Island', in *The Penguin Book of Irish Verse*, ed. Brendan Kennelly
    (Harmondsworth: Penguin, 1970), pp. 397–8 [1988, 2nd edn]

'Graves at Inishbofin', in *The New York Times Book of Verse*, ed. Thomas Lask (New
    York: Macmillan, 1970), pp. 110–11

'Droit de Seigneur 1820', in *Poems from Ireland*, ed. William Cole (New York:
    Thomas Y. Crowell, 1972), pp. 148–9

Excerpt from 'The Last Galway Hooker', in *The Sphere Book of Modern Irish Poetry*,
    ed. Derek Mahon (London: Sphere Books, 1972), pp. 167–8

'Seals at High Island'; 'The Reading Lesson', in *Soundings '72*, ed. Seamus Heaney
    (Belfast: Blackstaff Press, 1972), pp. 58–9

'Song for a Concrake', in *New Poems 1972–73: a P.E.N. anthology of contemporary
    poetry*, ed. Douglas Dunn (London: Hutchinson, 1973), p. 119

'The Reading Lesson', in *Choice: an anthology of Irish poetry selected by the poets
    themselves*, eds Desmond Egan and Michael Hartnett (The Curragh: Goldsmith
    Press, 1973), pp. 92–3

'Girl at the Seaside'; excerpts from *The Battle of Aughrim* ('Planter', 'Rapparees');
    'Little Hunger', in *The Faber Book of Irish Verse*, ed. John Montague (London:
    Faber & Faber, 1974), pp. 328–31

'High Island'; 'The Glass Dump Road'; 'Corncrake'; 'Firebug', in *Soundings 2: an
    anthology of new Irish poetry*, ed. Seamus Heaney (Belfast: Blackstaff Press,
    1974), pp. 48–51

'Girl at the Seaside'; excerpts from *The Battle of Aughrim* ('Planter', 'Rapparees');
    'Little Hunger', in *The Book of Irish Verse: an anthology of Irish poetry from the
    sixth century to the present*, ed. John Montague (New York: Macmillan, 1974),
    pp. 328–31

'Firebug', in *New Poems 1975: a P.E.N. anthology of contemporary poetry*, ed. Patricia
   Beer (London: Hutchinson, 1975), p. 129

Epilogue to 'The Cleggan Disaster' ('Years Later'); 'High Island', in *The Wolfhound
   Book of Irish Poems for Young People*, ed. Bridie Quinn and Seamus Cashman
   (Dublin: Wolfhound Press, 1975), pp. 122–4

'Walking on Sunday'; 'Pat Cloherty's Version of *The Maisie*'; 'The Reading Lesson';
   'The Woman of the House', in *Irish Poets 1924–1974*, ed. David Marcus (London:
   Pan Books, 1975), pp. 40–7

'Song for a Corncrake', in *Birds of Galway and Mayo* by Tony Whilde (Galway: Irish
   Wildbird Conservancy, 1977), p. 18

Excerpt from *The Battle of Aughrim* ('The Wolfhound'); 'The Reading Lesson';
   'Enigma'; 'For Sylvia Plath 1932–1963', in *A Prose and Verse Anthology of
   Modern Irish Writing*, ed. Grattan Freyer (Dublin: Irish Humanities Centre,
   1978), pp. 246–9

'Tony White'; 'The Price of Stone' as 'Stone Mania' [subsequently collected], in
   The First Ten Years: Dublin Arts Festival poetry, eds Peter Fallon and Dennis
   O'Driscoll (Dublin: Dublin Arts Festival, 1979), pp. 50–1

'High Island'; 'Granite Globe', in *Celebration: a salute to a visiting artist*, ed. Jim
   Fitzgerald (Dublin: Veritas, 1979), pp. 30, 34 an anthology published on the
   occasion of Pope John Paul II's visit to Ireland

'Sailing to an Island'; 'The Woman of the House'; 'The Last Galway Hooker'; excerpts
   from *The Battle of Aughrim* (Section 1, Now: 'On Battle Hill', 'Green Martyrs',
   'Orange March', 'Casement's Funeral', 'Historical Society', 'Slate', 'Inheritance',
   'Christening', 'History'); 'Seals at High Island'; 'Walking on Sunday'; 'Pat
   Cloherty's Version of *The Maisie*'; 'The Reading Lesson', 'Coppersmith';
   'Nocturne'; 'Trouvaille'; 'Care', in *Irish Poetry After Yeats*, ed. Maurice Harmon
   (Dublin: Wolfhound Press, 1979), pp. 122–35

'The Philosopher and the Birds'; 'The Poet on the Island'; excerpts from *The Battle of
   Aughrim* (extract from 'Legend', 'Mercenary', 'God's Dilemma'); 'Seals at High
   Island'; 'High Island'; 'Enigma'; 'Trouvaille', in *Contemporary Irish Poetry*, ed.
   Anthony Bradley (Berkeley: University Press of California, 1980), pp. 164–71

'Enigma'; 'Care'; 'Swallows'; 'Trouvaille'; 'Mary Ure'; 'The Price of Stone'
   [subsequently collected as 'Stone Mania'], in *Soft Day: a miscellany of
   contemporary Irish writing*, eds Peter Fallon and Seán Golden (Dublin:
   Wolfhound Press, 1980), pp. 68–72

'Morning Call'; 'Tony White at Inishbofin 1959'; 'Husbandry', in *The Writers: a
   sense of Ireland*, eds Andrew Carpenter and Peter Fallon (Dublin: O'Brien
   Press, 1980), pp. 139–41

'Pat Cloherty's Version of *The Maisie*', in the *Rattle Bag*, eds Seamus Heaney and
   Ted Hughes (London: Faber & Faber, 1982), p. 339

'Moonshine', in *Portraits of Poets*, ed. Sebastian Barker (Manchester: Carcanet Press, 1986), p. 95

Excerpts from *The Battle of Aughrim* ('Rapparees', 'Wolfhound', 'Green Martyrs', 'Orange March', 'Casement's Funeral'); 'High Island', in *The New Oxford Book of Irish Verse*, ed. Thomas Kinsella (Oxford: Oxford University Press, 1986), pp. 362–7

'Seals at High Island'; 'Sunup'; 'Moonshine'; 'A Nest in a Wall'; 'Displaced Person', in *The Long Embrace: twentieth century Irish love poems*, ed. Frank Ormsby (Belfast: Blackstaff Press, 1987), pp. 72–5

'The Philosopher and the Birds'; 'The Poet on the Island'; excerpts from *The Battle of Aughrim* ('Legend', 'Mercenary', 'God's Dilemma'); 'Seals at High Island'; 'High Island'; 'A Nest in a Wall'; 'Beehive Cell', in *Contemporary Irish Poetry*, ed. Anthony Bradley (Berkeley: University Press of California, 1988), pp. 164–71 [revised edn]

'Sri Lanka', in *In the Prison of His Days: a miscellany for Nelson Mandela on his 70th birthday*, ed. W.J. McCormack (Dublin: The Lilliput Press, 1988), p. 63

'Seals at High Island'; 'A Nest in a Wall'; 'Morning Call'; 'Tony White, 1930–1976'; 'Gym'; 'Elixir'; 'Roof-tree', in *Bitter Harvest: an anthology of contemporary Irish verse*, ed. John Montague (New York: Charles Scribner's Sons, 1989), pp. 26–31

'Sailing to an Island'; 'The Last Galway Hooker'; excerpts from *The Battle of Aughrim* ('Casement's Funeral', 'Slate', 'Rapparees', 'Luttrell's Death', 'Patrick Sarsfield's Portrait'); 'Seals at High Island'; 'The Reading Lesson'; 'Gate Lodge', in *The Penguin Book of Contemporary Irish Poetry*, eds Peter Fallon and Derek Mahon (London: Penguin, 1990), pp. 62–77

'Largesse', in *Irish Poetry of Faith and Doubt: the cold heaven*, ed. John F. Deane (Dublin: Wolfhound Press, 1990), pp. 143–4

'Pat Cloherty's Version of *The Maisie*', in *The Mayo Anthology*, ed. Richard Murphy (Castlebar: Mayo County Council, 1990), pp. 60–1

'The Last Galway Hooker'; excerpt from *The Battle of Aughrim* ('Casement's Funeral'); 'Seals at High Island'; 'Little Hunger'; 'Moonshine'; 'The Price of Stone' (also known as 'Stone Mania'); 'Wellington Testimonial'; 'Ice Rink'; 'Natural Son', in *The Field Day Anthology of Irish Writing*, ed. Seamus Deane (Derry: Field Day, 1991), pp. 1336–40

Excerpt from *The Battle of Aughrim* ('Orange March'); 'Amazement', in *A Rage for Order: poetry of the Northern Irish Troubles*, ed. Frank Ormsby (Belfast: Blackstaff Press, 1992), pp. 30–1, 148

'The Reading Lesson'; 'Song for a Corncrake'; 'The Pleasure Ground' [prose article], in *Molly Keane's Ireland: an anthology*, eds Molly Keane and Sally Phipps (London: Harper Collins, 1993), pp. 10–11, 64, 201–5

'Seals at High Island', in *Between Innocence and Peace: favourite poems of Ireland*, ed. Brendan Kennelly (Cork: Mercier Press, 1993), pp. 14–15

Excerpt from 'The Cleggan Disaster', in *Inishbofin: through time and tide*, ed. Kieran Concannon (Inishbofin: Inishbofin Development Association, 1993), p. 43

'Moonshine', in *Real Cool: poems to grow up with*, ed. Niall MacMonagle (Dublin: Marino Books, 1994), p. 43

'Sailing to an Island', in *Lifelines 2: letters from famous people about their favourite poem*, ed. Niall MacMonagle (Dublin: Town House, 1994), pp. 146–8

'Sailing to an Island'; 'The Poet on the Island'; 'Casement's Funeral' [from *The Battle of Aughrim*]; 'Seals at High Island'; 'Stormpetrel'; 'Morning Call'; 'Roof-tree'; 'Convenience'; 'Kylemore Castle'; 'Natural Son', in *Modern Irish Poetry: an anthology*, ed. Patrick Crotty (Belfast: Blackstaff, 1995), pp. 150–8

'Care', in *A Parcel of Poems for Ted Hughes on His Sixty-fifth Birthday, 17 August 1995* (London: Faber & Faber, 1995), pp. 48–9

'Walking on Sunday', in *The Clifden Anthology*, ed. Brendan Flynn (Clifden: Clifden Community Arts Week, 1995), pp. 48–9

'Sunup', in *Remembered Kisses: an illustrated anthology of Irish love poetry*, ed. Louis Bell (Dublin: Gill & Macmillan, 1996), p. 17

'Sunup', in *The Irish Eros: Irish short stories and poems on sexual themes*, ed. David Marcus (Dublin: Gill & Macmillan, 1996), pp. 215–16

Excerpts from *The Battle of Aughrim* ('Planter', 'Rapparees'); 'Pat Cloherty's Version of *The Maisie*', in *The Ireland Anthology*, ed. Seán Dunne (Dublin: Gill & Macmillan, 1997), pp. 27–9, 203–4

'The Reading Lesson', in *The Poolbeg Book of Irish Poetry for Children*, ed. Shaun Traynor (Dublin: Poolbeg, 1997), p. 125

Excerpt from *The Battle of Aughrim* ('Slate'), in *The Penguin Book of Poetry from Britain and Ireland*, eds Simon Armitage and Robert Crawford (Harmondsworth: Penguin, 1998), pp. 134–5

Excerpt from 'The Woman of the House'; 'Georgian Tenement', in *The Oxford Book of Ireland*, ed. Patricia Craig (Oxford: Oxford University Press, 1998), pp. 454, 492

'Roof-tree', in *Stream and Gliding Sun: a Wicklow anthology* (Wicklow: Wicklow County Council, 1998), p. 197

'Sailing to an Island', in *Watching the River Flow: a century, in Irish poetry*, eds Noel Duffy and Theo Dorgan (Dublin: Poetry Ireland, 1999), pp. 149–51

'Moonshine', in *The Whoseday Book: a unique diary for the millennium* (Dublin: Irish Hospice Foundation, 1999), unpaginated

'Moonshine', in *Ireland's Love Poems: wonder and a wild desire*, ed. A. Norman Jeffares (London: Kyle Cathie, 2000), p. 209

'Beehive Cell', in *The Oxford Book of Sonnets*, ed. John Fuller (Oxford: Oxford University Press, 2000), p. 310

'Lullaby', in *The Hip Flask: short poems from Ireland*, ed. Frank Ormsby (Belfast: Blackstaff Press, 2000), p. 28

'High Island'; 'Tony White at Inishbofin 1959', in *The Clifden Anthology*, ed. Brendan
    Flynn (Clifden: Clifden Community Arts Week, 2002), pp. 101–2
'Seals at High Island', in *A Treasury of Irish Verse*, ed. David Gibbon (Dublin: Gill
    & Macmillan, 2002), p. 114
'Seals at High Island', in *Staying Alive: real poems for unreal times*, ed. Neil Astley
    (Tarset: Bloodaxe, 2002), pp. 242–3
'Stormpetrel', in *20th-century Irish Verse*, ed. Michael Longley (London: Faber &
    Faber, 2002), p. 50
'Natural Son', in *Being Alive: the sequel to Staying Alive*, ed. Neil Astley (Tarset:
    Bloodaxe, 2004), pp. 124–5
'Beehive Cell', in *The Clifden Anthology*, ed. Brendan Flynn (Clifden: Clifden
    Community Arts Week, 2004), p. 118
'Doggerel for Emily', in *Something Beginning with P: new poems from Irish poets*, ed.
    Seamus Cashman (Dublin: O'Brien Press, 2004), p. 36
'High Island'; 'Walking on Sunday'; 'Tony White at Inishbofin 1959', in *100 Island
    Poems of Great Britain and Ireland*, ed. James Knox Whittet (Cullercoats: Iron
    Press, 2005), pp. 47–50
'Rite of Passage', in *Honouring the Word: poetry and prose, celebrating Maurice
    Harmon on His 80th birthday*, ed. Barbara Brown (Cliffs of Moher: Salmon
    Poetry, 2010), p. 25
'Seals at High Island'; 'Stormpetrel'; 'Morning Call', in *The Penguin Book of Irish
    Poetry*, ed. Patrick Crotty (London: Penguin, 2010), pp. 705–7 [1st edn]
'Doggerel for Emily', in *Dogs Singing: a tribute anthology*, ed. Jessie Lendennie
    (Cliffs of Moher: Salmon Poetry, 2010), p. 103
'The Reading Lesson', in *Island of Shadow: Irish poetry across the centuries*, ed. Brian
    Lalor (Dublin: Gill & Macmillan, 2011), pp. 160–1
'Sailing to an Island'; 'Girl at the Seaside', in *The Penguin Book of Irish Poetry*, ed.
    Patrick Crotty (London: Penguin, 2012), pp. 675–8 [2nd edn]
'Sailing to an Island'; 'The Last Galway Hooker'; excerpts from *The Battle of Aughrim*
    (Section 1, Now: 'On Battle Hill', 'History'; Section 2, Before: 'Legend', 'Planter',
    'Rapparees'; Section 3, During: 'St Ruth', 'The Winning Shot', 'Sarsfield', 'Luttrell',
    'Prisoner'; Section 4, After: 'The Wolfhound', 'Patrick Sarsfield's Portrait',
    'Battle Hill Revisited'); 'Seals at High Island'; 'Coppersmith'; 'Trouvaille';
    'Connemara Quay'; 'Friary', in *An Anthology of Modern Irish Poetry*, ed. Wes
    Davis (Cambridge, MA: Harvard University Press, 2013), pp. 193–213
Epilogue to 'The Cleggan Disaster' ('Years Later'), in *Best Loved Poems: favourite
    poems from the west of Ireland*, ed. Thomas F. Walsh (Dublin: Currach Press,
    2013), p. 84
'Nelson's Pillar'; 'Wellington Testimonial', in *If Ever You Go to Dublin Town: a
    map of Dublin, in poetry and song*, eds Pat Boran and Gerard Smyth (Dublin:
    Dedalus Press, 2014), pp. 94–5

Excerpt from *The Battle of Aughrim* ('Casement's Funeral'), in *Windharp: poems of Ireland since 1916*, ed. Niall MacMonagle (London: Penguin, 2015), pp. 75–6

(iv) Translations in Books, Anthologies and Journals

'Cinq extraits de La bataille d'Aughrim' ['Five Extracts from *The Battle of Aughrim*']: I.1 ['On Battle Hill']; I.6 ['Slate']; I.9 ['History']; IV.2 'The Reverend George Story Concludes *An Impartial History*' / 'Histoire Impartiale: Conclusion par le Révérend George Story'; IV.5 ['Battle Hill Revisted'], translated into French by Serge Fauchereau. *Ecrivains irlandais d'aujourd'hui: les lettres nouvelles, numéro special* (Paris: Mercure de France, 1973), pp. 124–35

'The Reading Lesson' / 'Lekcja Czytania'; 'The Poet on the Island' / 'Poeta na Wyspie'; 'The Wolfhound' / 'Wilczyca', translated into Polish by Bohdan Zadura and Jarosław Anders. *Literatura na Świecie* [Literature in the World], no. 4/60, April 1976, pp. 76–9

'The Reading Lesson' / 'Att Lära Sig Läsa', translated into Swedish by Marianne Levander. *Moderna språk*, vol. 71, 1977, pp. 65–7

'The Reading Lesson' / 'De leesles'; 'Ball's Cove' / 'Balls Kreek'; 'Husbandry' / 'Boerenleven'; 'Sunup' / 'Zonsopgang'; 'Shelter' / 'Beschutting', translated into Dutch by Ruud Hisgen and Adriaan van der Weel. *Ramp: Dat eeuwige verleden. Een overzicht van de Ierse letteren van nu (en toen)* 11–12, 1981, pp. 24–7. Reprinted in *Ierse stemmen: Bloemlezing van moderne schrijvers uit het West-Eiland*, eds Ruud Hisgen and Adriaan van der Weel (The Hague: Nijgh and Van Ditmar, 1981), pp. 46–57

'Largesse' / 'Largesse'; 'Amazement' / 'Stupeur'; 'Moonshine' / 'Petite bière'; 'Arsonist' / 'Incendiaire', translated into French by Serge Fauchereau. *Digraphe: aujourd'hui, la poésie Irlandaise*, ed. Serge Fauchereau, no. 27, June 1982, pp. 26–9

Care / Zorgzaamheid, translated into Dutch by Jan Eijkelboom (Amsterdam: Cornamona Press, 1983), 44pp.

Contents: 'To Gerald and Mary Cookson on their Silver Wedding' / 'Voor Gerald en Mary Cookson'; 'Moonshine' / 'Maneschijn'; 'Trouvaille' / 'Trouvaille'; 'Mary Ure' / 'Mary Ure'; 'Swallows' / 'Zwaluwen'; 'Shelter' / 'Beschutting'; 'Enigma' / 'Enigma'; 'Care' / 'Zorgzaamheid'; 'To Anya on New Year's Day 1977' / 'Voor Anya op nieuwjaarsdag'; 'Stone Mania' / 'Van steen bezeten'; 'Niches' / 'Nissen'; 'The Glass Door' / 'De glazen deur'; 'Husbandry' / 'Veeteelt'; 'A Nest in a Wall' / 'Een nest in de muur'; 'Tranquillity' / 'Rust'; 'Tony White at Inishbofin 1959' / 'Tony White op Inishbofin'; 'Double Negative' / 'Dubbel negatief'; 'Bookcase for *The Oxford English Dictionary*' / 'Boekenkast voor de Oxford English Dictionary'; 'Tony White' / 'Tony White'; 'Morning Call' / 'Ochtendbezoek'; 'Arsonist' / 'Brandstichter'; 'Elixir' / 'Elixer'; 'Amsterdam' / 'Amsterdam'; 'Altar'/ 'Altaar'; 'Displaced Person' / 'Displaced person'; 'Vertigo' / 'Duizeling'; 'Amazement' / 'Verbazing'; 'Visiting Hour' / 'Bezoekuur'; 'Natural Son' / 'Natuurlijke zoon'; 'Tourniquet' / 'Tourniquet', pp. 11–44

'High Island' / 'Hochinsel'; 'Granite Globe' / 'Granitkugel'; 'Pat Cloherty's Version
   of the *The Maisie*' / 'Wie Pat Cloherty vom Untergang der *Maisie* erzählte';
   'Largesse' / 'Großmut'; 'Travelling Man' / 'Fahrender'; 'The Reading Lesson'
   / 'Die Lesestunde', translated into German by Eva Bourke, Eoin Bourke and
   Friedrich Michael Dannenbauer. *Hundsrose: neue irische gedichte*, eds Eva
   Bourke, Eoin Bourke and Friedrich Michael Dannenbauer (Augsburg: Maro-
   Verlag, 1985), pp. 173–83
'On Battle Hill' / 'A Csata-Hegyen'; 'Green Martyrs' / 'Zöld Mártírok'; 'Orange
   March' / 'Narancsmenet', translated into Hungarian by Tótfalusi István.
   Nagyvilág, vol. 30, no. 5, May 1985, pp. 694–5
'Martial Law' / 'Loi Martiale'; 'Double Negative' / 'Double Negative'; 'High Island'
   / 'High Island'; 'The Glass Dump Road' / 'La Route de la Decharge de Verre';
   'Enigma' / 'Enigme'; 'The Cleggan Disaster: Years Later' / 'The Cleggan
   Disaster: Longtemps Après'; 'Firebug' / 'Le Pyromane'; 'Corncrake' / 'Râle des
   Genets', translated into French by Erlé Denez. *Poésies d'Irlande: anthologie*, ed.
   Denis Rigal (Marseille: Sud, 1987), pp. 135–51
'Sailing to an Island' / 'Varend naar een eiland'; 'Morning Call' / 'Ochtendbezoek';
   'Slate' / 'Leisten'; 'Patrick Sarsfield's Portrait' / 'Patrick Sarsfields portret';
   'Niches' / 'Nissen'; 'Stone Mania' / 'Van steen bezeten', translated into Dutch
   by Jan Eijkelboom. *Het dwingende verleden; Dertien moderne Ierse dichters*, ed.
   Peter Nijmeijer (Amsterdam: Meulenhoff, 1988), pp. 33–40
'Rapparees' / 'Mercenaires'; 'High Island' / 'High Island'; 'Moonshine' / 'Fariboles';
   'The Poet on the Island' / 'Le poète sur L'Île', translated into French by Patrick
   Hersant. *Anthologie de la poésie irlandaise du XXe siècle 1890–1900*, ed. Jean-
   Yves Masson (Paris: Verdier, 1996), pp. 428–33
'The Poet on the Island' / 'El Poeta en la Isla'; 'Stone Mania' / 'Piedra manía';
   'Amazement' / 'Asombro'; 'Amsterdam' / 'Amsterdam', translated into Spanish by
   Jorge Fondebrider. *Poesía irlandesa contemporánea*, eds Jorge Fondebrider and
   Gerardo Gambolini (Buenos Aires: Libros de Tierra Firme, 1999), pp. 153–60
'The Last Galway Hooker' / 'L'ultimo peschereccio di Galway', translated into Italian
   by Giovanna Mellini and Licia Governatori. *Almanacco letterario*, ed. Patrizia
   Consolo (Milan: Edizioni della Lisca, 1993), pp. 59–64
'Seals at High Island' / 'Foche a High Island', translated into Italian by Massimo
   Bacigalupo. *Poesia*, no. 190, 2005, p. 58
'The Archaeology of Love' / 'Kjæleikens Arkeologi'; 'Grounds' / 'Grunnar'; 'Largesse'
   / 'Generøsitet'; 'Travelling Man' / 'Ein Reisande'; 'Double Negative' / 'Dobbel
   Nekting'; 'Ball's Cove' / 'Balls Vik'; 'High Island' / 'Høg Øy'; 'Moonshine' /
   'Måneskin'; 'Swallows' / 'Svaler'; 'A Nest in a Wall' / 'Eit Reir i ein Mur'; 'Visiting
   Hour' / 'Visittid'; 'Natural Son' / 'Ein Uekte Son', translated into Norwegian by
   Knut Ødegård and Jostein Sæbøe. *Grøne dikt: 9 moderne irske lyrikarar*, eds
   Knut Ødegård and Jostein Sæbøe (Oslo: J.W. Cappelens Forlag, 2005), pp. 33–50

'Seals at High Island' / 'Tjulnji pri High Island', translated into Slovene by Veno Taufer. Čudovita usta: antologija sodobne irske poezije, ed. Mia Dintinjana (Ljubjana: Drustvo Apokalipsa, 2007), pp. 48–9

(v) Other Media

The Battle of Aughrim (Claddagh Records, 1969). [Spoken Word LP series, CCT 7 read by Cyril Cusack, C. Day Lewis, Ted Hughes, Margaret Robertson and Niall Tóibín, music composed by Seán Ó Riada]

'Seals at High Island', read by Adrian Hardiman, *Voices and Poetry of Ireland*, ed. Brian Molloy (London: Harper Collins, 2003), pp. 52–3 [CD2, Track 12]

PUBLISHED PROSE

(i) Literary Criticism and Memoir: Books

The Kick: a memoir (London: Granta, 2002), 379pp.

The Kick: a life among writers (London: Granta, 2003), 390pp.

The Kick: a life among writers (Dublin: The Lilliput Press, 2012) [e-book]

In Search of Poetry (Thame: Clutag Press, 2017), 159pp.

The Kick: a memoir of the poet Richard Murphy (Cork: Cork University Press, 2017), 360pp.

(ii) Memoir: Essays and extracts

'Charm of Eire', *Listener*, vol. 59, no. 1,503, 16 January 1958, pp. 119–20

'Deep Waters', *Listener*, vol. 67, no. 1,711, 11 January 1962, p. 85

'The Pleasure Ground', *Listener*, vol. 70, no. 1,794, 15 August 1963, pp. 237–40. Repr. *Writers on Themselves*, introduced by Herbert Read (London: BBC, 1964), pp. 62–6

'Sylvia Plath and Ted Hughes: a visit to the west of Ireland in 1962', *London Magazine*, vol. 29, nos 3–4, June/July 1989, pp. 31–43

'Introduction', in *The Mayo Anthology*, ed. Richard Murphy (Castlebar: Mayo County Council, 1990), pp. 9–11

'A Footnote to "Pat Cloherty's Version of *The Maisie*"', in *The Mayo Anthology*, ed. Richard Murphy (Castlebar: Mayo County Council, 1990), p. 62

'A Memoir of Sylvia Plath and Ted Hughes on a Visit to the West of Ireland in 1962', in *Bitter Fame: a life of Sylvia Plath* by Anne Stevenson (London: Penguin, 1990), pp. 348–58

'Photographs of Inishbofin – May 1960, *A dialogue between two boatsmen, Pat and Johnny*', *Poetry Ireland Review*, no. 37, winter 1992/93, pp. 23–4. Repr. *Poetry Ireland Review*, no. 50, summer 1996, pp. 119–20

'Preface', in *Inishbofin: through time and tide*, ed. Kieran Concannon (Inishbofin: Inishbofin Development Association, 1993): pp. ix–xiii

'On Writing "The God Who Eats Corn"', in *The Snow Path: tracks*, no. 10, ed. John F. Deane (Dublin: Dedalus Press, 1994), pp. 102–8

'Richard Murphy Looking Back at High Island', in *Voices of Connemara*, ed. Jane Stack (Clifden: Omey Union of Parishes, 1995), pp. 9–15

'Brief Encounters', *Granta*, no. 75, autumn 2001, pp. 7–27

'Getting a Kick', *Irish Times*, 18 May 2002, p. 39 [Weekend Supplement, p. 1]

'In the Presence of Grumpy Greatness', *Irish Times*, 6 December 2008, p. 13 [transcript of a talk recorded by Richard Murphy for the Oliver St John Gogarty Literary Festival, November 2008]

'Tea with Oliver St John Gogarty, Renvyle, 1951', *Poetry Ireland Review*, no. 96, December 2008, pp. 58–61

'Notes for Sonnets', *Poetry Ireland Review*, no. 104, September 2011, pp. 92–104

'Hewlett Johnson', *Times Literary Supplement*, no. 5,695, 25 May 2012, p. 6 [letter to the editor about *The Red Dean of Canterbury* by John Butler, reviewed in *TLS*, no. 5,693, 11 May 2012, p. 30]

'Transgressing into Poetry', *Poetry Ireland Review*, no. 107, September 2012, pp. 26–36

'Transgressing into Poetry', *Poetry Ireland Review*, no. 111, September 2013, pp. 117–33

'The Pleasure Ground', in *Poems 1952–2012* (Dublin: The Lilliput Press, 2013), pp. 13–16 [identical in *The Pleasure Ground: Poems 1952–2012*]

'Appendix', in *Poems 1952–2012* (Dublin: The Lilliput Press, 2013), pp. 243–72 [identical in *The Pleasure Ground: Poems 1952–2012*]

Contents: 'Author's note on the provenance of "Sailing to an Island"', p. 245; 'The provenance of "Wittgenstein and the Birds"', pp. 246–7; 'Author's note on "The Last Galway Hooker"', p. 248; 'Photographs of Inishbofin – May 1960, *A dialogue between two boatmen*', pp. 249–50; 'A note on the provenance of "The Cleggan Disaster"', pp. 251–3; 'Writing *The Battle of Aughrim*', pp. 254–9; 'A note on the provenance of *The God Who Eats Corn*', pp. 260–3; 'On the provenance of the High Island poems', pp. 264–72

Richard Murphy, 'From *The Price of Stone* Notebooks', *Archipelago*, no. 11, winter 2016, pp. 17–31

'My debt of gratitude to John Montague', *Irish Times*, 24 December 2016, p. 40 [Weekend Supplement, p. 12]

(iii) Literary Criticism and Reviews

Spectator, vol. 184, no. 6,357, (28 April 1950), p. 569 [commentary on T.S. Eliot's *The Cocktail Party* as poetic drama]

'The Pastoral Dream', Rev. of *England's Helicon* edited by Hugh Macdonald, *Spectator*, vol. 184, no. 6,359, 12 May 1950, pp. 658–60

'Mervyn Peake's Poetry', Rev. of *The Glassblowers* by Mervyn Peake, *Spectator*, vol. 184, no. 6,364, 16 June 1950, p. 834

'Two Poets', Rev. of *The Mongrel and Other Poems* by Ronald Duncan and *The Swarming of the Bees* by John Heath-Stubbs, *Spectator*, vol. 185, no. 6,369, 21 July 1950, p. 90

'Books and Writers', Rev. of *Collected Poems* by W.B. Yeats, *Spectator*, vol. 185, no. 6,372, 11 August 1950, p. 183

'MacLeish', Rev. of *Actfive and Other Poems* by Archibald MacLeish, *Spectator*, vol. 185, no. 6,374, 25 August 1950, pp. 247–8

'A New American Poet', Rev. of *Poems: 1938–1949* by Robert Lowell, *Spectator*, vol. 185, no. 6,385, 10 November 1950, p. 480

'Books and Writers', Rev. of *Ezra Pound* edited by Peter Russell and *Seventy Cantos* by Ezra Pound, *Spectator*, vol. 185, no. 6,386, 17 November 1950, p. 516

'Discovering Ireland', Rev. of *Leinster, Munster and Connaught* by Frank O'Connor, *Spectator*, vol. 185, no. 6,392, 29 December 1950, pp. 766–7

'Swinburne's Poetry', Rev. of *Selected Poems of Swinburne* edited by Edward Shanks and *Selected Poems* by Algernon Charles Swinburne, selected by Humphrey Hare, *Spectator*, vol. 186, no. 6,393, 5 January 1951, pp. 19–20

'American Poetry', Rev. of *The Oxford Book of American Verse* edited by F.O. Matthiessen, *Spectator*, vol. 186, no. 6,397, 2 February 1951, pp. 152–4

'An American Poet', Rev. of *The Collected Later Poems* by William Carlos Williams, *Times Literary Supplement*, no. 2,564, 23 March 1951, p. 178

'Footnotes to Yeats', Rev. of *The Lonely Tower* by T.R. Henn, *Spectator*, vol. 186, no. 6,404, 23 March 1951, pp. 190–2

'Before Yeats', Rev. of *Irish Poets of the Nineteenth Century* edited by Geoffrey Taylor, *Times Educational Supplement*, no. 1,876, 13 April 1951, p. 279

'A Storyteller in Verse', Rev. of *Collected Poems* by Robert Frost, *Spectator*, vol. 186, no. 6,410, 4 May 1951, pp. 594–6

'David Gascoyne's Poetry', Rev. of *A Vagrant* by David Gascoyne, *Spectator*, vol. 186, no. 6,413, 25 May 1951, pp. 694–6

'Books and Writers', Rev. of *Crisis in English Poetry, 1880–1940* by V. de S. Pinto, *Spectator*, vol. 187, no. 6,422, 27 July 1951, p. 131 [review essay]

'Why Has Narrative Poetry Failed?', *Listener*, vol. 46, no. 1,171, 9 August 1951, pp. 226–7

'A Dublin Poet', Rev. of *Reservations* by Valentin Iremonger, *Spectator*, vol. 187, no. 6,424, 10 August 1951, pp. 192–4

'Sentimental Journey', Rev. of *Connacht and the City of Galway* by Richard Hayward, *Times Literary Supplement*, no. 2,622, 2 May 1952, p. 229

'Spiritual Transformations', Rev. of *Collected Poems 1921–1951* by Edwin Muir, *Times Literary Supplement*, no. 2,631, 4 July 1952, p. 432

'Mr MacNeice's Poems', Rev. of *Ten Burnt Offerings* by Louis MacNeice, *Times Literary Supplement*, no. 2,636, 8 August 1952, p. 510

'The Music of Poetry', Rev. of *Selected Poems* by Wallace Stevens, *Spectator*, vol. 190, no. 6,503, 13 February 1953, pp. 191–2

'Poetry as Reportage', Rev. of *An Italian Visit* by C. Day Lewis, *Times Literary Supplement*, no. 2,666, 6 March 1953, p. 152

'The Critic and Society', Rev. of *The Responsibilities of the Critic* by F.O. Matthiessen, *Spectator*, vol. 190, no. 6,515, 8 May 1953, p. 582

'Drayton's Discovery of England', Rev. of *Poems of Michael Drayton*, *Times Literary Supplement*, no. 2,675, 8 May 1953, p. 303

'Appreciation of Milton', Rev. of *Milton's Act of Prosody* by S. Ernest Sprott, *Times Literary Supplement*, no. 2,676, 15 May 1953, p. 318

'A Study of Shakespeare', Rev. of *Shakespeare* by Henri Fluchère, *Spectator*, vol. 190, no. 6,516, 15 May 1953, pp. 648–50

'Donne and Milton', Rev. of *John Donne: the divine poems* edited by Helen Gardner and *The Poetical Works of John Milton* edited by Helen Darbishire, *Spectator*, vol. 190, no. 6,508, 20 May 1953, pp. 352–4

'Essay in Verse', Rev. of *Letter in a Bottle* by Gerald B. Walker, *Times Literary Supplement*, no. 2,682, 26 June 1953, p. 416

'The Clumsy Blue Bird', Rev. of *Selected Poems* by Idris Davis; *Famous Meeting* by Robert Gittings; *A Mask for Janus* by W.S. Merwin, *Spectator*, vol. 190, no. 6,522, 26 June 1953, p. 838

'Pastoral Poet', Rev. of *William Barnes of Dorset* by Giles Dugdale, *Times Literary Supplement*, no. 2,683, 3 July 1953, p. 430

'Young Poets and Writers', Rev. of *Springtime: an anthology of young poets and writers* edited by G.S. Fraser and Iain Fletcher, *Times Literary Supplement*, no. 2,684, 10 July 1953, p. 446

'Somewhat Like Poetry', Rev. of *The Singing Reel* by Moray McLaren, *Spectator*, vol. 191, no. 6,524, 10 July 1953, pp. 68–70

'Studying Poetry', Rev. of *The Anatomy of Poetry* by Marjorie Boulton, *Times Literary Supplement*, no. 2,687, 31 July 1953, p. 494

'The Mind of Coleridge', Rev. of *Coleridge: the Clark lectures, 1951–52* by Humphry House, *Spectator*, vol. 191, no. 6,527, 31 July 1953, pp. 133–4

'Wholesome!', Rev. of *J.P. Marquand, Esquire* by Philip Hamburger, *Spectator*, vol. 191, no. 6,533, 11 September 1953, p. 278

'The Art of the Translator', Rev. of *The Translations of Ezra Pound* by Ezra Pound, *Spectator*, vol. 191, no. 6,534, 18 September 1953, pp. 303–4

'The Sea! The Sea!', Rev. of *Journey into Wonder* by N.J. Berrill; *The Ocean River* by Henry Chapin and F.G. Walton Smith; *The Voyage of Waltzing Matilda* by Philip Davenport, *Spectator*, vol. 191, no. 65,36, 2 October 1953, pp. 372–3

'Random Pleasure', Rev. of *The Faber Book of Twentieth Century Verse* edited by John Heath-Stubbs and David Wright, *Spectator*, vol. 191, no. 6,542, 13 November 1953, pp. 543–4

'Landsman Hay', Rev. of *Memoirs of Robert Hay, 1789–1847* edited by M.D. Hay, *Listener*, vol. 50 no. 1,291, 26 November 1953, p. 917

'Impressions of Crete', Rev. of *The Stronghold* by Xan Fielding, *Spectator*, vol. 192, no. 6,550, 8 January 1954, pp. 49–50

'Ancient and Modern', Rev. of *The Winged Avengers: a verse drama* by David Bulwer Luytens, *Times Literary Supplement*, no. 2,738, 23 July 1954, p. 474

'A Life of Anecdotes', Rev. of *It Isn't This Time of Year at All* by Oliver St John Gogarty, *Spectator*, vol. 193, no. 6,586, 17 September 1954, pp. 346–8

'From the French', Rev. of *Selected Fables of La Fontaine* translated by Marianne Moore, *Times Literary Supplement*, no. 2,781, 17 June 1955, p. 331

'The Continual Sea', Rev. of *The Nightfishing* by W.S. Graham, *Times Literary Supplement*, no. 2,784, 8 July 1955, p. 379

'Three Modern Poets', *Listener*, vol. 54 no. 1,384, 8 Sept 1955, p. 373 [Theodore Roethke, Philip Larkin and Valentin Iremonger]

'Places and People', Rev. of *The River Steamer, and Other Poems* by E.J. Scovell, *Times Literary Supplement*, no. 2,830, 25 May 1956, p. 310

'The Atmosphere of Greece', Rev. of *Introducing Greece* edited by Francis King, *Times Literary Supplement*, no. 2,839, 27 July 1956, p. 452

'The Empty Tower at Ballylee', Rev. of *Explorations* by W.B. Yeats; *J.M. Synge, Collected Works, Vol 1: Poems*, ed. Robin Skelton; *The Dublin Diary of Stanislaus Joyce* ed. George Harris Healey, *Observer*, 7 October 1962, p. 29

'New Beauty from Old Clay', Rev of *Collected Poems* by Patrick Kavanagh, *New York Times Book Review*, 23 May 1965, p. 4

'Note on "The Reading Lesson"', in *Choice: an anthology of Irish poetry* edited by Desmond Egan and Michael Hartnett (The Curragh: Goldsmith Press, 1973), p. 92

'The Irish Situation', *New York Review of Books*, vol. 22, no. 6, 17 April 1975, p. 38 [reply by Richard Murphy to Donald Davie's review 'Cards of Identity', *New York Review of Books*, vol. 22, no. 3, 6 March 1975, pp. 10–11]

'The Art of Debunkery', Rev. of *High Windows* by Philip Larkin, *New York Review of Books*, vol. 22, no. 8, 15 May 1975, pp. 30–3. Repr. *The Snow Path: tracks*, no. 10, ed. John F. Deane (Dublin: Dedalus Press, 1994), pp. 87–96

'Poetry and Terror', Rev. of *North* by Seamus Heaney, *New York Review of Books*, vol. 23, no. 15, 30 September 1976, pp. 38–40. Repr. *Irish Pages*, vol. 8, no. 2, 2015, pp. 142–51 [Seamus Heaney Memorial Issue]

'To Celebrate Existence', Rev. of *Season Songs* by Ted Hughes, *Hibernia*, 17 December 1976, p. 20

'Fierce Games', Rev. of *Selected Poems 1950–1975* by Thom Gunn, *New York Review of Books*, vol. 27, no. 4, 20 March 1980, pp. 28–30

'Last Exit to Nature', Rev. of *New Selected Poems* by Ted Hughes; *Remains of Elmet* by Ted Hughes; *Cave Birds: an alchemical cave drama* by Ted Hughes; *Under the North Star* by Ted Hughes; *Moortown* by Ted Hughes, *New York Review of Books*, vol. 29, no. 10, 10 June 1982, pp. 38–40

'The Use of History in Poetry', in *The Uses of the Past: essays on Irish culture*, eds
   Audrey S. Eyler and Robert F. Garratt (Newark: University of Delaware Press,
   1988), pp. 19–23
'A Footnote on "The Strand"', in *The Mayo Anthology* edited by Richard Murphy
   (Castlebar: Mayo County Council, 1990), pp. 174–6
'Address to the International Writers' Conference in Dublin on 20th June 1991', in
   The Snow Path: tracks, no. 10, ed. John F. Deane (Dublin: Dedalus Press, 1994),
   pp. 97–101
'Foreword', in *Paintings by Anthony Murphy* by Anthony Murphy (Dublin:
   Jorgensen Fine Art, 2005), p. 2
'Crucial Collections: W.B. Yeats, *Last Poems* and Philip Larkin, *The Less Deceived*',
   Poetry Ireland Review, no. 86, May 2006, pp. 70–2
'Confronting Yeats', *Irish Pages*, vol. 4, no. 1, 2007, pp. 217–23 [a revised version
   of Richard Murphy's address at the opening of the 2007 Yeats International
   Summer School]
'Rejoice', *Poetry Ireland Review*, no. 116, September 2015, pp. 7–11 [abridged version
   of Richard Murphy's address to the 2007 Yeats International Summer School]

(iv) Interviews
With Isabel Healy, 'In Cleggan, Co. Galway, Isabel Healy Met Richard Murphy: a
   poet in a pink granite house', *Irish Press*, 3 November 1971, p. 9
With Rebecca Schull, 'Rebecca Schull Talks to the Poet Richard Murphy about His
   Recently Completed Additions to the W.B. Yeats Version of Sophocles' *King
   Oedipus* for the Abbey Theatre and About His Own Background', *Irish Times*,
   17 May 1973, p. 12
With John Boland, 'Relating to Our Past', *Irish Press*, 7 June 1973, p. 17
With Elgy Gillespie, 'Richard Murphy upon Omey', *Irish Times*, 21 November 1975,
   p. 10
With Cormac MacConnell, 'A Poet on His Own Island: annalist of the Galway
   hooker', *Irish Press*, 22 January 1976, p. 9
With Ciaran Carty, 'The Feel of a Real Person in a Real Place – That's Poetry',
   Sunday Independent, 4 March 1979, p. 29
With John Haffenden, 'Richard Murphy: a conversation in Connemara', *London
   Magazine*, vol. 19, no. 12, March 1980, pp. 9–23. Repr. in Haffenden, John,
   Viewpoints: poets in conversation with John Haffenden (London: Faber &
   Faber, 1981), pp. 143–56
With Fintan O'Toole, 'The Folly Became the Poem and It Turned Out To Be a
   Sonnet', *Sunday Tribune*, 17 July 1983, p. 12 ['Inside *Tribune*' section]
With Dennis O'Driscoll, 'Richard Murphy at Sixty', *Poetry Ireland Review*, no. 21,
   spring 1988, pp. 14–18
With Liam Robinson, 'Poet Who's at Home in Cleggan or Sri Lanka', *Irish Press*, 3
   June 1987, p. 8

With Licia Governatori, 'Il Fascino e il Mistero del Mare' ['The Fascination and Mystery of the Sea'], *Uomini e Libri: periodico bimestrale di critica ed informazione letteraria*, vol. 24, no. 121, 1988, pp. 15–16

With Rosita Boland, 'Embracing the World', *Irish Times*, 11 October 2000, p. 16

With David Wheatley, 'Richard Murphy: interview', *Metre*, no. 10, autumn 2001, pp. 141–55

With Shirley Kelly, 'The Ambition To Write a Poem Is Enough To Kill It', *Books Ireland*, no. 250, summer 2002, pp. 151–2

With Judy Murphy, 'Poet Richard Murphy Talks to Judy Murphy About His Life and Work, and His Funny, Quirky and Lyrical Memoir', *Irish Examiner*, 19 October 2002, pp. 92–3 [Weekend Supplement, pp. 28–9]

With Eugene O'Connell, 'Verse That Is Set in Stone', *Irish Times*, 14 August 2007, p. 13

With Ranga Chandrarathne, 'Meeting Richard Murphy: a true postcolonial?', *Sunday Observer*, 17 June 2007, http://archives.sundayobserver.lk/2007/06/17/spe02asp [accessed 29 September 2017]

With J.P. O'Malley, 'Interview with a Poet: Richard Murphy, an old *Spectator* hand', *Spectator*, 10 September 2013, https://blogs.spectator.co.uk/2013/09/interview-with-a-poet-richard-murphy-an-old-spectator-hand [accessed 29 September 2017]

With J.P. O'Malley, 'A Rebellious Son of the Ascendency Who Found His Voice in Connemara', *Irish Examiner*, 21 September 2013, p. 18

With Benjamin Keatinge, 'Richard Murphy in Sri Lanka: an interview', *Poetry Ireland Review*, no. 122, August 2017, pp. 86–93

WORKS ABOUT RICHARD MURPHY

(i) Books and Special Issues of Journals

Irish University Review: Richard Murphy special issue, ed. Maurice Harmon, vol. 7, no. 1, Spring 1977, pp. 1–117

[Contents: Maurice Harmon, 'Introduction: the poet and his background', pp. 7–10; Maurice Harmon, 'Biographical Note on Richard Murphy', pp. 11–17; Seamus Heaney, 'The Poetry of Richard Murphy', pp. 18–30; Richard Murphy, 'Seven Poems', pp. 31–5; J.G. Simms, 'The Battle of Aughrim: history and poetry', pp. 36–51; Michael Herity, 'The High Island Hermitage', pp. 52–69; Anthony Wilde, 'A Note on the Storm Petrel and Corncrake', pp. 70–2; Jonathan Williams, 'A Glossary to *The Battle of Aughrim* and *The God Who Eats Corn*', pp. 73–103; Mary FitzGerald, 'A Richard Murphy Bibliography', pp. 104–17]

Maurice Harmon (ed.), *Richard Murphy: a poet of two traditions* (Dublin: Wolfhound Press, 1978), 128pp

[Contents and pagination identical to *Irish University Review: Richard Murphy special issue* excepting two additional items: Maurice Harmon 'Editor's Preface', p. 6 and Maurice Harmon, 'Beginning With Words', pp. 118–28]

John F. Deane (ed.), 'Richard Murphy Special Feature', in *The Snow Path: tracks*, no. 10 (Dublin: Dedalus Press, 1994), pp. 61–138

[Contents: Rand Brandes, 'Drafting *The Price of Stone*: Richard Murphy's manuscripts for "Beehive Cell"', pp. 62–84; Eamon Grennan, 'Sense of Place', pp. 85–6; Richard Murphy, 'The Art of Debunkery', pp. 87–96; Richard Murphy, 'Address to the International Writers' Conference in Dublin on 20th June 1991', pp. 97–101; Richard Murphy, 'On Writing "The God Who Eats Corn"', pp. 102–8; Richard Murphy, 'The God Who Eats Corn', pp. 109–15; Joseph Sendry, 'The Poet as Interpreter: Richard Murphy's *The Mirror Wall*', pp. 116–38]

David Wheatley, Justin Quinn and Dennis O'Driscoll (eds), 'Richard Murphy Special Feature', *Metre*, no. 10, autumn 2001, pp. 127–55

[Contents: Thomas Kinsella, 'For Richard Murphy', p. 128; Jill Siddall, 'Grotesquely Free, Though Ruled by Symmetry', pp. 129–34; Declan Kiberd, 'Richard Murphy and Casement's Funeral', pp. 135–7; Bernard O'Donoghue, 'The Lost Link: Richard Murphy's early poetry', pp. 138–40; David Wheatley, 'Richard Murphy: interview', pp. 141–55]

(ii) Scholarly Articles: Book chapters

Edna Longley, 'Searching the Darkness: the poetry of Richard Murphy, Thomas Kinsella, John Montague, and James Simmons', in *Two Decades of Irish Writing: a critical survey*, ed. Douglas Dunn (Cheadle: Carcanet Press, 1975), pp. 118–53

James J. Lafferty, 'Perceptions of Roots: the historical dichotomy of Ireland as reflected in Richard Murphy's *The Battle of Aughrim* and John Montague's *The Rough Field*', in *Studies in Anglo-Irish Literature*, ed. Heinz Kosok (Bonn: Bouvier Verlag Herbert Grundmann, 1982), pp. 399–410

James D. Brophy, 'Richard Murphy: poet of nostalgia or *pietas?*', in *Contemporary Irish Writing*, eds James D. Brophy and Raymond J. Porter (Boston: Twayne, 1983), pp. 49–64

Terence Brown, 'Poets and Patrimony: Richard Murphy and James Simmons', in *Across the Roaring Hill: the Protestant imagination in modern Ireland*, eds Gerald Dawe and Edna Longley (Belfast: Blackstaff Press, 1985), pp. 182–95. Repr. Terence Brown, *Ireland's Literature* (Mullingar: The Lilliput Press, 1988), pp. 189–202

John Wilson Foster, 'The Landscape of Three Irelands: Hewitt, Murphy and Montague', in *Colonial Consequences: essays in Irish literature and culture*, by John Wilson Foster (Dublin: The Lilliput Press, 1991), pp. 149–67. Repr. *Contemporary Irish Poetry: a collection of critical essays*, ed. Elmer Andrews (Basingstoke: Macmillan, 1992), pp. 145–67. Repr. *Well Dreams: essays on John*

Montague, ed. Thomas Dillon Redshaw (Omaha, NE: Creighton University Press, 2004), pp. 95–112

Rand Brandes, 'A Shaping Music: Richard Murphy's *The Price of Stone*', in *Poetry in Contemporary Irish Literature*, ed. Michael Kenneally (Gerrards Cross: Colin Smythe, 1995), pp. 190–203

Eamon Grennan, 'Riddling Free: Richard Murphy's *The Price of Stone*', in *Facing the Music: Irish poetry in the twentieth century* by Eamon Grennan (Omaha, NE: Creighton University Press, 1999), pp. 232–40

Justin Quinn, 'Ireland's Empire: Richard Murphy, Derek Mahon, Michael Longley', in *The Cambridge Introduction to Modern Irish Poetry 1800–2000* (Cambridge: Cambridge University Press, 2008), pp. 113–29

Benjamin Keatinge, '"My Form Is Epicene": sexual ambiguity in the poetry of Richard Murphy', in *Essays in Irish Literary Criticism: themes of gender, sexuality, and corporeality*, eds Deirdre Quinn and Sharon Tighe-Mooney (Lampeter: Edwin Mellen Press, 2008), pp. 19–38

Eamonn Wall, 'Wings Beating on Stone: Richard Murphy's Ecology', in *Out of the Earth: ecocritical readings of Irish texts*, ed. Christine Cusick (Cork: Cork University Press, 2010), pp. 5–19. Repr. *Writing the Irish West: ecologies and traditions*, by Eamonn Wall (Notre Dame, IN: University of Notre Dame Press, 2011), pp. 51–69

Benjamin Keatinge, 'France, Ireland and the Jacobite Cause in Richard Murphy's *The Battle of Aughrim*', in *France and Ireland: notes and narratives*, eds Una Hunt and Mary Pierse (Bern: Peter Lang, 2015), pp. 159–76

John Goodby, 'Richard Murphy: last of the Anglo-Irish?', in *Irish Poetry Since 1950: from stillness into history* by John Goodby (Manchester: Manchester University Press, 2000), pp. 80–7

Benjamin La Farge, 'Richard Murphy', in *British Writers: supplement 5*, eds George Stade and Sarah Hannah Goldstein (New York: Charles Scribner's Sons, 1999), pp. 313–31

Benjamin Keatinge, 'Richard Murphy', in *The Cambridge Companion to Irish Poets*, ed. Gerald Dawe (Cambridge: Cambridge University Press, 2017), pp. 211–23

Benjamin Keatinge, 'The Archaeology of Love: Richard Murphy's Greece', in *Landscapes of Irish and Greek Poets: essays, poems, interviews*, ed. Joanna Kruczkowska (Oxford and Bern: Peter Lang, 2017), pp. 51–69

(iii) Scholarly Articles: Journals

Dennis O'Driscoll, 'The Poetry of Richard Murphy', *Poetry Australia*, no. 71, August 1979, pp. 70–5

Mark Kilroy, 'Richard Murphy's Connemara Locale', *Éire-Ireland*, vol. 15, no. 3, autumn 1980, pp. 127–34

Neal Bowers, 'Richard Murphy: the landscape of the mind', *Journal of Irish Literature*, vol. 11, no. 3, September 1982, pp. 33–42

Julian Moynihan, '*The Battle of Aughrim*: a commentary', *Irish University Review*, vol. 13, no. 1, spring 1983, pp. 103–13 [special issue: The Long Poem]

Joseph Sendry, 'The Poet as Builder: Richard Murphy's *The Price of Stone*', *Irish University Review*, vol. 15, no. 1, spring 1985, pp. 38–49

Terence Dewsnap, 'Richard Murphy's *Apologia*: The Price of Stone', *Canadian Journal of Irish Studies*, vol. 22, no. 1, July 1996, pp. 71–86

Elsa Meihuizen, 'Richard Murphy: a life in writing', *Literator*, vol. 27, no. 3, December 2006, pp. 157–74

Joseph Swann, 'The Historian, the Critic and the Poet: a reading of Richard Murphy's poetry and some questions of theory', *Canadian Journal of Irish Studies*, vol. 16, no. 1, July 1990, pp. 33–47

Bernard O'Donoghue, '"Pat Cloherty's Version of *The Maisie*", Richard Murphy', *Poems that Matter: 1950–2000*, ed. Peter Denman, *Irish University Review*, vol. 39, no. 2, autumn/winter 2009, pp. 239–45 Repr. *The Pleasure Ground: Poems 1952–2012*, by Richard Murphy (Tarset: Bloodaxe, 2013), pp. 273–9

Nicholas Meihuizen, 'The Poet, the Philosopher and the Birds: narrative, self and repetition in Richard Murphy', *English Academy Review: South African Journal of English Studies*, vol. 28, no. 1, 2011, pp. 53–63

Elsa Meihuizen, 'Richard Murphy: autobiography and the Connemara landscape', *Literator*, vol. 36, no. 2, August 2015, unpaginated, 7pp.

Robert Jocelyn, 'Living in a Dream: Richard Murphy and Connemara', *Galway Review*, no. 6, 2018, pp. 50–8

Benjamin Keatinge, 'Richard Murphy: a river of notebooks', *Agenda*, vol. 52, nos 1–2 (November 2018), pp. 135–8

Benjamin Keatinge, 'Murphy's Uncollected Poems: afterword', *Archipelago*, no. 12 spring 2019 , pp. 9–11

(iv) Selected Reviews: Early poems in anthologies, Dolmen editions and *The Archaeology of Love* (1955)

Thomas Kinsella, 'A Notable Irish Poet', *Irish Press*, 31 December 1955, p. 4 [review of *The Archaeology of Love*]

G.S. Fraser, 'Landscape Poetry', *Times Literary Supplement*, no. 2,813, 27 January 1956, p. 54 [review of *The Archaeology of Love*]

Donald S. Carne-Ross, 'Seventy-four Poets', *Times Literary Supplement*, no. 2,852, 26 October 1956, p. 635 [review of *Poetry Now: an anthology*, ed. G.S. Fraser, 1956]

John Hewitt, 'Poetry Review', *Threshold*, vol. 3, no. 2, summer 1959, pp. 92–6 [review of *The Woman of the House: an elegy*, 1959]

Richard Kell, 'Freedom-Preserving Disciplines', *Guardian*, 22 September 1961, p. 8 [review of *The Last Galway Hooker: a poem*, 1961]

Rudi Holzapfel, *The Kilkenny Magazine*, no. 5, autumn/winter 1961, p. 59 [review of *The Last Galway Hooker: a poem*, 1961]

John Hewitt, 'Poems and Verses from Ireland', *Threshold*, vol. 5, no. 2, autumn/ winter 1961–2), pp. 75–81 [review of *The Last Galway Hooker: a poem*, 1961]

(v) Selected Reviews: Sailing to an Island (Faber & Faber, 1963); *Sailing to an Island* (Chilmark Press, 1963)

Margaret Stanley Wrench, 'The Poet and the Sea', *Irish Times*, 23 February 1963, p. 8

P.N. Furbank, 'New Poetry', *Listener*, vol. 69, no. 1,771, 7 March 1963, p. 435

Austin Clarke, 'Verse from the Western World', *Irish Press*, 9 March 1963, p. 4

Norman MacCraig, 'Soaking Acorns', *New Statesman*, vol. 65, no. 1,670, 15 March 1963, pp. 387–8

Richard Kell, 'Plain Sailing', *Guardian*, 22 March 1963, p. 9

I[sabel] H[ealy], 'Tang of the Sea', *Irish Independent*, 13 April 1963, p. 12

Anon., 'Of Sea and Ships and Sailors', *Cork Examiner*, 13 June 1963, p. 4

Seamus Heaney, '"The Immortal Newsmen"', *Hibernia*, vol. 27, no. 7, July 1963, p. 17

George MacBeth, [untitled] *London Magazine*, vol. 3, no. 4, July 1963, pp. 87 9

Graham Martin, 'Recent Irish Poetry', *Review*, no. 8, August 1963, pp. 18–32

D.H.S., [untitled] *Dubliner*, vol. 2, no. 2, summer 1963, pp. 88–90

Thomas Lask, 'Books of the Times: end papers', *New York Times*, 25 October 1963, p. 29

Bruce Arnold, [untitled] *Books Abroad*, vol. 37, no. 4, autumn 1963, pp. 453–4

M.L. Rosenthal, 'Surrender to Despair', *New York Times Book Review*, 22 December 1963, pp. 4–5

Augustine Martin, [untitled] *Studies: an Irish quarterly review*, vol. 53, no. 109, spring 1964, pp. 95–9

Lorna Reynolds, [untitled] *University Review*, vol. 3, no. 4, spring 1964, pp. 60–1

John Flatley, 'Book Reviews', *Connaught Tribune*, 6 September 1968, p. 7

(vi) Selected Reviews: *The Battle of Aughrim* (Faber & Faber, 1968) and *The Battle of Aughrim* (Alfred A. Knopf, 1968)

Augustine Martin, 'Harvest of Poems', *Irish Press*, 5 October 1968, p. 10

P.J. Kavanagh, 'Love, Truth, and Ruth', *Guardian*, 11 October 1968, p. 9

John MacInerney, 'Richard Murphy: a search for identity', *St Stephen's*, vol. 2, no. 15 (Michaelmas Term 1968), pp. 29–34

Denis Donoghue, 'Digging for Ireland', *Times Literary Supplement*, no. 3,484, 5 December 1968, p. 1386

Gavin Ewart, 'Old Scores', *London Magazine*, vol. 8, no. 9, December 1968, pp. 92–5

John Jordan, 'Temps Perdu', *Hibernia*, vol. 32, no. 15, 13 December 1968, p. 18

Eavan Boland, 'Swift and Aughrim', *Irish Times*, 1 March 1969, p. 10

Stephen Wall, 'Chairing the Bard', *Review*, no. 20, March 1969, pp. 57–61

Padraic Colum, 'A War Won by Chance and Treachery', *New York Times Book Review*, 2 March 1969, p. 10

Basil Payne, 'Special Review: new poetry', *Studies: an Irish quarterly review*, vol. 58, no. 229, spring 1969, pp. 74–8

Daniel Hoffman, 'Constraints and Self-determinations', *Poetry*, vol. 114, no. 5, August 1969, pp. 335–44

Serge Faucherau, 'Tradition et Révolution dans la Poésie Irlandaise', *Critique*, no. 276, May 1970, pp. 438–56 [in French]

(vii) Selected Reviews: Sophocles, *Oedipus the King*, directed by Michael Cacoyannis with textual revisions by Richard Murphy, *Abbey Theatre*, Dublin, April 1973

Séamus Kelly [Quidnunc], 'An Irishman's Diary', *Irish Times*, 4 April 1973, p. 11

John Boland, 'Bouquets for Cacoyannis: superb playing at the Abbey', *Irish Press*, 5 April 1973, p. 3

Charles Lewsen, 'Cacoyannis Shows Little Daring', *The Times* [London], 6 April 1973, p. 15.

Rebecca Schull, 'The Preparation of *King Oedipus*', *Arts in Ireland*, vol. 2, no. 1, 1973, pp. 15–21

Desmond Rushe, 'Tatler's Parade: invisible mending', *Irish Independent*, 10 April 1973, p. 10

(viii) Selected Reviews: *High Island* (Faber & Faber, 1974) and *High Island: new and selected poems* (Harper & Row, 1974)

Brendan Kennelly, 'The Magic of the West', *Sunday Independent*, 8 December 1974, p. 16

Eavan Boland, 'Two Poets', *Irish Times*, 21 December 1974, p. 10

Robert Johnstone, 'Living in the Real World', *Fortnight*, no. 96, January 1975, p. 15

Colin Falck, 'Leaving Something Behind', *New Review*, vol. 1, no. 11, February 1975, pp. 69–71

Terry Eagleton, 'Reverberations', *Tablet*, vol. 229, no. 7,024, 15 February 1975, pp. 154–5

Donald Davie, 'Cards of Identity', *New York Review of Books*, vol. 22, no. 3, 6 March 1975, pp. 10–11

Roger Garfitt, 'Ceylon and Elsewhere', *London Magazine*, vol. 15, no. 1, April/May 1975, pp. 86–90

Maurice Harmon, [untitled] *Irish University Review*, vol. 5, no. 1, spring 1975, pp. 201–2

John Montague, 'Irish Landscape, with Myths', *Times Literary Supplement*, no. 3,825, 4 July 1975, p. 718

Seamus Deane, 'The Appetites of Gravity: contemporary Irish poetry', *Sewanee Review*, vol. 84, no. 1, winter 1976, pp. 199–208

Patrick King, [untitled] *Studies: an Irish quarterly review*, vol. 65, no. 257, spring 1976, pp. 80–2

Marianne Levander, [untitled] *Moderna Språk*, vol. 71, 1977, pp. 63–5 [in English]

(ix) Selected Reviews: *Selected Poems* (Faber & Faber, 1979)

Ciaran Carty, 'The Truth of What Happens', *Sunday Independent*, 4 March 1979, p. 29

Neil Corcoran, 'Poems Like Chrysanthemums', *PN Review 11*, vol. 6, no. 3, September 1980, pp. 56–7

Seamus Deane, 'The Long Ascendancy', *Honest Ulsterman*, no. 66, July/October 1980, pp. 66–9

(x) Selected Reviews: *The Price of Stone* (Faber & Faber, 1985)

Thomas McCarthy, 'Monument to Inner Space', *Irish Times*, 22 June 1985, p. 14

James Simmons, 'Sermons in Bricks and Mortar', *Fortnight*, no. 222, June/July 1985, p. 14

Terry Eagleton, 'From the Irish', *Poetry Review*, vol. 75, no. 2, August 1985, pp. 64–5

Peter Porter, 'Aussie Doom Watch', *Observer*, 11 August 1985, p. 21

Robert Greacen, 'Echoes from the Big House', *Books Ireland*, no. 97, October 1985, p. 169

Peter Denman, 'Allusive and Aloof, Quizzical and Detached', *Irish Literary Supplement*, vol. 4, no. 2, fall 1985, p. 15

Seán Dunne, 'Singing to the Stones', *Irish Press*, 2 November 1985, p. 9

Denis Donoghue, 'Ten Poets', *London Review of Books*, vol. 7, no. 19, November 1985, pp. 20–2

Bernard O'Donoghue, 'Structurally Speaking', *Times Literary Supplement*, no. 4,314, 6 December 1985, p. 1405

Eamon Grennan, 'Riddling Free', *Poetry Ireland Review*, no. 15, winter 1985–6, pp. 10–16

John Mole, 'Conceit and Concern', *Encounter*, vol. 66, no. 1, January 1986, pp. 55–61

Thomas D'Evelyn, 'A Builder of "Sound" Buildings', *Christian Science Monitor*, 16 April 1986, p. 21

Tom Clyde, 'Continuing the Slow Implosion', *Honest Ulsterman*, no. 81, spring/summer 1986, pp. 76–8

(xi) Selected Reviews: *The Price of Stone and Earlier Poems* (Wake Forest University Press, 1985) *New Selected Poems* (Faber & Faber, 1989), and *The Mirror Wall* (Wolfhound Press / Bloodaxe, 1989)

Robert J. Garratt, 'A Prize from Wake Forest Press', *Irish Literary Supplement*, vol. 5, no. 2, Fall 1986, p. 26

Seán Dunne, 'Uncovering Old, Rich Springs', *Cork Examiner*, 20 May 1989, p. 12

Ronnie Wathen, 'Among the Voluptuous Rocks', *Irish Independent*, 20 May 1989, p. 12

Peter Sirr, 'The Voyage Out', *Irish Times*, 24 June 1989, p. 28

Peter Denman, 'Archaelogies of Love' [*sic*], *Poetry Ireland Review*, no. 26, summer 1989, pp. 55–9

Sean O'Brien, 'Living Afterwards', *Times Literary Supplement*, no. 4,505, 4 August 1989, p. 850

Sam Burnside, 'Quiet Devotion to an Ideal', *Honest Ulsterman*, no. 87, summer/autumn 1989, pp. 76–9

Peter McDonald, 'Chalk and Cheese', *Irish Review*, no. 7, autumn 1989, pp. 92–7

James Simmons, 'Poetry Miscellany', *Linen Hall Review*, vol. 6, no. 2, autumn 1989, pp. 30–1

Leon McAuley, 'Lower-case Capitals Sound a Warning', *Fortnight*, no. 278, November 1989, p. 25

Brendan Hammill, 'Darkness Brightening', *Books Ireland*, no. 142, summer 1990, p. 109

Antoinette Quinn, 'Aughrim in Sri Lanka', *New Nation*, no. 7, 1989, p. 20

Neil Corcoran, 'Neil Corcoran Confronts the New Recklessness', *London Review of Books*, vol. 11, no. 18, September 1989, pp. 14–15

Thomas McCarthy, 'Perfect Pitch in a Poetic Voice', *Fortnight*, no. 276, September 1989, p. 25

Andrew Waterman, 'Golden Girls', *PN Review 71*, vol. 16, no. 3, January/February 1990, pp. 54–5

(xii) Selected Reviews: *Collected Poems 1952–2000* (Gallery Press/Wake Forest University Press, 2000)

Gerald Dawe, 'A Geography of the Mind', *Irish Times*, 11 November 2000, p. 53 [Weekend Supplement, p. 13].

Fred Johnston, 'Rooting Out the Rural', *Books Ireland*, no. 236, December 2000, pp. 354–5

John Boland, [untitled] *World of Hibernia*, vol. 6, no. 4, spring 2001, p. 16

Michael Leddy, [untitled] *World Literature Today*, vol. 75, nos. 3–4, summer/autumn 2001, pp. 155–6

Jill Siddall, 'Grotesquely Free, Though Ruled by Symmetry', *Metre*, no. 10, autumn 2001, pp. 129–34

Christina Hunt Mahony, [untitled] *Canadian Journal of Irish Studies*, vol. 27, no. 2 / vol. 28, no. 1, autumn/spring 2001–02, pp. 149–50

Justin Quinn, 'The Weather of Irish Poetry', *Sewanee Review*, vol. 111, no. 3, summer 2003, pp. 486–92

Floyd Skloot, [untitled] *Harvard Review*, no. 23, autumn 2002, pp. 171–3

Joseph Sendry, 'No Room for Wasted Effort', *Poetry Ireland Review*, no. 72, spring 2002, pp. 50–2

(xiii) Selected Reviews: *The Kick: a life among writers* (Granta, 2002/2003); *The Kick: a memoir of the poet Richard Murphy* (Cork University Press, 2017)

Stephen Dodd, 'A Kick from the Heart of the West', *Sunday Independent*, 19 May 2002, p. 82 [Living Supplement, p. 16]. Repr. as 'Richard Murphy', *Sunday Independent*, 4 February 2018, p. 28

John Montague, 'A Kick out of You', *Irish Times*, 22 June 2002, p. 44 [Weekend Supplement, p. 8].

Ruth Padel, 'He Misconstrued the Shepherd's Affection', *Literary Review*, no. 288, June 2002, pp. 37–8

Karl Miller, 'No-good Boyo Scores Elegantly', *Spectator*, vol. 289, no. 9,072, 22 June 2002, pp. 47–8

Ronan Farren, 'The Poet Lives on as Rebel and Man of Action', *Sunday Independent*, 21 July 2002, p. 18

Ciaran Carson, 'Murphy's Lore', *Guardian*, 3 August 2002, p. B10

Robert Greacen, 'Conventional Rebel', *Books Ireland*, no. 251, September 2002, pp. 202–4

Patrick Crotty, 'What a Strange Boy You Are', *Times Literary Supplement*, no. 5,192, 4 October 2002, pp. 26–7

John Banville, 'Keeping Busy', *New York Review of Books*, vol. 50, no. 8, 15 May 2003, pp. 33–5

Robert Tracy, 'A Vanished World', *Irish Literary Supplement*, vol. 23, no. 2, September 2003, pp. 23–4

Tara Stubbs, 'The Kick: a memoir of the poet', *Irish Studies Review*, vol. 26, no. 2, 2018, pp. 294–6

(xiv) Selected Reviews: *The Pleasure Ground: poems 1952–2012* (Bloodaxe Books, 2013); *Poems 1952–2012* (The Lilliput Press, 2013)

Michael Longley, 'The Lifelong Devotion of Richard Murphy', *Irish Times*, 17 August 2013, p. 45 [Weekend Supplement, p. 11]

Gerald Dawe, 'Outlasting Fashion', *Dublin Review of Books*, no. 43, October 2013, http://www.drb.ie/essays/outlasting-fashion [accessed 30 July 2017]

Peter Sirr, 'The Pleasure Ground', *Poetry Ireland Review*, no. 111, December 2013, pp. 134–6

Joseph Heininger, 'Memory and Imagination in Richard Murphy', *Irish Literary Supplement*, vol. 36, no. 2, spring 2017, p. 24

(xv) Selected Reviews: *In Search of Poetry* (Clutag Press, 2017)

Peter Sirr, 'In Search of Richard Murphy', *Irish Times*, p. 52 [Weekend Supplement, p. 12]

Peter Sirr, 'Stone Mad', *Poetry Ireland Review*, no. 122, August 2017, pp. 30–2

Benjamin Keatinge, 'In Search of Richard Murphy', *Dublin Review of Books*, no. 101, June 2018, http://drb.ie/essays/in-search-of-richard-murphy [accessed 21 June 2018]

(xvi) Other

Timothy Brownlow, 'Poet and Gentleman', *Hibernia*, vol. 31, no. 2, February 1967, p. 22

John Jordan, 'Magazine Scene', *Irish Press*, 30 June 1977, p. 6 [review of Maurice Harmon, ed., *Irish University Review: Richard Murphy special issue*, vol. 7, no. 1, spring 1977, pp. 1–117]

Gerard Smyth, 'Making of a Poet', *Irish Times*, 22 July 1978, p. 11 [review of Maurice Harmon, ed., *Richard Murphy: poet of two traditions*]

Paul Durcan, 'The Voyage of Richard Murphy', *Cork Examiner*, 30 April 1979, p. 6

Paul Durcan, 'The Voyage of Richard Murphy', *Cork Examiner*, 8 May 1979, p. 8 [different from article of same title listed above; review of Maurice Harmon, ed., *Richard Murphy: poet of two traditions*]

Gerald Dawe, 'Readings in Holland, *Irish Times*, 22 October 1981, p. 12

Richard J. Scott, *The Galway Hookers: working sailboats of Galway Bay* (Swords, Co. Dublin: Ward River Press, 1983), 127pp [contains information and photos of Richard Murphy's boats, the *Ave Maria* and the *True Light*]

Michael Viney, 'Names in the Landscape', *Irish Times*, 6 July 1985, p. 11 [a consideration of Tim Robinson's cartography of Connemara with reference to *The Price of Stone*]

Anon., 'Island Offered to Nation', *Connaught Tribune*, 18 October 1985, p. 1 [about Richard Murphy's offer to gift High Island to the Irish state]

Maurice Harmon, 'Richard Murphy', in *Dictionary of Literary Biography*, ed. Vincent Sherry, Jr (Detroit, MI: Gale Research Company, 1985) pp. 405–10

George Hetherington, 'Wittgenstein in Ireland: an account of his various visits from 1934 to 1949', *Irish University Review*, vol. 17, no. 2, autumn 1987, pp. 169–86

Daniel G. Marowski and Roger Matuz (eds), 'Richard Murphy 1927–', in *Contemporary Literary Criticism, vol. 41* (Detroit, MI: Gale Research Company, 1987), pp. 310–21 [digest and extracts of criticism and reviews of Richard Murphy's poetry to 1987]

Siobhan Dunlevy, 'Personality Profile: Richard Murphy', *Mayo News*, 28 March 1990, p. 10 [profile published on the occasion of Richard Murphy's appointment by Mayo County Council as writer-in-residence]

Fred Johnston, 'Reasonable Subjects', *Poetry Ireland Review*, no. 34, spring 1992, pp. 62–7 [review of Richard Murphy, ed., *The Mayo Anthology*]

Kellie Donovan Wilson, 'Richard Murphy (1927–)', in *Modern Irish Writers: a bio-critical sourcebook*, ed. Alexander G. Gonzalez (Westport, CT: Greenwood Press, 1997), pp. 258–62

Richard Wall, 'Rosroe, *Déjà Vu*. As Sole Inhabitant of the House by the Quay', in *Wittgenstein in Ireland* (London: Reaktion, 2000), pp. 83–105

Maurice Harmon, 'Richard Murphy: in good form', *Poetry Ireland News*, September/October 2007, unpaginated [p. 4]

Tim Robinson, 'Plague and Purity', in *Connemara: the last pool of darkness* (London: Penguin, 2008), pp. 195–208 [chapter on Richard Murphy and High Island]

Maria Johnston, 'Sylvia Plath's Vital Presence in Contemporary Irish Poetry', *Plath Profiles*, vol. 2, summer 2009, pp. 8-34

Gail Crowther, '"The wild beauty I found there": Plath's Connemara', *Plath Profiles*, vol. 4, summer 2011, pp. 208–19

The Other Irish Travellers, documentary film directed by Fiona Murphy, Journeyman Pictures, 2012

Emmanuel Kehoe, 'The Other Island of the Anglo-Irish', *Sunday Business Post*, 23 December 2012, pp. 38–9 [review of *The Other Irish Travellers* by Fiona Murphy, broadcast on BBC Four, 16 December 2012]

Joe Kennedy, 'Sea Gypsies Mew in the Night', *Sunday Independent*, 23 June 2013, p. 35 [some background to the poem 'Stormpetrel']

John Burnside, 'Special Commendation for *The Pleasure Ground: poems 1952–2012* by Richard Murphy', *Bulletin of the Poetry Book Society*, summer 2013, p. 17

His Chosen Islands, radio documentary produced by Julien Clancy and Claire Cunningham, Rockfinch Productions, 2017 [first broadcast on Friday, 4 August 2017 at 7pm on RTÉ Lyric FM]

Gerald Dawe, 'Richard Murphy at 90: a poet of other people', *Irish Times*, 23 October 2017, https://www.irishtimes.com/culture/books/richard-murphy-at-90-a-poet-of-other-people-13265705 [accessed 10 November 2017]

Sam Miller, *Fathers* (London: Jonathan Cape, 2017) [contains information on friendship between Richard Murphy and Tony White]

John Fanning, 'Wittgenstein in Ireland: the Irish poetic response', *Galway Review*, no. 6, 2018, pp. 63–71

(xvii) Obituaries and Tributes

Martin Doyle, 'President Leads Tributes to Poet Richard Murphy', *Irish Times*, 31 January 2018, https://www.irishtimes.com/culture/books/president-leads-tributes-to-poet-richard-murphy-13375383 [accessed 21 June 2018]

Tributes from: President Michael D. Higgins, Mary O'Malley, Theo Dorgan, Bernard O'Donoghue, Caitríona O'Reilly, Eiléan Ní Chuilleanáin, Maria Johnston, Ben Keatinge, Jessica Traynor, Christine Murray, Maureen Kennelly, Thomas McCarthy, Eavan Boland, Maurice Harmon, Gerald Dawe, Peter Sirr, John McAuliffe, Frank Shovlin, Mike Collins, Michael Longley.

'Poet and Aosdána Member Richard Murphy Dies', *Irish Times*, 1 February 2018, p. 9 [News]

'Anglo-Irish Poet Who Wrote to Unite', *Irish Times*, 3 February 2018, p. 12 [obituary]

'Standing Apart', *Irish Times*, 3 February 2018, p. 15 [editorial]

'Richard Murphy and the Apples of Thoor Ballylee', *Yeats Thoor Ballylee Society*, 7 February 2018, https://yeatsthoorballylee.org/2018/02/07/richard-murphy-and-the-apples-of-thoor-ballylee [accessed 21 June 2018] [tribute]

Michael Viney, 'How the West Gave a Poet His Dream and Identity', *Irish Times*, 17 February 2018, p. 47 [Weekend Supplement, p. 7]

'Richard Murphy, Poet', *Herald* [Glasgow], 17 February 2018, http://www.heraldscotland.com/news/16029497Obituary_-_Richard_Murphy__poet [accessed 21 June 2018] [obituary]

'Anglo-Irish Poet who Berated the Colonial System and was Troubled by a Sexual Ambivalence', *Daily Telegraph*, 26 February 2018, p. 27 [obituary]

'Acclaimed Irish Poet Whose Marriage Was Open and Loyalties Divided', *The Times* [Ireland edition], 10 March 2018, p. 30 [obituary]

'Acclaimed Anglo-Irish Poet with Loyalties that Were Divided and Companionable Ways that Were Appreciated by Men and Women Alike', *The Times* [UK edition], 12 March 2018, p. 49 [obituary]

Benjamin Keatinge, 'Richard Murphy 1927–2018', *Dublin Review of Books*, no. 98, March 2018, http://drb.ie/essays/richard-murphy-1927-2018 [accessed 21 June 2018] [tribute]

Mary O'Malley, 'Richard Murphy', *PN Review 240*, vol. 44, no. 4, March–April 2018, pp. 3–4 [tribute]

Benjamin Keatinge, 'His Chosen Islands: Richard Murphy', *Orbis*, no. 185, autumn 2018, p. 33 [tribute]

Gerald Dawe, 'To Stay for Ever: remembering Richard Murphy', *Poetry Ireland Review*, no. 127, April 2019, pp. 72–4 [tribute]

Works Cited

INTRODUCTION

Ackerley, J.R., *The Letters of J.R. Ackerley*, ed. Neville Braybrooke (London: Gerald Duckworth & Company Ltd, 1975)

Brown, Terence, 'Poets and Patrimony: Richard Murphy and James Simmons', in *Ireland's Literature* (Mullingar: The Lilliput Press, 1988), pp. 189–202

Bushe, Paddy (ed.), *Voices at the World's Edge: Irish poets on Skellig Michael* (Dublin: Dedalus Press, 2013)

Crotty, Patrick (ed.), *Modern Irish Poetry: an anthology* (Belfast: Blackstaff Press, 1995)

Dawe, Gerald, 'Anecdotes Over a Jar', in *The Proper Word: collected criticism*, ed. Nicholas Allen (Omaha, NE: Creighton University Press, 2007), pp. 107–16

Dawe, Gerald, 'Richard Murphy at 90: a poet of other people', *Irish Times*, 23 October 2017, online edition

Doyle, Martin, 'President Leads Tributes to Poet Richard Murphy', *Irish Times*, 31 January 2018, online edition

Gillespie, Elgy, 'Richard Murphy upon Omey', *Irish Times*, 21 November 1975, p. 10

Haffenden, John, *Viewpoints: poets in conversation with John Haffenden* (London: Faber & Faber, 1981)

Longley, Edna, 'Searching the Darkness: Richard Murphy, Thomas Kinsella, John Montague and James Simmons', in *Two Decades of Irish Writing: a critical survey*, ed. Douglas Dunn (Cheadle: Carcanet Press, 1975), pp. 118–53

Longley, Michael, 'The West', in *One Wide Expanse: writings from the Ireland Chair of Poetry* (Dublin: UCD Press, 2015), pp. 43–62

O'Malley, Mary, *Where the Rocks Float* (Cliffs of Moher: Salmon Poetry, 1993)

O'Malley, Mary, *Asylum Road* (Cliffs of Moher: Salmon Poetry, 2001)

O'Malley, Mary, *The Boning Hall: new and selected poems* (Manchester: Carcanet Press, 2002)

Randolph, Jody Allen (ed.), *Close to the Next Moment: interviews from a changing Ireland* (Manchester: Carcanet Press, 2010)

DIVISION AND DISTRESS IN THE POETRY OF RICHARD MURPHY

Murphy, Richard, 'Notes for Sonnets', *Poetry Ireland Review*, no. 104, September 2011, pp. 92–104

Murphy, Richard, 'Transgressing into Poetry', *Poetry Ireland Review*, no. 107, September 2012, pp. 26–36

Murphy, Richard, 'Transgressing into Poetry', *Poetry Ireland Review*, no. 111, December 2013, pp. 117–33

Murphy, Richard, *In Search of Poetry* (Thame: Clutag Press, 2017)

Schull, Rebecca, 'Rebecca Schull Talks to the Poet Richard Murphy About His Recently Completed Additions to the W.B. Yeats Version of Sophocles' *King Oedipus* for the Abbey Theatre and About His Own Background', *Irish Times*, 17 May 1973, p. 12

RICHARD MURPHY'S PLAINSTYLES

Davie, Donald, 'Cards of Identity', *New York Review of Books*, vol. 22, no. 3, 6 March 1975, pp. 10–11

Gregory, Augusta, *Seventy Years: being the autobiography of Lady Gregory*, ed. Colin Smythe (Gerrards Cross: Colin Smythe, 1974)

Heaney, Seamus, *New Selected Poems 1966-1987* (London: Faber & Faber, 1990)

Kavanagh, Patrick, *A Poet's Country: selected prose*, ed. Antoinette Quinn (Dublin: The Lilliput Press, 2003)

Murphy, Richard, *The Mirror Wall* (Dublin: Wolfhound Press, 1989)

O'Donoghue, Bernard, '"Pat Cloherty's Version of *The Maisie*", Richard Murphy', in 'Poems that Matter: 1950–2000', ed. Peter Denman, *Irish University Review*, vol. 39, no. 2, autumn/winter 2009, pp. 239–45

Ong, W.J., *Ramus: method and the decay of dialogue* (Cambridge, MA: Harvard University Press, 1958)

Randall, James and Seamus Heaney, 'An Interview with Seamus Heaney', *Ploughshares*, vol. 5, no. 3, 1979, pp. 7–22

Wordsworth, William, 'Preface to Lyrical Ballads' (1802), in *Wordsworth and Coleridge: lyrical ballads*, eds R.L. Brett and A.R. Jones (London: Routledge, 2005), pp. 233–58

Yeats, W.B., *Autobiographies* (London: Macmillan, 1955)

Yeats, W.B., *Essays and Introductions* (London: Macmillan, 1961)

'AS IF THE SUN SHONE': LOVE AND LOSS IN RICHARD MURPHY'S POEMS

Haffenden, John (ed.), *Viewpoints: poets in conversation with John Haffenden* (London: Faber & Faber, 1981)

Larkin, Philip, *Collected Poems* (London: Faber & Faber, 2003)

Murphy, Richard, 'The Art of Debunkery', *New York Review of Books*, vol. 22, no. 8, 15 May 1975, pp. 30–3

RICHARD MURPHY'S ISLAND LIVES

Boelhower, William, 'The Rise of the New Atlantic Studies Matrix', *American Literary History*, vol. 20, nos 1–2, 2008, pp. 83–101

Boey, Kim Cheng, 'Sailing to an Island: contemporary Irish poetry visits the western islands', *Shima: the international journal of research into island cultures*, vol. 2, no. 2, 2008, pp. 19–41

Brown, Terence, 'MacNeice's Ireland, MacNeice's Islands', in *Literature and Nationalism*, eds Vincent Newey and Ann Thompson (Liverpool: Liverpool University Press, 1991), pp. 225–38

Chamberlin, J. Edward, *Island: how islands transform the world* (London: Elliott & Thompson, 2013)

Clark, Heather, 'Leaving Barra, Leaving Inishmore: islands in the Irish Protestant imagination', *Canadian Journal of Irish Studies*, vol. 35, no. 2, fall 2009, pp. 30–5

Conkling, Philip, 'On Islanders and Islandness', *Geographical Review*, vol. 97, no. 2, April 2007, pp. 191–201

Cunliffe, Barry, *Facing the Ocean: the Atlantic and its peoples 8000 BC to AD 1500* (Oxford: Oxford University Press, 2001)

Deleuze, Gilles, *Desert Islands and Other Texts 1953–74*, trans. Michael Taormina, ed. David Lapoujade (Los Angeles, CA: Semiotext(e), 2004)

Grennan, Eamonn, 'Riddling Free: Richard Murphy's *The Price of Stone*', in *Facing the Music: Irish poetry in the twentieth century* by Eamonn Grennan (Omaha, NE: Creighton University Press, 1999), pp. 232–40

Harmon, Maurice, 'Biographical Note on Richard Murphy', *Irish University Review*, vol. 7, no. 1, spring 1977, pp. 11–17

Hay, Pete, 'What the Sea Portends: a reconsideration of contested island tropes', *Island Studies Journal*, vol. 8, no. 2, 2013, pp. 209–32

Hoare, Philip, *The Sea Inside* (London: Fourth Estate, 2013)

Miller, Liam, *Dolmen XXV: an illustrated bibliography of the Dolmen Press 1951–76* (Dublin: The Dolmen Press, 1976)

Murphy, Richard, *The Last Galway Hooker* (Dublin: The Dolmen Press, 1961)

Murphy, Richard, *Sailing to an Island* (London: Faber & Faber, 1963)

Murphy, Richard, *High Island* (London: Faber & Faber, 1974)

O'Donoghue, Bernard, 'The Lost Link: Richard Murphy's early poetry', *Metre*, no. 10, autumn 2001, pp. 138–40

O'Malley, J.P., 'A Rebellious Son of the Ascendancy Who Found His Voice in Connemara', *Irish Examiner*, 21 September 2013, p. 18

Pugh, Jonathan, 'Island Movements: thinking with the archipelago', *Island Studies Journal*, vol. 8, no. 1, May 2013, pp. 9–24

Stratford, Elaine, Godfrey Baldacchino, Elizabeth McMahon, Carol Farbotko and Andrew Harwood, 'Envisioning the Archipelago', *Island Studies Journal*, vol. 6, no. 2, November 2011, pp. 113–30

Symons, Arthur, *Cities and Seacoasts and Islands* (London: W. Collins & Sons, 1918)

Synge, J.M., *The Aran Islands* (Dublin: Maunsel Press, 1907)

Synge, J.M., *Collected Works, Vol. 3: plays book 1*, ed. Ann Saddlemyer (Gerrards Cross: Colin Smythe, 1982)

Wall, Eamonn, 'Wings Beating on Stone: Richard Murphy's ecology', in *Out of the Earth: ecocritical readings of Irish texts*, ed. Christine Cusick (Cork: Cork University Press, 2010), pp. 5–19

Yamashiro, Shin, *American Sea Literature: seascapes, beach narratives, and underwater explorations* (New York: Palgrave Macmillan, 2014)

FLUID GEOGRAPHIES: RICHARD MURPHY'S POETICS OF PLACE

Bowers, Neal, 'Richard Murphy: the landscape of the mind', *Journal of Irish Literature*, vol. 11, no. 3, September 1982, pp. 33–41

Brown, Terence, 'Poets and Patrimony: Richard Murphy and James Simmons', in *Ireland's Literature: selected essays* (Mullingar: The Lilliput Press, 1988), pp. 189–202

Deleuze, Gilles and Félix Guattari, *A Thousand Plateaus: capitalism and schizophrenia*, trans. Brian Massumi (London: Continuum, 2004)

Foster, John Wilson, 'The Landscape of Three Irelands: Hewitt, Murphy and Montague', in *Contemporary Irish Poetry: a collection of critical essays*, ed. Elmer Andrews (London: Macmillan, 1992), pp. 145–68

Foster, Roy F., *Paddy and Mr. Punch: connections in Irish and English history* (Harmondsworth: Penguin, 1995)

Foucault, Michel, 'Of Other Spaces: utopias and heterotopias', trans. Jay Miskowiec, *Diacritics*, vol. 16, no. 1, spring 1986, pp. 22–7

Goodby, John, *Irish Poetry Since 1950: from stillness into history* (Manchester: Manchester University Press, 2000)

Harmon, Maurice, 'Introduction: the poet and his background', in *Richard Murphy: poet of two traditions*, ed. Maurice Harmon (Dublin: Wolfhound Press, 1978), pp. 7–10

Kilroy, Mark, 'Richard Murphy's Connemara Locale', *Éire-Ireland*, vol. 15, no. 3, autumn 1980, pp. 127–33

Kirmayer, Laurence J., 'Landscapes of Memory: trauma, narrative, and dissociation', in *Tense Past: cultural essays in trauma and memory*, eds Paul Antze and Michael Lambek (London: Routledge, 1996), pp. 173–98

Moynaghan, Julian, *Anglo-Irish: the literary imagination in a hyphenated culture* (Princeton, NJ: Princeton University Press, 1995)

Murphy, Richard, 'Afternoon at Home', *Listener*, vol. 49, no. 1,258, 9 April 1953, p. 594

Murphy, Richard, 'Charm of Eire', *Listener*, vol. 59, no. 1,503, 16 January 1958, pp. 119–20

Murphy, Richard, 'The Pleasure Ground', *Listener*, vol. 70, no. 1,794, 15 August 1963, pp. 237–40

Murphy, Richard, 'Notes for Sonnets', *Poetry Ireland Review*, no. 104, September 2011, pp. 92–104

Murphy, Richard, 'Transgressing into Poetry', *Poetry Ireland Review*, no. 111, September 2013, pp. 117–33

Murphy, Richard, *In Search of Poetry* (Thame: Clutag Press, 2017)

Vance, Norman, *Irish Literature: a social history* (Oxford: Basil Blackwell, 1990)

Westphal, Bertrand, 'Foreword', in *Geocritical Explorations: space, place, and mapping in literary and cultural studies*, ed. Robert T. Tally, Jr (New York: Palgrave Macmillan, 2011), pp. ix–xv

Westphal, Bertrand, *Geocriticism: real and fictional spaces*, trans. Robert T. Tally, Jr (New York: Palgrave Macmillan, 2011)

Yeats, W.B., *The Poems*, ed. Daniel Albright (London: Everyman, 1992)

RICHARD MURPHY: RADIO POET

Allison, Jonathan (ed.), *Letters of Louis MacNeice* (London: Faber & Faber, 2010)

Bloom, Emily C., 'Channel Paddlers: 1950s Irish drama on the British airwaves', *Éire-Ireland*, vol. 50, nos. 1–2, spring/summer 2015, pp. 45–64

Bridson, D.G., *Prospero and Ariel: the rise and fall of radio. A personal recollection* (London: Victor Gollancz, 1971)

Cohen, Debra Rae, Michael Coyle and Jane Lewty (eds), *Broadcasting Modernism* (Gainesville, FL: University Press of Florida, 2009)

Davie, Donald, 'Cards of Identity', *New York Review of Books*, vol. 22, no. 3, 6 March 1975, pp. 10–11

Feldman, Matthew, Erik Tonning and Henry Mead (eds), *Broadcasting in the Modernist Era* (London: Bloomsbury, 2014)

Giddings, Robert, 'Radio in Peace and War', in *Literature and Culture in Modern Britain, Volume II: 1930–1955*, ed. Gary Day (London: Longman, 1997), pp. 132–67

Haffenden, John, *Viewpoints: poets in conversation with John Haffenden* (London: Faber & Faber, 1981)

Heaney, Seamus, 'The Poetry of Richard Murphy', *Irish University Review*, vol. 7, no. 1, spring 1977, pp. 18–30

Leader, Zachary (ed.), *The Movement Reconsidered: essays on Larkin, Amis, Gunn, Davie and their contemporaries* (Oxford: Oxford University Press, 2009)

Long, Paul, '"Ephemeral Work": Louis MacNeice and the moment of "pure radio"', *Key Words*, no. 7, 2009, pp. 73–91

MacNeice, Louis, *Selected Plays of Louis MacNeice*, eds Alan Heuser and Peter McDonald (Oxford: Oxford University Press, 1993)

Morin, Emilie, "'I beg your pardon?' W.B. Yeats, Audibility and Sound Transmission', in *Yeats's Mask: Yeats annual no. 19*, eds Margaret Mills Harper and Warwick Gould (Cambridge: Open Book Publishers, 2013), pp. 191–219

Moynihan, Julian, '*The Battle of Aughrim*: a commentary', *Irish University Review*, vol. 13, no. 1, spring 1983, pp. 103–13

Murphy, Richard, 'A New American Poet', *Spectator*, vol. 185, no. 6,385, 10 November 1950, p. 480

Murphy, Richard, 'Books and Writers', *Spectator*, vol. 185, no. 6,386, 17 November 1950, p. 516

Murphy, Richard, 'Why Has Narrative Poetry Failed?', *Listener*, vol. 46, no. 1,171, 9 August 1951, pp. 226–7

O'Donoghue, Bernard, "'Pat Cloherty's Version of *The Maisie*", Richard Murphy', *Irish University Review*, vol. 39, no. 3, autumn/winter 2009, pp. 239–45

Ó Lochlainn, Colm (ed.), *Irish Street Ballads* (Dublin: The Three Candles, 1939)

Orwell, George, 'Poetry and the Microphone' (1945), in *The Collected Essays, Journalism and Letters of George Orwell, II: my country right or left, 1940–1943*, eds Sonia Orwell and Ian Angus (Harmondsworth: Penguin, 1970) pp. 374–82

Scott, J.D., 'In the Movement', *Spectator*, vol. 193, no. 6,588, 1 October 1954, pp. 399–400

Whitehead, Kate, *The Third Programme: a literary history* (Oxford: Clarendon Press, 1989)

'BYGONE CANON, BYGONE SPLEEN': RICHARD MURPHY AS A CONFLICT POET IN *THE BATTLE OF AUGHRIM*

Deane, Seamus, *A Short History of Irish Literature* (London: Hutchinson, 1986)

Eyler, Audrey S. and Robert F. Garratt (eds), *The Uses of the Past: essays on Irish culture* (Newark: University of Delaware Press, 1988)

Goodby, John, *Irish Poetry since 1950: from stillness into history* (Manchester: Manchester University Press, 2000)

Harmon, Maurice and Roger McHugh, *Short History of Anglo-Irish Literature from Its Origins to the Present Day* (Dublin: Wolfhound Press, 1982)

Kiberd, Declan, 'Richard Murphy and Casement's Funeral', *Metre*, no. 10, autumn 2001, pp. 135–7

Longley, Edna, 'Searching the Darkness: Richard Murphy, Thomas Kinsella, John Montague and James Simmons', in *Two Decades of Irish Writing: a critical survey*, ed. Douglas Dunn (Cheadle: Carcanet Press, 1975), pp. 118–53

Wheatley, David, 'Richard Murphy: interview', *Metre*, no. 10, autumn 2001, pp. 135–55

Williams, Jonathan, 'A Glossary to *The Battle of Aughrim* and *The God Who Eats Corn*', *Irish University Review*, vol. 7, no. 1, spring 1977, pp. 73-103

Wilson Foster, John, 'The Landscape of Three Irelands: Hewitt, Murphy and Montague', in *Contemporary Irish Poetry: a collection of critical essays*, ed. Elmer Kennedy-Andrews (Basingstoke: Macmillan, 1992), pp. 145–68

RICHARD MURPHY'S POETRY OF AFTERMATH

Armstrong, Karen, *Fields of Blood* (New York: Alfred A. Knopf, 2014)

Childs, John, *The Williamite Wars in Ireland* (London: Continuum, 2007)

Foster, R.F., 'Book of the Irish', *Times Literary Supplement*, no. 5,911, 15 July 2016, pp. 10–11

Harmon, Maurice, 'Biographical Note on Richard Murphy', *Irish University Review*, vol. 7, no. 1, spring 1977, pp. 11–17

Murphy, Richard, *Sailing to an Island* (London: Faber & Faber, 1963)

Murphy, Richard, 'The Pleasure Ground', in *Writers on Themselves* (London: British Broadcasting Corporation, 1964), pp. 62–6

Murphy, Richard, 'Notes for Sonnets', *Poetry Ireland Review*, no. 104, September 2011, pp. 92–104

Murphy, Richard, 'Extract: Transgressing into Poetry', *Poetry Ireland Review*, no. 107, September 2012, pp. 26–33

Murphy, Richard, 'Essay: Transgressing into Poetry', *Poetry Ireland Review*, no. 111, September 2013, pp. 117–33

Murphy, Richard, 'Rejoice', *Poetry Ireland Review*, no. 116, September 2015, pp. 7–11

Oxford English Dictionary, Compact Edition: complete text reproduced micrographically, 2 vols, 2nd printing (New York: Oxford University Press, 1972)

Oxford English Dictionary, 20 vols, 2nd edn (Oxford: Clarendon Press, 1989)

Wills, A.J., *An Introduction to the History of Central Africa*, 4th edn (New York: Oxford University Press, 1985)

'IN A PARADISE FOR WHITE GODS HE GROWS OLD': THE INSTABILITY OF PASTORAL SPACE IN RICHARD MURPHY'S 'THE GOD WHO EATS CORN'

Bowers, Neal, 'Richard Murphy: the landscape of the mind', *Journal of Irish Literature*, vol. 11, no. 3, September 1982, pp. 33–41

Brophy, James D., 'Richard Murphy: poet of nostalgia or *pietas*?', in *Contemporary Irish Writing*, eds James D. Brophy and Raymond J. Porter (Boston: Twayne, 1983), pp. 49–64

Brown, Terence, 'Poets and Patrimony: Richard Murphy and James Simmons', in *Ireland's Literature: selected essays* (Mullingar: The Lilliput Press, 1988), pp. 189–202

Ettin, Andrew V., *Literature and the Pastoral* (New Haven, CT: Yale University Press, 1984)

Johnston, Dillon and Guinn Batten, 'Contemporary Poetry in English: 1940–2000', in *The Cambridge History of Irish Literature, Vol. II: 1890–2000*, eds Margaret Kelleher and Philip O'Leary (Cambridge: Cambridge University Press, 2006), pp. 357–420

Lefebvre, Henri, *The Production of Space*, trans. Donald Nicholson-Smith (Malden, MA: Blackwell, 1991)

Murphy, Richard, 'The Pleasure Ground', *Listener*, vol. 70, no. 1,794, 15 August 1963, pp. 237–40

Murphy, Richard, *Collected Poems* (Oldcastle: The Gallery Press, 2000)

Soja, Edward W., *Postmodern Geographies: the reassertion of space in critical social theory* (London: Verso, 1989)

'LIKE FISH UNDER POETRY'S BEAKS': RICHARD MURPHY AND TED HUGHES

Crotty, Patrick, 'What a strange boy you are', *Times Literary Supplement*, no. 5,192, 4 October 2002, pp. 26–7

Heaney, Seamus, 'The Poetry of Richard Murphy', in *Richard Murphy: poet of two traditions*, ed. Maurice Harmon (Dublin: Wolfhound Press, 1978), pp. 18–30

Hughes, Ted, 'Ted Hughes, the Poet, Introduces Another in His Series of Extracts from Great Books He Believes All Children Will Enjoy and Remember', *Sunday Times*, 16 September 1962, Colour Section, p. 18

Hughes, Ted, *Poetry in the Making* (London: Faber & Faber, 1967)

Hughes, Ted, *Gaudete* (London: Faber & Faber, 1977)

Hughes, Ted, *Flowers and Insects* (London: Faber & Faber, 1986)

Hughes, Ted, *The Letters of Ted Hughes*, ed. Christopher Reid (London: Faber & Faber, 2007)

Kilroy, Mark, 'Richard Murphy's Connemara Locale', *Éire-Ireland*, vol. 15, no. 3, autumn 1980, pp. 127–34

Murphy, Richard, 'The Empty Tower at Ballylee', *Observer*, 7 October 1962, Books Section, p. 29

Murphy, Richard, *High Island* (London: Faber & Faber, 1974)

Murphy, Richard, 'To Celebrate Existence', *Hibernia*, 17 December 1976, p. 20

Murphy, Richard, *In Search of Poetry* (Thame: Clutag Press, 2017)

Stevenson, Anne, *Bitter Fame: a life of Sylvia Plath*, with additional material by Lucas Myers, Dido Merwin, and Richard Murphy (London: Viking, 1989)

Wall, Eamonn, 'Wings Beating on Stone: Richard Murphy's ecology', in *Out of the Earth: ecocritical readings of Irish texts*, ed. Christine Cusick (Cork: Cork University Press, 2010), pp. 5–19

'THE LYRIC BARRIER': RICHARD MURPHY'S AMERICA

Berryman, John, *The Dream Songs* (New York: Farrar, Straus & Giroux, 1969)
Lowell, Robert, *Collected Prose* (New York: Farrar, Straus & Giroux, 1987)
Lowell, Robert, *Collected Poems*, eds Frank Bidart and David Gewanter (New York: Farrar, Straus & Giroux, 2003)
Murphy, Richard, 'A New American Poet', *Spectator*, 10 November 1950, p. 32
Murphy, Richard, 'Why Has Narrative Poetry Failed?', *Listener*, vol. 46, no. 1,171, 9 August 1951, pp. 226–7
Murphy, Richard, 'The Poet on the Island', *Dubliner*, vol. 1, no. 6, January/February 1963, pp. 51–2
Murphy, Richard, *Sailing to an Island* (London: Faber & Faber, 1963)
Murphy, Richard, *Collected Poems* (Oldcastle: The Gallery Press, 2000)
Murphy, Richard, 'Excerpt: Notes for Sonnets', *Poetry Ireland Review*, no. 104, September 2011, pp. 92–104
Murphy, Richard, 'Extract: Transgressing into Poetry', *Poetry Ireland Review*, no. 107, September 2012, pp. 26–36
Murphy, Richard, 'Essay: Transgressing into Poetry', *Poetry Ireland Review*, no. 111, December 2013, pp. 117–33
Murphy, Richard, 'Rejoice', *Poetry Ireland Review*, no. 116, September 2015, pp. 7–11
Perkins, David, *A History of Modern Poetry, Volume II: modernism and after* (Cambridge, MA: Belknap Press, 1989)
Roethke, Theodore, 'The Shy Man', *Dubliner*, vol. 1, no. 4, July/August 1962, p. 51
Roethke, Theodore, 'Gob Music', *Dubliner*, vol. 1, no. 4, July/August 1962, pp. 52–3
Roethke, Theodore, *The Collected Poems of Theodore Roethke* (New York: Anchor Press/Doubleday, 1975)
Rosenthal, M.L., *The Modern Poets: a critical introduction* (New York: Oxford University Press, 1965)
Young, Vernon, 'The Worst Possible Ordeal', *New Criterion*, vol. 1, no. 6, 1 January 1983, p. 79

WHAT PRICE STONE? THE SHAPING OF INHERITANCE INTO FORM IN RICHARD MURPHY'S *THE PRICE OF STONE* SONNET SEQUENCE

Bloom, Harold (ed.), *Percy Bysshe Shelley* (New York: Chelsea House, 2001)
Delanty, Greg and Paul McLoughlin, 'An Interview with Greg Delanty', *Poetry Ireland Review*, no. 90, June 2007, pp. 23–9

Gillis, Alan, 'The Modern Irish Sonnet', in *The Oxford Handbook of Modern Irish Poetry*, eds Fran Brearton and Alan Gillis (Oxford: Oxford University Press, 2012), pp. 567–87

Heaney, Seamus, 'The Poetry of Richard Murphy', in *Richard Murphy: poet of two traditions*, ed. Maurice Harmon (Dublin: Wolfhound, 1978), pp. 18–30

Hirsch, Edward, and Eavan Boland (eds), *The Making of a Sonnet* (New York: W.W. Norton, 2008)

Longley, Edna, 'Searching the Darkness: Richard Murphy, Thomas Kinsella, John Montague and James Simmons', in *Two Decades of Irish Writing*, ed. Douglas Dunn (Cheadle: Carcanet Press, 1975), pp. 118–53

Moore, Marianne, *Complete Poems*, ed. Clive Driver (London: Faber & Faber, 1987)

Murphy, Richard, 'Excerpt: Notes for Sonnets', *Poetry Ireland Review*, no. 104, October 2011, pp. 92–104

Murphy, Richard, 'Extract: Transgressing into Poetry', *Poetry Ireland Review*, no. 107, September 2012, pp. 26–33

Murphy, Richard, 'Writing *The Battle of Aughrim*', in *The Pleasure Ground: poems 1952–2012* (Tarset: Bloodaxe, 2013), pp. 254–9

Murphy, Richard, *In Search of Poetry* (Thame: Clutag Press, 2017)

O'Donoghue, Bernard, 'Critique of "Pat Cloherty's Version of *The Maisie*"', in *Richard Murphy, The Pleasure Ground: poems 1952–2012* (Tarset: Bloodaxe, 2013), pp. 273–9

Ricks, Christopher, *The Force of Poetry* (Oxford: Oxford University Press, 1999)

Sendry, Joseph, 'The Poet as Builder: Richard Murphy's *The Price of Stone*', *Irish University Review*, vol. 15, no. 1, spring 1985, pp. 38–49

Wu, Duncan (ed.), *Romanticism: an anthology* (Oxford: Wiley-Blackwell, 2002)

EXPOSURE AND OBSCURITY: THE CRUISING SONNETS IN RICHARD MURPHY'S *THE PRICE OF STONE*

Ackerley, J.R., *My Father and Myself* [1968] (London: Pimlico, 1992)

Brandes, Rand, 'Drafting *The Price of Stone*: Richard Murphy's manuscripts for "Beehive Cell"', in *The Snow Path: tracks 10*, ed. John F. Deane (Dublin: Dedalus Press, 1994), pp. 62–84

Keatinge, Benjamin, '"My form is epicene": sexual ambiguity in the poetry of Richard Murphy', in *Essays in Irish Literary Criticism: themes of gender, sexuality and corporeality*, eds Sharon Tighe-Mooney and Deirdre Quinn (Lampeter: Edwin Mellen Press, 2008), pp. 19–38

Murphy, Richard, 'Notes for Sonnets', *Poetry Ireland Review*, no. 104, September 2011, pp. 92–104

Murphy, Richard, 'Transgressing into Poetry', *Poetry Ireland Review*, no. 107, September 2012, pp. 26–36

Murphy, Richard, 'Transgressing into Poetry', *Poetry Ireland Review*, no. 111, December 2013, pp. 117–33

Murphy, Richard, *In Search of Poetry* (Thame: Clutag Press, 2017)

O'Malley, J.P., 'Interview with a Poet: Richard Murphy, an old *Spectator* hand', *Spectator*, http://blogs.spectator.co.uk/2013/09/interview-with-a-poet-richard-murphy-an-old-spectator-hand/ [accessed 12 November 2017]

Siddall, Jill, 'Grotesquely Free, Though Ruled by Symmetry', *Metre*, no. 10, autumn 2001, pp. 129–34

'TO SEEM A WHITE KING'S GEM': RICHARD MURPHY'S SRI LANKAN POEMS AND IRISH POSTCOLONIAL STUDIES

Deane, Seamus, 'The Long Ascendancy', *Honest Ulsterman*, no. 66, July–October 1980, pp. 66–9

Gibbons, Luke, *Gaelic Gothic: race, colonization and Irish culture* (Galway: Arlen House, 2004)

Goodby, John, 'Richard Murphy: last of the Anglo-Irish?', in *Irish Poetry Since 1950: from stillness into history* (Manchester: Manchester University Press, 2000), pp. 80–7

Heaney, Seamus, 'The Poetry of Richard Murphy', in *Richard Murphy: poet of two traditions*, ed. Maurice Harmon (Dublin: Wolfhound Press, 1978), pp. 18–30

Innes, C.L., 'Postcolonial Studies and Ireland', in *Comparing Postcolonial Literatures: dislocations*, eds Ashok Bery and Patricia Murray (Basingstoke: Macmillan, 2000), pp. 21–30

Keatinge, Benjamin, 'Richard Murphy in Sri Lanka: an interview', *Poetry Ireland Review*, no. 122, August 2017, pp. 86–93

Kiberd, Declan, 'Richard Murphy and Casement's Funeral', *Metre*, no. 10, autumn 2001, pp. 135–7

Lennon, Joseph, 'Irish Orientalism: an overview', in *Ireland and Postcolonial Theory*, eds Clare Carroll and Patricia King (Cork: Cork University Press, 2003)

Llosa, Mario Vargas, *The Dream of the Celt*, trans. Edith Grossman (London: Faber & Faber, 2012)

Mizutani, Satoshi, 'Hybridity and History: a critical reflection on Homi K. Bhabha's post-historical thoughts', *Ab Imperio*, no. 4, 2013, pp. 27–48

Murphy, Richard, *The Mirror Wall* (Dublin: Wolfhound Press, 1989)

Murray, Melanie A., *Island Paradise: the myth. An examination of contemporary Caribbean and Sri Lankan writing* (Amsterdam: Rodopi, 2009)

O'Driscoll, Dennis, 'Richard Murphy at Sixty', *Poetry Ireland Review*, no. 21, spring 1988, pp. 14–18

Quinn, Antoinette, 'Aughrim in Sri Lanka', *New Nation*, no. 7, 1989, p. 20

Young, Robert J.C., *Colonial Desire: hybridity in theory, culture and race* (London: Routledge, 1995)

THE KICK AND THE GENRE OF ANGLO-IRISH AUTOBIOGRAPHY

Brown, Terence, 'Poets and Patrimony: Richard Murphy and James Simmons', in *Across a Roaring Hill: the Protestant imagination in modern Ireland*, eds Gerald Dawe and Edna Longley (Belfast: Blackstaff Press, 1985), pp. 182–95

Deane, Seamus, 'Autobiography and Memoirs 1890–1988: introduction', in *The Field Day Anthology of Irish Writing, Vol. III* (Derry: Field Day, 1991), pp. 380–3

Freeman, Mark, *Rewriting the Self: history, memory, narrative* (London: Routledge, 1993)

Grubgeld, Elizabeth, *Anglo-Irish Autobiography: class, gender, and the forms of narrative* (Syracuse: Syracuse University Press, 2004)

Grubgeld, Elizabeth, 'Life Writing in the Twentieth Century', in *The Cambridge Companion to the Irish Novel*, ed. John Wilson Foster (Cambridge: Cambridge University Press, 2006), pp. 223–37

Haffenden, John, *Viewpoints: poets in conversation with John Haffenden* (London: Faber & Faber, 1981)

Heaney, Seamus, 'The Poetry of Richard Murphy', *Irish University Review: Richard Murphy special issue*, vol. 7, no. 1, spring 1977, pp. 18–30

Kenneally, Michael, 'The Autobiographical Imagination and Irish Literary Autobiographies', in *Critical Approaches to Anglo-Irish Literature*, eds Michael Allen and Angela Wilcox (Gerrards Cross: Colin Smythe, 1989), pp. 111–31

Kiberd, Declan, *Inventing Ireland* (London: Vintage, 1996)

Lynch, Claire, *Irish Autobiography: stories of self in the narrative of a nation* (Bern: Peter Lang, 2009)

Murphy, Richard, 'The Pleasure Ground', in *Writers on Themselves* (London: BBC, 1964), pp. 62–6

O'Malley, J.P., 'Interview with a Poet: Richard Murphy, an old *Spectator* hand', http://blogs.spectator.co.uk/2013/09/interview-with-a-poet-richard-murphy-an-old-spectator-hand/ [accessed 12 November 2017]

Yeats, W.B., *Autobiographies*, eds William H. O'Donnell and Douglas N. Archibald (New York: Scribner, 1999)

Index